CANADIAN CRIMINAL CASES

SELECTED HIGHLIGHTS

CRM 2300·B

Wade Deisman
#202B - 25 University
University of Ottawa
Ottawa, ON
562-5800-2843

CANADIAN CRIMINAL CASES

SELECTED HIGHLIGHTS

SIMON VERDUN-JONES

SIMON FRASER UNIVERSITY

THOMSON

NELSON

Australia   Canada   Mexico   Singapore   Spain   United Kingdom   United States

Canadian Cataloguing in Publication Data

Canadian criminal cases
ISBN 0-7747-3594-5

1. Criminal law — Canada — Cases. I. Verdun-Jones, Simon N. (Simon Nicholas), 1947- .

KE8808.5C35 1999   345.71   C98-932219-X
KF9220.ZA2C35 1999

New Editions Editor: Megan Mueller
Developmental Editor: Lise Dupont
Production Editor: Carolyn McLarty
Senior Production Co-ordinator: Sue-Ann Becker

Copy Editor: First Folio Resource Group, Inc.
Cover Design: FIZZZ Design, Inc.
Typesetting and Assembly: Carolyn Hutchings
Printing and Binding: Webcom

Cover Art: Paul Beliveau, *La 8e demeure: les impossibles choix, la 9e demeure: l'autre choix*, 1989. Acrylique sur toile. 213,5 x 305. Transparency provided by Musée du Québec. Reproduced with permission of the artist.

Nelson Thomson Learning
1120 Birchmount Road, Scarborough, Ontario, M1K 5G4
Customer Service
Toll-Free Tel.: 1-800-730-2214
Toll-Free Fax: 1-800-730-2215

This book was printed in Canada.

2 3 4 5   05 04 03 02

TO EVELEEN ROWENA

PREFACE

Courts and camps are the only places to learn the world in.   Lord Chesterfield (1747)

This casebook was conceived as a vehicle for introducing students to a select number of judicial decisions that have played a substantial role in shaping the fabric of contemporary criminal law in Canada.

There would almost certainly be a general consensus among the teachers of criminal law that, from a student's point of view, a case-oriented approach is an extremely effective method of structuring the study of this subject. Indeed, any investigation of the general principles of criminal law needs to be supplemented with an analysis of the specific details of particular decided cases if students are to be left with an adequate understanding of exactly how criminal law applies to situations that may arise in their everyday lives. Learning the basic principles of criminal law without acquiring some familiarity with specific cases could be compared to learning the principles of creative writing without ever reading a novel!

Traditionally, the only available collections of Canadian criminal cases have been those specifically prepared for law students. Most of these volumes, containing at least a thousand pages of relatively small print, reproduce extracts from literally hundreds of different cases. While such an abundance of material may be perfectly appropriate for students training to become lawyers, it is clearly not suited to the needs of students in disciplines such as criminology, criminal justice, and law and security. The present volume has been devised to meet the needs of the latter group of students who may wish to acquaint themselves with some of the leading cases in Canadian criminal law without

having to purchase an encyclopedic casebook that significantly exceeds their academic requirements and inevitably strains their available funds.

This casebook makes available to students extracts from forty-two leading cases in Canadian criminal law. Thirty-six of these cases were decided by the Supreme Court of Canada and the remainder by various provincial courts of appeal. Each of the cases has been heavily edited in order to reduce them — from the reader's point of view — to a reasonable length. However, an attempt has also been made to retain enough of the judges' words to provide students with a genuine appreciation of the complexity of the legal issues and factual circumstances that generally constitute the background for major decisions made by the appellate courts. In addition, the author has endeavoured to perform this editorial task with a view to ensuring that the selected cases provide students with a genuine feel of how criminal law actually operates in real-life situations. In short, it is hoped that the essential characteristics and "colour" of each case have ultimately been preserved in spite of far-reaching pruning.

This book has been designed to be used either independent of, or in conjunction with, an introductory textbook of Canadian criminal law. In particular, it may serve as a useful adjunct to the author's *Criminal Law in Canada: Cases, Questions, and the Code*, Second Edition (Toronto: Harcourt Brace & Company, Canada, 1997). The chapters in the present casebook are organized in exactly the same manner as those in *Criminal Law in Canada*, permitting students to develop well-coordinated study plans by following a reading of each chapter in the textbook with a reading of the corresponding chapter in the casebook. In addition, the reader of the present casebook may wish to refer to *Criminal Law in Canada* because it contains a glossary that provides definitions of key terms used by the courts, as well as brief guides to the structure of the Canadian system of criminal courts and the method of citing decided cases.

Naturally, any selection of decided cases reflects the personal predilections of the individual who is making the choices. However, it is hoped that the present selection does encompass a representative group of important cases that have made significant contributions to the development of Canadian Criminal Law. The author would be more than grateful to receive suggestions of cases that should (or should not) be included in subsequent editions of this casebook, as it is his strong aspiration that the present volume should be developed into a truly effective instrument for learning Canadian criminal law.

ACKNOWLEDGEMENTS

This book could not have been completed without the generous support and unfailing encouragement of Heather McWhinney, Senior Acquisitions Editor at Harcourt Brace & Company, Canada. Although it soon became apparent to the author that there is much more to the editing of decided cases than meets the novice's eye, Heather's proverbial patience and constructive criticism provided exactly the right degree of support to ensure that the project was completed on a positive note.

I also wish to express my thanks for the excellent editorial work undertaken by staff at Harcourt Brace & Company, Canada. In particular, I would like to mention the splendid efforts of Megan Mueller, who was involved in the early stages of the development of the casebook and never failed to offer wise and helpful advice. In addition, I owe a special debt to Lise Dupont, who succeeded Megan Mueller in the role of Developmental Editor and worked tirelessly to ensure that the casebook would become the best possible learning resource for students. Indeed, Lise's efforts to prevent the length of the casebook from careening out of control were

truly admirable and her patient and shrewd advice proved to be invaluable. In short, I have been extraordinarily fortunate in having been able to rely on such an accomplished and supportive editorial staff.

Finally, a number of reviewers played a significant role in improving the content of *Canadian Criminal Cases: Selected Highlights*. I would like to thank Dale Dearden (Kwantlen University College), Jessie Horner (Kwantlen University College), James Ketchen (Laurentian University), David MacAlister (Kwantlen University College), Oliver R. Stoetzer (Fanshaw College), and Brian Young (Camosun College).

A NOTE TO THE STUDENT

This book contains *edited* Canadian criminal cases. To access the original, unedited cases (some of which are hundreds of pages long), please refer to the Table of Case Citations provided at the end of this book. The cases can be found in law libraries, and many of them can also be accessed through the Internet.

CONTENTS

Chapter 1
Introduction to Canadian Criminal Law 1

INTRODUCTION 1

CASE 1
Regina v. Hydro-Québec 2

CASE 2
Morgentaler, Smolig, and Scott v. The Queen 7

CASE 3
Regina v. Butler 16

Chapter 2
The *Actus Reus* Elements of a Criminal Offence 27

INTRODUCTION 27

CASE 4
Regina v. Hatfield 28

CASE 5
Regina v. Cooper 31

CASE 6
Regina v. Parks 36

CASE 7
Smithers v. The Queen 45

CASE 8
Harbottle v. The Queen 49

CASE 9
Regina v. Kitching and Adams 54

CASE 10
Rodriguez v. British Columbia (Attorney-General) 59

Chapter 3
The Mental Element in Criminal Law: Subjective Liability 69

INTRODUCTION 69

CASE 11
Théroux v. The Queen 70

CASE 12
Sansregret v. The Queen 77

CASE 13
Regina v. Oluwa 83

CASE 14
Regina v. Martineau 88

Chapter 4
The Mental Element in Criminal Law:
Objective Liability 93

INTRODUCTION 93

CASE 15
Regina v. DeSousa 95

CASE 16
Regina v. Creighton 100

CASE 17
Regina v. Hundal 112

CASE 18
Regina v. Tutton and Tutton 118

CASE 19
Waite v. The Queen 125

Chapter 5
The Special Case of Regulatory
Offences: Strict and Absolute Liability in
Canada 129

INTRODUCTION 129

CASE 20
Regina v. City of Sault Ste. Marie 130

CASE 21
Reference re: Section 94(2) of the Motor Vehicle
Act 137

CASE 22
Wholesale Travel Group Inc. v. The Queen 141

Chapter 6
Modes of Participation in Crime 153

INTRODUCTION 153

CASE 23
Greyeyes v. The Queen 154

CASE 24
Regina v. Logan et al. 160

CASE 25
Regina v. Ancio 165

CASE 26
United States of America and Minister of Justice
v. Dynar 170

CASE 27
Gladstone et al. v. The Queen 180

Chapter 7
Mental Disorder as a Defence:
The Verdict of Not Criminally
Responsible on Account of Mental
Disorder (NCRMD) 183

INTRODUCTION 183

CASE 28
Chaulk v. The Queen 184

CASE 29
Regina v. Swain 193

CASE 30
Regina v. LePage 204

CASE 31
Jacquard v. The Queen 212

Chapter 8
Defences to a Criminal Charge: Part I
Mistake of Fact, Intoxication, Necessity,
and Duress 217

INTRODUCTION 217

CASE 32
Regina v. Park 219

CASE 33
Daviault v. The Queen 229

CASE 34
Regina v. Robinson 239

CASE 35
Perka et al. v. The Queen 248

CASE 36
Hibbert v. The Queen 257

CASE 37
Regina v. Langlois 268

Chapter 9
Defences to a Criminal Charge:
Part II Provocation, Self-Defence,
and Consent 275

INTRODUCTION 275

CASE 38
Thibert v. The Queen 276

CASE 39
Lavallee v. The Queen 282

CASE 40
Regina v. Pétel 291

CASE 41
Jobidon v. The Queen 295

CASE 42
Regina v. Leclerc 305

Table of Case Citations 311

Introduction to Canadian Criminal Law

INTRODUCTION

The three cases excerpted in Chapter 1 address some significant issues that pervade the entire fabric of Canadian criminal law. It is particularly desirable to acquaint oneself with these basic issues because they provide the key to understanding the complex process through which the criminal law is shaped and refined by the decisions of both legislators and judges.

Regina v. Hydro-Québec (1997) illustrates the nature and scope of the exclusive power to enact criminal law that has been assigned to the Parliament of Canada under the terms of section 91(27) of the Constitution Act, 1867.

The Morgentaler, Smolig, and Scott case (1988) demonstrates the remarkable degree of discretionary power that has been placed in the hands of the Canadian judiciary as a consequence of the enactment of the Canadian Charter of Rights and Freedoms in 1982. Indeed, in this case, the Supreme Court of Canada took the bold step of striking down the provisions of the Criminal Code relating to therapeutic abortions on the basis that these provisions were invalid under the Charter.

The *Butler* case (1992) is now the leading authority on the interpretation of the obscenity provisions of the Criminal Code (section 163). The case is significant insofar as it effectively demonstrates that rights under the Charter are not absolute: indeed, section 1 of the Charter may be used to save provisions that infringe on Charter rights, such as freedom of expression [section 2(b)], if these provisions constitute a reasonable limit that "can be demonstrably justified in a free and democratic society." Section 1, therefore, grants to Canadian courts the power to balance the interests of the individual citizen with those of society as a whole and the *Butler* case dramatically illustrates the circumstances in which the Supreme Court of Canada is prepared to use this formidable power. Furthermore, the *Butler* case is important because it demonstrates the extent to which the Supreme Court of Canada is willing to place a considerable degree of emphasis on the need for the criminal law to be "responsive to women's realities." This significant theme is also reflected in the *Park* (1995) and *Lavallee* (1990) cases (excerpted in Chapters 8 and 9 respectively).

CASE

1

Regina v. Hydro-Québec

SUPREME COURT OF CANADA   SEPTEMBER 18, 1997

BACKGROUND

Hydro-Québec was charged with two offences under section 6(a) of the Chlorobiphenyls Interim Order, P.C. 1989–296, issued under the provisions of sections 34 and 35 of the Canadian Environmental Protection Act, R.S.C. 1985, c. 16 (4th Supp.). The offences related to the alleged dumping of polychlorinated biphenyls (PCBs) into a river in Québec. Before the summary conviction court judge, Hydro-Québec brought a motion seeking to have both the interim order and the relevant federal legislative provisions declared *ultra vires* the Parliament of Canada on the basis that they did not fall under any of the heads of federal jurisdiction articulated by section 91 of the Constitution Act, 1867. The judge granted this motion and the Crown appealed to the Québec Superior Court, which dismissed the appeal. The Crown's subsequent appeal to the Québec Court of Appeal was also dismissed, and it then appealed to the Supreme Court of Canada.

MAIN ISSUE

Did the interim order and the relevant federal legislation, under which the order was issued, constitute a valid exercise of the federal criminal law power under section 91(27) of the Constitution Act, 1867?

JUDGMENTS

The *majority* judgment was delivered by Justice La Forest (with whom Justices L'Heureux-Dubé, Gonthier, Cory, and McLachlin agreed). The *dissenting* judgment of Chief Justice Lamer (with whom Justices Iacobucci, Sopinka, and Major agreed) has been omitted.

85 La Forest J.: — This Court has in recent years been increasingly called upon to consider the interplay between federal and provincial legislative powers as they relate to environmental protection. Whether viewed positively as strategies for maintaining a clean environment, or negatively as measures to combat the evils of pollution, there can be no doubt that these measures relate to a public purpose of superordinate importance, and one in which all levels of government and numerous organs of the international community have become increasingly engaged.

87 This latest case in which this Court is required to define the nature of legislative powers over the environment is of major significance. The narrow issue raised is the extent to and manner in which the federal Parliament may control the amount of and conditions under which Chlorobiphenyls (PCBs) — substances well known to

pose great dangers to humans and the environment generally — may enter into the environment. However, the attack on the federal power to secure this end is not really aimed at the specific provisions respecting PCBs. Rather, it puts into question the constitutional validity of its enabling statutory provisions. What is really at stake is whether Part II ("Toxic Substances") of the Canadian Environmental Protection Act, R.S.C. 1985, c. 16 (4th Supp.), which empowers the federal Ministers of Health and of the Environment to determine what substances are toxic and to prohibit the introduction of such substances into the environment except in accordance with specified terms and conditions, falls within the constitutional power of Parliament.

Facts

88 The case arose in this way. The respondent Hydro-Québec allegedly dumped polychlorinated biphenyls (PCBs) into the St. Maurice River in Québec in early 1990. On June 5, 1990, it was charged with two infractions under s. 6(a) of the Chlorobiphenyls Interim Order, P.C. 1989–296 (hereafter "Interim Order"), which was adopted and enforced pursuant to ss. 34 and 35 of the Canadian Environmental Protection Act. On July 23, 1990, the respondent pleaded not guilty to both charges before the Court of Québec.

89 On March 4, 1991, the respondent Hydro-Québec brought a motion before Judge Michel Babin seeking to have ss. 34 and 35 of the Act as well as s. 6(a) of the Interim Order itself declared *ultra vires* the Parliament of Canada on the ground that they do not fall within the ambit of any federal head of power set out in s. 91 of the Constitution Act, 1867. The Attorney-General of Québec intervened in support of the respondent's position. Judge Babin granted the motion on August 12, 1991, and an appeal to the Québec Superior Court was dismissed by Trottier J. on August 6, 1992. A further appeal to the Court of Appeal of Québec was dismissed on February 14, 1995. Leave to appeal to this Court was granted on October 12, 1995.

Constitutional Questions

97 On December 21, 1995, Lamer C.J. framed the following constitutional question:

> Do s. 6(a) of the Chlorobiphenyls Interim Order, P.C. 1989–296, and the enabling legislative provisions, ss. 34 and 35 of the Canadian Environmental Protection Act, R.S.C. 1985, c. 16 (4th Supp.), fall in whole or in part within the jurisdiction of the Parliament of Canada to make laws for the peace, order and good government of Canada pursuant to s. 91 of the Constitution Act, 1867, or its criminal law jurisdiction under s. 91(27) of the Constitution Act, 1867, or otherwise fall within its jurisdiction?

The Issues

108 In this Court, the appellant Attorney-General of Canada seeks to support the impugned provisions of the Act on the basis of the national concern doctrine under the peace, order and good government clause of s. 91, or under the criminal law power under s. 91(27) of the Constitution Act, 1867. The respondent Hydro-Québec and the *mis en cause* Attorney-General of Québec dispute this. In broad terms, they say that the provisions are so invasive of provincial powers that they cannot be justified either under the national dimensions doctrine or under the criminal law power. The attack on the validity of the provisions under the latter power is also supported, most explicitly by the intervener the Attorney-General for Saskatchewan, on the ground that they are, in essence, of a regulatory and not of a prohibitory character. Finally, I repeat that while the Interim Order precipitated the litigation, there is no doubt that the respondent and mis en cause as well as their supporting interveners are after bigger game — the enabling provisions.

110 In my view, the impugned provisions are valid legislation under the criminal law power — s. 91(27) of the Constitution Act, 1867. It thus becomes unnecessary to deal with the national concern doctrine, which inevitably raises profound issues respecting the federal structure of our Constitution which do not arise with anything like the same intensity in relation to the criminal law power.

The Criminal Law Power

118 Section 91(27) of the Constitution Act, 1867 confers the exclusive power to legislate in relation to criminal law on Parliament. The nature and ambit of this power has recently been the subject of a detailed analytical and historical examination in *RJR-MacDonald Inc. v. Canada (Attorney-General)*, [1995] 3 S.C.R. 199 at p. 240, 100 C.C.C. (3d) 449, 127 D.L.R. (4th) 1, where it was described as it has for many years, as being "*plenary in nature*" (emphasis added).

119 What appears from the analysis in *RJR-MacDonald* is that as early as 1903, the Privy Council, in *Attorney-General for Ontario v. Hamilton Street Railway Co.*, [1903] A.C. 524 at pp. 528–29, 7 C.C.C. 326, had made it clear that the power conferred on Parliament by s. 91(27) is "the criminal law in its *widest sense*" (emphasis added). Consistently with this approach, the Privy Council in *Proprietary Articles Trade Association v. Attorney-General for Canada*, [1931] A.C. 310, 55 C.C.C. 241, [1931] 2 D.L.R. 1 (hereafter PATA), at p. 324, defined the criminal law power as including any prohibited act with penal consequences. As it put it, at p. 324: "The criminal quality of an act cannot be discerned . . . by reference to any standard but one: Is the act prohibited with penal consequences?" This approach has been consistently followed ever since and, as *RJR-MacDonald* relates, it has been applied by the courts in a wide variety of settings. Accordingly, it is entirely within the discretion of Parliament to determine what evil it wishes by penal prohibition to suppress and what threatened interest it thereby wishes to safeguard, to adopt the terminology of Rand J. in *Reference re: Validity of Section 5(a) of the Dairy Industry Act*, [1949] S.C.R. 1 D.L.R. 433 (the *Margarine Reference*), at p. 49.

121 The Canadian Charter of Rights and Freedoms apart, only one qualification has been attached to Parliament's plenary power over criminal law. The power cannot be employed colourably. Like other legislative powers, it cannot, as Estey J. put it in *Scowby v. Glendinning*, [1986] 2 S.C.R. 226 at p. 237, 29 C.C.C. (3d) 1, 32 D.L.R. (4th) 161, "permit Parliament, simply by legislating in the proper form, to colourably invade areas of exclusively provincial legislative competence." To determine whether such an attempt is being made, it is, of course, appropriate to enquire into Parliament's purpose in enacting the legislation. As Estey J. noted in *Scowby*, at p. 237, since the *Margarine Reference*, it has been "accepted that some legitimate public purpose must underlie the prohibition." Estey J. then cited Rand J.'s words in the *Margarine Reference* (at p. 49) as follows:

> A crime is an act which the law, with appropriate penal sanctions, forbids; but as prohibitions are not enacted in a vacuum, we can properly look for some evil or injurious or undesirable effect upon the public against which the law is directed. That effect may be in relation to social, economic or political interests; and the legislature has had in mind to suppress the evil or to safeguard the interest threatened.

I simply add that the analysis in *Scowby* and the *Margarine Reference* was most recently applied by this Court in *RJR-MacDonald, supra*, at pp. 240–41.

122 In the *Margarine Reference, supra*, at p. 50, Rand J. helpfully set forth the more usual purposes of a criminal prohibition in the following passage:

> Is the prohibition . . . enacted with a view to a public purpose which can support it as being in relation to criminal law? *Public peace, order, security, health, morality: these are the ordinary though not exclusive ends served by that law . . .*

[Emphasis added.] See also *Morgentaler, supra*, [1993] 3 S.C.R. 463 at p. 489; *RJR-MacDonald, supra*, at p. 241. As the final clause in the passage just cited indicates, the listed purposes by no means exhaust the purposes that may legitimately support valid criminal legislation.

123 I entertain no doubt that the protection of a clean environment is a public purpose within Rand J.'s formulation in the *Margarine Reference*, cited *supra*, sufficient to support a criminal prohibition. It is surely an "interest threatened" which Parliament can legitimately "safeguard," or to put it another way, pollution is an "evil" that Parliament can legitimately seek to suppress. Indeed, as I indicated at the outset of these reasons, it is a public purpose of superordinate importance; it constitutes one of the major challenges of our time. It would be surprising indeed if Parliament could not exercise its plenary power over criminal law to protect this interest and to suppress the evils associated with it by appropriate penal prohibitions.

127 As is stated in the preamble to the Act under review, "Canada must be able to fulfil its international obligations in respect of the environment." I am confident that Canada can fulfil its international obligations, in so far as the toxic substances sought to be prohibited from entering into the environment under the Act are concerned, by use of the criminal law power. The purpose of the criminal law is to underline and protect our fundamental values. The stewardship of the environment is a fundamental value of our society and Parliament may use its criminal law power to underline that value. The criminal law must be able to keep pace with and protect our emerging values.

130 I conclude that Parliament may validly enact prohibitions under its criminal law power against specific acts for the purpose of preventing pollution or, to put it in other terms, causing the entry into the environment of certain toxic substances. I quite understand that a particular prohibition could be so broad or all-encompassing as to be found to be, in pith and substance, really aimed at regulating an area falling within the provincial domain and not exclusively at protecting the environment. A sweeping prohibition like this (and this would be equally true of one aimed generally at the protection of health) would, in

any case, probably be unworkable. But the attack here ultimately is that the impugned provisions grant such a broad discretion to the Governor in Council as to permit orders that go beyond federal power. I can imagine very nice issues being raised concerning this matter under certain types of legislation, though in such a case one would tend to interpret the legislation narrowly if only to keep it within constitutional bounds. But one need not go so far here. For, it seems to me, as we shall see, when one carefully peruses the legislation, it becomes clear enough that Parliament has stayed well within its power.

131 Though I shall deal with this issue in more detail once I come to consider the legislation, it is well at this point to recall that the use of the federal criminal law power in no way precludes the provinces from exercising their extensive powers under s. 92 to regulate and control the pollution of the environment either independently or to supplement federal action. The situation is really no different from the situation regarding the protection of health where Parliament has for long exercised extensive control over such matters as food and drugs by prohibitions grounded in the criminal law power. This has not prevented the provinces from extensively regulating and prohibiting many activities relating to health. The two levels of government frequently work together to meet common concerns.

157 Since I have found the empowering provisions, ss. 34 and 35, to be *intra vires*, the only attack that could be brought against any action taken under them would be that such action went beyond the authority granted by those provisions; in the present case, for example, such an attack might consist in the allegation that PCBs did not pose "a significant danger to the environment or to human life or health" justifying the making of the Interim Order. This would seem to me to be a tall order. The fact that PCBs are highly toxic substances should require no demonstration. This has become well known to the general public and is supported by an impressive array of scientific studies at both the national and international levels.

158 From what appears in these studies, one can conclude that PCBs are not only highly toxic but long lasting and very slow to break down in water, air or soil. They do dissolve readily in fat tissues and other organic compounds, however, with the result that they move up the food chain through birds and other animals and eventually to humans. They pose significant risks of serious harm to both animals and humans. As well they are extremely mobile. They evaporate from soil and water and are transported great distances through the atmosphere. High levels of PCBs have been found in a variety of arctic animals living thousands of kilometres from any major source of PCBs. The extent of the dangers they pose is reflected in the fact that they were the first substance sought to be controlled in Canada under the Environmental Contaminants Act, *supra*, R.S.C. 1985, C.E–12, the predecessor of the present legislation. They were also the first substance regulated in the United States under the Toxic Substances Control Act, 15 U.S.C. § 2605(c). And because of the trans-boundary nature of the threat, they were the first substances targeted for joint action by Canada, the United States and Mexico through the Commission for Environmental Cooperation established under the North American Free Trade Agreement.

Disposition

161 I would allow the appeal with costs, set aside the judgment of the Court of Appeal of Québec and order that the matter be returned to the Court of summary convictions to be dealt with in accordance with the Act. I would answer the constitutional question as follows:

Q. Do s. 6(a) of the Chlorobiphenyls Interim Order, P.C. 1989–296, and the enabling legislative provisions, ss. 34 and 35 of the Canadian Environmental Protection Act, R.S.C. 1985, c. 16 (4th Supp.), fall in whole or in part within the jurisdiction of the Parliament of Canada to make laws for the peace, order and good government of Canada pursuant to s. 91 of the Constitution Act, 1867, or its criminal law jurisdiction under s. 91(27) of the Constitution Act, 1867, or otherwise fall within its jurisdiction?

A. Yes. They fall wholly within Parliament's power to enact laws under s. 91(27) of the Constitution Act, 1867. It is not necessary to consider the first issue.

Appeal allowed.

Morgentaler, Smolig, and Scott v. The Queen

SUPREME COURT OF CANADA   JANUARY 28, 1988

BACKGROUND

The three accused, who were all doctors working in a clinic that provided abortion services in Toronto, were charged with conspiracy to procure a miscarriage contrary to section 251(1) [now section 287(1)] and section 423(1)(d) [now section 465(1)(c)] of the Criminal Code. At their trial, they were acquitted by a jury. However, the Crown appealed against the acquittals. The Ontario Court of Appeal allowed the appeal and ordered a new trial. The accused appealed to the Supreme Court against the judgment of the Court of Appeal and contended that section 251 [now section 287] was invalid and of no effect because it infringed section 7 of the Charter.

MAIN ISSUE

A number of constitutional and Charter issues were raised before the Supreme Court of Canada. However, the major issue was whether section 251 [now section 287] of the Criminal Code infringed section 7 of the Charter and, if so, whether it could be saved by the application of section 1 of the Charter.

JUDGMENTS

Five of the seven members of the Supreme Court ruled that section 251 [now section 287] infringed section 7 of the Charter and that it could not be saved by section 1 of the Charter. However, while they were all agreed on the outcome of the case, they articulated different reasons for reaching this decision. Extracts from the *concurring* judgments of Chief Justice Dickson (with whom Justice Lamer agreed) and Justice Wilson are reproduced below. The *concurring* judgment of Justice Beetz (with whom Justice Estey agreed) and the *dissenting* judgment of Justice McIntyre (with whom Justice La Forest agreed) have been omitted.

DICKSON, C.J.C.: — The principal issue raised by this appeal is whether the abortion provisions of the Criminal Code infringe the "right to life, liberty and security of the person and the right not to be deprived thereof except in accordance with the principles of fundamental justice" as formulated in s. 7 of the Canadian Charter of Rights and Freedoms.

During argument before this court, counsel for the Crown emphasized repeatedly that it is not the role of the judiciary in Canada to evaluate the wisdom of legislation enacted by our democratically elected representatives, or to second-guess difficult policy choices that confront all governments.

Although no doubt it is still fair to say that courts are not the appropriate forum for articulating complex and controversial programmes of public policy, Canadian courts are now charged with the crucial obligation of ensuring that the legislative initiatives pursued by our Parliament and legislatures conform to the democratic values expressed in the Canadian Charter of Rights and Freedoms. As Justice McIntyre states in his reasons for judgment [*post*, p. 529 (omitted)], ". . . the task of the court in this case is not to solve nor seek to solve what might be called the abortion issue, but simply to measure the content of s. 251 against the Charter."

Procedural History

The three appellants are all duly qualified medical practitioners who together set up a clinic in Toronto to perform abortions upon women who had not obtained a certificate from a therapeutic abortion committee of an accredited or approved hospital as required by s. 251(4). The doctors had made public statements questioning the wisdom of the abortion laws in Canada and asserting that a woman has an unfettered right to choose whether or not an abortion is appropriate in her individual circumstances.

Indictments were preferred against the appellants charging that they conspired with each other between November, 1982, and July, 1983, with intent to procure the miscarriage of female persons, using an induced suction technique to carry out that intent, contrary to ss. 423(1)(d) and 251(1) of the Criminal Code.

Counsel for the appellants moved to quash the indictment or to stay the proceedings before pleas were entered on the grounds that s. 251 of the Criminal Code was *ultra vires* the Parliament of Canada, infringed ss. 2(a), 7 and 12 of the Charter, and was inconsistent with s. 1(b) of the Canadian Bill of Rights. The trial judge, Parker A.C.J.H.C., dismissed the motion, and an appeal to the Ontario Court of Appeal was dismissed. The trial proceeded before Parker A.C.J.H.C. and a jury, and the three accused were acquitted. The Crown appealed the acquittal to the Court of Appeal and the appellants filed a cross-appeal. The Court of Appeal allowed the appeal, set aside the verdict of acquittal and ordered a new trial. The court held that the cross-appeal related to issues already raised in the appeal, and the issues were therefore examined as part of the appeal.

Section 7 of the Charter

A. Interpreting s. 7

The goal of Charter interpretation is to secure for all people "the full benefit of the Charter's protection." To attain that goal, this court has held consistently that the proper technique for the interpretation of Charter provisions is to pursue a "purposive" analysis of the right guaranteed. A right recognized in the Charter is "to be understood, in other words, in the light of the interests it was meant to protect."

B. Security of the Person

The law has long recognized that the human body ought to be protected from interference by others. At common law, for example, any medical procedure carried out on a person without that person's consent is an assault. Only in emergency circumstances does the law allow others to make decisions of this nature. Similarly, art. 19 of the Civil Code of Lower Canada provides that "[t]he human person is inviolable" and that "[n]o person may cause harm to the person of another without his consent or without being authorized by law to do so." "Security of the person," in other words, is not a value alien to our legal landscape. With the advent of the Charter, security of the person has been elevated to the status of a constitutional norm. This is not to say that the various forms of protection accorded to the human body by the common and civil law occupy a similar status. "Security of the person" must be given content in a manner sensitive to its constitutional position. The above examples are simply illustrative of our respect for individual physical integrity.

The case-law leads me to the conclusion that state interference with bodily integrity and serious state-imposed psychological stress, at least in the criminal law context, constitute a breach of security of the person.

I wish to reiterate that finding a violation of security of the person does not end the s. 7 inquiry. Parliament could choose to infringe security of the person if it did so in a manner consistent with the principles of fundamental justice. The present discussion should therefore be seen as a threshold inquiry and the conclusions do not dispose definitively of all the issues relevant to s. 7. With that caution, I have no difficulty in concluding that the encyclopedic factual submissions addressed to us by counsel in the present appeal establish beyond any doubt that s. 251 of the Criminal Code is *prima facie* a violation of the security of the person of thousands of Canadian women who have made the difficult decision that they do not wish to continue with a pregnancy.

At the most basic, physical and emotional level, every pregnant woman is told by the section that she cannot submit to a generally safe medical procedure that might be of clear benefit to her unless she meets criteria entirely unrelated to her own priorities and aspirations. Not only does the removal of decision-making power threaten women in a physical sense; the indecision of knowing whether an abortion will be granted inflicts emotional stress. Section 251 clearly interferes with a woman's bodily integrity in both a physical and emotional sense. Forcing a woman, by threat of criminal sanction, to carry a foetus to term unless she meets certain criteria unrelated to her own priorities and aspirations, is a profound interference with a woman's body and thus a violation of security of the person. Section 251, therefore, is required by the Charter to comport with the principles of fundamental justice.

Although this interference with physical and emotional integrity is sufficient in itself to trigger a review of s. 251 against the principles of fundamental justice, the operation of the decision-making mechanism set out in s. 251 creates additional glaring breaches of security of the person. The evidence indicates that s. 251 causes a certain amount of delay for women who are successful in meeting its criteria. In the context of abortion, any unnecessary delay can have profound consequences on the woman's physical and emotional well-being.

The first factor to consider is that different medical techniques are employed to perform abortions at different stages of pregnancy. The testimony of expert doctors at trial indicated that in the first 12 weeks of pregnancy, the relatively safe and simple suction dilation and curettage method of abortion is typically used in North America. From the 13th to the 16th week, the more dangerous dilation and evacuation procedure is performed, although much less often in Canada than in the United States. From the 16th week of pregnancy, the instillation method is commonly employed in Canada. This method requires the intra-amniotic introduction of prostoglandin, urea, or a saline solution, which causes a woman to go into labour, giving birth to a foetus which is usually dead, but not invariably so. The uncontroverted evidence showed that each method of abortion progressively increases risks to the woman.

The second consideration is that even within the periods appropriate to each method of abortion, the evidence indicated that the earlier the abortion was performed, the fewer the complications and the lower the risk of mortality. For example, a study emanating from the centre for disease control in Atlanta confirmed that "D & E [dilation and evacuation] procedures performed at 13 to 15 weeks' gestation were nearly 3 times safer than those performed at 16 weeks or later." Even more revealing were the over-all mortality statistics evaluated by Drs. Cates and Grimes. They concluded from their study of the relevant data that: "Anything that contributes to delay in performing abortions increases the complication rates by 15% to 30%, and the chance of dying by 50% for each week of delay." These statistics indicate clearly that even if he average delay caused by s. 251 *per arguendo* is of only a couple of weeks' duration, the effects upon any particular woman can be serious and, occasionally, fatal.

It is no doubt true that the over-all complication and mortality rates for women who undergo abortions are very low, but the increasing risks caused by delay are so clearly established that I have no difficulty in concluding that the delay in obtaining therapeutic abortions caused by the mandatory procedures of s. 251 is an infringement of the purely physical aspect of the individual's right to security of the person.

The above physical interference caused by the delays created by s. 251, involving a clear risk of damage to the physical well-being of a woman, is sufficient, in my view, to warrant inquiring whether s. 251 comports with the principles of fundamental justice. However, there is yet another infringement of security of the person. It is clear from the evidence that s. 251 harms the psychological integrity of women seeking abortions.

I have already noted that the instillation procedure requires a woman actually to experience labour and to suffer through the birth of a foetus that is usually but not always dead. Statistics from 1982 indicated that 33.4% of second trimester abortions in Ontario were done by instillation, and the Powell report revealed, at p. 36, that even in 1986 there persisted a high incidence of second trimester abortions in Ontario. The psychological injury caused by delay in obtaining abortions, much of which must be attributed to the procedures set out in s. 251, constitutes an additional infringement of the right to security of the person.

In summary, s. 251 is a law which forces women to carry a foetus to term contrary to their own priorities and aspirations and which imposes serious delay causing increased physical and psychological trauma to those women who meet its criteria. It must, therefore, be determined whether that infringement is accomplished in accordance with the principles of fundamental justice, thereby saving s. 251 under the second part of s. 7.

C. The Principles of Fundamental Justice

In outline, s. 251 operates in the following manner. Subsection (1) creates an indictable offence for any person to use any means with the intent "to procure the miscarriage of a female person." Subsec-

tion (2) establishes a parallel indictable offence for any pregnant woman to use or to permit any means to be used with the intent "to procure her own miscarriage." The crucial provision for the purposes of the present appeal is s-s. (4) which states that the offences created in s-ss. (1) and (2) "do not apply" in certain circumstances. In *Morgentaler (1975)*, at p. 493 C.C.C., p. 205 D.L.R., p. 673 S.C.R., a majority of this court held that the effect of s. 251(4) was to afford "a complete answer and defence to those who respect its terms."

The procedure surrounding the defence is rather complex. A pregnant woman who desires to have an abortion must apply to the "therapeutic abortion committee" of an "accredited or approved hospital." Such a committee is empowered to issue a certificate in writing stating that, in the opinion of the majority of the committee, the continuation of the pregnancy would be likely to endanger the pregnant woman's life or health. Once a copy of the certificate is given to a qualified medical practitioner who is not a member of the therapeutic abortion committee, he or she is permitted to perform an abortion on the pregnant woman and both the doctor and the woman are freed from any criminal liability.

The Badgley report contains a wealth of detailed information which demonstrates, however, that many of the most serious problems with the functioning of s. 251 are created by procedural and administrative requirements established in the law.

The seemingly neutral requirement of s. 251(4) that at least four physicians be available to authorize and to perform an abortion meant in practice that abortions would be absolutely unavailable in almost one quarter of all hospitals in Canada.

Even if a hospital is eligible to create a therapeutic abortion committee, there is no requirement in s. 251 that the hospital need do so. The Badgley committee discovered that in 1976, of the 559 general hospitals which met the procedural requirements of s. 251, only 271 hospitals in Canada, or only 20.1% of the total, had established a therapeutic abortion committee (p. 105).

Even though the Badgley report was issued 10 years ago, the relevant statistics do not appear to be out of date. More recent data exists for Ontario. In the Powell report, it was noted that in 1986 only 54% of accredited acute care hospitals in the province had therapeutic abortion committees. In five counties there were no committees at all (p. 24). Of the 95 hospitals with committees, 12 did not do any abortions in 1986 (p. 24).

A further flaw with the administrative system established in s. 251(4) is the failure to provide an adequate standard for therapeutic abortion committees which must determine when a therapeutic abortion should, as a matter of law, be granted. Subsection (4) states simply that a therapeutic abortion committee may grant a certificate when it determines that a continuation of pregnancy would be likely to endanger the "life or health" of the pregnant woman. It was noted above that "health" is not defined for the purposes of the section.

Various expert doctors testified at trial that therapeutic abortion committees apply widely differing definitions of health. For some committees, psychological health is a justification for therapeutic abortion; for others it is not. Some committees routinely refuse abortions to married women unless they are in physical danger, while for other committees it is possible for a married women to show that she would suffer psychological harm if she continued with a pregnancy, thereby justifying an abortion. It is not typically possible for women to know in advance what standard of health will be applied by any given committee.

When the decision of the therapeutic abortion committee is so directly laden with legal consequences, the absence of any clear legal standard to be applied by the committee in reaching its decision is a serious procedural flaw.

The combined effect of all of these problems with the procedure stipulated in s. 251 for access to therapeutic abortions is a failure to comply with the principles of fundamental justice. In *Reference re: s. 94(2) of Motor Vehicle Act*, Lamer J. held, at p. 302 C.C.C., p. 550 D.L.R., p. 503 S.C.R., that "the principles of fundamental justice are to be found in the basic tenets of our legal system." One of the basic tenets of our system of criminal justice is that when Parliament creates a defence to a criminal charge, the defence should not be illusory or so difficult to attain as to be practically illusory.

Consider then the case of a pregnant married woman who wishes to apply for a therapeutic abortion certificate because she fears that her psychological health would be impaired seriously if she carried the foetus to term. The uncontroverted evidence reveals that there are many areas in Canada where such a woman would simply not have access to a therapeutic abortion. She may live in an area where no hospital has four doctors; no therapeutic abortion committee can be created. Equally, she may live in a place where the treatment functions of the nearby hospitals do not satisfy the definition of "accredited hospital" in s. 251(6). Or she may live in a province where the provincial government has imposed such stringent requirements on hospitals seeking to create therapeutic abortion committees that no hospital can qualify. Alternatively, our hypothetical woman may confront a therapeutic abortion committee in her local hospital which defines "health" in purely physical terms or which refused to countenance abortions for married women. In each of these cases, it is the administrative structures and procedures established by s. 251 itself that would in practice prevent the woman from gaining the benefit of the defence held out to her in s. 251(4).

Parliament must be given room to design an appropriate administrative and procedural structure for bringing into operation a particular defence to criminal liability. But if that structure is "so manifestly unfair, having regard to the decisions it is called upon to make, as to violate the principles of *fundamental* justice," that structure must be struck down. In the present case, the structure — the system regulating access to therapeutic abortions — is manifestly unfair. It contains so many potential barriers to its own operation that the defence it creates will in many circumstances be practically unavailable to women who would *prima facie* qualify for the defence, or at least would force such women to travel great distances at substantial expense and inconvenience in order to benefit from a defence that is held out to be generally available.

I conclude that the procedures created in s. 251 of the Criminal Code for obtaining a therapeutic abortion do not comport with the principles of fundamental justice. For the reasons given earlier, the deprivation of security of the person caused by s. 251 as a whole is not in accordance with the second clause of s. 7. It remains to be seen whether s. 251 can be justified for the purposes of s. 1 of the Charter.

Section 1 Analysis

I think the protection of the interests of pregnant women is a valid governmental objective, where life and health can be jeopardized by criminal sanctions. Like Beetz and Wilson JJ., I agree that protection of foetal interests by Parliament is also a valid governmental objective. It follows that balancing these interests, with the lives and health of women a major factor, is clearly an important governmental objective.

I am equally convinced, however, that the means chosen to advance the legislative objectives of s. 251 do not satisfy any of the three elements of the proportionality component of *R. v. Oakes*. The evidence has led me to conclude that the infringement of the security of the person of pregnant women caused by s. 251 is not accomplished in accordance with the principles of fundamental justice. It has been demonstrated that the procedures and administrative structures created by s. 251 are often arbitrary and unfair. The procedures established to implement the policy of s. 251 impair s. 7 rights far more than is necessary because they hold out an illusory defence to many women who would *prima facie* qualify under the exculpatory provisions of s. 251(4). In other words, many women whom Parliament professes not to wish to subject to criminal liability will nevertheless be forced by the practical unavailability of the supposed defence to risk liability or to suffer other harm such as a traumatic late abortion caused by the delay inherent in the s. 251 system. Finally, the effects of the limitation upon the s. 7 rights of many pregnant women are out of proportion to the objective sought to be achieved. Indeed, to the

extent that s. 251(4) is designed to protect the life and health of women, the procedures it establishes may actually defeat that objective. The administrative structures of s. 251(4) are so cumbersome that women whose health is endangered by pregnancy may not be able to gain a therapeutic abortion, at least without great trauma, expense and inconvenience.

I conclude, therefore, that the cumbersome structure of s-s. (4) not only unduly subordinates the s. 7 rights of pregnant women but may also defeat the value Parliament itself has established as paramount, namely, the life and health of the mother. As I have noted, counsel for the Crown did contend that one purpose of the procedures required by s-s. (4) is to protect the interests of the foetus. State protection of foetal interests may well be deserving of constitutional recognition under s. 1. Still, there can be no escape from the fact that Parliament has failed to establish either a standard or a procedure whereby any such interests might prevail over those of the woman in a fair and non-arbitrary fashion.

Section 251 of the Criminal Code cannot be saved, therefore, under s. 1 of the Charter.

Conclusion

Section 251 of the Criminal Code infringes the right to security of the person of many pregnant women. The procedures and administrative structures established in the section to provide for therapeutic abortions do not comply with the principles of fundamental justice. Section 7 of the Charter is infringed and that infringement cannot be saved under s. 1.

In *Morgentaler (1975)*, at p. 496 C.C.C., pp. 207–8 D.L.R., p. 676 S.C.R., the court held that "s. 251 contains a comprehensive code on the subject of abortions, unitary and complete within itself." Having found that this "comprehensive code" infringes the Charter, it is not the role of the court to pick and choose among the various aspects of s. 251 so as effectively to re-draft the section. The appeal should therefore be allowed and s. 251

as a whole struck down under s. 52(1) of the Constitution Act, 1982.

WILSON J.: — At the heart of this appeal is the question whether a pregnant woman can, as a constitutional matter, be compelled by law to carry the foetus to term. The legislature has proceeded on the basis that she can be so compelled and, indeed, has made it a criminal offence punishable by imprisonment under s. 251 of the Criminal Code, R.S.C. 1970, c. C-34, for her or her physician to terminate the pregnancy unless the procedural requirements of the section are complied with.

1. The Right of Access to Abortion

(a) THE RIGHT TO LIBERTY

The Charter is predicated on a particular conception of the place of the individual in society. An individual is not a totally independent entity disconnected from the society in which he or she lives. Neither, however, is the individual a mere cog in an impersonal machine in which his or her values, goals and aspirations are subordinated to those of the collectivity. The individual is a bit of both. The Charter reflects this reality by leaving a wide range of activities and decisions open to legitimate government control while at the same time placing limits on the proper scope of that control. Thus, the rights guaranteed in the Charter erect around each individual, metaphorically speaking, an invisible fence over which the state will not be allowed to trespass. The role of the courts is to map out, piece by piece, the parameters of the fence.

The Charter and the right to individual liberty guaranteed under it are inextricably tied to the concept of human dignity. The idea of human dignity finds expression in almost every right and freedom guaranteed in the Charter. Individuals are afforded the right to choose their own religion and their own philosophy of life, the right to choose with whom they will associate and how they will express themselves, the right to choose where they will live and what occupation they will pursue. These are all examples of the basic theory underlying the Charter, namely, that the state will respect choices made by individuals and, to the greatest extent possible, will avoid subordinating these choices to any one conception of the good life.

Thus, an aspect of the respect for human dignity on which the Charter is founded is the right to make fundamental personal decisions without interference from the state. This right is a critical component of the right to liberty.

The question then becomes whether the decision of a woman to terminate her pregnancy falls within this class of protected decision. I have no doubt that it does. This decision is one that will have profound psychological, economic and social consequences for the pregnant woman. The circumstances giving rise to it can be complex and varied and there may be, and usually are, powerful considerations militating in opposite directions. It is a decision that deeply reflects the way the woman thinks about herself and her relationship to others and to society at large. It is not just a medical decision; it is a profound social and ethical one as well. Her response to it will be the response of the whole person.

It is probably impossible for a man to respond, even imaginatively, to such a dilemma not just because it is outside the realm of his personal experience (although this is, of course, the case) but because he can relate to it only by objectifying it, thereby eliminating the subjective elements of the female psyche which are at the heart of the dilemma. Women's needs and aspirations are only now being translated into protected rights. The right to reproduce or not to reproduce which is in issue in this case is one such right and is properly perceived as an integral part of modern woman's struggle to assert *her* dignity and worth as a human being.

Given then that the right to liberty guaranteed by s. 7 of the Charter gives a woman the right to decide for herself whether or not to terminate her pregnancy, does s. 251 of the Criminal Code violate this right? Clearly it does. The purpose of the section is to take the decision away from the woman and give it to a committee. Furthermore, as the Chief Justice correctly points out, the committee bases its decision on "criteria entirely unrelated to [the pregnant women's] priorities and aspirations." The fact that the decision whether a woman will be allowed to terminate her pregnancy is in the hands of a committee is just as great a violation of the woman's right to personal autonomy in decisions of an intimate and private nature as it would be if a committee were established to decide whether a woman should be allowed to continue her pregnancy. Both these arrangements violate the woman's right to liberty by deciding for her something that she has the right to decide for herself.

(b) THE RIGHT TO SECURITY OF THE PERSON

The present legislative scheme for the obtaining of an abortion clearly subjects pregnant women to considerable emotional stress as well as to unnecessary physical risk. I believe, however, that the flaw in the present legislative scheme goes much deeper than that. In essence, what it does is assert that the woman's capacity to reproduce is not to be subject to her own control. It is to be subject to the control of the state. She may not choose whether to exercise her existing capacity or not to exercise it. This is not, in my view, just a matter of interfering with her right to liberty in the sense (already discussed) of her right to personal autonomy in decision-making, it is a direct interference with her physical "person" as well. She is truly being treated as a means — a means to an end which she does not desire but over which she has no control. She is the passive recipient of a decision made by others as to whether her body is to be used to nurture a new life. Can there by anything that comports less with human dignity and self-respect? How can a woman in this position have any sense of security with respect to her person? I believe that s. 251 of the Criminal Code deprives the pregnant woman of her right to security of the person as well as her right to liberty.

2. The Scope of the Right under s. 7

(a) THE PRINCIPLES OF FUNDAMENTAL JUSTICE

A deprivation of the s. 7 right which has the effect of infringing a right guaranteed elsewhere in the Charter cannot be in accordance with the principles of fundamental justice.

In my view, the deprivation of the s. 7 right with which we are concerned in this case offends s. 2(a) of the Charter. I say this because I believe that the decision whether or not to terminate a pregnancy is essentially a moral decision, a matter of conscience. I do not think there is or can be any dispute about that. The question is: whose conscience? Is the conscience of the woman to be paramount or the conscience of the state? I believe, for the reasons I gave in discussing the right to liberty, that in a free and democratic society it must be the conscience of the individual. Indeed, s. 2(a) makes it clear that this freedom belongs to "everyone", i.e., to each of us individually. I quote the section for convenience:

> 2. Everyone has the fundamental freedoms:
>   (a) freedom of conscience and religion;

It seems to me, therefore, that in a free and democratic society "freedom of conscience and religion" should be broadly construed to extend to conscientiously-held beliefs, whether grounded in religion or in a secular morality. Indeed, as a matter of statutory interpretation, "conscience" and "religion" should not be treated as tautologous if capable of independent, although related, meaning. Accordingly, for the state to take sides on the issue of abortion, as it does in the impugned legislation by making it a criminal offence for the pregnant woman to exercise one of her options, is not only to endorse but also to enforce, on pain of further loss of liberty through actual imprisonment, one conscientiously-held view at the expense of another. It is to deny freedom of conscience to some, to treat them as means to an end, to deprive them, as Professor MacCormick puts it, of their "essential humanity." Can this comport with fundamental justice?

Legislation which violates freedom of conscience in this manner cannot, in my view, be in accordance with the principles of fundamental justice within the meaning of s. 7.

(b) SECTION 1 OF THE CHARTER

In my view, the primary objective of the impugned legislation must be seen as the protection of the foetus. It undoubtedly has other ancillary objectives, such as the protection of the life and health of pregnant women, but I believe that the main objective advanced to justify a restriction on the pregnant woman's s. 7 right is the protection of the foetus. I think this is a perfectly valid legislative objective.

The question is: at what point in the pregnancy does the protection of the foetus become such a pressing and substantial concern as to outweigh the fundamental right of the woman to decide whether or not to carry the foetus to term? At what point does the state's interest in the protection of the foetus become "compelling" and justify state intervention in what is otherwise a matter of purely personal and private concern?

A developmental view of the foetus supports a permissive approach to abortion in the early stages of pregnancy and a restrictive approach in the later stages. In the early stages the woman's autonomy would be absolute; her decision, reached in consultation with her physician, not to carry the foetus to term would be conclusive. The state would have no business inquiring into her reasons. Her reasons for having an abortion would, however, be the proper subject of inquiry at the later stages of her pregnancy when the state's compelling interest in the protection of the foetus would justify it in prescribing conditions. The precise point in the development of the foetus at which the state's interest in its protection becomes "compelling" I leave to the informed judgment of the legislature, which is in a position to receive guidance on the subject from all the relevant disciplines. It seems to me, however, that it might fall somewhere in the second trimester.

Section 251 of the Criminal Code takes the decision away from the woman at *all* stages of her pregnancy. It is a complete denial of the woman's constitutionally protected right under s. 7, not merely a limitation on it. It cannot, in my opinion, meet the proportionality test in *Oakes*. It is not sufficiently tailored to the legislative objective and does not impair the woman's right "as little as possible." It cannot be saved under s. 1.

Appeal allowed; acquittals restored.

REGINA v. BUTLER

SUPREME COURT OF CANADA   FEBRUARY 27, 1992

BACKGROUND

In 1987, Butler operated a video store in Winnipeg. He rented so-called "hard core" videos and
magazines as well as "sexual paraphernalia." He
was charged with numerous counts of offences,
contrary to section 163 of the Criminal Code.
The trial judge convicted Butler on 8 counts relating to 8 films but acquitted him on 242 other
counts. The Crown appealed against the acquittals to the Manitoba Court of Appeal, while the
accused appealed against his convictions. The
Court of Appeal allowed the Crown's appeal and
entered convictions against Butler on all counts.
Butler then appealed to the Supreme Court of
Canada against the judgment of the Court of
Appeal.

MAIN ISSUES

(1) Does section 163 of the Criminal Code violate
the guarantee to freedom of expression, enshrined
in Section 2(b) of the Charter? If section 163 of
the Code does violate this guarantee, is it nevertheless saved by the application of Section 1 of the
Charter? (2) What is the appropriate test for
determining whether there has been "undue
exploitation of sex," as defined by section 163(8)
of the Code?

JUDGMENTS

The judgment of the *majority* of the members of
the Supreme Court of Canada was delivered by Justice Sopinka (with whom Chief Justice Lamer and
Justices La Forest, Cory, McLachlin, Stevenson and
Iacobucci agreed). The separate, *concurring* judgment of Justice Gonthier (with whom Justice
L'Heureux-Dubé agreed) has been omitted.

SOPINKA J.: — This appeal calls into question the
constitutionality of the obscenity provisions of
the Criminal Code, R.S.C. 1985, c. C-46, s. 163.
They are attacked on the ground that they contravene s. 2(b) of the Canadian Charter of Rights
and Freedoms. The case requires the Court to
address one of the most difficult and controversial
of contemporary issues, that of determining
whether, and to what extent, Parliament may
legitimately criminalize obscenity. I propose to
begin with a review of the facts which gave rise to
this appeal, as well of the proceedings in the lower
courts.

3. Issues

The following constitutional questions are raised
by this appeal:

1. Does s. 163 of the Criminal Code of Canada, R.S.C., 1985, c. C-46, violate s. 2(b) of the Canadian Charter of Rights and Freedoms?
2. If s. 163 of the Criminal Code of Canada, R.S.C., 1985, c. C-46, violates s. 2(b) of the Canadian Charter of Rights and Freedoms, can s. 163 of the Criminal Code of Canada be demonstrably justified under s. 1 of the Canadian Charter of Rights and Freedoms as a reasonable limit prescribed by law?

4. Analysis

B. Judicial Interpretation of s. 163(8)

The first case to consider the current provision was *R. v. Brodie* (1962), 132 C.C.C. 161, 32 D.L.R. (2d) 507, [1962] S.C.R. 681. The majority of this court found in that case that D.H. Lawrence's novel *Lady Chatterley's Lover* was not obscene within the meaning of the Code. The *Brodie* case laid the groundwork for the interpretation of s. 163(8) by setting out the principal tests which should govern the determination of what is obscene for the purposes of criminal prosecution.

(a) SECTION 163(8) TO BE EXCLUSIVE TEST

In the words of Judson J. (at p. 179):

> I think that the new statutory definition does give the Court an opportunity to apply tests which have some certainty of meaning and are capable of objective application and which do not so much depend as before upon the idiosyncrasies and sensitivities of the tribunal of fact, whether judge or jury. We are now concerned with a Canadian statute which is exclusive of all others.

Any doubt that s. 163(8) was intended to provide an exhaustive test of obscenity was settled in *Dechow v. The Queen* (1997), 35 C.C.C. (2d) 22, 76 D.L.R. (3d) 1, [1978] 1 SC.R. 951. Laskin C.J.C. stated (at p. 30):

> I am not only satisfied to regard s. 159(8) [now s. 163(8)] as prescribing an exhaustive test of obscenity in respect of a publication which has sex as a theme or characteristic but I am also of the opinion that this Court should apply that test in respect of other provisions of the Code, such as ss. 163 and 164, in cases in which the allegation of obscenity revolves around sex considerations.

In the *Dechow* case, the majority ascribed a liberal meaning to the term "publication," and found that the sex devices in question were "publications," as the accused had made such objects "publicly known" and had produced and issued such articles for public sale. Furthermore in *R. v. Germain* (1985), 21 C.C.C. (3d) 289, 21 D.L.R. (4th) 296, [1985] 2 S.C.R. 241, La Forest J., with whom a majority of the court agreed on this point, held that the word "obscene" must be given the same meaning whether the articles are publications under s. 159(1) (now s. 163(1)) or matter covered by s. 159(2)(a) (now s. 163(2)(a)). As a consequence, it is now beyond dispute that s. 163(8) provides the exhaustive test of obscenity with respect to publications and objects which exploit sex as a dominant characteristic.

(b) TESTS OF "UNDUE EXPLOITATION OF SEX"

In order for the work or material to qualify as "obscene," the exploitation of sex must not only be its dominant characteristic, but such exploitation must be "undue." In determining when the exploitation of sex will be considered "undue," the courts have attempted to formulate workable tests. The most important of these is the "community standard of tolerance" test.

(i) "COMMUNITY STANDARD OF TOLERANCE" TEST
In *Brodie*, Judson J. accepted the view espoused notably by the Australian and New Zealand courts that obscenity is to be measured against "community standards."

The community standards test has been the subject of extensive judicial analysis. It is the standards of the community as a whole which must be considered and not the standards of a small segment of that community, such as the university community where a film was shown.

Our court was called upon to elaborate the community standards test in *R. v. Towne Cinema Theatres Ltd.* (1985), 18 C.C.C. 3(d) 193 at p. 205, 18 D.L.R. (4th) 1, [1985] 1 S.C.R. 494. Dickson C.J.C. reviewed the case law and found:

> The cases all emphasize that it is a standard of *tolerance*, not taste, that is relevant. What matters is not what Canadians think is right for themselves to see. What matters is what Canadians would not abide other Canadians seeing because it would be beyond the contemporary Canadian standard of tolerance to allow them to see it.
>
> Since the standard is tolerance, I think the audience to which the allegedly obscene material is targeted must be relevant. The operative-standards are those of the Canadian community as a whole, but since what matters is what other people may see, it is quite conceivable that the Canadian community would tolerate varying degrees of explicitness depending upon the audience and the circumstances.

(Emphasis in original.)

Therefore, the community standards test is concerned not with what Canadians would not tolerate being exposed to themselves, but what they would not tolerate *other* Canadians being exposed to. The minority view was that the tolerance level will vary depending on the manner, time, and place in which the material is presented as well as the audience to whom it is directed. The majority opinion on this point was expressed by Wilson J. in the following passage (at p. 215):

> It is not, in my opinion, open to the courts under s. 159(8) of the Criminal Code to characterize a movie as obscene if shown to one constituency but not if shown to another. . . In my view, a movie is either obscene under the Code based on a national community standard of tolerance or it

is not. If it is not, it may still be the subject of provincial regulatory control.

(ii) "DEGRADATION OR DEHUMANIZATION" TEST

There has been a growing recognition in recent cases that material which may be said to exploit sex in a "degrading or dehumanizing" manner will necessarily fail the community standards test. Borins Co. Ct. J. expressed this view in *R. v. Doug Rankine Co. Ltd.* (1983), 9 C.C.C. (3d) 53 at p. 70, 36 C.R. (3d) 154 (Ont. Co. Ct.):

> . . . films which consist substantially or partially of scenes which portray violence and cruelty in conjunction with sex, particularly where the performance of indignities degrade and dehumanize the people upon whom they are performed, exceed the level of community tolerance.

Subsequent decisions, such as *R. v. Ramsingh* (1984), 14 C.C.C. (3d) 230, 29 Man. R. (2d) 110 (Q.B.), and *R. v. Wagner* (1985), 43 C.R. (3d) 318, 36 Alta. L.R. (2d) 301 (Q.B.), held that material that "degraded" or "dehumanized" any of the participants would exceed community standards even in the absence of cruelty and violence.

Among other things, degrading or dehumanizing materials place women (and sometimes men) in positions of subordination, servile submission or humiliation. They run against the principles of equality and dignity of all human beings. In the appreciation of whether material is degrading or dehumanizing, the appearance of consent is not necessarily determinative. Consent cannot save materials that otherwise contain degrading or dehumanizing scenes. Sometimes the very appearance of consent makes the depicted acts even more degrading or dehumanizing.

This type of material would, apparently, fail the community standards test not because it offends against morals but because it is perceived by public opinion to be harmful to society, particularly to women. While the accuracy of this perception is not susceptible of exact proof, there is a substantial body of opinion that holds that the portrayal of persons being subjected to degrading or dehumanizing sexual treatment results in harm, particularly to women and therefore to society as a whole. It would be reasonable to conclude that there is an appreciable risk of harm to society in the portrayal of such material. The effect of the evidence on public opinion was summed up by Wilson J. in *Towne Cinema, supra*, as follows (at pp. 217–18):

> The most that can be said, I think, is that the public has concluded that exposure to material which degrades the human dimensions of life to a subhuman or merely physical dimension and thereby contributes to a process of moral desensitization must be harmful in some way.

In *Towne Cinema*, Dickson C.J.C. considered the "degradation" or "dehumanization" test to be the principal indicator of "undueness" without specifying what role the community tolerance test plays in respect of this issue. He did observe, however, that the community might tolerate some forms of exploitation that caused harm that were nevertheless undue.

> Sex-related publications which portray persons in a degrading manner as objects of violence, cruelty or other forms of dehumanizing treatment, may be "undue" for the purpose of s. 159(8). No one should be subject to the degradation and humiliation inherent in publications which link sex with violence, cruelty, and other forms of dehumanizing treatment. It is not likely that at a given moment in a society's history, such publications will be tolerated...
>
> However, as I have noted above, there is no necessary coincidence between the undueness of publications which degrade people by linking violence, cruelty or other forms of dehumanizing treatment with sex, and the community standard of tolerance. Even if certain sex-related materials were found to be within the standard of tolerance of the community, it would still be necessary to ensure that they were not "undue" in some other

sense, for example in the sense that they portray persons in a degrading manner as objects of violence, cruelty, or other forms of dehumanizing treatment.

(Emphasis in original.)

(iii) "INTERNAL NECESSITIES TEST" OR "ARTISTIC DEFENCE"
In determining whether the exploitation of sex is "undue," Judson J. set out the test of "internal necessities" in *Brodie, supra* (at p. 181):

> What I think is aimed at is excessive emphasis on the theme for a base purpose. But I do not think that there is undue exploitation if there is no more emphasis on the theme than is required in the serious treatment of the theme of a novel with honesty and uprightness. That the work under attack is a serious work of fiction is to me beyond question. It has none of the characteristics that are often described in judgments dealing with obscenity — dirt for dirt's sake, the leer of the sensualist, depravity in the mind of an author with an obsession for dirt, pornography, an appeal to a prurient interest, etc. The section recognizes that the serious-minded author must have freedom in the production of a work of genuine artistic and literary merit and the quality of the work, as the witnesses point out and common sense indicates, must have real relevance in determining not only a dominant characteristic but also whether there is undue exploitation.

As counsel for the Crown pointed out in his oral submissions, the artistic defence is the last step in the analysis of whether the exploitation of sex is undue. Even material which by itself offends community standards will not be considered "undue," if it is required for the serious treatment of a theme.

Accordingly, the "internal necessities" test, or what has been referred to as the "artistic defence," has been interpreted to assess whether the exploitation of sex has a justifiable role in advancing the plot or the theme, and in considering the work as a whole, does not merely represent "dirt for dirt's sake" but has a legitimate role when measured by the internal necessities of the work itself.

(iv) THE RELATIONSHIP OF THE TESTS TO EACH OTHER

This review of jurisprudence shows that it fails to specify the relationship of the tests one to another. Failure to do so with respect to the community standards test and the degrading or dehumanizing test, for example, raises a serious question as to the basis on which the community acts in determining whether the impugned material will be tolerated. With both these tests being applied to the same material and apparently independently, we do not know whether the community found the material to be intolerable because it was degrading or dehumanizing, because it offended against morals, or on some other basis. In some circumstances, a finding that the material is tolerable can be overruled by the conclusion by the court that it causes harm and is therefore undue. Moreover, is the internal necessities test dominant so that it will redeem material that would otherwise be undue or is it just one factor? Is this test applied by the community or is it determined by the court without regard for the community? This hiatus in the jurisprudence has left the legislation open to attack on the ground of vagueness and uncertainty. That attack is made in this case. This lacuna in the interpretation of the legislation must, if possible, be filled before subjecting the legislation to Charter scrutiny.

Pornography can be usefully divided into three categories: (1) explicit sex with violence, (2) explicit sex without violence but which subjects people to treatment that is degrading or dehumanizing, and (3) explicit sex without violence that is neither degrading nor dehumanizing. Violence in this context includes both actual physical violence and threats of physical violence. Relating these three categories to the terms of s. 163(8) of the Code, the first, explicit sex coupled with violence, is expressly mentioned. Sex coupled with crime, horror, or cruelty will sometimes involve violence. Cruelty, for instance, will usually do so. But, even in the absence of violence, sex coupled with crime, horror, or cruelty may fall within the second category. As for category (3), subject to the exception referred to below, it is not covered.

The courts must determine as best they can what the community would tolerate others being exposed to on the basis of the degree of harm that may flow from such exposure. Harm in this context means that it predisposes persons to act in an antisocial manner as, for example, the physical or mental mistreatment of women by men, or, what is perhaps debatable, the reverse. Antisocial conduct for this purpose is conduct which society formally recognizes as incompatible with its proper functioning. The stronger the inference of a risk of harm the lesser the likelihood of tolerance. The inference may be drawn from the material itself or from the material and other evidence. Similarly, evidence as to the community standards is desirable but not essential.

In making this determination with respect to the three categories of pornography referred to above, the portrayal of sex coupled with violence will almost always constitute the undue exploitation of sex. Explicit sex which is degrading or dehumanizing may be undue if the risk of harm is substantial. Finally, explicit sex that is not violent and neither degrading nor dehumanizing is generally tolerated in our society and will not qualify as the undue exploitation of sex unless it employs children in its production.

If material is not obscene under this framework, it does not become so by reason of the person to whom it is or may be shown or exposed nor by reason of the place or manner in which it is shown. The availability of sexually explicit materials in theatres and other public places is subject to regulation by competent provincial legislation. Typically, such legislation imposes restrictions on the material available to children.

The foregoing deals with the interrelationship of the "community standards test" and "the degrading or dehumanizing" test. How does the "internal necessities" test fit into this scheme? The need to apply this test only arises if a work contains sexually explicit material that by itself would constitute the undue exploitation of sex. The portrayal of sex must then be viewed in context to determine whether that is the dominant theme of the work as a whole. Put another way, is undue exploitation of sex the main object of the work or is this portrayal of sex essential to a wider artistic, literary, or other similar purpose? Since the threshold determination must be made on the basis of community standards, that is, whether the sexually explicit aspect is undue, its impact when considered in context must be determined on the same basis. The court must determine whether the sexually explicit material when viewed in the context of the whole work would be tolerated by the community as a whole. Artistic expression rests at the heart of freedom of expression values and any doubt in this regard must be resolved in favour of freedom of expression.

C. Does s. 163 Violate 2(b) of the Charter?

In this case, both the purpose and effect of s. 163 are specifically to restrict the communication of certain types of materials based on their content. In my view, there is no doubt that s. 163 seeks to prohibit certain types of expressive activity and thereby infringes s. 2(b) of the Charter.

I would conclude that the first constitutional question should be answered in the affirmative.

D. Is s. 163 Justified under s. 1 of the Charter?

(a) IS S. 163 A LIMIT PRESCRIBED BY LAW?

The appellant argues that the provision is so vague that it is impossible to apply it. Vagueness must be considered in relation to two issues in this appeal: (1) is the law so vague that it does not qualify as "a limit prescribed by law," and (2) is it so imprecise that it is not a reasonable limit?

Standards which escape precise technical definition, such as "undue," are an inevitable part of the law. The Criminal Code contains other such standards. Without commenting on their constitutional validity, I note that the terms "indecent," "immoral," and "scurrilous," found in ss. 167, 168,

173, and 175, are nowhere defined in the Code. It is within the role of the judiciary to attempt to interpret these terms. If such interpretation yields an intelligible standard, the threshold test for the application of s. 1 is met. In my opinion, the interpretation of s. 163(8) in prior judgments that I have reviewed, as supplemented by these reasons, provides an intelligible standard.

(b) OBJECTIVE

The respondent argues that there are several pressing and substantial objectives which justify overriding the freedom to distribute obscene materials. Essentially, these objectives are the avoidance of harm resulting from antisocial attitudinal changes that exposure to obscene material causes and the public interest in maintaining a "decent society." On the other hand, the appellant argues that the objective of s. 163 is to have the state act as "moral custodian" in sexual matters and to impose subjective standards of morality.

I cannot agree with the suggestion of the appellant that Parliament does not have the right to legislate on the basis of some fundamental conception of morality for the purposes of safeguarding the values which are integral to a free and democratic society.

As the respondent and many of the interveners have pointed out, much of the criminal law is based on moral conceptions of right and wrong and the mere fact that a law is grounded in morality does not automatically render it illegitimate. In this regard, criminalizing the proliferation of materials which undermine another basic Charter right may indeed be a legitimate objective.

In my view, however, the overriding objective of s. 163 is not moral disapprobation but the avoidance of harm to society. In *Towne Cinema*, Dickson C.J.C. stated (at p. 204): "It is harm to society from undue exploitation that is aimed at by the section, not simply lapses in propriety or good taste."

The harm was described in the following way in the Report on Pornography by the Standing Committee on Justice and Legal Affairs (MacGuigan Report) (1978) (at p. 18:4):

The clear and unquestionable danger of this type of material is that it reinforces some unhealthy tendencies in Canadian society. The effect of this type of material is to reinforce male–female stereotypes to the detriment of both sexes. It attempts to make degradation, humiliation, victimization, and violence in human relationships appear normal and acceptable. A society which holds that egalitarianism, non-violence, consensualism, and mutuality are basic to any human interaction, whether sexual or other, is clearly justified in controlling and prohibiting any medium of depiction, description or advocacy which violates these principles.

This being the objective, is it pressing and substantial? Does the prevention of the harm associated with the dissemination of certain obscene materials constitute a sufficiently pressing and substantial concern to warrant a restriction on the freedom of expression? In this regard, it should be recalled that in *R. v. Keegstra* (1990), 61 C.C.C. (3d) 1, [1990] 3 S.C.R. 697, 1 C.R. (4th) 129, this court unanimously accepted that the prevention of the influence of hate propaganda on society at large was a legitimate objective.

This court has thus recognized that the harm caused by the proliferation of materials which seriously offend the values fundamental to our society is a substantial concern which justifies restricting the otherwise full exercise of the freedom of expression. In my view, the harm sought to be avoided in the case of the dissemination of obscene materials is similar. In the words of Nemetz C.J.B.C. in *R. v. Red Hot Video Ltd.* (1985), 18 C.C.C. (3d) 1 at p. 8, 45 C.R. (3d) 36, 15 C.R.R. 206 (B.C.C.A.), there is a growing concern that the exploitation of women and children, depicted in publications and films, can, in certain circumstances, lead to "abject and servile victimization." As Anderson J.A. also noted in that same case, if true equality between male and female persons is to be achieved, we cannot ignore the threat to equality resulting from exposure to audiences of certain types of violent and degrading material. Materials portraying women as a class as objects for sexual exploitation and abuse have a negative impact on "the individual's sense of self-worth and acceptance."

In reaching the conclusion that legislation proscribing obscenity is a valid objective which justifies some encroachment on the right to freedom of expression, I am persuaded in part that such legislation may be found in most free and democratic societies.

Finally, it should be noted that the burgeoning pornography industry renders the concern even more pressing and substantial than when the impugned provisions were first enacted. I would therefore conclude that the objective of avoiding the harm associated with the dissemination of pornography in this case is sufficiently pressing and substantial to warrant some restriction on full exercise of the right to freedom of expression. The analysis of whether the measure is proportional to the objective must, in my view, be undertaken in light of the conclusion that the objective of the impugned section is valid only in so far as it relates to the harm to society associated with obscene materials. Indeed, the section as interpreted in previous decisions and in these reasons is fully consistent with that objective. The objective of maintaining conventional standards of propriety, independently of any harm to society, is no longer justified in light of the values of individual liberty which underlie the Charter. This, then, being the objective of s. 163, which I have found to be pressing and substantial, I must now determine whether the section is rationally connected and proportional to this objective. As outlined above, s. 163(8) criminalizes the exploitation of sex and sex and violence, when, on the basis of the community test, it is undue. The determination of when such exploitation is undue is directly related to the immediacy of a risk of harm to society which is reasonably perceived as arising from its dissemination.

(c) PROPORTIONALITY

(i) GENERAL

The proportionality requirement has three aspects:

(1) the existence of a rational connection between the impugned measures and the objective;

(2) minimal impairment of the right or freedom; and

(3) a proper balance between the effects of the limiting measures and the legislative objective.

In assessing whether the proportionality test is met, it is important to keep in mind the nature of expression which has been infringed.

The values which underlie the protection of freedom of expression relate to the search for truth, participation in the political process, and individual self-fulfilment. The Attorney-General for Ontario argues that of these, only "individual self-fulfilment," and only in its most base aspect, that of physical arousal, is engaged by pornography. On the other hand, the civil liberties groups argue that pornography forces us to question conventional notions of sexuality and thereby launches us into an inherently political discourse.

A proper application of the test should not suppress what West refers to as "good pornography." The objective of the impugned provision is not to inhibit the celebration of human sexuality. However, it cannot be ignored that the realities of the pornography industry are far from the picture which the B.C. Civil Liberties Association would have us paint. Shannon J., in *R. v. Wagner, supra,* described the materials more accurately when he observed (at p. 331):

> Women, particularly, are deprived of unique human character or identity and are depicted as sexual playthings, hysterically and instantly responsive to male sexual demands. They worship male genitals and their own value depends upon the quality of their genitals and breasts.

In my view, the kind of expression which is sought to be advanced does not stand on an equal footing with other kinds of expression which directly engage the "core" of the freedom of expression values.

This conclusion is further buttressed by the fact that the targeted material is expression which is motivated, in the overwhelming majority of cases, by economic profit.

I will now turn to an examination of the three basic aspects of the proportionality test.

(ii) RATIONAL CONNECTION

The message of obscenity which degrades and dehumanizes is analogous to that of hate propaganda. As the Attorney-General of Ontario has argued in its factum, obscenity wields the power to wreak social damage in that a significant portion of the population is humiliated by its gross misrepresentations.

Accordingly, the rational link between s. 163 and the objective of Parliament relates to the actual causal relationship between obscenity and the risk of harm to society at large. On this point, it is clear that the literature of the social sciences remains subject to controversy.

The recent conclusions of *Pornography and Prostitution in Canada: Report of the Special Committee on Pornography and Prostitution* (1985) (the Fraser Report), vol. 1, could not postulate any causal relationship between pornography and the commission of violent crimes, the sexual abuse of children, or the disintegration of communities and society. This is in contrast to the findings of the MacGuigan Report, *ibid.*

While a direct link between obscenity and harm to society may be difficult, if not impossible, to establish, it is reasonable to presume that exposure to images bears a causal relationship to changes in attitudes and beliefs.

In the face of inconclusive social science evidence, the approach adopted by our court in *Irwin Toy v. Québec (Attorney-General)* (1989), 58 D.L.R. (4th) 577, 25 C.P.R. (3d) 417, [1989] 1 S.C.R. 927, is instructive. In that case, the basis for the legislation was that television advertising directed at young children is *per se* manipulative. The court made it clear that in choosing its mode of intervention, it is sufficient that Parliament had a *reasonable basis* (at p. 626):

> In the instant case, the court is called upon to assess competing social science evidence respecting

the appropriate means for addressing the problem of children's advertising. The question is whether the government had a reasonable basis, on the evidence tendered, for concluding that the ban on all advertising directed at children impaired freedom of expression as little as possible given the government's pressing and substantial objective.

And at p. 623: " . . . the court also recognized that the government was afforded a margin of appreciation to form legitimate objectives based on somewhat inconclusive social science evidence."

I am in agreement with Twaddle J.A. who expressed the view that Parliament was entitled to have a "reasoned apprehension of harm" resulting from the desensitization of individuals exposed to materials which depict violence, cruelty, and dehumanization in sexual relations.

Accordingly, I am of the view that there is a sufficiently rational link between the criminal sanction — which both demonstrates our community's disapproval of the dissemination of materials that potentially victimize women and restricts the negative influence such materials have on changes in attitudes and behaviour — and the objective.

(iii) MINIMAL IMPAIRMENT

In determining whether less intrusive legislation may be imagined, this court stressed in *Reference re: ss. 193 and 195.1 (1) (c) of Criminal Code* (1990), 56 C.C.C. (3d) 65, [1990] 1 S.C.R. 1123, 77 C.R. (3d) 1 (the *Prostitution Reference*), that it is not necessary that the legislative scheme be the "perfect" scheme, but that it be appropriately tailored *in the context of the infringed right* (at p. 75). Furthermore, in *Irwin Toy, supra*, Dickson C.J.C., Lamer and Wilson JJ. stated (at pp. 629–30):

> While evidence exists that other less intrusive options reflecting more modest objectives were available to the government, there is evidence establishing the necessity of a ban to meet the objectives the government had reasonably set. This court will not, in the name of minimal

impairment, take a restrictive approach to social science evidence and require legislatures to choose the least ambitious means to protect vulnerable groups.

There are several factors which contribute to the finding that the provision minimally impairs the freedom which is infringed.

First, the impugned provision does not proscribe sexually explicit erotica without violence that is not degrading or dehumanizing. It is designed to catch material that creates a risk of harm to society. It might be suggested that proof of actual harm should be required. It is apparent from what I have said above that it is sufficient in this regard for Parliament to have a reasonable basis for concluding that harm will result and this requirement does not demand actual proof of harm.

Secondly, materials which have scientific, artistic, or literary merit are not captured by the provision. As discussed above, the court must be generous in its application of the "artistic defence." The existence of an accompanying economic motive does not, of itself, deprive a work of significance as an example of individual or artistic expression.

Thirdly, in considering whether the provision minimally impairs the freedom in question, it is legitimate for the court to take into account Parliament's past abortive attempts to replace the definition with one that is more explicit. The attempt to provide exhaustive instances of obscenity has been shown to be destined to fail (Bill C-54, 2nd Sess., 33rd Parl.). It seems that the only practicable alternative is to strive towards a more abstract definition of obscenity which is contextually sensitive and responsive to progress in the knowledge and understanding of the phenomenon to which the legislation is directed. In my view, the standard of "undue exploitation" is therefore appropriate. The intractable nature of the problem and the impossibility of precisely defining a notion which is inherently elusive makes the possibility of a more explicit provision remote. In this light, it is appropriate to question whether, and at what cost, greater legislative precision can be demanded.

Fourthly, while the discussion in this appeal has been limited to the definition portion of s. 163, I would note that the impugned section, with the possible exception of s-s. (1), which is not in issue here, has been held by this court not to extend its reach to the private use or viewing of obscene materials.

Accordingly, it is only the public distribution and exhibition of obscene materials which is in issue here.

It is also submitted that there are more effective techniques to promote the objectives of Parliament. For example, if pornography is seen as encouraging violence against women, there are certain activities which discourage it — counselling rape victims to charge their assailants, provision of shelter and assistance for battered women, campaigns for laws against discrimination on the grounds of sex, education to increase the sensitivity of law enforcement agencies and other governmental authorities. In addition, it is submitted that education is an under-used response.

However, given the gravity of the harm, and the threat to the values at stake, I do not believe that the measure chosen by Parliament is equalled by the alternatives which have been suggested. Education, too, may offer a means of combating negative attitudes to women, just as it is currently used as a means of addressing other problems dealt with in the Code. However, there is no reason to rely on education alone. Serious social problems such as violence against women require multi-pronged approaches by government. Education and legislation are not alternatives but complements in addressing such problems. There is nothing in the Charter which requires Parliament to choose between such complementary measures.

(iv) BALANCE BETWEEN EFFECTS OF LIMITING MEASURES AND LEGISLATIVE OBJECTIVE

The final question to be answered in the proportionality test is whether the effects of the law so severely trench on a protected right that the legislative objective is outweighed by the infringement. The infringement on freedom of expression is confined to a measure designed to prohibit the distribution of sexually explicit materials accompanied by violence, and those without violence that are degrading or dehumanizing. As I have already concluded, this kind of expression lies far from the core of the guarantee of freedom of expression. It appeals only to the most base aspect of individual fulfilment, and it is primarily economically motivated.

The objective of the legislation, on the other hand, is of fundamental importance in a free and democratic society. It is aimed at avoiding harm, which Parliament has reasonably concluded will be caused directly or indirectly, to individuals, groups such as women and children, and consequently to society as a whole, by the distribution of these materials. It thus seeks to enhance respect for all members of society, and non-violence and equality in their relations with each other.

I therefore conclude that the restriction on freedom of expression does not outweigh the importance of the legislative objective.

5. Conclusion

I conclude that while s. 163(8) infringes s. 2(b) of the Charter, freedom of expression, it constitutes a reasonable limit and is saved by virtue of the provisions of s. 1. The trial judge convicted the appellant only with respect to materials which contained scenes involving violence or cruelty intermingled with sexual activity or depicted lack of consent to sexual contact or otherwise could be said to dehumanize men or women in a sexual context. The majority of the Court of Appeal, on the other hand, convicted the appellant on all charges.

I would answer the constitutional questions as follows:

Question 1: Does s. 163 of the Criminal Code of Canada, R.S.C., 1985, c. C-46, violate s. 2(b) of the Canadian Charter of Rights and Freedoms?

Answer: Yes.

Question 2: If s. 163 of the Criminal Code of Canada, R.S.C., 1985, c. C-46, violates s. 2(b) of the Canadian Charter of Rights and Freedoms, can s. 163 of the Criminal Code of Canada be demonstrably justified under s. 1 of the Canadian Charter of Rights and Freedoms as a reasonable limit prescribed by law?

Answer: Yes.

Appeal allowed; new trial ordered.

The *Actus Reus* Elements of a Criminal Offence

INTRODUCTION

For the purpose of academic analysis, the elements of a criminal offence have traditionally been divided into two categories: the *mens rea* elements and the *actus reus* elements. The *mens rea* elements consist of all of the mental (state-of-mind) requirements that the Crown must prove in order to achieve the conviction of an accused person who is charged with a criminal offence. The *actus reus* elements, by way of contrast, consist of all the *other* (non-mental) elements of the offence that must be established before an accused person may be convicted. However, it is becoming increasingly common for judges and legal scholars to include the requirement of *voluntariness* among the *actus reus* elements of a criminal offence.

The seven cases excerpted in Chapter 2 illustrate various elements of the *actus reus* component of criminal offences. The *Hatfield* case (1997) is an example of an exception to the general principle that conduct is an essential element of the *actus reus* of a criminal offence. In this particular case, the offence concerned is that of being in care and control of a motor vehicle while impaired by alcohol or a drug (section 253 of the Code).

The *Cooper* case (1993) illustrates the application of the important principle that the *actus reus* and *mens rea* elements of an offence must coincide before an individual may be convicted of a serious crime. In addition, the *Parks* case (1992) underscores the critical requirement that there be *voluntariness* of action on the part of the accused before he or she may be convicted of an offence. More specifically, this case examines the nature of the defence of automatism and the distinction between the defences of automa-

tism and "not criminally responsible on account of mental disorder" (NCRMD).

The remainder of the cases in this chapter focus on various aspects of the law concerning *causation*. In particular, they all concern situations in which the accused is charged with an offence that requires the Crown to prove that he or she *caused* the death of another person. The *Smithers* case (1977) established the rule of causation that applies to all homicide offences other than first degree murder under section 231(5) of the Criminal Code: the Crown must prove that the accused's conduct constituted a contributing cause of death, outside of the "de minimis range." On the other hand, in the *Harbottle* case (1993), the Supreme Court of Canada ruled that a more onerous test of causation (namely, the "substantial and integral cause" test) must be applied when the accused is charged with first degree murder under the provisions of section 231(5) of the Code.

The *Kitching and Adams* case (1976) raises the question of whether the chain of causation in a homicide case may be broken by the intervention of third parties who can be considered to have contributed, in some way, to the death of the victim. In this case, the intervention consisted of allegedly improper medical treatment that was administered after the two accused had seriously wounded the victim. Finally, the *Rodriguez* case (1993) addresses the difficult issues that arise when medical treatment accelerates the death of an individual who may be suffering from a terminal illness. In this particular instance, the question before the Supreme Court of Canada was whether the assisted suicide provision of the Criminal Code [section 241(b)] is valid under the Charter.

Regina v. Hatfield

ONTARIO COURT OF APPEAL   APRIL 3, 1997

BACKGROUND

The accused was charged with the offences of being in care and control of a motor vehicle while his ability to operate the vehicle was impaired by alcohol or a drug [section 253(a) of the Criminal Code], and being in care and control of a motor vehicle while having a blood-alcohol level of more than 80 milligrams of alcohol in 100 millilitres of blood [section 253(b)]. At Hatfield's trial in the Ontario Court (Provincial Division), both charges were dismissed. The Crown appealed to the summary conviction appeal court which set aside the dismissal and entered a conviction in relation to the charge of impairment (the "over 80" charge was stayed). The accused appealed to the Ontario Court of Appeal.

MAIN ISSUE

The presumption of care and control contained in section 258(1)(a) of the Criminal Code applies when the accused person occupies the seat or position ordinarily occupied by a person who operates a motor vehicle. Does the statutory presumption of care of control apply to the particular set of facts in this case?

JUDGMENT

The judgment of the court was delivered by Justice Goudge. The other members of the Court of Appeal were Justices Abella and Finlayson.

....

GOUDGE, J.A.: — On March 10, 1995, the appellant was tried in the Ontario Court (Provincial Division) upon an information alleging that he, on or about the 7th day of July, in the year 1994, at the Town of Pickering, in the said region:

1. Unlawfully did, while his ability to operate a motor vehicle was impaired by alcohol or a drug, have the care or control of a motor vehicle, contrary to s. 253(a) of the Criminal Code; and

2. Unlawfully did have the care or control of a motor vehicle, having consumed alcohol in such a quantity that the concentration thereof in his blood exceeded 80 milligrams of alcohol in 100 millilitres of blood, contrary to s. 253(b) of the Criminal Code.

At the conclusion of the trial both charges were dismissed.

The Crown appealed and, on December 12, 1995, the summary conviction appeal court set aside the dismissal, entered a conviction in respect of the charge of impairment and stayed the "over 80" charge.

The appellant, having been granted leave, appeals his conviction to this court.

The facts are straightforward. At about 9:00 P.M. on July 7, 1994, two Durham Region regional police officers noticed the appellant's car parked in an industrial parking lot in Pickering. The driver's seat was fully reclined. The appellant was sitting in the driver's seat so that only a portion of his head was visible to the approaching officers above the bottom of the window line of the vehicle. The key was in the ignition. The headlights and radio were on but the engine was not running.

The appellant testified that he had been drinking at a restaurant, and that upon leaving drove for about one-quarter of a mile before deciding he was not fit to drive. He then pulled into the parking lot, planning to stay there and sleep until he felt able to continue driving. He was awakened by the arrival of the two police officers.

The officers made a breath demand and the breathalyzer results were that the appellant had 180 and 170 milligrams of alcohol per 100 millilitres of blood in respect of the two tests taken, both significantly above the permitted level of 80 milligrams in 100 millilitres of blood. The appellant does not contest that he was impaired when the police officers arrived.

Section 253 of the Criminal Code reads in part as follows:

> 253. Every one commits an offence who operates a motor vehicle . . . or has the care or control of a motor vehicle . . . whether it is in motion or not,
>
> > (a) while the person's ability to operate the vehicle . . . is impaired by alcohol or a drug; or
> >
> > (b) having consumed alcohol in such a quantity that the concentration in the person's blood exceeds eighty milligrams of alcohol in one hundred millilitres of blood.

Section 258(1)(a), which creates a rebuttable presumption, is also germane to this matter. In relevant part, it reads as follows:

> 258(1) In any proceedings under subsection 255(1) in respect of an offence committed under section 253 or in any proceedings under subsection 255(2) or (3),
>
> > (a) where it is proved that the accused *occupied the seat or position ordinarily occupied by a person who operates a motor vehicle . . . the accused shall be deemed to have had the care or control of the vehicle . . . unless the accused establishes that the accused did not occupy that seat or position for the purpose of setting the vehicle . . . in motion . . .* [Emphasis added.]

It is clear that the appellant was significantly impaired. The only issue, therefore, was whether the appellant had the necessary care and control of the vehicle to sustain the conviction imposed by the summary conviction appeal court.

At trial, the Provincial Court judge held that the appellant did not have care or control of his car. The trial judge declined to apply the presumption created by s. 258(1)(a) because, on the facts of this case, he was not certain that a driver's seat, when fully reclined, could be said to be a "seat ordinarily occupied by the driver." He then went on to find that care or control could not be established beyond a reasonable doubt. In doing so, he appeared to rely primarily on the fact that the driver's seat was in a reclined position and, secondly, on his view that the facts in this case closely parallelled those in *R. v. Toews* (1985), 21 C.C.C. (3d) 24 (S.C.C.). In that case the Supreme Court concluded that an accused lying across the front seat of a vehicle, with his head by the passenger door and asleep in a sleeping bag, neither triggered the presumption of s. 258 nor demonstrated, apart from the presumption, the necessary acts of care or control to establish the offence.

The summary conviction appeal court held that the trial judge erred in law in failing to apply the presumption section. He further held that the trial judge erred in relying on *R. v. Toews*, where the facts were significantly different from those in *Toews*. He concluded that not only did the presumption apply but, even if it did not, the appellant had care or control of the vehicle.

In my view the summary conviction appeal court was correct in determining that, as a matter of law, the presumption provided for by s. 258(1) applies in this case. The language of the section requires that the accused occupy the seat ordinarily occupied by the driver. In this case, the appellant was in the driver's seat. On the plain language of the section, the presumption is therefore triggered. The fact that the seat was fully reclined does not, in my view, negate the application of the presumption. In *R. v. Toews* the Supreme Court of Canada said at p. 28:

> I would agree that to occupy the seat ordinarily occupied by the driver within the meaning of s. 237(1), one need not be sitting straight up with hands on the steering wheel and in all respects be ready to drive. The fact that some movement or adjustment of position might be required to enable a person to take the steering wheel and drive the car will not necessarily be such a departure from the occupation of the driver's seat that it will deprive the Crown of the right to rely on the presumption.

Where all that is necessary is for the occupant to bring the driver's seat up to its vertical position, the presumption must apply unless rebutted.

The appellant, however, argues that, on the facts of this case, the presumption is rebutted. He argues that the appropriate time to address the appellant's purpose in occupying the driver's seat is on the arrival of the police officers. On the facts of this case, he argues that the appellant's purpose at that point was to sleep, not to put the vehicle in motion.

In my view, on a correct reading of s. 258(1)(a) the presumption of care or control cannot be rebutted in this case. The broad purpose of the presumption section was set out by the Supreme Court of Canada in *R. v. Whyte* (1988), 42 C.C.C. (3d) 97 at 115, in the following language:

> Parliament wished to discourage intoxicated people from even placing themselves in a position

where they could set a vehicle in motion while at the same time providing a way for a person to avoid liability when there was a reason for entering the vehicle other than to set it in motion.

It seems to me that, where an intoxicated person is discovered occupying the driver's seat of a vehicle, the presumption will apply unless the person can demonstrate that his or her occupancy began without the purpose of setting the vehicle in motion.

On the appellant's reading of the section, an accused could escape the presumption by showing, on being apprehended by the police, no requisite intention by reason only that, being asleep, he was without intent to drive. Such a reading would not manifest a legislative intention to discourage intoxicated people from ever getting behind the wheel in the first place but rather a legislative intention to encourage intoxicated people, once behind the wheel and on the road, to pull off.

In summary, therefore, it is my view that to rebut the presumption of care or control the appellant must show that his occupancy began without the purpose of setting the vehicle in motion. The evidence here was entirely to the opposite effect. The appellant occupied the driver's seat in order to drive the vehicle away from the restaurant where he had been drinking. He intended to continue driving when he decided that he was no longer impaired.

As a matter of law, therefore, I conclude on the facts of this case that the presumption of care or control applies and cannot, on the evidence, be rebutted.

It is therefore unnecessary to pass on the finding of the summary conviction appeal court that even without the presumption the appellant had care or control of his vehicle.

In the result, the appellant was properly convicted of being in care or control of his motor vehicle while impaired. I would dismiss the appeal.

Appeal dismissed.

Regina v. Cooper

SUPREME COURT OF CANADA   JANUARY 21, 1993

BACKGROUND

Cooper was convicted of murder at his trial. His appeal to the Newfoundland Court of Appeal was allowed and a new trial was ordered. The Crown subsequently appealed to the Supreme Court of Canada, which allowed the appeal and restored Cooper's conviction.

MAIN ISSUE

Did the necessary *mens rea* for murder coincide with the *actus reus* for this offence?

JUDGMENT

The *majority* judgment of the court was delivered by Justice Cory (with whom Justices L'Heureux-Dubé, Sopinka, Gonthier, McLachlin, and Iacobucci agreed). The *dissenting* judgment of Chief Justice Lamer has been omitted.

CORY J.: — At issue, on this appeal, is the nature of the intent required to found a conviction for murder pursuant to s. 212(a)(ii) of the Criminal Code, R.S.C. 1970, c. C-34, (now R.S.C. 1985, c. C-46, s. 229(a)(ii)).

Factual Background

The respondent Lyndon Cooper and the deceased Deborah Careen lived in Labrador City, Newfoundland. At one time, they had been friends and lovers. On January 30, 1988, they met at a gathering place known as the K-Bar in Labrador City. Although by this time the respondent was living with somebody else, they spent the evening together at the bar. There is no doubt that they consumed a considerable amount of alcohol. Eventually, Cooper, the deceased and a mutual friend left the bar in a taxi. After they dropped off the friend, they continued in the cab to the residence of another of Cooper's friends where he borrowed a Jeep. Cooper then drove the deceased to the secluded parking lot of a power station.

At the parking lot, the respondent testified that he and the deceased engaged in some form of consensual sexual activity. He said that they began to argue at one point and that the deceased struck him. At this he became angry. He hit the deceased and grabbed her by the throat with both hands and shook her. He stated that this occurred in the front seat of the Jeep. He then said that he could recall nothing else until he woke in the back seat and found the body of the deceased beside him. He had no recollection of causing her death. He pushed her

Adapted from *R. v. Cooper* (1993), 78 C.C.C. (3d), pp. 292–302. Copyright © 1993 by *Canada Law Book*. Reprinted with permission.

body out of the Jeep and drove away. Later during the drive to his home, he found one of her shoes in the vehicle and threw it out the window into the snow.

The expert evidence established that the deceased had in fact been struck twice. However, these blows could not have killed her. Rather, death was caused by "a classic pattern of one-handed manual strangulation." That same evidence confirmed that death by strangulation can occur as quickly as 30 seconds after contact with the throat and that a drunken victim is likely to die from asphyxiation more quickly than a sober one. Nonetheless, the presence of *petechial haemorrhages* on the neck of the deceased and the finding that the hyoid bone in her throat was not fractured suggested to the expert that death occurred rather more slowly, probably after two minutes of pressure.

The position of the defence was that the respondent was so drunk that he blacked out shortly after he started shaking her with both hands. Thus, it was said that the respondent (i) did not have the required intent to commit murder, or, alternatively, (ii) did not foresee that holding someone by the neck was likely to cause death.

Analysis

THE NATURE OF THE INTENT REQUIRED TO SECURE A CONVICTION UNDER S. 212(a)(ii)

Section 212(a)(ii) provides:

> 212. Culpable homicide is murder
>> (a) where the person who causes the death of a human being
>>
>> ....
>>
>> (ii) means to cause him bodily harm that he knows is likely to cause his death, and is reckless whether death ensues or not;

This section was considered in *R. v. Nygaard* (1989), 51 C.C.C. (3d) 417, [1989] 2 S.C.R.

1074, 72 C.R. (3d) 257. On the issue of the requisite intent, the court was unanimous. At p. 435, it was said: The essential element is that of intending to cause bodily harm of such a grave and serious nature that the accused knew that it was likely to result in the death of the victim. The aspect of recklessness is almost an afterthought . . .

The aspect of recklessness can be considered an afterthought since, to secure a conviction under this section, it must be established that the accused had the intent to cause such grievous bodily harm that he knew it was likely to cause death. One who causes bodily harm that he knows is likely to cause death must, in those circumstances, have a deliberate disregard for the fatal consequences which are known to be likely to occur. That is to say he must, of necessity, be reckless whether death ensues or not.

The concept of recklessness was considered by this court in *R. v. Sansregret* (1985), 18 C.C.C. (3d) 223, 17 D.L.R. (4th) 577, [1985] 1 S.C.R. 570. At p. 233 it was said:

> [Recklessness] is found in the attitude of one who, aware that there is danger that his conduct could bring about the result prohibited by the criminal law, nevertheless persists, despite the risk. It is, in other words, the conduct of one who sees the risk and who takes the chance.

The same words can apply to s. 212(a)(ii) with this important addition: it is not sufficient that the accused foresee simply a *danger* of death; the accused must foresee a *likelihood* of death flowing from the bodily harm that he is occasioning the victim.

It is for this reason that it was said in *Nygaard* that there is only a "slight relaxation" in the *mens rea* required for a conviction for murder under s. 212(a)(ii) as compared to s. 212(a)(i). The position was put in this way at p. 436:

> . . . [where] two accused form the intent to repeatedly and viciously strike a person in the head with a baseball bat realizing full well that the victim will probably die as a result. Nonetheless they

continue with the bone-splintering, skull-shattering assault. The accused . . . must have committed as grave a crime as the accused who specifically intends to kill . . . I would conclude that the crime defined in s. 212(a)(ii) [now 229(a)(ii)] can properly be described as murder and on a "culpability scale" it varies so little from s. 212(a)(i) as to be indistinguishable.

The intent that must be demonstrated in order to convict under s. 212(a)(ii) has two aspects. There must be (a) subjective intent to cause bodily harm; (b) subjective knowledge that the bodily harm is of such a nature that it is likely to result in death. It is only when those two elements of intent are established that a conviction can properly follow.

WHAT DEGREE OF CONCURRENCY IS REQUIRED BETWEEN THE WRONGFUL ACT AND THE REQUISITE *MENS REA*?

There can be no doubt that under the classical approach to criminal law it is the intent of the accused that makes the wrongful act illegal. It is that intent which brings the accused within the sphere of blameworthiness and justifies the penalty or punishment which is imposed upon him for the infraction of the criminal law. The essential aspect of *mens rea* and the absolute necessity that it be present in the case of murder was emphasized by Lamer J. (as he then was) in *R. v. Vaillancourt* (1987), 39 C.C.C. (3d) 118, 47 D.L.R. (4th) 399, [1987] 2 S.C.R. 636. At p. 133, he stated: "It may well be that, as a general rule, the principles of fundamental justice require proof of a subjective *mens rea* with respect to the prohibited act, in order to avoid punishing the "morally innocent."

The essential element of a subjectively guilty mind in order to convict a person of murder was again emphasized in *R. v. Martineau* (1990), 58 C.C.C. (3d) 353, [1990] 2 S.C.R. 633, 79 C.R. (3d) 129.

However, not only must the guilty mind, intent, or *mens rea*, be present, it must also be concurrent with the impugned act. Professor D. Stuart has referred to this as "the simultaneous principle": see *Canadian Criminal Law*, 2nd ed. (1987), p. 305. The principle has been stressed in a number of cases. For example, in *R. v. Droste* (1979), 49 C.C.C. (2d) 52, 18 C.R. (3d) 64 (Ont. C.A.), the accused had intended to murder his wife by pouring gasoline over the interior of the car and setting fire to it while she was within it. Before he could light the gasoline, the car crashed into a bridge and ignited prematurely. As a result, both his children were killed rather than his wife. He was charged with their murder and convicted. On appeal, Arnup J.A., speaking for the Court of Appeal in directing a new trial, stated at pp. 53–4:

> . . . the trial Judge did not instruct the jury of the necessity of the Crown showing that at the time of the occurrence at the bridge, the appellant, intending to kill his wife, had done an act with that intention, and in the course of doing so his children were killed. *In short, he did not tell them that the* mens rea *and the* actus reus *must be concurrent . . .*

(Emphasis added.)

Yet, it is not always necessary for the guilty act and the intent to be completely concurrent. See for example *Fagan v. Metropolitan Police Commissioner*, [1968] 3 All E.R. 442 (Q.B.). In that case a motorist stopped his car on the foot of a police officer. This was apparently done by accident. When the officer, not unreasonably, asked the accused to move the car, he at first refused but eventually did move on. It was determined that while the first action of stopping was innocent of criminal intent, it acquired the necessary *mens rea* when the accused was made aware that the car was resting on the officer's foot and still refused to move. James J., concurring in the result, stated at p. 445: "It is not necessary that *mens rea* should be present at the inception of the *actus reus*; it can be superimposed on an existing act."

There is, then, the classic rule that at some point the *actus reus* and the *mens reas*, or intent, must coincide. Further, I would agree with the conclusion of James J. that an act (*actus reus*) which may be innocent or no more than careless at the outset can become criminal at a later stage when the accused acquires knowledge of the nature of the act and still refuses to change his course of action.

The determination of whether the guilty mind, or *mens rea*, coincides with the wrongful act will depend to a large extent upon the nature of the act. For example, if the accused shot the victim in the head or stabbed the victim in the chest with death ensuing a few minutes after the shooting or stabbing, then it would be relatively easy to infer that the requisite intent, or *mens rea*, coincided with the wrongful act (*actus reus*) of shooting or stabbing. As well, a series of acts may form part of the same transaction. For example, the repeated blows of the baseball bat continuing over several minutes are all part of the same transaction. In those circumstances, if the requisite intent coincides at any time with the sequence of blows, then that could be sufficient to found a conviction.

An example of a series of acts that might be termed a continuous transaction appears in *Meli v. The Queen*, [1954] 1 W.L.R. 228 (P.C.). There the accused intended to kill the deceased, and to this end struck a number of blows. The effect of the blows was such that the accused thought the victim was dead and threw the body over a cliff. However, it was not the blows but rather the exposure suffered by the victim while he lay at the base of the cliff that resulted in the death. It was argued on behalf of the accused that when there was the requisite *mens rea* (during the beating), death did not ensue, and when death did ensue, there was no longer any intention to kill. The Judicial Committee of the Privy Council concluded that the entire episode was one continuing transaction that could not be subdivided in that way. At some point, the requisite *mens rea* coincided with the continuing series of wrongful acts that constituted the transaction. As a result, the conviction for murder was sustained. I agree with that conclusion.

APPLICATION OF THE "CONTEMPORANEOUS" PRINCIPLES TO THIS CASE

There is no question that in order to obtain a conviction the Crown must demonstrate that the accused intended to cause bodily harm he knew was ultimately so dangerous and serious that it was likely to result in the death of the victim. But that intent need not persist throughout the entire act of strangulation. When Cooper testified that he seized the victim by the neck, it was open to the jury to infer that by those actions he intended to cause her bodily harm that he knew was likely to cause her death. Since breathing is essential to life, it would be reasonable to infer the accused knew that strangulation was likely to result in death. I would stress that the jury was, of course, not required to make such an inference but, on the evidence presented, it was open to them to do so.

Did the accused possess such a mental state after he started strangling the victim? Here, death occurred between 30 seconds and two minutes after he grabbed her by the neck. It could be reasonably inferred by the jury that, when the accused grabbed the victim by the neck and shook her, there was, at that moment, the necessary coincidence of the wrongful act of strangulation and the requisite intent to do bodily harm that the accused knew was likely to cause her death. Cooper was aware of these acts before he "blacked out." Thus, although the jury was under no compulsion to do so, it was nonetheless open to them to infer that he knew he was causing bodily harm and knew it was so dangerous to the victim that it was likely to cause her death. It was sufficient that the intent and the act of strangulation coincided at some point. It was not necessary that the requisite intent continue throughout the entire two minutes required to cause the death of the victim.

In order to obtain a conviction under s. 212(a)(ii), the Crown must prove that the accused caused and intended to cause bodily harm that he knew was likely to cause the death of the victim. If death results from a series of wrongful acts that are part of a single transaction, then it must be established that the requisite intent coincided at some point with the wrongful acts.

On this issue the trial judge correctly instructed the jury when he stated:

> When he grabbed her by the neck and shook her, did he intend to cause her bodily harm, which he knew was likely to cause her death and was reckless whether death ensued or not? In other words, he wouldn't have to be there until she died . . . He could formulate all of that intent at that point in time, even th[o]ugh he doesn't remember the final outcome.

It was on this ground that the Court of Appeal directed the new trial. Although it can never be determinative of the issue, it is significant that defence counsel at trial took no objection to this or any other aspect of the charge. In any event, for the reasons set out earlier, I must disagree with the Court of Appeal's conclusion on this issue. A new trial should not have been granted on this ground.

THE KNOWLEDGE OF THE LIKELIHOOD OF DEATH

The appellant seeks to uphold the order directing a new trial on two other grounds. The first, and the more important of these, is the issue raised before the Court of Appeal that the trial judge did not adequately instruct the jury that the Crown must establish that Cooper *knew* that the bodily injury that he was inflicting was likely to cause the death of the victim. I cannot agree with that contention.

It is true that from one or two excerpts from the charge, the jury could have inferred that an intent to cause bodily harm was all that was required in order to convict. Yet on numerous occasions the trial judge stated and repeated that the jurors had to be satisfied beyond a reasonable doubt that Cooper meant to cause bodily harm that he *knew* was likely to cause death and was reckless whether death ensued or not.

When the charge is looked at as a whole, there can be no doubt that the jury understood what was required in order to convict under s. 212(a)(ii). It has been said before but bears repeating that it would be difficult if not impossible to find a perfect charge. Directions to the jury need not, as a general rule, be endlessly dissected and subjected to minute scrutiny and criticism. Rather, the charge must be read as a whole. The directions to the jury must, of course, set out the position of the Crown and defence, the legal issues involved, and the evidence that may be applied in resolving the legal issues and ultimately in determining the guilt or innocence of the accused. At the end of the day, the question must be whether an appellate court is satisfied that the jurors would adequately understand the issues involved, the law relating to the charge the accused is facing, and the evidence they should consider in resolving the issues. I am satisfied that in this case the charge meets all these basic requirements. Particularly, the law pertaining to the legal issues was correctly placed before the jury. Any errors were immediately and repeatedly corrected.

Upon a careful reading and review of the charge as a whole, I am satisfied that there were no errors committed by the trial judge that would justify a new trial.

In the result, I would set aside the order of Court of Appeal directing a new trial and restore the conviction.

Appeal allowed; conviction restored.

Regina v. Parks

SUPREME COURT OF CANADA   AUGUST 27, 1992

BACKGROUND

At his trial, the accused was charged with the murder of his mother-in-law and the attempted murder of his father-in-law. He was acquitted by a jury on both charges. The Crown appealed to the Ontario Court of Appeal, which dismissed the appeal. The Crown then appealed to the Supreme Court of Canada against the judgment of the Court of Appeal.

MAIN ISSUES

Should sleepwalking (somnambulism) be categorized as a "disease of the mind" for the purposes of drawing a distinction between the defences of NCRMD (not criminally responsible on account of mental disorder) and automatism? If an accused person is acquitted on the basis of a successful defence of automatism, should he or she nevertheless be liable to continuing restraints on his or her liberty in order to protect the public from the potential danger posed by the accused's presence in the community?

JUDGMENTS

On the question of whether the accused should have been acquitted by reason of automatism or mental disorder, the *majority* judgment was delivered by Chief Justice Lamer (with whom Justices La Forest, L'Heureux-Dubé, Sopinka, Gonthier, Cory, McLachlin, and Iacobucci concurred). On the question of whether the case should be returned to the trial judge for the purpose of determining whether restrictions should be placed on Parks' liberty, the *majority* judgment was delivered by Justice McLachlin (with whom Justices La Forest, L'Heureux-Dubé, Sopinka, Gonthier, and Iacobucci concurred), while a *dissenting* judgment was delivered by Chief Justice Lamer (with whom Justice Cory agreed). Extracts from the judgments of Chief Justice Lamer, Justice La Forest, and Justice McLachlin are included below. However, the separate judgment of Justice Sopinka has been omitted.

....

LAMER C.J.C. (dissenting in part): — In the small hours of the morning of May 24, 1987, the respondent, aged 23, attacked his parents-in-law, Barbara Ann and Denis Woods, killing his mother-in-law with a kitchen knife and seriously injuring his father-in-law. The incident occurred at the home of his parents-in-law while they were both asleep in bed. Their residence was 23 km. from that of the respondent, who went there by car. Immediately after the incident, the respondent went to the nearby police station, again driving his own car. He told the police:

> I just killed someone with my bare hands; Oh my God, I just killed someone; I've just killed two people; My God, I've just killed two people with my hands; My God, I've just killed two people. My hands; I just killed two people. I killed them; I just killed two people; I've just killed my mother- and father-in-law. I stabbed and beat them to death. It's all my fault.

At the trial the respondent presented a defence of automatism, stating that at the time the incidents took place he was sleepwalking. The respondent has always slept very deeply and has always had a lot of trouble waking up. The year prior to the events was particularly stressful for the respondent. His job as a project coordinator for Revere Electric required him to work ten hours a day. In addition, during the preceding summer the respondent had placed bets on horse races which caused him financial problems. To obtain money he also stole some $30 000 from his employer. The following March his boss discovered the theft and dismissed him. Court proceedings were brought against him in this regard. His personal life suffered from all of this. However, his parents-in-law, who were aware of the situation, always supported him. He had excellent relations with them: he got on particularly well with his mother-in-law, who referred to him as the "gentle giant." His relations with his father-in-law were more distant, but still very good. In fact, a supper at their home was planned for May 24 to discuss the respondent's problems and the solutions he intended to suggest. Additionally, several members of his family suffer or have suffered from sleep problems such as sleepwalking, adult enuresis, nightmares, and sleep-talking.

The respondent was charged with the first degree murder of Barbara Ann Woods and the attempted murder of Denis Woods.

The trial judge chose to put only the defence of automatism to the jury, which first acquitted the respondent of first degree murder and then of second degree murder. The judge also acquitted the respondent of the charge of attempted murder for the same reasons. The Court of Appeal unanimously upheld the acquittal.

Analysis

This court has only ruled on sleepwalking in an *obiter dictum* in *R. v. Rabey* (1980), 54 C.C.C. (2d) 1, 114 D.L.R. (3d) 193, [1980] 2 S.C.R. 513. The court found that sleepwalking was not a "disease of the mind" in the legal sense of the term and gave rise to a defence of automatism. Should the court maintain this position?

In *Rabey* this court affirmed the judgment of the Ontario Court of Appeal, 37 C.C.C. (2d) 461 at pp. 472–3, 79 D.L.R. (3d) 414 at p. 425, 40 C.R.N.S. 46, in which Martin J.A. defined the expression "disease of the mind":

> "Disease of the mind" is a legal term, not a medical term of art; although a legal concept, it contains a substantial medical component as well as a legal or policy component.
>
> The legal or policy component relates to (a) the scope of the exemption from criminal responsibility to be afforded by mental disorder or disturbance, and (b) the protection of the public by the control and treatment of persons who have caused serious harms while in a mentally disordered or disturbed state. The medical component of the term, generally, is medical opinion as to how the mental condition in question is viewed or characterized medically. Since the medical component of the term reflects or should reflect the state of medical knowledge at a given time, the concept of "disease of the mind" is capable of evolving with increased medical knowledge with respect to mental disorder or disturbance.

As Martin J.A. pointed out, Canadian and foreign courts and authors have recognized that sleepwalking is not a disease of the mind: "Sleepwalking appears to fall into a separate category. Unconscious behaviour in a state of somnambulism is non-insane automatism . . ."

A large part of the defence evidence in this case was medical evidence. Five physicians were heard: Dr. Roger James Broughton, a neurophysiologist and specialist in sleep and sleep disorders, Dr. John Gordon Edmeads, a neurologist, Dr. Ronald Frederick Billings, a psychiatrist, Dr. Robert Wood Hill, a forensic psychiatrist, and finally, Dr. Frank Raymond Ervin, a neurologist and psychiatrist.

The medical evidence in the case at bar showed that the respondent was in fact sleepwalking when he committed the acts with which he is charged. All the expert witnesses called by the defence said that in their opinion Parks was sleepwalking when the events occurred. This is what Dr. Broughton said:

> Q. . . . assuming for a moment that Mr. Parks caused the death of Barbara Woods, did you, sir, reach an opinion as to his condition at the time he caused that death?
>
> A. Yes. My opinion is that he did it during a sleepwalking episode.

Though sceptical at the outset, the expert witnesses unanimously stated that at the time of the incidents the respondent was not suffering from any mental illness and that, medically speaking, sleepwalking is not regarded as an illness, whether physical, mental, or neurological.

They also unanimously stated that a person who is sleepwalking cannot think, reflect, or perform voluntary acts:

> Q. Is there any evidence that a person could formulate a plan while they were awake and then in some way ensure that they carry it out in their sleep?
>
> A. No, absolutely not. No. Probably the most striking feature of what we know of what goes on in the mind during sleep is that it's very independent of waking mentation in terms of its objectives and so forth. There is a lack of control of directing our minds in sleep compared to wakefulness. In the waking state, of course, we often

voluntarily plan things, what we call volition — that is, we decide to do this as opposed to that — and there is no evidence that this occurs during the sleepwalking episode. There usually is — well, they are precipitated. They are part of an arousal, an incomplete arousal process during which all investigators have concluded that volution [*sic*] is not present.

> Q. And assuming he was sleepwalking at the time, would he have the capacity to intend?
>
> A. No.
>
> Q. Would he have appreciated what he was doing?
>
> A. No, he would not.
>
> Q. Would he have understood the consequences of what he was doing?
>
> A. No, he would not.
>
> Q. Would he have been able to stop what he was doing?
>
> A. No, I do not believe that he would. I think it would all have been an unconscious activity, uncontrolled and unmeditated.

The evidence also disclosed that sleepwalking was very common, almost universal, among children, and that 2 to 2.5% of "normal" adults had sleepwalked at least once. Dr. Hill further noted that he found it significant that there were several sleepwalkers in the respondent's family.

Dr. Broughton, for his part, indicated that he had never known of sleepwalkers who had acted violently who had repeated this kind of behaviour.

In cross-examination he also added that sleepwalking episodes in which violent acts are committed are not common. Further, on being questioned about a cure or treatment, Dr. Broughton answered that the solution was sleep hygiene, which involved eliminating factors that precipitated sleepwalking such as stress, lack of sleep, and violent physical exercise.

Dr. Ervin in his turn stated that during the slow wave sleep stage the cortex, which is the part of the brain that controls thinking and voluntary movement, is essentially in coma. When a person is sleepwalking, the movements he makes are controlled by other parts of the brain and are more or less reflexive:

> We put our recording electrodes on the top of the head after all so we are looking at the cortical matter and what is happening there. That part of the brain is effectively in coma, that is, it is highly synchronized, very slow. It looks like the ocean waves rolling along, suggesting that all those nerve cells are no longer doing their busy integrated — or they are cut off. They are not working. What is left? What is left is those deep structures evolved some time back, evolved very competently in lower animals to handle the whole set of problems of moving about in the world and responding to stimuli reflexly [*sic*] more or less, going places, eating things, doing things, and so on.

Three very important points emerge from this testimony: (1) the respondent was sleepwalking at the time of the incident; (2) sleepwalking is not a neurological, psychiatric, or other illness: it is a sleep disorder very common in children and also found in adults; (3) there is no medical treatment as such, apart from good health practices, especially as regards sleep. It is important to note that this expert evidence was not in any way contradicted by the prosecution, which as the trial judge observed did have the advice of experts who were present during the testimony given by the defence experts and whom it chose not to call.

I am of the view that in the instant case, based on the evidence and the testimony of the expert witnesses heard, the trial judge did not err in leaving the defence of automatism rather than that of insanity with the jury, and that the instant appeal should be dismissed. For a defence of insanity to have been put to the jury, together with or instead of a defence of automatism, as the case may be, there would have had to have been in the record evidence tending to show that sleepwalking was the cause of the respondent's state of mind. As we have just seen, that is not the case here. This is not to say that sleepwalking could never be a disease of the mind, in another case on different evidence.

As I see it, however, that does not end the matter. Although the expert witnesses were unanimous in saying that sleepwalkers are very rarely violent, I am still concerned by the fact that as the result of an acquittal in a situation like this (and I am relieved that such cases are quite rare), the accused is simply set free without any consideration of measures to protect the public, or indeed the accused himself, from the possibility of a repetition of such unfortunate occurrences. In the case of an outright acquittal, should there not be some control? And if so, how should this be done? I am of the view that such control could be exercised by means of the common law power to make an order to keep the peace vested in any judge or magistrate.

Accordingly, such a power exists. The question remains whether it should be exercised in the case of the respondent Parks, or at least whether its exercise should be considered. I am of the view that this approach should be considered. As I have already said, despite the unanimous and uncontradicted evidence that the chances of such an occurrence taking place again are for all practical purposes nil, I feel that all necessary measures should be taken to ensure that such an event does not recur. After all, before this tragic incident occurred, the probability of Mr. Parks' killing someone while in a somnambulistic state was infinitesimal. Yet this is precisely what took place. Furthermore, the evidence at trial was not adduced with a view to determining whether an order would be justified and to determine the appropriate conditions of such an order. Thus, for example, an order might be made requiring Parks to do certain things suggested by a specialist in sleep disorders, for example to report to him periodically. In appropriate cases of outright acquittals on grounds of automatism, measures that would reinforce sleep hygiene, and thereby provide greater safety for others, should always be considered. If the trial judge considers that making such an order would be in the interest of the public, he should so advise the parties and consider whatever evidence and submissions are tendered. In those situations where an order is made, it should be complied with in the same way as any other order of the court.

I would, therefore, refer this matter back to the trial judge so that he can hear the parties on this point and decide, upon the evidence before him, whether such an order is appropriate. If this proves to be the case, it will be up to the trial judge to determine the content of the order.

I would, accordingly, dismiss this appeal and uphold the acquittal of the respondent but refer the matter back to the trial judge for him to decide on the making of an order to keep the peace on certain conditions, pursuant to the "preventive justice" power which he possesses.

LA FOREST J.: — In his reasons, the Chief Justice finds that the evidence and expert testimony from the trial of the accused support the trial judge's decision to instruct the jury on non-insane automatism. I agree with this finding, but, in my view, that is not the end of the matter. In distinguishing between automatism and insanity, the trial judge must consider more than the evidence; there are overarching policy considerations as well. Of course, the evidence in each case will be highly relevant to this policy inquiry.

Automatism occupies a unique place in our criminal law system. Although spoken of as a "defence," it is conceptually a sub-set of the voluntariness requirement, which in turn is part of the *actus reus* component of criminal liability. A useful introduction is found in the dissenting reasons of Dickson J. (as he then was) in *R. v. Rabey* (1980), 54 C.C.C. (2d) 1 at p. 9, 114 D.L.R. (3d) 193 at pp. 200–1, [1980] 2 S.C.R. 513:

> Although the word "automatism" made its way but lately to the legal stage, it is basic principle that absence of volition in respect of the act involved is always a defence to a crime. A defence that the act is involuntary entitles the accused to a complete and unqualified acquittal. That the defence of automatism exists as a middle ground between criminal responsibility and legal insanity is beyond question. Although spoken as a defence,

in the sense that it is raised by the accused, the Crown always bears the burden of proving a voluntary act.

One qualification to this statement should be noted. When the automatistic condition stems from a disease of the mind that has rendered the accused insane, then the accused is not entitled to a full acquittal, but to a verdict of insanity. The condition in that instance is referred to as insane automatism, and the distinction between it and non-insane automatism is the crucial issue in this appeal.

When a defence of non-insane automatism is raised by the accused, the trial judge must determine whether the defence should be left with the trier of fact. This will involve two discrete tasks. First, he or she must determine whether there is some evidence on the record to support leaving the defence with the jury. Thus an evidential burden rests with the accused, and the mere assertion of the defence will not suffice. If the proper foundation is present, the judge moves to the second task: he or she must consider whether the condition alleged by the accused is, in law, non-insane automatism. If the trial judge is satisfied that there is some evidence pointing to a condition that is in law non-insane automatism, then the defence can be left with the jury. The issue for the jury is one of fact: did the accused suffer from or experience the alleged condition at the relevant time? Because the Crown must always prove that an accused has acted voluntarily, the onus rests on the prosecution at this stage to prove the absence of automatism beyond a reasonable doubt.

In the present case, there is no question that the accused has laid the proper foundation for the defence of automatism. The expert testimony reviewed by the Chief Justice is more than adequate on that score. At issue here is the question of law: is sleepwalking properly classified as non-insane automatism, or does it stem from a disease of the mind, thereby leaving only the defence of insanity for the accused? When considering this question, s. 16(4) of the Criminal Code, R.S.C. 1985, c. C-46, should be recalled:

16(4) Every one shall, until the contrary is proved, be presumed to be and to have been sane.

If the accused pleads automatism, the Crown is then entitled to raise the issue of insanity, but the prosecution then bears the burden of proving that the condition in question stems from a disease of the mind.

In Canada, the approach to distinguishing between insane and non-insane automatism was settled by this court's judgment in *Rabey*. The majority in that case endorsed the reasons of Martin J.A. in the Ontario Court of Appeal, 37 C.C.C. (2d) 461 at pp. 472–3, 79 D.L.R. (3d) 414 at p. 425, 40 C.R.N.S. 46. These reasons provide what has become the accepted formula for determining whether a mental condition stems from a disease of the mind. Because "disease of the mind" is a legal concept, a trial judge cannot rely blindly on medical opinion. On this point Martin J.A. states the following:

> If the question what particular mental conditions or mental disorders constitute disease of the mind were to be determined by the opinion of medical witnesses, then the scope of the defence of insanity under s. 16 of the Code would vary according to the choice of expert witnesses called to testify, since the existence of disease of the mind, apart from natural imbecility, constitutes the necessary foundation for insanity, and it is abundantly clear that medical opinions differ as to what mental conditions constitute a disease of the mind.
>
> I take the true principle to be this: It is for the Judge to determine what mental conditions are included within the term "disease of the mind," and whether there is any evidence that the accused suffered from an abnormal mental condition comprehended by that term. The evidence of medical witnesses with respect to the cause, nature, and symptoms of the abnormal mental condition from which the accused is alleged to suffer, and how that condition is viewed and characterized from the medical point of view, is highly relevant to the judicial determination of whether

such a condition is capable of constituting a "disease of the mind." The opinions of medical witnesses as to whether an abnormal mental state does or does not constitute a disease of the mind are not, however, determinative, since what is a disease of the mind is a legal question . . .

This position is beyond dispute, as similar statements were expressed by both the majority and minority judgments rendered by this court.

Another problem with relying solely on medical opinion is the lack of consensus within the medical community on the scope and meaning of "mental disease." In part because of the imprecision of medical science in this area, the legal community reserves for itself the final determination of what constitutes a "disease of the mind." This is accomplished by adding the "legal or policy component" to the inquiry.

A review of the cases on automatism reveals two distinct approaches to the policy component of the disease of the mind inquiry. These may be labelled the "continuing danger" and "internal cause" theories: see Colvin, *Principles of Criminal Law*, 2nd ed. (1991), at p. 293. At first glance these approaches may appear to be divergent, but in fact they stem from a common concern for public safety. This was recognized by Martin J.A., who referred to "protection of the public" as a focus of the policy inquiry.

The "continuing danger" theory holds that any condition likely to present a recurring danger to the public should be treated as insanity. The "internal cause" theory suggests that a condition stemming from the psychological or emotional make-up of the accused, rather than some external factor, should lead to a finding of insanity. The two theories share a common concern for recurrence, the latter holding that an internal weakness is more likely to lead to recurrent violence than automatism brought on by some intervening external cause.

It would appear that the "internal cause" approach has gained a certain ascendancy in both Canadian and English jurisprudence. The theory was the basis for deciding *Rabey*, where the distinction was described by Martin J.A. as follows:

In general, the distinction to be drawn is between a malfunctioning of the mind arising from some cause that is primarily internal to the accused, having its source in his psychological or emotional make-up, or in some organic pathology, as opposed to a malfunctioning of the mind which is the transient effect produced by some specific external factor such as, for example, concussion. Any malfunctioning of the mind, or mental disorder having its source primarily in some subjective condition or weakness internal to the accused (whether fully understood or not), may be a "disease of the mind" if it prevents the accused from knowing what he is doing, but transient disturbances of consciousness due to certain specific external factors do not fall within the concept of disease of the mind ... Particular transient mental disturbances may not, however, be capable of being properly categorized in relation to whether they constitute "disease of the mind," on the basis of a generalized statement, and must be decided on a case by case basis.

The "internal cause" approach has been criticized as an unfounded development of the law, and for the odd results the external/internal dichotomy can produce. These criticisms have particular validity if the "internal cause" theory is held out as the definitive answer to the disease of the mind inquiry. However, it is apparent from the cases that the theory is really meant to be used only as an analytical tool, and not as an all-encompassing methodology.

As Martin J.A. suggested in *Rabey*, somnambulism is an example of a condition that is not well suited to analysis under the "internal cause" theory. The poor fit arises because certain factors can legitimately be characterized as either internal or external sources of automatistic behaviour. For example, the Crown in this case argues that the causes of the respondent's violent sleepwalking were entirely internal, a combination of genetic susceptibility and the ordinary stresses of everyday life (lack of sleep, excessive afternoon exercise, and a high stress level due to personal problems). These "ordinary stresses" were ruled out as external factors by this

court in *Rabey* (although by a narrow majority). However, the factors that for a waking individual are mere ordinary stresses can be differently characterized for a person who is asleep, unable to counter with his conscious mind the onslaught of the admittedly ordinary strains of life. One could argue that the particular amalgam of stress, excessive exercise, sleep deprivation, and sudden noises in the night that causes an incident of somnambulism is, for the sleeping person, analogous to the effect of a concussion upon a waking person, which is generally accepted as an external cause of non-insane automatism. In the end, the dichotomy between internal and external causes becomes blurred in this context, and is not helpful in resolving the inquiry.

The continuing danger approach stems from an *obiter* comment of Lord Denning in *Bratty v. A.-G. for Northern Ireland*, [1963] A.C. 386 (H.L.), where he proposes the following test for distinguishing between insane and non-insane automatism, at p. 412:

> It seems to me that any mental disorder which has manifested itself in violence and is prone to recur is a disease of the mind. At any rate, it is the sort of disease for which a person should be detained in hospital rather than be given an unqualified acquittal.

Lord Denning's casual proposition has not been universally accepted, although some elements of the theory remain today. It was questioned in *R. v. Quick*, [1973] 3 All E.R. 347 C.C.A. , at pp. 351–2, and legal academics have questioned the utility of the test. As well, medical authorities have doubted the ability of their profession to predict recurrent dangerousness. In *Rabey*, Martin J.A. doubted the merit of Lord Denning's test, noting, at p. 476, C.C.C., p. 428 D.L.R., that the converse of Denning's proposition was surely not good law. He stated:

> It would be quite unreasonable to hold that a serious mental disorder did not constitute a disease of the mind because it was unlikely to recur. To so

hold would be to exclude from the exemption from responsibility afforded by insanity, persons, who by reason of a severe mental disorder, were incapable of appreciating the nature and quality of the act or of knowing that it was wrong, if such mental disorder was unlikely to recur.

The majority of this court approved these comments, and Dickson J. in dissent conceded the point, at p. 17 C.C.C., p. 208 D.L.R.:

A test of proneness to recur does not entail the converse conclusion, that if the mental malady is not prone to recur it cannot be a disease of the mind. A condition, organic in nature, which causes an isolated act of unconscious violence could well be regarded as a case of temporary insanity.

Since *Rabey*, the House of Lords has revisited the question of disease of the mind. In *R. v. Sullivan*, [1984] A.C. 156 at p. 172, Lord Diplock, speaking for a unanimous court, commented as follows:

The purpose of the legislation relating to the defence of insanity, ever since its origin in 1800, has been to protect society against recurrence of the dangerous conduct. The duration of a temporary suspension of the mental faculties of reason, memory, and understanding, particularly if, as in Mr. Sullivan's case, it is recurrent, cannot on any rational ground be relevant to the application by the courts of the M'Naghten Rules, though it may be relevant to the course adopted by the Secretary of State, to whom the responsibility for how the defendant is to be dealt with passes after the return of the special verdict of "not guilty by reason of insanity."

(My emphasis.) This passage, while not entirely clear, appears to endorse the consideration of recurrence as a non-determinative factor in the insanity inquiry. Lord Diplock states that the *duration* of the condition in question is not a relevant consideration: a disease of the mind can be temporary or permanent. He also suggests that the relative impermanence of a condition is particularly incon-

sequential *if the condition is prone to recur*. A necessary corollary of these statements is the more general proposition that recurrence suggests insanity, but the absence of recurrence does not preclude it. This view of the law was stated explicitly in *R. v. Burgess*, [1991] 2 All E.R. 769 at p. 774 (C.C.A.):

It seems to us that if there is a danger of recurrence, that may be an added reason for categorising the condition as a disease of the mind. On the other hand, the absence of the danger of recurrence is not a reason for saying that it cannot be a disease of the mind. Subject to that possible qualification, we respectfully adopt Lord Denning's suggested definition.

In my view, the Court of Appeal has properly stated the law on this point. Recurrence is but one of a number of factors to be considered in the policy phase of the disease of the mind inquiry. Moreover, the absence of a danger of recurrence will not automatically exclude the possibility of a finding of insanity.

In this case, then, neither of the two leading policy approaches determines an obvious result. It is clear from the evidence that there is almost no likelihood of recurrent violent somnambulism. A finding of insanity is therefore less likely, but the absence of a continuing danger does not mean that the respondent must be granted an absolute acquittal. At the same time, the "internal cause" theory is not readily applicable in this case. It is therefore necessary to look further afield.

It seems unlikely that the recognition of somnambulism as non-insane automatism will open the floodgates to a cascade of sleepwalking defence claims. First of all, the defence of somnambulism has been recognized, albeit in *obiter* discussion, in an unbroken line of cases stretching back at least a century, yet I am unaware of any current problem with specious defence claims of somnambulistic automatism. Indeed, this case and *Burgess* are among the few appellate decisions in which the status of somnambulism was a question to be decided. Moreover, it is very difficult to feign sleepwalking — precise symptoms and medical histories beyond the control of the accused must be presented to the trier of fact, and, as in this case, the accused will be subjected to a battery of medical tests. Finally, a comprehensive listing of the *indicia* of sleepwalking can be consulted by both the court and the medical experts.

It may be that some will regard the exoneration of an accused through a defence of somnambulism as an impairment of the credibility of our justice system. Those who hold this view would also reject insane automatism as an excuse from criminal responsibility. However, these views are contrary to certain fundamental precepts of our criminal law: only those who act voluntarily with the requisite intent to commit an offence should be punished by criminal sanction. The concerns of those who reject these underlying values of our system of criminal justice must accordingly be discounted.

In the end, there are no compelling policy factors that preclude a finding that the accused's condition was one of non-insane automatism. I noted earlier that it is for the Crown to prove that somnambulism stems from a disease of the mind; neither the evidence nor the policy considerations in this case overcome the Crown's burden in that regard. Committal under s. 614(2) of the Criminal Code is therefore precluded, and the accused should be acquitted.

As I noted at the outset, it is apparent that the medical evidence in this case is not only significant in its own right, but also has an impact at several stages of the policy inquiry. As such, I agree with the Chief Justice that in another case on different evidence, sleepwalking might be found to be a disease of the mind. As Dickson J. commented in *Rabey*, at p. 31 C.C.C., p. 223 D.L.R.:

> What is disease of the mind in the medical science of today may not be so tomorrow. The Court will establish the meaning of disease of the mind on the basis of scientific evidence as it unfolds from day to day. The Court will find as a matter of fact

in each case whether a disease of the mind, so defined, is present.

On the question of a possible imposition of an order to keep the peace, I am in agreement with the reasons of both Sopinka and McLachlin JJ. I would not refer this matter back to the trial judge.

McLACHLIN J.: — I share the Chief Justice's concern that notwithstanding the justice of an acquittal in this case and the evidence that a recurrence is highly unlikely, great care should be taken to avoid the possibility of a similar episode in the future. However, I also have concerns about the appropriateness of referring the matter back at this stage for a supervisory order in the circumstances of this case.

In addition to the difficult issues raised by an order restricting a person's liberty on account of an act for which he has been acquitted, I have concerns whether further proceedings are appropriate in the circumstances before us. Mr. Parks has been living in the shadow of these charges since May 24, 1987, over five years. His acquittal is now confirmed. We are told he has been making courageous efforts to re-establish his life. Should he now be embroiled in a further set of proceedings concerned, not with his guilt or innocence, but with the maintenance of his liberty?

Generally, the courts do not grant remedies affecting the liberty of the subject unless they are asked to do so by the Crown, which is charged with instituting such legal processes as it deems appropriate having regard to the public interest and fairness to the individual involved. In the absence of an application by the Crown, I hesitate to remit the case for consideration of further measures against the accused.

I add that the possibility of supervisory orders in this situation may be a matter which Parliament would wish to consider in the near future.

Appeal dismissed.

CASE

7

Smithers v. The Queen

SUPREME COURT OF CANADA   MAY 17, 1977

BACKGROUND

Smithers was convicted at his trial of manslaughter. His appeal to the Ontario Court of Appeal was dismissed. Smithers' further appeal to the Supreme Court of Canada was also dismissed.

MAIN ISSUES

What is the appropriate test of causation in a case involving a charge of manslaughter?

JUDGMENT

The judgment of the Supreme Court of Canada was delivered by Justice Dickson. (The other members of the Court were Chief Justice Laskin and Justices Martland, Judson, Ritchie, Spence, Pigeon, Beetz, and de Grandpré.)

....

DICKSON, J.: — This is an appeal from a judgment of the Court of Appeal for Ontario dismissing an appeal brought by the appellant from his conviction by Judge and jury on a charge of manslaughter. The indictment alleges that the appellant did unlawfully kill Barrie Ross Cobby by kicking him.

On February 18, 1973, a hockey game was played between the Applewood Midget Team and the Cooksville Midget Team at the Cawthra Park Arena in the Town of Mississauga. The leading player on the Applewood team was the deceased, Barrie Cobby, 16 years of age; the leading player on the Cooksville team was the appellant. The game was rough, the players were aggressive and feelings ran high. The appellant, who is black, was subjected to racial insults by Cobby and other members of the Applewood team. Following a heated and abusive exchange of profanities, the appellant and Cobby were both ejected from the game. The appellant made repeated threats that he was going to "get" Cobby. Cobby was very apprehensive and left the arena at the end of the game, some 45 minutes later, accompanied by eight or ten persons including friends, players, his coach, and the team's manager. The appellant repeated his threats and challenges to fight as the group departed. Cobby did not take up the challenge. Instead, he hurried toward a waiting car. The appellant caught up with him at the bottom of the outside steps and directed one or two punches to Cobby's head. Several of Cobby's team mates grabbed the appellant and held him. Cobby, who had taken no steps to defend himself, was observed to double up and stand back while the appellant struggled to free himself from those holding him. While Cobby was thus bent over, and approximately two to four feet from the appellant, the appellant delivered what was described as a

Adapted from *R. v. Smithers* (1977), 34 C.C.C. (2d), pp. 428–434. Copyright © 1977 by *Canada Law Book*. Reprinted with permission.

45

hard, fast kick to Cobby's stomach area. Only seconds elapsed between the punching and the kick. Following the kick, Cobby groaned, staggered towards his car, fell to the ground on his back, and gasped for air. Within five minutes he appeared to stop breathing. He was dead upon arrival at the Mississauga General Hospital.

Doctor David Brunsdon, who performed an autopsy, testified that, in his opinion, death was due to the aspiration of foreign materials present from vomiting. He defined aspiration as the breathing, or taking in, of foreign material through the windpipe into the lungs. It appears from the medical evidence that aspiration is generally due to barbiturate overdosage, alcohol intoxication, motor vehicle accidents or epilepsy. One medical witness testified to the possibility of spontaneous aspiration, whereby foreign material may be aspirated without any precipitating cause. This witness had seen three such cases out of the 900 to 1000 cases of aspiration he had experienced. In none of the three cases was the aspiration preceded by a blow. The consensus among the doctors was that spontaneous aspiration was a rare and unusual cause of death in the case of a healthy teenager such as Cobby. Normally, when a person vomits, the epiglottis folds over to prevent the regurgitated stomach contents from entering the air passage. In the instant case this protective mechanism failed.

I agree with the majority view in the Ontario Court of Appeal that the issue as to the cause of death was properly and sufficiently delineated by the trial Judge. It was not an unduly complicated issue. The assault by the appellant upon the deceased boy was undoubtedly an unlawful act. The principal issue was whether the appellant had committed homicide by directly or indirectly, by any means, causing the death of Cobby and whether such homicide was culpable for the reason that it was caused by an unlawful act. The Crown quite properly chose to establish causation principally through medical evidence and the doctors, men of high professional standing, understandably were disinclined to speak in absolute terms.

Doctor Brunsdon testified as to the effect of a sudden blow in the abdominal area. He said:

> I couldn't say always, but it certainly, I think, would be predisposed to regurgitation. I am certainly not going to say it would happen in every case, but I think it could be predisposed to.

During cross-examination, Dr. Brunsdon used the expressions "very possible" and "very probable" to describe the cause and effect of the kick and the vomiting. As to the relationship of the kick and aspiration, he said: "I can amplify that a bit. It is a rare condition, but the kick would have made it more likely to aspirate."

The jury was not limited to the evidence of the medical experts. In considering the issue of causation, the jury had the benefit of uncontradicted evidence of a number of lay witnesses to the effect that the appellant kicked the deceased boy in the stomach area, that the kick was followed by immediate distress, and that the death occurred within minutes. This was cogent evidence to which the jury could apply common sense in considering the issue of causality. In my opinion, the first ground of appeal cannot be maintained.

The second ground, not unrelated to the first ground, is that the Court of Appeal erred in holding that there was evidence on the basis of which the jury was entitled to find that it had been established beyond a reasonable doubt that the kick caused the death. This broad question is unfortunately phrased, in that it leaves doubt whether the issue raised is one of sufficiency of evidence, a question of fact to which the jurisdiction of this Court does not extend, or an entire absence of evidence upon which a finding could be made that the kick caused the death, a question of law. The appellant's factum tends to remove the uncertainty by subsuming, within the broad question, three narrower questions. The first of these is whether the jury were restricted to a consideration of the expert medical evidence in making their determination on the issue of causation. It is conceded that the jury was entitled to consider all of the evidence, expert and lay, in their deliberations with respect to the issue of causation, but on the precise question of whether or not the kick caused the vomiting or the aspiration, it is contended the jury was restricted to the medical evidence. It seems to me to be a novel proposition, subversive of the usual jury procedure, that on a particular issue the jury should be denied the evidence of certain witnesses. I have difficulty also in reconciling the concession that the jury is entitled to consider all of the evidence on the issue of causation but something less than all the evidence when considering the only causative questions in the case, namely, whether the kick caused the vomiting and whether the kick caused the aspiration.

It is important in considering the issue of causation in homicide to distinguish between causation as a question of fact and causation as a question of law. The factual determination is whether A caused B. The answer to the factual question can only come from the evidence of witnesses. It has nothing to do with intention, foresight or risk. In certain types of homicide, jurors need little help from medical experts. Thus, if D shoots P or stabs him and death follows within moments, there being no intervening cause, jurors would have little difficulty in resolving the issue of causality from their own experience and knowledge.

Expert evidence is admissible, of course, to establish factual cause. The work of expert witnesses in an issue of this sort, as Granville Williams has pointed out ("Causation in Homicide," [1957] *Crim. L.R.* 429 at p. 431), is "purely diagnostic and does not involve them in metaphysical subtleties"; it does not require them to distinguish between what is a "cause," i.e., a real and contributing cause of death, and what is merely a "condition," i.e., part of the background of the death. Nor should they be expected to say, where two or more causes combine to produce a result, which of these causes contributes the more.

In the case at bar, the Crown had the burden of showing factual causation, that beyond a reasonable doubt the kick caused the death. In my view the trial Judge did not err in failing to instruct the

jury that in determining that issue they could consider only the medical evidence. The issue of causation is for the jury, and not the experts. The weight to be given to the evidence of the experts was entirely for the jury. In the search for truth, the jury was entitled to consider all of the evidence, expert and lay, and accept or reject any part of it. Non-medical testimony is available to both the Crown and the accused, and in the instant case, lay evidence was vital to the defence raised by the appellant. That evidence tended to show that all the circumstances preceding the kick were such as to create in the deceased boy a highly emotional state which might well have given rise to spontaneous vomiting, unassociated with the kick.

The second sub-question raised is whether there was evidence on the basis of which the jury was entitled to find that it had been established beyond a reasonable doubt that the kick caused the death. In answer to this question it may shortly be said that there was a very substantial body of evidence, both expert and lay, before the jury indicating that the kick was at least a contributing cause of death, outside the *de minimis* range, and that is all that the Crown was required to establish. It is immaterial that the death was in part caused by a malfunctioning epiglottis to which malfunction the appellant may, or may not, have contributed. No question of remoteness or of incorrect treatment arises in this case.

The third sub-question is whether there was evidence from which the jury was entitled to find that it had been established beyond a reasonable doubt that the kick caused the aspiration. It is contended that the burden on the Crown was to prove beyond a reasonable doubt that the kick caused both the vomiting and the aggravated condition of aspiration. I do not agree. A person commits homicide, according to s. 205(1) of the Code, when directly or indirectly, by any means, he causes the death of a human being. Once evidence had been led concerning the relationship between the kick and the vomiting, leading to aspiration of stomach contents and asphyxia, the contributing condition of a malfunctioning epiglottis would not prevent conviction for manslaughter. Death may have been unexpected, and the physical reactions of the victim unforeseen, but that does not relieve the appellant.

It is a well-recognized principle that one who assaults another must take his victim as he finds him. An extreme example of the application of the principle will be found in the English case of *R. v. Blaue*, [1975] 1 W.L.R. 1411, in which the Court upheld a conviction for manslaughter where the victim's wounds were only fatal because of her refusal, on religious grounds, to accept a blood transfusion. The Court rejected the argument that the victim's refusal had broken the chain of causation between the stabbing and the death.

Although causation in civil cases differs from that in a criminal case, the "thin skulled man" may appear in the criminal law as in the civil law. The case of *R. v. Nicholson* (1926), 47 C.C.C. 113, 59 N.S.R. 323, will serve as an illustration. In that case, the accused dealt the deceased man two heavy blows. The man who was struck was in poor physical condition. His heart was abnormally small and he was suffering from Bright's disease. An eminent medical specialist was asked if the blow or blows could cause death, given the condition of the body which was described, and he said it was possible. The blow might be one of the causes. Over-indulgence in alcohol, bad health, and the blow and tussle combined, in his opinion, to account for the result. The appeal for conviction was dismissed. Even if the unlawful act, alone, would not have caused the death, it was still a legal cause so long as it contributed in some way to the death. I myself presided at a jury trial in which the accused, one Alan Canada, following an argument, struck his brother lightly on the head with a piece of firewood as a result of which the brother died some time later without regaining consciousness. The medical evidence showed that the bony structure of his skull was unusually thin and fragile. The accused, on the advice of counsel, pleaded guilty to a charge of manslaughter and I have never considered that he was wrong in doing so.

I would conclude this point by saying that, although Dr. Hillsdon Smith thought that once vomiting had been induced, aspiration in these circumstances was no more than an accident, both Dr. Brunsdon and Dr. Butt acknowledged that the kick may have contributed to the epiglottal malfunction.

I would dismiss the appeal.

Harbottle v. The Queen

SUPREME COURT OF CANADA   SEPTEMBER 30, 1993

BACKGROUND

Harbottle was convicted at his trial of first degree murder. His appeal was dismissed by the Ontario Court of Appeal. Harbottle's subsequent appeal to the Supreme Court of Canada was also dismissed.

MAIN ISSUE

What is the appropriate test of causation when an accused person is charged with first degree murder by virtue of section 214(5) [now section 231(5)] of the Criminal Code?

JUDGMENT

The judgment of the Supreme Court of Canada was delivered by Justice Cory. (The other members of the Court were Chief Justice Lamer and Justices La Forest, L'Heureux-Dubé, Sopinka, Gonthier, McLachlin, Iacobucci, and Major.)

....

CORY J.: — The appellant James Harbottle together with his friend Shawn Ross forcibly confined Elaine Bown. While she was still confined with her hands tied, Shawn Ross strangled her while Harbottle held her legs to prevent her from continuing to kick and struggle. What must be determined on this appeal is

whether Harbottle's participation was such that he can be found guilty of first degree murder pursuant to the provisions of s. 214(5) of the Criminal Code, R.S.C. 1970, c. C-34.

Factual Background

The disposition of this appeal requires the sordid factual background to be set out in some detail. The body of Elaine Bown, a 17-year-old high school student from Font Hill, Ontario, was discovered by firefighters called to a fire at 5 Lowther Avenue in Toronto in the early morning hours of July 12, 1988. She was lying on her back with her hands tied above her head. She had been strangled and the remains of a brown brassiere were found around her neck. There were copious quantities of semen in her vagina. Her blood tested negative for alcohol and drugs.

This young girl was, for some strange reason, attracted by the street life of Toronto and would hitchhike into the city from Font Hill on weekends. How she met her sad fate is best described in the chilling words of the appellant uttered during a videotaped statement to the police. The appellant told the officers that prior to the rape and killing there had been no sexual activity between the victim and Ross. On the morning of the killing, Ross and the appellant woke the victim and asked if she

....

wanted to accompany them to get some food and she said no. They left her and went to the Scott Mission to get a bag lunch. They then went to the clothing room and got some clothes. Ross then indicated to the appellant his intentions.

In a statement to the police, the appellant recounted in grim detail the sordid sequence of events which included the sexual assault, forcible confinement, and, ultimately, the murder of the victim. His words reveal a brutish insensitivity to human suffering and death. The appellant related that while they were returning from the Scott Mission, Ross told him he was going to assault the victim sexually. When they returned to the house on Lowther Avenue, Harbottle gave Ross his knife which Ross used to cut off Elaine Bown's clothes. Harbottle then watched while Ross raped her and perpetrated the most cruel and demeaning acts upon her.

The forcible confinement and murder of the victim are depicted in the statement of the appellant in these chilling words:

> He cut her, put an "X" on her chest and uh, with a razor, and then stabbed her with a knife in the arm. And uh, after that — well, he tied her up too and stuff and gagged her. And then after that he — me and him went into another room actually and uh, I said now what are you going to do? You cut her up and stuff and uh, he said why don't we kill her. And uh, I said well I don't know, maybe. And then he said well why not. And I said okay, fine. And I carried her downstairs and what not. And then I said why don't we kill her nicely, you know. I didn't want her to go through any pain or anything. So he said why don't we cut her wrists. And I said go for it. And she said she didn't want to die. He said well I'm going to have to do it. So he started slashing her wrists but she pulled away what not, so he couldn't do that. So then he said why don't we strangle her. And I said go for it then. *And he cut off her bra, take her bra, wrapped it around her neck. I grabbed her leg cause she started kicking and [Ross] strangled her to death.* Then we put her under the

couch and we left and went and panhandled for some glue and got a little high on glue. Then went back — back about 3 o'clock in the morning or something like that and torched the place . . .

(Emphasis added.)

That it was essential for the appellant to intervene and to enable Ross to strangle the victim might be readily surmised from a comparison of the size of Ross and Elaine Bown. At the time of the murder, Shawn Ross was 17 years old, 5'7" tall, and weighed only 130 lb. Elaine Bown was 5'4" tall and weighed 140 lb. This may give an indication of the importance and significance of the actions of Harbottle in holding her legs. The length and intensity of the struggle is also evidenced by the extensive bruising of the victim's neck which is typical of grabbing injuries and a sign of throttling.

Analysis

Section 214 is designed to impose the longest possible term of imprisonment without eligibility for parole upon those who commit the most grievous murders. It is concerned with contract killers, with those who murder police and correctional officers, with those who murder after due planning and premeditation, and with those who murder while committing crimes of domination.

To this effect, the portions of s. 214(5) relevant to this case provide that:

> 214(5) Irrespective of whether a murder is planned and deliberate on the part of any person, murder is first degree murder in respect of a person when *the death is caused* by that person while committing or attempting to commit an offence under one of the following sections:
>
> . . . .
>
> (b) section 246.1 (sexual assault);
> (c) section 246.2 (sexual assault with a weapon, threats to a third party or causing bodily harm);

(d) section 246.3 (aggravated sexual assault); or

(e) section 247 (kidnapping and forcible confinement).

(Emphasis added.)

What must be determined is the meaning of the words "when the death is caused by that person" as they appear in s. 214(5).

History of s. 214(5) and Its Present Wording

It was the position of the appellant, based upon the reasons of the minority in the Court of Appeal, that the legislative history of s. 214(5) compels an extremely narrow interpretation of the words "death is caused." It is contended that the subsection is applicable only to a person who diagnostically occasions the death of the victim. This reasoning is based upon the amendments resulting from the Criminal Law Amendment Act (No. 2), 1976, S.C. 1974–75–76, c. 105, s. 4. That legislation changed the relevant wording of the section from "by his own act caused or assisted in causing the death" to "when the death is caused by that person," the wording which is still found in the current section. From this, it is argued that, since the new wording does not include "assisted," those who were simply parties to the murder could not be included. With respect I cannot accept that position.

The difficulties caused by such an interpretation can be readily appreciated when the old and new wording is juxtaposed:

Old — "by his own act caused or assisted in causing the death"

New — "when the death is caused by that person." It can be seen that Parliament deleted both the words "his own act" and "caused or assisted in causing" and replaced them simply with the word "caused." That single word is, in my view, broad enough to include both perpetrators and those who assist in the murder and come within the purview of the substantial cause test I will set out later. On its face, the use of the wording "by that person" in

the last version of the section cannot, in my view, have the same limiting effect as the previous formulation, "by his own act."

On the other hand, the Crown contends that the phrase in s. 214(5), "when the death is caused by that person," is no more than an adoption by reference of the wording of s. 212(a) (now s. 229(a)) and not a distinct causation requirement. That provision states that culpable homicide is murder "where *the person who causes the death* of a human being" means to cause his death. Neither can I accept that position. If Parliament had wished to accomplish this result it could have stated that murder was to be first degree murder "when the murder is committed by that person while committing" an offence of domination. Instead it reiterated a causation requirement within s. 214(5) and effect must be given to that additional phrase.

The question which does arise is precisely what causal effect is required by the phrase "death . . . caused by that person." I think, with respect, that the physically caused test advocated by the majority of the Court of Appeal is too restrictive. In the case at bar, it would be unreasonable to suggest that, in order to be liable under s. 214(5), Harbottle must have pathologically caused the death of the victim by pulling one end of the brassiere strap while his co-accused pulled the other. I find it impossible to distinguish between the blameworthiness of an accused who holds the victim's legs, thus allowing his co-accused to strangle her and the accused who performs the act of strangulation.

Object of the Section

At the outset, it is important to remember that when s. 214(5) comes into play it is in essence a sentencing provision. First degree murder is an aggravated form of murder and not a distinct substantive offence: see *R. v. Farrant*, (1983), 4 C.C.C. (3d) 354, 147 D.L.R. (3d) 511, [1983] 1 S.C.R. 124. It is only to be considered *after* the jury has concluded that the accused is guilty of murder by causing the death of the victim. An accused found guilty of second degree murder will receive a mandatory life sentence. What the jury must then determine is whether such aggravating circumstances exist that they justify ineligibility for parole for a quarter of a century. It is at this point that the requirement of causation set out in s. 214(5) comes into play. The gravity of the crime and the severity of the sentence both indicate that a *substantial and high* degree of blameworthiness, above and beyond that of murder, must be established in order to convict an accused of first degree murder.

Substantial Cause Test

Accordingly, I suggest a restrictive test of *substantial* cause should be applied under s. 214(5). That test will take into account the consequences of a conviction, the present wording of the section, its history, and its aim to protect society from the most heinous murderers.

The consequences of a conviction for first degree murder and the wording of the section are such that the test of causation for s. 214(5) must be a strict one. In my view, an accused may only be convicted under the subsection if the Crown establishes that the accused has committed an act or series of acts which are of such a nature that they must be regarded as a substantial and integral cause of the death.

The substantial causation test requires that the accused play a very active role — usually a physical role — in the killing. Under s. 214(5), the actions of the accused must form an essential, substantial and integral part of the killing of the victim. Obviously, this requirement is much higher than that described in *R. v. Smithers* (1977), 34 C.C.C. (2d) 427, 75 D.L.R. (3d) 321, [1978] 1 S.C.R. 506, which dealt with the offence of manslaughter. There it was held at p. 435 C.C.C., p. 329 D.L.R., that sufficient causation existed where the actions of the accused were "a contributing cause of death, outside the *de minimis* range." That case demonstrates the distinctions in the degree of causation required for the different homicide offences.

While the intervening act of another will often mean that the accused is no longer the substantial cause of the death under s. 214(5), there will be instances where an accused could well be the substantial cause of the death without physically causing it. For example, if one accused with intent to kill locked the victim in a cupboard while the other set fire to that cupboard, then the accused who confined the victim might be found to have caused the death of the victim pursuant to the provisions of s. 214(5). Similarly, an accused who fought off rescuers in order to allow his accomplice to complete the strangulation of the victim might also be found to have been a substantial cause of the death.

Therefore, an accused may be found guilty of first degree murder pursuant to s. 214(5) if the Crown has established beyond a reasonable doubt that:

(1) the accused was guilty of the underlying crime of domination or of attempting to commit that crime;

(2) the accused was guilty of the murder of the victim;

(3) the accused participated in the murder in such a manner that he was a substantial cause of the death of the victim;

(4) there was no intervening act of another which resulted in the accused no longer being substantially connected to the death of the victim; and

(5) the crimes of domination and murder were part of the same transaction; that is to say, the death was caused while committing the offence of domination as part of the same series of events.

It would be appropriate to charge a jury in those terms.

Application of These Principles to This Case

The facts of this case clearly established that Harbottle was a substantial and an integral cause of the death of Elaine Bown. It will be remembered that Ross, who actually strangled the victim, weighed only 130 lb. and was about 5' 7" in height. Elaine Bown, although three inches shorter, was 10 lb. heavier. There was no indication in her blood of any alcohol or drugs so that it can be inferred that she was not impaired. Rather, the bruising on her neck indicates she struggled valiantly. Indeed, it is apparent that even when her hands were bound, she successfully resisted the attempts of both Ross and Harbottle to cut her wrists. There is every reason to believe that, had it not been for Harbottle's holding her legs, she would have been able to resist the attempts to strangle her. In those circumstances, it is difficult to believe that Ross could have strangled her in the absence of the assistance of Harbottle.

The evidence adduced clearly established all the elements of the test. The appellant was guilty (1) of at least one enumerated offence of domination (forcible confinement); (2) he participated in and was found guilty of the murder; (3) his participa-tion in the murder was such that he was a substantial and integral cause of the death of the victim; (4) there was no intervening act of another which resulted in the accused's no longer being substantially connected to the death of the victim; and (5) the crimes of domination and murder were part of the same series of acts or transaction.

Further, after a careful review of the charge, I would agree with the majority of the Court of Appeal that the directions to the jury by the trial judge were eminently fair and adequately covered all the requisite elements of the offences of domination, murder and first degree murder.

Disposition

As the court indicated at the conclusion of the hearing, the appeal must be dismissed.

Appeal dismissed.

Regina v. Kitching and Adams

MANITOBA COURT OF APPEAL

OCTOBER 26, 1976

BACKGROUND

Kitching and Adams were convicted at their trial of the manslaughter of D.G. Junor. Their appeal against conviction was subsequently dismissed by the Manitoba Court of Appeal. However, their appeals against sentence were allowed by the Court of Appeal. (Kitching's sentence was reduced from four years' imprisonment to two years less a day, and Adams' sentence, from five to three years.)

MAIN ISSUE

In what circumstances may the chain of causation in a homicide case be severed by intervening medical treatment?

JUDGMENTS

The *majority* judgment on the question of the convictions was delivered by Justice Matas (with whom Chief Justice Freedman and Justices Monnin and Hall agreed). Justice O'Sullivan delivered a *concurring* judgment on the question of the convictions. On the matter of the sentences, the *majority* judgment was that of Justice O'Sullivan (with whom Chief Justice Freedman and Justice Hall agreed), while Justice Matas (with whom Justice Monnin joined forces) *dissented.*

MATAS, J.A. (dissenting as to sentence): — Appellants, Adams and Kitching, were charged with causing the death of D.G. Junor by means of an unlawful act, thereby committing manslaughter. They were convicted on the charge after a trial before Hunt, J., and a jury, and were sentenced to penitentiary for five years and four years respectively. This is an appeal from conviction and sentence.

Around midnight, July 23, 1975, Junor was seen at the Vibrations Discotheque, a bar attached to St. Charles Hotel in Winnipeg. Junor ordered a drink, and shortly after was seen sitting in a chair with his feet up on another chair, his head slouched forward and his chin resting on his chest. (It became known later that Junor had a blood-alcohol reading of 267 mg. per 100 ml. of blood.) One of the waiters employed at the Vibrations tried to rouse him but was unsuccessful.

Within a few minutes Junor was taken outside by two men and dropped onto the concrete sidewalk. A cab driver stationed near the hotel saw the manoeuvre and said that when Junor was dropped, his face hit the sidewalk, making a sound which was described as: "Just a squishy sound, like, say a tomato hitting against concrete."

An ambulance was called. On arrival, the ambulance attendant examined Junor, did not detect any sign of life and tried resuscitative procedures. Junor was taken to the Health Sciences Centre, with the procedures being continued. On arrival at the hospital, shortly after 1:00 A.M., on July 24th, Junor was examined by Dr. Donan, the resident in charge of the intensive care unit. Dr. Donan noted that the patient had no respiration, pulse, nor activity of the heart. Seven minutes after continued resuscitative procedures, a pulse was obtained and respiration was restored. Junor was admitted to the intensive care unit. During the early morning he was attached to a respirator and to several monitoring devices.

At 7:00 A.M., July 24th, Dr. Tweed, an anaesthetist, examined Junor and found he was deeply unconscious, totally unresponsive to voice or deep painful stimulation and with no significant neurological signs. When removed from the respirator he breathed spontaneously but his breathing was shallow and inadequate. Doctor Tweed diagnosed a brain injury. At 11:30 P.M., the same day, Dr. Tweed found, in summary, that Junor had a complete absence of function at any level of his brain and that his outlook for recovery was hopeless.

Doctor A.J. Gomori, a neurologist, was called in as a consultant and examined Junor in the early afternoon of July 24th, and at 11:00 A.M. on July 25th. On the second examination, Dr. Gomori found Junor was unable to breathe on his own, there was no evidence of response to external painful stimuli and there were no reflexes; Dr. Gomori could not detect any brain stem function; all of this indicated "brain death" and no chance of any recovery.

In the early afternoon of July 25th, Junor suffered a cardiac arrest, which normally would have ended his life. However, Junor's bodily functions were maintained until his kidneys could be removed for transplant purposes. The purpose of maintaining the bodily functions, latterly, was to preserve Junor's organs, not his life. After removal of the kidneys, the artificial respirator was turned off; the EKG, monitoring the heart, continued to show electrical activity for 13 minutes.

The formal death certificate was completed upon removal of the kidneys.

Doctor J.R. Taylor, a pathologist, conducted an autopsy on the morning of July 26, 1975. He said there were two major findings: two hairline fractures of the base of the skull and extensive degenerative changes within the brain itself. The injuries to the skull and brain were consistent with a fall. According to Dr. Taylor, the principal injury was "the brain lesion the total and absolute death of the brain." Doctor Taylor summarized his findings as follows:

> Well, as I have said, at the time of autopsy I found several things. He had an absence of kidneys for one thing. Incidentally, he had evidence of highly bronchial pneumonia. Thirdly, he had, and most significantly to my mind, he had evidence of severe and irreversible brain injury at the time of death. How that injury came about can be interpreted in one of two ways. At least, but primarily, it was, I think, due to a blow which was sufficient to crack his skull. It was sufficient to produce subaracnoid hemorrhage, and it might, but I can't prove this, it might have been sufficient at the time to have damaged this man's brain. It could have damaged the hyperthalamous, or some other part of the brain. At the time of autopsy all I can suggest is one of two pathways of this finding of the final condition of the brain. Either it was caused at the time of the initial injury or the death of the brain was a result of a sequence of events starting with the injury and the brain swelling, compression of blood vessels, and from the compression of the blood vessels to the death of the brain, with the same final end result. At the time of autopsy it is not possible to say when or which pathway this man took. I think it would require other evidence of the state of his nervous system, the function especially of his hyperthalamous at the time that he was admitted, to be able to elucidate, and at this point I cannot expand on that factor.

The jury heard detailed evidence on the several tests given Junor and his progressive medical condition from all the doctors who were called by the Crown; as well, there was an exhaustive exploration of the difficult criteria for determining death and the basis for use of those criteria.

Adams' notice of appeal listed 28 grounds of alleged error and Kitching's notice of appeal set out 22 grounds.

5. There were a series of objections made to the summing up with respect to ss. 207 to 209 of the Criminal Code dealing with questions of death which might have been prevented, death from treatment of injury, and acceleration of death. It was part of appellants' case that it was something which the doctors had done, or omitted to do, arising from the kidney transplant, which brought about the death of Junor. In my view, the argument is without merit.

The question of the cause of death was left to the jury for their decision. They obviously decided, after weighing all the evidence, including the extensive medical testimony and the Judge's charge, that Junor had died as a result of acts of appellants. In my view, the learned Judge, if anything, gave more credence than was warranted to the defence that death was caused by the doctors, in respect of the transplant.

I would apply the provisions of s. 613(1)(b)(iii) of the Code and hold that there has been no substantial wrong or miscarriage of justice. I am satisfied that the evidence against appellants was such that the jury, charged as it should have been, could not, as reasonable men, have done otherwise than find appellants guilty.

In the result, I would dismiss the appeal from conviction.

O'SULLIVAN, J.A.: — I agree with my brother Matas on the question of the appeal from conviction. Whatever errors there may have been in the course of the trial, there has been no substantial wrong or miscarriage of justice.

I would like to add something about the medical evidence which occupied more than half the time of the trial.

Counsel for the accused argued that their clients should not be convicted of manslaughter because there was a possibility on the evidence that the deceased, Mr. Junor, was killed not as a result of the acts of the accused, but as a result of the acts of doctors at Health Sciences Centre in Winnipeg, who removed the deceased's kidneys and shut off a life-supporting ventilator.

The actions of the accused took place on July 24, 1975, about 1:00 A.M., when Mr. Junor was dropped on the sidewalk while being taken out of the Vibrations.

On July 25, 1975, about 1:00 P.M., the deceased's heart was beating spontaneously and his lungs were breathing with the help of a ventilator.

At that time the deceased's body was taken to an operating room and both kidneys were removed for potential transplantation.

About 2:10 P.M., following removal of the kidneys, the ventilator was shut off. The heart continued to beat on its own for 13 minutes. Then the heart stopped beating.

It was only after the kidneys were removed that Dr. W.A. Tweed certified the death of Mr. Junor. No one at Health Sciences Centre had pronounced him dead before the removal of his kidneys.

The contentions of counsel raise far-reaching questions of law relating to death, its definition, and the time of death.

By traditional criteria, there is no question that Mr. Junor was alive when his kidneys were removed. Traditionally, both law and medicine have been unanimous in saying that it is not safe to pronounce a man dead until after his vital functions have ceased to operate. The heart has always been regarded as a vital organ.

Since the introduction of organ transplantation, however, many physicians and moralists have sought to establish new and different criteria for determining the time and the fact of death.

It is apparent that the fresher the kidneys, the better chance the recipient will have. It is apparent that in the case of a heart transplant, there is no use transplanting a dead heart. The heart must be alive if the recipient of it is to have any chance of life. The problem facing medicine and society in recent years is how do you get a living heart out of a dead body? If a person is not dead until after his heart ceases to function, it is practically impossible to imagine a successful heart transplant except by taking a living heart out of a still living person. But this is abhorrent to the conscience of many people.

So a substantial body of medical opinion has come forward with the suggestion that the concept of death itself should be redefined.

Some have said, if a man is "as good as dead," we will call him "dead" and then there will be no ethical problem about taking out his vital organs.

Some doctors have said that a person is as good as dead, and is therefore dead, if he is in such a condition that it can be predicted with confidence that he will never again be able to be restored to meaningful life.

Others have advanced the proposition that death is not an event but a process and, when the process of death reaches a stage where a doctor is of the opinion that the process is irreversible, the person should be declared dead.

Doctor Tweed advanced this view in this case before the jury, and the learned trial Judge appears to have adopted it for he said to the jury: "It appears that death is a process, not an event, as I stated earlier."

This is a most controversial statement at variance with centuries of religious tradition. It is a statement vigorously disputed in many medico-legal books, for example, in *Grey's Attorney's Textbook of Medicine* at para. 29.11. Religion has taught us that death is an event. Dying may be a process, but death is an event. Except for some small sects, such as those in Rumania, who believe that death is a process during which the soul is in a state of suspended animation (hence, perhaps residing in vampire bats), the overwhelming weight of religious teaching all over the world is that the moment of death occurs when the soul leaves the body. This is true not only of Christians who believe in the personal immortality of the individual soul and the immediacy of judgment after death, but also of eastern religions which believe in the transmigration of souls at the moment of death.

Furthermore, by common consent, it has been held by all civilized people that no one, for however laudable a purpose, has the right to dispatch a dying man so as to hasten his death. Most moralists agree that it is not wrong to withhold extraordinary treatment to prolong the life of a dying man. It is not wrong to let him die. But directly to dispatch him by cutting out his heart or his lungs or his kidneys is contrary to every principle of civilized morality, as held by large numbers of citizens.

Another large body of medical opinion, I think the most substantial body, accept the fact that death is an event and not a process. They say that the criteria for "defining" death are really criteria for determining the manifestations of death. It is true that the fact of death is manifested where all the vital signs, including heartbeat, have ceased. But, they say, it is equally true that the fact of death is manifested if all activity of the brain has ceased for a sufficient period of time. If the brain of a man is dead, then it is safe to say that the whole man is dead. It is the activities operated through the brain which differentiate man from an animal. If the brain is dead, he is dead.

This approach has gained widespread support not only among doctors but among moralists as well and has received legislative recognition in some States and in the Province of Manitoba.

This opinion does not proceed on the principle that if a man will surely die, then it is safe to call him already dead. It operates on the principle that if a man's brain is dead, he is dead.

The trouble is that it is not always obvious when brain death occurs. There are well documented cases where a man's brain has shown absolutely no sign of activity for two days or more and yet he has recovered and survived. This is particularly so where a man has ingested large quantities of central nervous system depressants such as barbiturates.

There has been a great deal of debate about this subject and the debate is likely to go on for some time.

Many eminent physicians, including an *ad hoc* committee of doctors of Harvard University, have established certain criteria for determining brain death. Among the requirements are flat EEG's taken 24 hours apart. The possibility of barbiturate consumption being excluded, they say that if there is no sign of brain activity during a 24-hour period, it is then safe to say that the brain is dead and, hence, that the man is dead.

In the case of the deceased, Mr. Junor, the Harvard criteria were not followed. Twenty-four hours before the kidney transplant, there was evidence of brain stem activity. Neither were the criteria proposed by Cornell University doctors followed.

Faced with the difficulties inherent in establishing universally acceptable criteria for determining brain death, many doctors have said that the safe course is to have at least two doctors certify death before allowing removal of vital organs.

Thus, a world assembly on medicine held in Australia in 1968 said: "If transplantation of an organ is involved, the decision that death exists should be made by two or more physicians, and the physician determining the moment of death should in no way be immediately concerned with the performance of the transplantation."

Many hospitals have regulations requiring such certificates of death prior to removal of vital organs. According to the evidence, the Health Sciences Centre has no such protection for potential donors.

These questions are important and they may have to be considered by the Courts some day. In my opinion, however, they were not properly before the Court in the case before us.

The legal and ethical implications of the conduct of doctors are no doubt under constant and careful review by peer review committees, by the Colleges of Physicians and Surgeons, and by others.

I think it is regrettable that the doctors at Health Sciences Centre were subjected to the lengthy questioning in this case. I do not think that the trial in this case, or in cases similar to it, affords a suitable forum for discussing these important questions.

I think that counsel for the accused proceeded on a fundamental misconception of the law. They assumed that, if it could be shown that death resulted in this case from the removal of the kidneys, then the accused should be acquitted because there would be a reasonable doubt that they had been the cause of death.

The assumption underling counsel's conduct in this case is that there can be only one cause of death. I think the law is that the conduct of a defendant in a criminal trial need not be shown to be the sole or "the effective" cause of a crime. It is sufficient if it is a cause.

Sections 207 to 209 of the Criminal Code extend liability in certain cases; they do not affect the principle that it is not necessary to prove that a criminal is the sole cause of his crime.

I think the authorities are clear that there may be two or more independent operative causes of death.

Without in this case criticizing the doctors of Health Sciences Centre or suggesting that they were guilty of any improper conduct, I am of the opinion that their conduct was irrelevant to the questions before the jury. Even if it could be shown that the actions of the doctors constituted an operative cause of Mr. Junor's death — and I emphasize that I do not suggest that the evidence would support such a conclusion — still, that would not exonerate the accused unless the evidence left a reasonable doubt that the accused's actions also constituted an operative cause of the deceased's death.

On that question, the evidence was overwhelming. Whether or not the kidneys had been removed, the deceased could not have lasted more than a short period of time even with artificial assistance.

The jury had to decide not whether the doctors were ethical or not but simply did the accused cause the death of the deceased by unlawful means. The question of causation was put to the jury plainly; they decided that the accused did cause the death. The evidence was overwhelmingly in favour of their verdict.

While agreeing with my brother Matas on the issue of conviction, I disagree with respect on the subject of sentence.

Accordingly, I would uphold the conviction but vary the sentences as indicated.

Appeals from conviction dismissed; appeals from sentence allowed.

Rodriguez v. British Columbia (Attorney-General)

SUPREME COURT OF CANADA   SEPTEMBER 30, 1993

BACKGROUND

Ms. Rodriguez applied to the B.C. Supreme Court for a declaration that section 241(b) of the Criminal Code was invalid because it infringed her rights under sections 7, 12, and 15(1) of the Charter. The application was rejected and Ms. Rodriguez's subsequent appeals to the B.C. Court of Appeal and the Supreme Court of Canada were dismissed.

MAIN ISSUE

Is section 241(b), which makes it an offence to assist a person to commit suicide, invalid under the Charter?

JUDGMENTS

The *majority* judgment was delivered by Justice Sopinka (with whom Justices La Forest, Gonthier, Iacobucci, and Major agreed). *Dissenting* judgments were delivered by Chief Justice Lamer, Justice McLachlin (with whom Justice L'Heureux-Dubé agreed), and Justice Cory. The judgments of Justices McLachlin and Cory have been omitted.

LAMER C.J.C. (dissenting): —

Facts

The facts of this case are straightforward and well known. Sue Rodriguez is a 42-year-old woman living in British Columbia. She is married and the mother of an 8 1/2 -year-old son. Ms. Rodriguez suffers from amyotrophic lateral sclerosis (ALS), which is widely known as Lou Gehrig's disease; her life expectancy is between 2 and 14 months but her condition is rapidly deteriorating. Very soon she will lose the ability to swallow, speak, walk, and move her body without assistance. Thereafter she will lose the capacity to breathe without a respirator, to eat without a gastrotomy, and will eventually become confined to a bed.

Ms. Rodriguez knows of her condition, the trajectory of her illness, and the inevitability of how her life will end; her wish is to control the circumstances, timing, and manner of her death. She does not wish to die so long as she still has the capacity to enjoy life. However, by the time she no longer is able to enjoy life, she will be physically unable to terminate her life without assistance. Ms. Rodriguez seeks an order which will allow a qualified medical

Adapted from *Rodriquez v. British Columbia* (Attorney-General) (1993), 85 C.C.C. (3d), pp. 21–22, 31, 60–84. Copyright © 1993 by *Canada Law Book*. Reprinted with permission.

practitioner to set up technological means by which she might, by her own hand, at the time of her choosing, end her life.

Relevant Statutory Provisions

The relevant provision of the Criminal Code is as follows:

> 241. Every one who
>> (a) counsels a person to commit suicide, or
>> (b) aids or abets a person to commit suicide,
>> whether suicide ensues or not, is guilty of an indictable offence and liable to imprisonment for a term not exceeding fourteen years.

Analysis

I find that s. 241(b) of the Criminal Code infringes s. 15(1) of the Charter. In my view, persons with disabilities who are or will become unable to end their lives without assistance are discriminated against by that provision since, unlike persons capable of causing their own deaths, they are deprived of the option of choosing suicide. I further find that s. 1 of the Charter does not save s. 241(b) of the Criminal Code. The means chosen to carry out the legislative purpose of preventing possible abuses do not in my opinion impair as little as reasonably possible the right to equality enshrined in s. 15(1) of the Charter.

In view of my findings under s. 15(1), I need not address the constitutionality of the legislation under ss. 7 or 12 of the Charter.

SOPINKA J: —

I. Section 7

The most substantial issue in this appeal is whether s. 241(b) infringes s. 7 in that it inhibits the appellant in controlling the timing and manner of her death. I conclude that while the section impinges on the security interest of the appellant, any resulting deprivation is not contrary to the principles of fundamental justice. I would come to the same conclusion with respect to any liberty interest which may be involved.

The appellant argues that, by prohibiting anyone from assisting her to end her life when her illness has rendered her incapable of terminating her life without such assistance, by threat of criminal sanction, s. 241(b) deprives her of both her liberty and her security of the person. The appellant asserts that her application is based upon (a) the right to live her remaining life with the inherent dignity of a human person, (b) the right to control what happens to her body while she is living, and (c) the right to be free from governmental interference in making fundamental personal decisions concerning the terminal stages of her life. The first two of these asserted rights can be seen to invoke both liberty and security of the person; the latter is more closely associated with only the liberty interest.

(a) LIFE, LIBERTY AND SECURITY OF THE PERSON

The appellant seeks a remedy which would assure her some control over the time and manner of her death. While she supports her claim on the ground that her liberty and security of the person interests are engaged, a consideration of these interests cannot be divorced from the sanctity of life, which is one of the three Charter values protected by s. 7.

None of these values prevail *a priori* over the others. All must be taken into account in determining the content of the principles of fundamental justice and there is no basis for imposing a greater burden on the propounder of one value as against that imposed on another.

Section 7 involves two stages of analysis. The first is as to the values at stake with respect to the individual. The second is concerned with possible limitations of those values when considered in conformity with fundamental justice. In assessing the first aspect, we may do so by considering whether there has been a violation of Ms. Rodriguez's security of the person and we must consider this in light of the other values I have mentioned.

Sanctity of life, as we will see, has been understood historically as excluding freedom of choice in the self-infliction of death and certainly in the involvement of others in carrying out that choice. At the very least, no new consensus has emerged in society opposing the right of the state to regulate the involvement of others in exercising power over individuals ending their lives.

The appellant suggests that for the terminally ill, the choice is one of time and manner of death rather than death itself since the latter is inevitable. I disagree. Rather it is one of choosing death instead of allowing natural forces to run their course. The time and precise manner of death remain unknown until death actually occurs. There can be no certainty in forecasting the precise circumstances of a death. Death is, for all mortals, inevitable. Even when death appears imminent, seeking to control the manner and timing of one's death constitutes a conscious choice of death over life. It follows that life as a value is engaged even in the case of the terminally ill who seek to choose death over life.

Indeed, it has been abundantly pointed out that such persons are particularly vulnerable as to their life and will to live, and great concern has been expressed as to their adequate protection, as will be further set forth.

I do not draw from this that in such circumstances life as a value must prevail over security of person or liberty as these have been understood under the Charter, but that it is one of the values engaged in the present case.

In my view, then, the judgments of this court in *R. v. Morgentaler* (1988), 37 C.C.C. (3d) 449, 44 D.L.R. (4th) 385, [1988] 1 S.C.R. 30 (S.C.C.) can be seen to encompass a notion of personal autonomy involving, at the very least, control over one's bodily integrity free from state interference and freedom from state-imposed psychological and emotional stress. There is no question, then, that personal autonomy, at least with respect to the right to make choices concerning one's own body, control over one's physical and psychological integrity, and basic human dignity are encompassed within security of the person, at least to the extent of freedom from criminal prohibitions which interfere with these.

The effect of the prohibition in s. 241(b) is to prevent the appellant from having assistance to commit suicide when she is no longer able to do so on her own. She fears that she will be required to live until the deterioration from her disease is such that she will die as a result of choking, suffocation or pneumonia caused by aspiration of food or secretions. She will be totally dependent upon machines to perform her bodily functions and completely dependent upon others. Throughout this time, she will remain mentally competent and able to appreciate all that is happening to her. Although palliative care may be available to ease the pain and other physical discomfort which she will experience, the appellant fears the sedating effects of such drugs and argues, in any event, that they will not prevent the psychological and emotional distress which will result from being in a situation of utter dependence and loss of dignity. That there is a right to choose how one's body will be dealt with, even in the context of beneficial medical treatment, has long been recognized by the common law. To impose medical treatment on one who refuses it constitutes battery, and our common law has recognized the right to demand that medical treatment which would extend life be withheld or withdrawn. In my view, these considerations lead to the conclusion that the prohibition in s. 241(b) deprives the appellant of autonomy over her person and causes her physical pain and psychological stress in a manner which impinges on the security of her person. The appellant's security interest (considered in the context of the life and liberty interest) is therefore engaged, and it is necessary to determine whether there has been any deprivation thereof that is not in accordance with the principles of fundamental justice.

(b) THE PRINCIPLES OF FUNDAMENTAL JUSTICE

In this case, it is not disputed that in general s. 241(b) is valid and desirable legislation which fulfils the government's objectives of preserving life and protecting the vulnerable. The complaint is that the legislation is over-inclusive because it does not exclude from the reach of the prohibition those in the situation of the appellant who are terminally ill and mentally competent but cannot commit suicide on their own. It is also argued that the extension of the prohibition to the appellant is arbitrary and unfair as suicide itself is not unlawful, and the common law allows a physician to withhold or withdraw life-saving or life-maintaining treatment on the patient's instructions and to administer palliative care which has the effect of hastening death. The issue is whether, given this legal context, the existence of a criminal prohibition on assisting suicide for one in the appellant's situation is contrary to principles of fundamental justice.

The appellant asserts that it is a principle of fundamental justice that the human dignity and autonomy of individuals be respected, and that to subject her to needless suffering in this manner is to rob her of her dignity. The importance of the concept of human dignity in our society was enunciated by Cory J. (dissenting, Lamer C.J.C. concurring) in *Kindler v. Canada (Minister of Justice)* (1991), 67 C.C.C. (3d) 1 at pp. 33–4, 84 D.L.R. (4th) 438 at pp. 470–1, [1991] 2 S.C.R. 779. Respect for human dignity underlies many of the rights and freedoms in the Charter.

That respect for human dignity is one of the underlying principles upon which our society is based is unquestioned. I have difficulty, however, in characterizing this in itself as a principle of fundamental justice within the meaning of s. 7. While respect for human dignity is the genesis for many principles of fundamental justice, not every law that fails to accord such respect runs afoul of these principles. To state that "respect for human dignity and autonomy" is a principle of fundamental justice, then, is essentially to state that the deprivation of the appellant's security of the person is contrary to principles of fundamental justice because it deprives her of security of the person. This interpretation would equate security of the person with

a principle of fundamental justice and render the latter redundant.

Where the deprivation of the right in question does little or nothing to enhance the state's interest (whatever it may be), it seems to me that a breach of fundamental justice will be made out, as the individual's rights will have been deprived for no valid purpose.

The issue here, then, can be characterized as being whether the blanket prohibition on assisted suicide is arbitrary or unfair in that it is unrelated to the state's interest in protecting the vulnerable, and that it lacks a foundation in the legal tradition and societal beliefs which are said to be represented by the prohibition.

Section 241(b) has as its purpose the protection of the vulnerable who might be induced in moments of weakness to commit suicide. This purpose is grounded in the state interest in protecting life and reflects the policy of the state that human life should not be depreciated by allowing life to be taken. This policy finds expression not only in the provisions of our Criminal Code which prohibit murder and other violent acts against others notwithstanding the consent of the victim, but also in the policy against capital punishment and, until its repeal, attempted suicide. This is not only a policy of the state, however, but is part of our fundamental conception of the sanctity of human life.

The principle of sanctity of life is no longer seen to require that all human life be preserved at all costs. Rather, it has come to be understood, at least by some, as encompassing quality of life considerations, and to be subject to certain limitations and qualifications reflective of personal autonomy and dignity. An analysis of our legislative and social policy in this area is necessary in order to determine whether fundamental principles have evolved such that they conflict with the validity of the balancing of interests undertaken by Parliament.

(i) HISTORY OF THE SUICIDE PROVISIONS

At common law, suicide was seen as a form of felonious homicide that offended both against God and the King's interest in the life of his citizens.

Thus, until 1823, English law provided that the property of the suicide be forfeited and his body placed at the cross-roads of two highways with a stake driven through it.

However, given the practical difficulties of prosecuting the successful suicide, most prohibitions centred on attempted suicide; it was considered an offence and accessory liability for assisted suicide was made punishable. In England, this took the form of a charge of accessory before the fact to murder or murder itself until the passage of the Suicide Act, 1961 (U.K.), c. 60, which created an offence of assisting suicide which reads much like our s. 241. In Canada, the common law recognized that aiding suicide was criminal (G.W. Burbidge, *A Digest of the Criminal Law of Canada* (1890), at p. 224) and this was enshrined in the first Criminal Code, S.C. 1892, c. 29, s. 237. It is, with some editorial changes, the provision now found in s. 241.

The associated offence of attempted suicide has an equally long pedigree in Canada, found in the original Code at s. 238 and continued substantively unaltered until its repeal by S.C. 1972, c. 13, s. 16. The fact of this decriminalization does not aid us particularly in this analysis, however. Unlike the situation with the partial decriminalization of abortion, the decriminalization of attempted suicide cannot be said to represent a consensus by Parliament or by Canadians in general that the autonomy interest of those wishing to kill themselves is paramount to the state interest in protecting the life of its citizens. Rather, the matter of suicide was seen to have its roots and its solutions in sciences outside the law, and for that reason not to mandate a legal remedy. Since that time, there have been some attempts to decriminalize assistance to suicide through private members bills, but none has been successful.

(ii) MEDICAL CARE AT THE END OF LIFE

Canadian courts have recognized a common law right of patients to refuse consent to medical treatment, or to demand that treatment, once commenced, be withdrawn or discontinued: *Ciarlariello v. Schacter* (1993), 100 D.L.R. (4th) 609, [1993] 2 S.C.R. 119, 15 C.C.L.T. (2d) 209 (S.C.C.). This right has been specifically recognized to exist even if the withdrawal from or refusal of treatment may result in death (*Nancy B. v. Hôtel-Dieu de Québec* (1992), 69 C.C.C. (3d) 450, 86 D.L.R. (4th) 385, [1992] R.J.Q. 361 (Que. S.C.); *Mallette v. Shulman* (1990), 67 D.L.R. (4th) 321, 2 C.C.L.T. (2d) 1, 72 O.R. (2d) 417 (Ont. C.A.).

Following Working Paper 28, the Law Reform Commission recommended in its 1983 report to the Minister of Justice that the Criminal Code be amended to provide that the homicide provisions not be interpreted as requiring a physician to undertake medical treatment against the wishes of a patient, or to continue medical treatment when such treatment "has become therapeutically useless," or from requiring a physician to "cease administering appropriate palliative care intended to eliminate or to relieve the suffering of a person, for the sole reason that such care or measures are likely to shorten the life expectancy of this person" (Report 20, *Euthanasia, Aiding Suicide and Cessation of Treatment* (1983), at p. 35).

The Law Reform Commission had discussed in the Working Paper the possibility of the decriminalization of assisted suicide in the following terms, at pp. 53–54:

> First of all, the prohibition in [s. 241] is not restricted solely to the case of the terminally ill patient, for whom we can only have sympathy, or solely to his physician or a member of his family who helps him to put an end to his suffering. The section is more general and applies to a variety of situations for which it is much more difficult to feel sympathy. Consider, for example, a recent incident, that of inciting to mass suicide. What of the person who takes advantage of another's depressed state to encourage him to commit suicide, for his own financial benefit? What of the person who, knowing an adolescent's suicidal tendencies, provides him with large enough quantities of drugs to kill him? The "accomplice" in these cases cannot be considered morally blameless. Nor can one conclude that the criminal law should not

punish such conduct. To decriminalize completely the act of aiding, abetting or counselling suicide would therefore not be a valid legislative policy. But could it be in the case of the terminally ill?

The probable reason why legislation has not made an exception for the terminally ill lies in the fear of the excesses or abuses to which liberalization of the existing law could lead. As in the case of "compassionate murder," decriminalization of aiding suicide would be based on the humanitarian nature of the motive leading the person to provide such aid, counsel or encouragement. As in the case of compassionate murder, moreover, the law may legitimately fear the difficulties involved in determining the true motivation of the person committing the act.

Aiding or counselling a person to commit suicide, on the one hand, and homicide, on the other, are sometimes extremely closely related. Consider, for example, the doctor who holds the glass of poison and pours the contents into the patient's mouth. Is he aiding him to commit suicide? Or is he committing homicide, since the victim's willingness to die is legally immaterial? There is reason to fear that homicide of the terminally ill for ignoble motives may readily be disguised as aiding suicide.

It can be seen, therefore, that while both the House of Lords and the Law Reform Commission of Canada have great sympathy for the plight of those who wish to end their lives so as to avoid significant suffering, neither has been prepared to recognize that the active assistance of a third party in carrying out this desire should be condoned, even for the terminally ill. The basis for this refusal is twofold it seems — first, the active participation by one individual in the death of another is intrinsically morally and legally wrong, and second, there is no certainty that abuses can be prevented by anything less than a complete prohibition. Creating an exception for the terminally ill might therefore frustrate the purpose of the legislation of protecting the vulnerable because adequate guidelines to control abuse are difficult or impossible to develop.

(iii) REVIEW OF LEGISLATION IN OTHER COUNTRIES

A brief review of the legislative situation in other western democracies demonstrates that in general, the approach taken is very similar to that which currently exists in Canada. Nowhere is assisted suicide expressly permitted, and most countries have provisions expressly dealing with assisted suicide which are at least as restrictive as our s. 241.

(iv) CONCLUSION ON PRINCIPLES OF FUNDAMENTAL JUSTICE

What the preceding review demonstrates is that Canada and other western democracies recognize and apply the principle of the sanctity of life as a general principle which is subject to limited and narrow exceptions in situations in which notions of personal autonomy and dignity must prevail. However, these same societies continue to draw distinctions between passive and active forms of intervention in the dying process, and with very few exceptions, prohibit assisted suicide in situations akin to that of the appellant. The task then becomes to identify the rationales upon which these distinctions are based and to determine whether they are constitutionally supportable.

The distinction between withdrawing treatment upon a patient's request, such as occurred in the *Nancy B.* case, on the one hand, and assisted suicide, on the other, has been criticized as resting on a legal fiction — that is, the distinction between active and passive forms of treatment. The criticism is based on the fact that the withdrawal of life supportive measures is done with the knowledge that death will ensue, just as is assisting suicide, and that death does in fact ensue as a result of the action taken.

Other commentators, however, uphold the distinction on the basis that in the case of withdrawal of treatment, the death is "natural" — the artificial forces of medical technology which have kept the patient alive are removed and nature takes its course. In the case of assisted suicide or euthanasia, however, the course of nature is interrupted, and death results *directly* from the human action taken.

Whether or not one agrees that the active vs. passive distinction is maintainable, however, the fact remains that under our common law, the physician has no choice but to accept the patient's instructions to discontinue treatment. To continue to treat the patient when the patient has withdrawn consent to that treatment constitutes battery (*Ciarlariello* and *Nancy B.*, *supra*). The doctor is therefore not required to make a choice which will result in the patient's death as he would be if he chose to assist a suicide or to perform active euthanasia.

The fact that doctors may deliver palliative care to terminally ill patients without fear of sanction, it is argued, attenuates to an even greater degree any legitimate distinction which can be drawn between assisted suicide and what are currently acceptable forms of medical treatment. The administration of drugs designed for pain control in dosages which the physician knows will hasten death constitutes active contribution to death by any standard. However, the distinction drawn here is one based upon intention — in the case of palliative care, the intention is to ease pain, which has the effect of hastening death, while in the case of assisted suicide, the intention is undeniably to cause death. In my view, distinctions based upon intent are important, and in fact form the basis of our criminal law. While factually the distinction may, at times, be difficult to draw, legally it is clear. The fact that in some cases the third party will, under the guise of palliative care, commit euthanasia or assist in suicide and go unsanctioned due to the difficulty of proof cannot be said to render the existence of the prohibition fundamentally unjust.

The principles of fundamental justice cannot be created for the occasion to reflect the court's dislike or distaste of a particular statute. While the principles of fundamental justice are concerned with more than process, reference must be made to principles which are "fundamental" in the sense that they would have general acceptance among reasonable people. From the review that I have conducted above, I am unable to discern anything approaching unanimity with respect to the issue before us. Regardless of one's personal views as to whether the

distinctions drawn between withdrawal of treatment and palliative care, on the one hand, and assisted suicide, on the other, are practically compelling, the fact remains that these distinctions are maintained and can be persuasively defended. To the extent that there is a consensus, it is that human life must be respected and we must be careful not to undermine the institutions that protect it.

This consensus finds legal expression in our legal system which prohibits capital punishment. This prohibition is supported, in part, on the basis that allowing the state to kill will cheapen the value of human life, and thus the state will serve, in a sense, as a role model for individuals in society. The prohibition against assisted suicide serves a similar purpose. In upholding the respect for life, it may discourage those who consider that life is unbearable at a particular moment, or who perceive themselves to be a burden upon others, from committing suicide. To permit a physician to lawfully participate in taking life would send a signal that there are circumstances in which the state approves of suicide.

I also place some significance in the fact that the official position of various medical associations is against decriminalizing assisted suicide (Canadian Medical Association, British Medical Association, Council of Ethical and Judicial Affairs of the American Medical Association, World Medical Association, and the American Nurses Association). Given the concerns about abuse that have been expressed and the great difficulty in creating appropriate safeguards to prevent these, it cannot be said that the blanket prohibition on assisted suicide is arbitrary or unfair, or that it is not reflective of fundamental values at play in our society. I am thus unable to find that any principle of fundamental justice is violated by s. 241(b).

II. Section 12

Section 12 of the Charter provides as follows:

> 12. Everyone has the right not to be subjected to any cruel and unusual treatment or punishment.

In order to come within the protection of s. 12, the appellant must demonstrate two things: first, that she is subjected to treatment or punishment at the hands of the state, and second, that such treatment or punishment is cruel and unusual. In this case, the appellant alleges that the prohibition on assisted suicide has the effect of imposing upon her cruel and unusual treatment in that the prohibition subjects her to prolonged suffering until her natural death or requires that she end her life at an earlier point while she can still do so without help. In my opinion, it cannot be said that the appellant is subjected by the state to any form of punishment within the meaning of s. 12. The question of whether the appellant is subjected to "treatment," however, is less clear.

The degree to which "treatment" in s. 12 may apply outside the context of penalties imposed to ensure the application and enforcement of the law has not been definitively determined by this Court.

For the purposes of the present analysis, I am prepared to assume that "treatment" within the meaning of s. 12 may include that imposed by the state in contexts other than that of a penal or *quasi*-penal nature. However, it is my view that a mere prohibition by the state on certain action, without more, cannot constitute "treatment" under s. 12. In the present case, the appellant is simply subject to the edicts of the Criminal Code, as are all other individuals in society. The fact that, because of the personal situation in which she finds herself, a particular prohibition impacts upon her in a manner which causes her suffering does not subject her to "treatment" at the hands of the state. The starving person who is prohibited by threat of criminal sanction from "stealing a mouthful of bread" is likewise not subjected to "treatment" within the meaning of s. 12 by reason of the theft provisions of the Code, nor is the heroin addict who is prohibited from possessing heroin by the provisions of the Narcotic Control Act, R.S.C. 1985, c. N-1. There must be some more active state process in operation, involving an exercise of state control over the individual, in order for the state action in question, whether it be positive action, inaction or

prohibition, to constitute "treatment" under s. 12. In my view, to hold that the criminal prohibition in s. 241(b), without the appellant being in any way subject to the state administrative or justice system, falls within the bounds of s. 12 stretches the ordinary meaning of being "subjected to . . . treatment" by the state.

For these reasons, in my view, s. 241(b) does not violate s. 12.

III. Section 15

The Chief Justice concludes that disabled persons who are unable to commit suicide without assistance are discriminated against contrary to s. 15 in that they are deprived of a benefit or subjected to a burden by virtue of s. 241(b) of the Criminal Code. Since I am of the opinion that any infringement is clearly saved under s. 1 of the Charter, I prefer not to decide these issues in this case. They are better left to a case in which they are essential to its resolution. Rather, I will assume that s. 15 of the Charter is infringed and consider the application of s. 1.

IV. Section 1

I agree with the Chief Justice that s. 241(b) has "a clearly pressing and substantial legislative objective" grounded in the respect for and the desire to protect human life, a fundamental Charter value. I elaborated on the purpose of s. 241(b) earlier in these reasons in my discussion of s. 7.

On the issue of proportionality, which is the second factor to be considered under s. 1, it could hardly be suggested that a prohibition on giving assistance to commit suicide is not rationally connected to the purpose of s. 241(b). The Chief Justice does not suggest otherwise. Section 241(b) protects all individuals against the control of others over their lives. To introduce an exception to this blanket protection for certain groups would create an inequality. As I have sought to demonstrate in my discussion of s. 7, this protection is grounded on a substantial consensus among western countries, medical organizations, and our own Law Reform Commission that, in order to effectively protect life and those who are vulnerable in society, a prohibition without exception on the giving of assistance to commit suicide is the best approach. Attempts to fine tune this approach by creating exceptions have been unsatisfactory and have tended to support the theory of the "slippery slope." The formulation of safeguards to prevent excesses has been unsatisfactory and has failed to allay fears that a relaxation of the clear standard set by the law will undermine the protection of life and will lead to abuses of the exception.

The foregoing is also the answer to the submission that the impugned legislation is overbroad. There is no halfway measure that could be relied upon with assurance to fully achieve the legislation's purpose; first, because the purpose extends to the protection of the life of the terminally ill. Part of this purpose, as I have explained above, is to discourage the terminally ill from choosing death over life. Secondly, even if the latter consideration can be stripped from the legislative purpose, we have no assurance that the exception can be made to limit the taking of life to those who are terminally ill and genuinely desire death.

In light of the significant support for the type of legislation under attack in this case and the contentious and complex nature of the issues, I find that the government had a reasonable basis for concluding that it had complied with the requirement of minimum impairment. This satisfies this branch of the proportionality test, and it is not the proper function of this court to speculate as to whether other alternatives available to Parliament might have been preferable.

It follows from the above that I am satisfied that the final aspect of the proportionality test, balance between the restriction and the government objective, is also met. I conclude, therefore, that any infringement of s. 15 is clearly justified under s. 1 of the Charter.

V. Disposition

I agree with the sentiments expressed by the justices of the British Columbia Court of Appeal — this case is an upsetting one from a personal perspective. I have the deepest sympathy for the appellant and her family, as I am sure do all of my colleagues, and I am aware that the denial of her application by this court may prevent her from managing the manner of her death. I have, however, concluded that the prohibition occasioned by s. 241(b) is not contrary to the provisions of the Charter.

In the result, the appeal is dismissed, but without costs.

The constitutional questions are answered as follows:

Question 1: Does s. 241(b) of the Criminal Code of Canada infringe or deny, in whole or in part, the rights and freedoms guaranteed by ss. 7, 12 and 15(1) of the Canadian Charter of Rights and Freedoms?

Answer: No, except as to s. 15 in respect of which an infringement is assumed.

Question 2: If so, is it justified by s. 1 of the Canadian Charter of Rights and Freedoms and therefore not inconsistent with the Constitution Act, 1982?

Answer: As to ss. 7 and 12, no answer is required. As to s. 15, the answer is yes.

Appeal dismissed.

The Mental Element in Criminal Law: Subjective Liability

INTRODUCTION

Chapters 3 and 4 present cases that illuminate the *mens rea* requirements of a criminal offence. There are two forms of *mens rea* in criminal law: *subjective* and *objective*. In Chapter 4, objective *mens rea* is examined.

Subjective *mens rea* is based on what was "actually going on in the accused's head" at the time of the alleged offence. The major forms of subjective *mens rea* are intention and knowledge, recklessness, and wilful blindness. In addition, there are certain offences which require the Crown to prove some special mental element, such as "fraud," *in addition to* intention and knowledge, etc.

In the important case of *Théroux* (1993), the Supreme Court of Canada examined the subjective *mens rea* elements required in relation to a charge of fraud under section 380 of the Criminal Code. The Supreme Court ruled that, in addition to subjective intention and knowledge, the Crown must prove that the accused acted "fraudulently" and it established a working definition of the meaning of this term. Both the *Sansregret* (1985) and *Oluwa* (1996) cases articulate the nature of, and differences between, the concepts of recklessness and wilful blindness.

In *Martineau* (1990), the Supreme Court of Canada ruled that there is a (very limited) number of offences in relation to which the Crown must prove a minimal degree of *mens rea* in order to preserve the validity of such offences under the Charter. In this important case, it was held that the minimum *mens rea* requirement for murder in Canada is *subjective foresight of death* on the part of the accused.

Théroux v. The Queen

SUPREME COURT OF CANADA   APRIL 8, 1993

BACKGROUND

Théroux was convicted at his trial of thirteen counts of fraud. His subsequent appeal to the Québec Court of Appeal was dismissed. Théroux appealed against the judgment of the Court of Appeal to the Supreme Court of Canada.

MAIN ISSUES

(1) What is the *mens rea* element for the offence of fraud under section 380 of the Criminal Code? (2) Is it a defence to a charge of fraud that the accused subjectively believed that his or her conduct was not dishonest?

JUDGMENTS

Justice McLachlin (with whom Justices La Forest, Gonthier, and Cory agreed) delivered the judgment of the *majority* of the members of the Supreme Court of Canada. The *concurring* judgment of Justice Sopinka (with whom Chief Justice Lamer and Justice L'Heureux-Dubé agreed) has been omitted.

McLACHLIN J.: — This appeal requires the court to consider the elements of the offence of fraud, and in particular the mental element, or *mens rea*, necessary to sustain a conviction for fraud. The question is whether a belief that, in the end, a dishonest practice will not result in loss to the victims of that practice, negates the guilty mind necessary to establish the offence of fraud.

Facts

The appellant, Robert Théroux, was a businessman involved in residential construction in the province of Québec. He operated through a company called Les Habitations Co-Hab Inc. Although a personal bankruptcy prevented him from serving as a director of Co-Hab, Théroux was the directing mind, or *âme dirigeante*, of the company.

The charges arise out of two residential housing projects Co-Hab undertook through its subsidiaries, one in Laprairie and one in Ste-Catherine. Sales to prospective home buyers were solicited from a trailer located on the Laprairie site. Co-Hab's representative at this site entered into agreements for the purchase of the residences with a number of individuals, collecting deposits from them.

The contracts were made and the deposits taken on the basis of a representation by Co-Hab that the deposits were insured by the Fédération de construction du Québec. The representation was made orally. It was backed up by a certificate of participation in the insurance program posted on the trailer wall, which had been furnished to Co-Hab before it completed the application process. In addition, a brochure describing the insurance program was distributed to most of the depositors.

In fact, the representations that the deposits were insured were false. Co-Hab never paid the premiums due on a first application for participation in the insurance program; a second application was never completed. The trial judge found that Théroux, as the directing mind of Co-Hab, was responsible for these misrepresentations.

The company, which was to have built the residences, became insolvent and could not complete the project. Some of the depositors got their money back, but most lost the entire amount.

The Issue

There is no doubt that the appellant deliberately practised a deceitful act, constituting the *actus reus* of the offence of fraud. The issue is whether the fact that he honestly believed that the projects would be completed negates the guilty mind, or *mens rea*, of the offence. This requires this court to examine the question of what constitutes the *mens rea* for the offence of fraud.

Discussion

1. Introduction

Fraud, as a substantive offence, was introduced in Canada only in 1948. Before this date, conspiracy to defraud was a criminal offence, but fraud committed by one person was not. In 1948 (S.C. 1948, c. 39, s. 13), s. 444 of the Criminal Code, R.S.C. 1927, c. 36, was amended to delete the "conspiracy" requirement and create the general offence of fraud. In the years following, there have been only minor amendments to the section.

It has been said that a single precept underlies the offence of fraud: "commercial affairs are to be

conducted honestly" (J. D. Ewart, *Criminal Fraud* (1986), at p. 9). The courts, in the decades since the adoption of the new offence, have moved to develop a jurisprudence which conforms to this central tenet. Nevertheless, the generality of the language of the section coupled with the lack of jurisprudential antecedents created uncertainty as to the elements of the offence. In 1978, this court provided a comprehensive definition of the *actus reus* of the offence in *R. v. Olan* (1978), 41 C.C.C. (2d) 145, 86 D.L.R. (3d) 212, [1978] 2 S.C.R. 1175. But uncertainty remained about what was required to establish the *mens rea* of the offence, the issue raised in this case. Is the test for guilty mind objective or subjective? More particularly, does an honest belief that no one will be harmed establish the absence of *mens rea*? Again, must the accused subjectively believe that his or her act is dishonest before he or she will have the required *mens rea*?

2. The *Actus Reus* of Fraud

Since the *mens rea* of an offence is related to its *actus reus*, it is helpful to begin the analysis by considering the *actus reus* of the offence of fraud. Speaking of the *actus reus* of this offence, Dickson J. (as he then was) set out the following principles in *Olan* [at p. 150, paraphrase]:

(i) the offence has two elements: dishonest act and deprivation;
(ii) the dishonest act is established by proof of deceit, falsehood or "other fraudulent means";
(iii) the element of deprivation is established by proof of detriment, prejudice, or risk of prejudice to the economic interests of the victim, caused by the dishonest act.

Olan marked a broadening of the law of fraud in two respects. First, it overruled previous authority which suggested that deceit was an essential element of the offence. Instead, it posited the general concept of dishonesty, which might manifest itself in deceit, falsehood, or some other form of dishonesty.

Just as what constitutes a lie or a deceitful act for the purpose of the *actus reus* is judged on the objective facts, so the "other fraudulent means" in the third category is determined objectively, by reference to what a reasonable person would consider to be a dishonest act. Second, *Olan* made it clear that economic loss was not essential to the offence; the imperilling of an economic interest is sufficient even though no actual loss has been suffered. By adopting an expansive interpretation of the offence, the court established fraud as an offence of general scope capable of encompassing a wide range of dishonest commercial dealings.

Subsequent cases followed *Olan*'s lead, fleshing out the elements of the offence set out in *Olan* in a broad and purposive manner. One of the first questions which arose was whether the third type of dishonest conduct, "other fraudulent means," was a super-added element that the Crown must prove in addition to proving either deceit or falsehood. This was rejected in *R. v. Doren* (1982), 66 C.C.C. (2d) 448, 135 D.L.R. (3d) 258, 36 O.R. (2d) 114 (C.A.); see also *R. v. Kirkwood* (1983), 5 C.C.C. (3d) 393, 148 D.L.R. (3d) 323, 42 O.R. (2d) 65 (C.A.). In a number of subsequent cases, courts have defined the sort of conduct which may fall under this third category of other fraudulent means to include the use of corporate funds for personal purposes, non-disclosure of important facts, exploiting the weakness of another, unauthorized diversion of funds, and unauthorized arrogation of funds or property. As noted above, where it is alleged that the *actus reus* of a particular fraud is "other fraudulent means," the existence of such means will be determined by what reasonable people consider to be dishonest dealing. In instances of fraud by deceit or falsehood, it will not be necessary to undertake such an inquiry; all that need be determined is whether the accused, as a matter of fact, represented that a situation was of a certain character, when, in reality, it was not.

A further question, whether it was necessary for the accused to have profited by the fraud, had been uniformly answered in the negative prior to *Olan*. In *Olan*, this court affirmed this rule at pp. 150–1.

3. The *Mens Rea* of Fraud

(i) DOCTRINAL CONSIDERATIONS

This brings us to the *mens rea* of fraud. What is the guilty mind of fraud? At this point, certain confusions inherent in the concept of *mens rea* itself become apparent. It is useful initially to distinguish between the mental element or elements of a crime and the *mens rea*. The term *mens rea*, properly understood, does not encompass all of the mental elements of a crime. The *actus reus* has its own mental element; the act must be the voluntary act of the accused for the *actus reus* to exist. *Mens rea*, on the other hand, refers to the guilty mind, the wrongful intention, of the accused. Its function in criminal law is to prevent the conviction of the morally innocent — those who do not understand or intend the consequences of their acts. Typically, *mens rea* is concerned with the consequences of the prohibited *actus reus*. Thus in the crimes of homicide, we speak of the consequences of the voluntary act — intention to cause death, or reckless and wilfully blind persistence in conduct which one knows is likely to cause death. In other offences, such as dangerous driving, the *mens rea* may relate to the failure to consider the consequences of inadvertence.

This brings me to the question of whether the test for *mens rea* is subjective or objective. Most scholars and jurists agree that, leaving aside offences where the *actus reus* is negligence or inadvertence and offences of absolute liability, the test for *mens rea* is subjective. The test is not whether a reasonable person would have foreseen the consequences of the prohibited act, but whether the accused subjectively appreciated those consequences at least as a possibility. In applying the subjective test, the court looks to the accused's intention and the facts as the accused believed them to be: G. Williams, *Textbook of Criminal Law*, 2nd ed. (1983), pp. 727–8.

Two collateral points must be made at this juncture. First, as Williams underlines, this inquiry has nothing to do with the accused's system of values. A person is not saved from conviction because he or she believes there is nothing wrong with what he or she is doing. The question is whether the accused subjectively appreciated that certain consequences would follow from his or her acts, not whether the accused believed the acts or their consequences to be moral. Just as the pathological killer would not be acquitted on the mere ground that he failed to see his act as morally reprehensible, so the defrauder will not be acquitted because he believed that what he was doing was honest.

The second collateral point is the oft-made observation that the Crown need not, in every case, show precisely what thought was in the accused's mind at the time of the criminal act. In certain cases, subjective awareness of the consequences can be inferred from the act itself, barring some explanation casting doubt on such inference. The fact that such an inference is made does not detract from the subjectivity of the test.

Having ventured these general comments on *mens rea*, I return to the offence of fraud. The prohibited act is deceit, falsehood, or some other dishonest act. The prohibited consequence is depriving another of what is or should be his, which may, as we have seen, consist in merely placing another's property at risk. The *mens rea* would then consist in the subjective awareness that one was undertaking a prohibited act (the deceit, falsehood, or other dishonest act) which could cause deprivation in the sense of depriving another of property or putting that property at risk. If this is shown, the crime is complete. The fact that the accused may have hoped the deprivation would not take place, or may have felt there was nothing wrong with what he or she was doing, provides no defence. To put it another way, following the traditional criminal law principle that the mental state necessary to the offence must be determined by reference to the external acts which constitute the *actus* of the offence (see Williams, *ibid.*, c. 3), the proper focus in determining the *mens rea* of fraud is to ask whether the accused intentionally committed the prohibited acts (deceit, falsehood, or other dishonest act) knowing or desiring the consequences proscribed by the offence (deprivation, including the risk of depriva-

tion). The personal feeling of the accused about the morality or honesty of the act or its consequences is no more relevant to the analysis than is the accused's awareness that the particular acts undertaken constitute a criminal offence.

This applies as much to the third head of fraud, "other fraudulent means," as to lies and acts of deceit. Although other fraudulent means have been broadly defined as means which are "dishonest," it is not necessary that an accused personally consider these means to be dishonest in order that he or she be convicted of fraud for having undertaken them. The "dishonesty" of the means is relevant to the determination whether the conduct falls within the type of conduct caught by the offence of fraud; what reasonable people consider dishonest assists in the determination whether the *actus reus* of the offence can be made out on particular facts. That established, it need only be determined that an accused knowingly undertook the acts in question, aware that deprivation, or risk of deprivation, could follow as a likely consequence.

I have spoken of knowledge of the consequences of the fraudulent act. There appears to be no reason, however, why recklessness as to consequences might not also attract criminal responsibility. Recklessness presupposes knowledge of the likelihood of the prohibited consequences. It is established when it is shown that the accused, with such knowledge, commits acts which may bring about these prohibited consequences, while being reckless as to whether or not they ensue.

These doctrinal observations suggest that the *actus reus* of the offence of fraud will be established by proof of:

1. the prohibited act, be it an act of deceit, a falsehood or some other fraudulent means; and
2. deprivation caused by the prohibited act, which may consist in actual loss or the placing of the victim's pecuniary interests at risk.

Correspondingly, the *mens rea* of fraud is established by proof of:

1. Subjective knowledge of the prohibited act; and
2. Subjective knowledge that the prohibited act could have as a consequence the deprivation of another (which deprivation may consist in knowledge that the victim's pecuniary interests are put at risk).

Where the conduct and knowledge required by these definitions are established, the accused is guilty whether he actually intended the prohibited consequence or was reckless as to whether it would occur.

The inclusion of risk of deprivation in the concept of deprivation in *Olan* requires specific comment. The accused must have subjective awareness, at the very least, that his or her conduct will put the property or economic expectations of others at risk. As noted above, this does not mean that the Crown must provide the trier of fact with a mental snapshot proving exactly what was in the accused's mind at the moment the dishonest act was committed. In certain cases, the inference of subjective knowledge of the risk may be drawn from the facts as the accused believed them to be. The accused may introduce evidence negating that inference, such as evidence that his deceit was part of an innocent prank, or evidence of circumstances which led him to believe that no one would act on his lie or deceitful or dishonest act. But in cases like the present one, where the accused tells a lie knowing others will act on it and thereby puts their property at risk, the inference of subjective knowledge that the property of another would be put at risk is clear.

(ii) JURISPRUDENTIAL CONSIDERATIONS

The view of *mens rea* suggested above accords with earlier rulings of this Court which rejected the notion that the accused's subjective appreciation of his or her dishonesty is relevant to the *mens rea* of fraud.

While the authorities are far from consistent, the better view is that the accused's belief that the conduct is not wrong or that no one will in the end be hurt affords no defence to a charge of fraud.

(iii) PRAGMATIC CONSIDERATIONS

Pragmatic considerations support the view of *mens rea* proposed above. A person who deprives another person of what the latter has should not escape criminal responsibility merely because, according to his moral or her personal code, he or she was doing nothing wrong or because of a sanguine belief that all will come out right in the end. Many frauds are perpetrated by people who think there is nothing wrong in what they are doing or who sincerely believe that their act of placing other people's property at risk will not ultimately result in actual loss to those persons. If the offence of fraud is to catch those who actually practise fraud, its *mens rea* cannot be cast so narrowly as this. As stated in *R. v. Allsop* (1976), 64 Cr. App. R. 29, approved by this court in *Olan*, at p. 150:

> Generally the primary objective of fraudsmen is to advantage themselves. The detriment that results to their victims is secondary to that purpose and incidental. It is "intended" only in the sense that it is a contemplated outcome of the fraud that is perpetrated.

The law of fraud must be sufficiently broad to catch this secondary incident of the defrauder's purpose or it will be of little avail.

This approach conforms to the conception of the offence of fraud which imbues this court's decision in *Olan*. *Olan* points the way to a conception of fraud broad enough in scope to encompass the entire panoply of dishonest commercial dealings. It defines the *actus reus* accordingly; the offence is committed whenever a person deceives, lies, or otherwise acts dishonestly, and that act causes deprivation (including risk of deprivation) to another. To adopt a definition of *mens rea* which requires subjective awareness of dishonesty and a belief that actual deprivation (as opposed to risk of deprivation) will result, is inconsistent with Olan's definition of the *actus reus*. The effect of such a test would be to negate the broad thrust of *Olan* and confine the offence of fraud to a narrow ambit, capable of catching only a small portion of the dishonest commercial dealing which *Olan* took as the target of the offence of fraud.

The question arises whether the definition of *mens rea* for fraud which I have proposed may catch conduct which does not warrant criminalization. I refer to the fear, reflected in the appellate decisions adopting a narrower definition of the required *mens rea*, that the reach of the offence of fraud may be extended beyond criminal dishonesty to catch sharp or improvident business practices which, although not to be encouraged, do not merit the stigma and loss of liberty that attends the criminal sanction. The concern is that any misrepresentation or practice which induces an incorrect understanding or belief in the minds of customers, or which causes deprivation, will become criminal. As Marshall J.A. put it in *R. v. Mugford* (1990), 58 C.C.C. (3d) 172 at pp. 175–6, 86 Nfld. & P.E.I. R. 91, 10 W.C.B. (2d) 448 (Nfld. C.A.):

> . . . it is not sufficient to base fraud merely upon a finding that the appellant induced a state of mind in his customers which was not correct. Any misrepresentation may have that effect. Criminal dishonesty extends further . . .

> . . . .

> It would be a startling extension of criminal liability if every statement urging the public to purchase one's wares because only a limited supply remains were by itself to be visited with criminal sanction.

This poses starkly the critical question: does a view of the offence of fraud, which catches a broad range of dishonest commercial dealing, also catch conduct which should not be regarded as criminal, but rather left to the civil sanction?

In my view, the approach to the offence of fraud adopted in *Olan* and perused in these reasons does not take us out of the proper domain of the criminal sanction. To establish the *actus reus* of fraud, the Crown must establish beyond a reasonable doubt that the accused practised deceit, lied, or committed some other fraudulent act. Under the third head of the offence, it will be necessary to show that the impugned act is one which a reasonable person would see as dishonest. Deprivation or the risk of deprivation must then be shown to have occurred as a matter of fact. To establish the *mens rea* of fraud, the Crown must prove that the accused knowingly undertook the acts which constitute the falsehood, deceit, or other fraudulent means, and that the accused was aware that deprivation could result from such conduct.

The requirement of intentional fraudulent action excludes mere negligent misrepresentation. It also excludes improvident business conduct or conduct which is sharp in the sense of taking advantage of a business opportunity to the detriment of someone less astute. The accused must intentionally deceive, lie, or commit some other fraudulent act for the offence to be established. Neither a negligent misstatement nor a sharp business practice will suffice, because in neither case will the required intent to deprive by fraudulent means be present. A statement made carelessly, even if it is untrue, will not amount to an intentional falsehood, subjectively appreciated. Nor will any seizing of a business opportunity, which is not motivated by a person's subjective intent to deprive by cheating or misleading others, amount to an instance of fraud. Again, an act of deceit which is made carelessly without any expectation of consequences, as for example, an innocent prank or a statement made in debate which is not intended to be acted upon, would not amount to fraud because the accused would have no knowledge that the prank would put the property of those who heard it at risk. We are left then with deliberately practised fraudulent acts which, in the knowledge of the accused, actually put the property of others at risk. Such conduct may be appropriately criminalized, in my view.

4. Application of the Law on this Appeal

The trial judge found that the appellant deliberately lied to his customers by means of verbal misrepresentations, a certificate of participation in the insurance scheme, and brochures advising that the scheme protected all deposits. The lies were told in order to induce potential customers to enter into contracts for the homes the appellant was selling and to induce them to give him their money as deposits on the purchase of these homes. The trial judge also found that the appellant knew at the time he made these falsehoods that the insurance for the deposits was not in place. Finally, he found that the appellant genuinely believed that the homes would be built and hence that there was no risk to the depositors. "No risk" used in this sense is the equivalent of saying the appellant believed the risk would not materialize.

Applying the principles discussed above, these findings establish that the appellant was guilty of fraud. The *actus reus* of the offence is clearly established. The appellant committed deliberate falsehoods. Those falsehoods caused or gave rise to deprivation. First, the depositors did not get the insurance protection they were told they would get. That, in itself, is a deprivation sufficient to estab-lish the *actus reus* fraud. Second, the money they gave to the appellant's company was put at risk, a risk which in most cases materialized. Again, this suffices to establish deprivation.

The *mens rea* too is established. The appellant told the depositors they had insurance protection when he knew that they did not have that protection. He knew this to be false. He knew that by this act he was depriving the depositors of something they thought they had, insurance protection. It may also be inferred from his possession of this knowledge that the appellant knew that he was placing the depositors' money at risk. That established, his *mens rea* is proved. The fact that he sincerely believed that in the end the houses would be built and that the risk would not materialize cannot save him.

Disposition

I would dismiss the appeal.

Appeal dismissed.

Sansregret v. The Queen

SUPREME COURT OF CANADA   MAY 9, 1985

BACKGROUND

Sansregret was charged with the offences of rape, unlawful confinement, robbery, breaking and entering with intent to commit an indictable offence, and possession of a weapon. At his trial before a Judge of the County Court of Winnipeg, he was acquitted of rape but was convicted of breaking and entering, and unlawful confinement. The Crown appealed against the acquittal on the rape charge to the Manitoba Court of Appeal, which allowed the appeal and entered a conviction of rape against Sansregret. Sansregret appealed to the Supreme Court of Canada against the judgment of the Court of Appeal. Note that the offence of rape no longer exists in the Criminal Code: today, the accused would be charged with one of the three forms of sexual assault defined in sections 271, 272, and 273 of the Code.

MAIN ISSUE

To what extent does the existence of recklessness or wilful blindness on the part of the accused disqualify him or her from relying on the defence of mistake of fact?

JUDGMENTS

The judgment of the Supreme Court of Canada was delivered by Justice McIntyre. The other members of the Court were Chief Justice Dickson and Justices Estey, Chouinard, Lamer, Wilson, and Le Dain.

....

McINTYRE J.: — The appellant, a man in his early 20s, and the complainant, a woman of 31 years, had lived together in the complainant's house for about a year before the events of October 15, 1982. Their relationship had been one of contention and discord with violence on the part of the appellant: "slappings" or "roughing up" in his description, "blows" in hers. The appellant had left the house for short periods and in September, 1982, the complainant decided to end the affair. She told the appellant to leave and he did.

On September 23, 1982, some days after his dismissal, the appellant broke into the house at about 4:30 A.M. He was "raging" at her and furious because of his expulsion. He terrorized her with a file-like instrument with which he was armed. She was fearful of what might occur, and, in order to calm him down, she held out some hope of a reconciliation, and they had intercourse. A report was made to the police of this incident, the complainant asserting she had been raped, but no proceedings were taken. The appellant's probation officer became involved and there was evidence that he had asked the complainant not to press the matter, presumably because it would interfere with the appellant's probation.

On October 15, 1982, again at about 4:30 A.M., the appellant broke into the complainant's house through a basement window. She was alone, and, awakened by the entry, she seized the bedroom telephone in an effort to call the police. The appellant picked up a butcher knife in the kitchen and came into the bedroom. He was furious and violent. He accused her of having another boyfriend; pulled the cord of the telephone out of the jack and threw it into the living-room; threatened her with the knife and ordered her to take off her night-dress and made her stand in the kitchen doorway, naked save for a jacket over her shoulders, so he could be sure where she was while he repaired the window to conceal his entry from the police, should they arrive. He struck her on the mouth with sufficient force to draw blood, and on three occasions rammed the knife-blade into the wall with great force, once very close to her. He told her that if the police came, he would put the knife through her, and added that if he had found her with a boyfriend, he would have killed them both. At one point he tied her hands behind her back with a scarf. The complainant said she was in fear for her life and sanity.

By about 5:30 A.M., after an hour of such behaviour by the appellant, she tried to calm him down. She pretended again that there was some hope of reconciliation if the appellant would settle down and get a job. This had the desired effect. He calmed down, and, after some conversation, he joined her on the bed and they had intercourse. The complainant swore that her consent to the intercourse was solely for the purpose of calming him down, to protect herself from further violence. This, she said, was something she had learned from earlier experience with him. In her evidence she said:

I didn't consent at any time.

I was very afraid. My whole body was trembling. I was sure I would have a nervous breakdown. I came very, very close to losing my mind. All I knew was I had to keep this man calm or he would kill me.

At about 6:45 A.M., after further conversation with the appellant, she got dressed and prepared to leave for work. She had a business appointment at 8:00 A.M. She drove the appellant to a location which he chose, and in the course of the journey he returned her keys and some money that he had taken from her purse upon his arrival in the early morning. Upon dropping him off, she drove immediately to her mother's home where she made a complaint of rape. The police were called and the appellant was arrested that evening.

On the facts of this case, briefly summarized above, at first glance it may appear strange indeed that a defence of mistake of fact could be suggested, let alone made out. To appreciate how the issue arises, reference must be made to the finding of fact at trial and to the judgments given in the Court of Appeal.

The trial judge described the complainant as a bright, sophisticated woman, articulate, capable, and well employed. She considered that the appellant was neither particularly intelligent nor "verbal," and expressed surprise that any intimate relationship had ever arisen between them. She described the events of September 23, 1982, a month before the events in question, and she considered there was no evidence that the appellant knew she had complained of rape as a result of that incident. Comment will be made on this question later. She then referred to the defence of mistake of fact, and said:

If there were any evidence before me that the accused was aware on October 15th that the complainant had considered the sexual relations of September 23rd, 1982, to have been non-consensual, I would have rejected this defence out of hand. There is no such evidence. I can speculate, but that is not proof.

She described in detail the events of October 15th and said that she accepted the complainant's version in so far as it differed from the appellant's, but she observed that in many respects his evidence confirmed hers. She continued:

I am satisfied beyond any doubt that the accused broke and entered the complainant's residence on October 15, motivated primarily by jealousy and I do not doubt for a moment that, had the complainant had a man there, the knife would have been used aggressively. Having not found another man, he was bound and determined to make the complainant hear what he had to say to her by confining her unlawfully. He certainly broke and entered the dwelling house with the intent to commit an indictable offence therein, and he certainly took possession of the butcher knife for purposes dangerous to the public peace.

Having entered the house and discovering that the complainant was on the phone, being unsure about whether or not she had called the police, two things became paramount. One was to cover up the evidence of his break in so that it would not be visible from the street and to cover up his presence in the house by reducing it to darkness. The second was to prevent the escape of the complainant, or her use of the telephone, particularly probable events while he was outside putting the basement window back on the house. What better way to confine her than to take her car keys, her house keys, her money, to strip her naked, to bind her hands and to force her to stand by the back door and whistle so he could hear where she was.

I find that the accused forced the complainant to strip and tied her hands not by way of preliminaries to an intended rape, but by way of confining the complainant. I similarly find the forced taking of her keys and money to be part of the unlawful confinement.

She said that once the appellant became satisfied that the police would not come, he set out to convince the complainant to reconcile. She accepted the evidence of the complainant that she was absolutely terrified, and that her consent was given solely to protect herself from further violence or death. She told him the things he wanted to hear regarding reconciliation, and she reassured him that no other man was of interest to her. Then the trial judge continued:

As I said, no rational person could have been under any honest mistake of fact. However, people have an uncanny ability to blind themselves to much that they don't want to see, and to believe in the existence of facts as they would wish them to be. The accused says that, notwithstanding the reign of terror which preceded their chat, notwithstanding that he held a knife while they talked, notwithstanding that he did most of the talking and that the complainant's answers were clearly equivocal, he presumed and believed that everything between them was peachy. This, notwithstanding that three weeks earlier, on a replay of the same sort of evening, his probation officer became involved and the complainant moved out of her house. Very honestly, despite my confidence in the ability of people to blind themselves to reality, and even if the accused had not lied about other parts of his testimony, I would have been hard pressed to credit the honesty of his belief.

However, his honest belief finds support in the testimony of the complainant. She knows him and in her opinion, notwithstanding all the objective facts to the contrary, he did believe that everything was back to normal between them by the time of the sexual encounter. His subsequent behaviour as well attests to that fact.

I do not like the conclusion which this leads me to. There was no real consent. There was submission as a result of a very real and justifiable fear. No one in his right mind could have believed that the complainant's dramatic about-fact [*sic*] stemmed from anything other than fear. But the accused did. He saw what he wanted to see, heard what he wanted to hear, believed what he wanted to believe.

The facts in *R. v. Pappajohn* (1977) 38 C.C.C. (2d) 106 are quite dissimilar to those in this case. The dictum of the Supreme Court of Canada, however, is clear and broad and in no way seems to limit itself to the peculiar circumstances of that case. Perhaps the Crown will appeal this decision to obtain some direction from the Supreme Court on whether it was that court's intention to cover situations where an accused, who demonstrates the clarity and shrewdness this accused showed in securing his own safety at the outset, can turn around and, because it does not suit his wishes, can go wilfully blind to the obvious, shortly thereafter. In any event, the ratio of *Pappajohn* is clear and it leaves me no alternative but to acquit.

To summarize, the trial judge found that the appellant did not enter the house with the intent to make a sexual assault on the complainant; that the complainant consented to intercourse only because of the fear engendered by the threats of the appellant and to save herself; and that the appellant honestly believed that the complainant was giving a free and genuine consent to intercourse. She found as well that the complainant, who knew the appellant, also believed in the honesty, of his belief.

Before this Court the appellant contended that he never suspected, and never had cause to suspect, that the consent had been given because of his threats. He argued that all the facts and all findings of the trial judge supported this proposition. He denied wilful blindness and recklessness and contended that the *Pappajohn* case was decisive in his favour.

The defence of mistake of fact has been said to rest on the proposition that the mistaken belief, honestly held, deprives the accused of the requisite *mens rea* for the offence. The question of the *mens rea* required for a conviction of rape was considered by Dickson J. in this Court in *Pappajohn*. Concluding upon this point, he said:

> In summary, intention or recklessness must be proved in relation to all elements of the offence, including absence of consent. This simply extends to rape the same general order of intention as in other crimes.

I would conclude then that the *mens rea* for rape under s. 143(a) of the Code must involve knowledge that the woman is not consenting, or recklessness as to whether she is consenting or not, and for s. 143(b)(i), knowledge that the consent was given because of threats or fear of bodily harm, or recklessness as to its nature. It would follow, as has been held by the majority of this Court in *Pappajohn*, that an honest belief on the part of the accused, even though unreasonably held, that the woman was consenting to intercourse freely and voluntarily and not because of threats, would negate the *mens rea* under s. 143(b)(i) of the Code and entitle the accused to an acquittal.

The concept of recklessness as a basis for criminal liability has been the subject of much discussion. Negligence, the failure to take reasonable care, is a creature of the civil law and is not generally a concept having a place in determining criminal liability. Nevertheless, it is frequently confused with recklessness in the criminal sense and care should be taken to separate the two concepts. Negligence is tested by the objective standard of the reasonable man. A departure from his accustomed sober behaviour by an act or omission which reveals less than reasonable care will involve liability at civil law but forms no basis for the imposition of criminal penalties. In accordance with well-established principles for the determination of criminal liability, recklessness, to form a part of the criminal *mens rea*, must have an element of the subjective. It is found in the attitude of one who, aware that there is danger that his conduct could bring about the result prohibited by the criminal law, nevertheless persists, despite the risk. It is, in other words, the conduct of one who sees the risk and who takes the chance. It is in this sense that the term "recklessness" is used in the criminal law and it is clearly distinct from the concept of civil negligence.

On the face of it, one would have thought that a man who intimidates and threatens a woman and thereafter obtains her consent to intercourse would know that the consent was obtained as a result of the threats. If specific knowledge of the nature of the consent was not attributable to him in such circumstances, then one would think that at the very least recklessness would be. It might be said then that this case could have been disposed of on the basis of recklessness. The trial judge, however, did not do so because of her application of the "mistake of fact" defence.

There was indeed an abundance of evidence before the trial judge upon which a finding of recklessness could have been made. After a stormy period of cohabitation, the complainant dismissed the appellant from her house in September, 1982, thus demonstrating her rejection of him. He broke into the house on September 23rd and there went through a performance which led to an act of intercourse with a consent given by the complainant out of fear for her life. This incident led to a report to the police and the involvement of the appellant's probation officer. In the early morning hours of October 15th he again broke into the house and repeated his earlier performance, which provided the basis for the present charges.

Sansregret admitted that he knew his probation officer had called the complainant with respect to the September incident and that he knew that he was not welcome in her house. There was then evidence that the appellant knew of her attitude towards him; knew that she had complained to the police with respect to the September 23rd incident, and knew that it was only the intervention of his parole officer which prevented charges from being laid after that incident. I therefore disagree with the trial judge who, in my opinion, was in error in not drawing the inference that the appellant knew that the complainant had complained of rape as a result of the incident on September 23rd.

It is evident that the trial judge would have convicted the appellant of rape had it not been for the defence of mistake of fact. She considered that the belief in the consent expressed by the appellant was an honest one and therefore on the basis of *Pappajohn v. The Queen* (1980), 52 C.C.C. (2d) 481, 111 D.L.R. (3d) 1, [1980] 2 S.C.R. 120, even if it were unreasonably held, as it is clear she thought it was, he was entitled to his acquittal. This application of the defence of mistake of fact would be supportable were it not for the fact that the trial judge found in addition that the appellant had been wilfully blind to reality in his behaviour on October 15th. Such a finding would preclude the application of the

defence and lead to a different result. It is my opinion then that the trial judge erred in this matter in that, though she made the requisite findings of fact that the appellant was wilfully blind to the consequences of his acts, she did not apply them according to law.

The idea of wilful blindness in circumstances such as this has been said to be an aspect of recklessness. While this may well be true, it is wise to keep the two concepts separate because they result from different mental attitudes and lead to different legal results. A finding of recklessness in this case could not override the defence of mistake of fact. The appellant asserts an honest belief that the consent of the complainant was not caused by fear and threats. The trial judge found that such an honest belief existed. In the facts of this case, because of the reckless conduct of the appellant, it could not be said that such a belief was reasonable but, as held in *Pappajohn*, the mere honesty of the belief will support the "mistake of fact" defence, even where it is unreasonable. On the other hand, a finding of wilful blindness as to the very facts about which the honest belief is now asserted would leave no room for the application of the defence because, where wilful blindness is shown, the law presumes knowledge on the part of the accused, in this case knowledge that the consent had been induced by threats.

Wilful blindness is distinct from recklessness because, while recklessness involves knowledge of a danger or risk and persistence in a course of conduct which creates a risk that the prohibited result will occur, wilful blindness arises where a person who has become aware of the need for some inquiry declines to make the inquiry because he does not wish to know the truth. He would prefer to remain ignorant. The culpability in recklessness is justified by consciousness of the risk and by proceeding in the face of it, while in wilful blindness it is justified by the accused's fault in deliberately failing to inquire when he knows there is reason for inquiry.

This case reveals, in my view, an appropriate set of circumstances for the application of the "wilful blindness" rule. I have outlined the circumstances which form the background. I have referred to the findings of the trial judge that the appellant blinded himself to the obvious and made no inquiry as to the nature of the consent which was given. If the evidence before the court was limited to the events of October 15th, it would be difficult indeed to infer wilful blindness. To attribute criminal liability on the basis of this one incident would come close to applying a constructive test to the effect that he should have known she was consenting out of fear. The position, however, is changed when the evidence reveals the earlier episode and the complaint of rape which it caused, knowledge of which, as I have said, had clearly reached the accused. Considering the whole of the evidence then, no constructive test of knowledge is required. The appellant was aware of the likelihood of the complainant's reaction to his threats. To proceed with intercourse in such circumstances constitutes, in my view, self-deception to the point of wilful blindness.

In my view, it was error on the part of the trial judge to give effect to the "mistake of fact" defence in these circumstances where she had found that the complainant consented out of fear and the appellant was wilfully blind to the existing circumstances, seeing only what he wished to see. Where the accused is deliberately ignorant as a result of blinding himself to reality, the law presumes knowledge, in this case knowledge of the nature of the consent. There was therefore no room for the operation of this defence.

This is not to be taken as a retreat from the position taken in *Pappajohn* that the honest belief need not be reasonable. It is not to be thought that any time an accused forms an honest though unreasonable belief he will be deprived of the defence of mistake of fact. This case rests on a different proposition. Having wilfully blinded himself to the facts before him, the fact that an accused may be enabled to preserve what could be called an honest belief, in the sense that he has no specific knowledge to the contrary, will not afford a defence because, where the accused becomes deliberately blind to the existing facts, he is fixed by law with actual knowledge and his belief in another state of facts is irrelevant.

I would dismiss the appeal.

Appeal dismissed.

Regina v. Oluwa

BRITISH COLUMBIA COURT OF APPEAL   MAY 16, 1996, AND AUGUST 14, 1996

BACKGROUND

At his trial, Oluwa was convicted of the offences of importing heroin and possession of heroin for the purpose of trafficking. He appealed against his convictions to the B.C. Court of Appeal.

MAIN ISSUES

(1) What are the *mens rea* elements that the Crown must prove in relation to a charge of importing heroin? (2) In what circumstances may wilful blindness or recklessness be considered sufficient *mens rea* for conviction of such an offence? (3) When may knowledge be inferred from the surrounding circumstances of the case?

JUDGMENTS

The *majority* judgment was delivered by Chief Justice McEachern (with whom Justice Goldie agreed). The *dissenting* judgment of Justice Donald has been omitted.

1 McEACHERN C.J.B.C. (GOLDIE J.A. concurring): — No one but lawyers and judges would have any difficulty deciding that the appellant, whom I shall call "the accused," imported nearly a pound of heroin into Canada when he arrived at the Vancouver International Airport on Japanese Airlines Flight No. 12 from Tokyo on November 19, 1993. This would especially be so when, upon being informed by a customs officer that he would be X-rayed, the accused admitted, as was later confirmed, that he had that quantity of packaged heroin in his stomach and intestines.

2 The accused was charged and convicted by Fratkin, Prov. Ct. J., with importing heroin into Canada and of possessing heroin in Canada for the purpose of trafficking. He was sentenced to four years on each count, to be served concurrently. He has served a portion of his sentence, and is now at liberty on parole. He is appealing his conviction.

A. Factual Overview

5 Japan Airlines ("JAL") Flight No. 12 flies from Tokyo to Mexico City with an approximately one and one-half hour scheduled stopover in Vancouver. Counsel agree that there is no mention on a passenger's ticket that Flight No. 12 stops in Vancouver. During the stopover, the plane is cleaned and refueled. Regulations require that all passengers deplane and wait in the transit departure facility (the "TDF") of the Vancouver International Airport. The facility doubles as a waiting-room for those passengers who are joining the flight to Mexico City in Vancouver.

6 Although Canada customs and immigration officers do not always attend to check in-transit passengers as they enter the TDF, the evidence disclosed that the officers will target the in-transit passengers of flights they consider to be "high risk" for drug smuggling or other offences. JAL flight No. 12 is one such "high risk" flight.

7 The accused was a passenger on JAL Flight No. 12 on November 19, 1993. While in flight, all passengers were asked to fill out a Canada Customs E311 Form, which requests statistical and other information. As an "in-transit" passenger, the accused was required to deplane in Vancouver and to wait in the TDF. As he was making his way to the TDF, the accused was approached by a customs officer who asked for his E311 and his passport. The officer admits that he had no information about the accused prior to stopping him. The accused handed over his E311, but explained that his passport and airline tickets had been taken by JAL officials in Tokyo. JAL staff turned the documents over to the officer. Both the E311 and the passport were in the name "Victor M. Topping" and listed an address in London, England. Information on the passport disclosed that the accused had been travelling in Thailand and Malaysia, both known "source countries" for narcotics. On inspection, the passport appeared to have been tampered with.

8 During this initial exchange, the customs officers became suspicious and began to ask the accused some routine questions. The accused was unable to answer simple questions about the area of London in which he claimed he lived. He was uncertain about his place of birth: first, he claimed to have been born in Jamaica; then he claimed to have been born in Bootle, which he incorrectly stated to be in Wales rather than in England. He claimed that a friend in Mexico City had purchased his ticket for him, but he was unable to provide any information about that friend.

9 It was later learned that the accused is a native Nigerian who had been travelling in Asia on a false British passport. He says he bought the passport two years ago in Lagos, Nigeria, for $400. He admits he had been warned twice by JAL officials,

once in Malaysia and once in Tokyo, that they suspected his passport was false. They told him that if he continued to use the passport to travel, he could be detained. The accused elected to continue his flight notwithstanding the warnings. JAL officials confiscated his passport and ticket and placed them in an envelope marked "deportee," and gave the envelope to the JAL pilot to pass on to the proper authorities.

10 The officers decided to search the accused's luggage and obtained authorization from a superior to remove it from the plane. This decision ultimately and inevitably meant that the accused would not be able to continue on the same flight to Mexico City.

12 The accused was read his Charter rights and was twice offered legal counsel, which he declined. The accused and his luggage were taken to a search room on another level of the airport. The bag was then searched in the accused's presence. The contents of the bag further aroused the suspicion of the customs officers. Although the search was negative for actual narcotics, several narcotics "indicators" were found: a package of rubber gloves (which are often used as "balloons" in which drugs are stored and which are then swallowed or "stuffed" into body cavities); Vaseline and Lubriderm lotion (which are often used as lubricants by both "swallowers" and "stuffers"); "Preparation H" ointment; laxatives; and hair remover and tension bandages (often used by "body packers"). The officers were not satisfied with the accused's explanations for each of the indicators. They determined that they had sufficient grounds for a personal search, as the above items were consistent with the accused being a "swallower" (i.e. a narcotics courier who smuggles drugs in his intestinal tract).

13 While the baggage search was being conducted, one of the customs officers took the accused's passport to an immigration officer, whose preliminary tests indicated that it had been tampered with.

14 The officers obtained authorization to conduct a personal search of the accused pursuant to s. 98 of the Customs Act, R.S.C. 1985, c. 1 (2nd

Supp.). When the accused had removed all his clothing, the officers conducted a visual search of his person; the officers reported variously that there was "some damage" or "disturbance" in the accused's anal area.

15 Because the officers believed the accused was probably a "swallower" of narcotics, they asked him to consent to have an X-ray taken of his stomach. At this point, the accused requested a lawyer. After he had spoken to a lawyer over the telephone, the accused declined to give consent to an X-ray.

16 The customs officers then contacted the R.C.M.P. airport drug squad, and informed them that they had a possible drug "swallower" in custody. The R.C.M.P. officers believed they had grounds to arrest the accused for importing a narcotic into Canada and so arrested him, giving him the usual caution. The accused was taken to the Richmond R.C.M.P. detachment, where he was photographed and fingerprinted, and then to the Richmond General Hospital. Just before an X-ray was to be taken, the accused informed one of the officers that he had drugs in his stomach. He also told the officer his real name, the name of his contact in Mexico, and explained that the source of these drugs was in Thailand.

17 The accused then signed a consent to be X-rayed. The X-ray confirmed the presence of packages in his stomach and intestines.

18 The accused eventually passed 35 small packages and two larger ones, which contained a total of 437.9 grams of 80% plus pure heroin. There was evidence that the accused would have died within 60 seconds if any one of these packages had ruptured inside him.

C. Substantive Offences

1. The Offence of "Importing"

(a) WERE THE REQUISITE ELEMENTS OF THE OFFENCE OF IMPORTING ESTABLISHED BY THE EVIDENCE?

73 It was held in *R. v. Salvador, Wannamaker, Campbell and Nunes* (1981), 59 C.C.C. (2d) 521 at p. 540, 21 C.R. (3d), 1, 45 N.S.R.(2d) 192 (C.A.), that the *actus reus* of the offence of importing is the voluntary bringing of a narcotic into Canada from abroad. Knowledge, or imputed knowledge, that the drugs would be imported into Canada is part of the *actus reus* of the offence. *Mens rea* is found in the basic intent to knowingly bring narcotics into Canada from abroad.

74 The basis of the appellant's argument is that the requisite *mens rea* to import narcotics into Canada has not been shown because there is no direct evidence he knew he would be coming to Canada or intended to come here. In other words, it is the defence's position that there is no evidence the appellant knew his flight would be stopping in Canada.

82 The trial judge in this case concluded that:

> There is no direct evidence that the accused knew he was coming into Canada, save and except, the E311 card that would have been filled out while he is aboard J.A.L. incoming to Vancouver. What inferences are to be found from the evidence presented that proves beyond a reasonable doubt that the accused voluntarily entered Canada.[*sic*] This presupposes that the accused knew he was coming to Canada. If he did not know he was coming into Canada, how could he exercise his free will, so the argument goes with regard to Mr. Sanders. There is nothing on the tickets or itinerary that indicates Canada as a destination or stop along the way. The accused, getting on the J.A.L. flight, that is J.A.L. 12, was like any other traveller. You go where the plane takes you with your destination foremost in mind. I am of the view that the accused has voluntarily agreed to go where that plane will take him. To put it simply, I am of the opinion, based on the evidence, that the accused, by getting on J.A.L. 12, is deemed to have voluntarily accepted the normal routing of that plane, whether he knew the route or not.

83 The trial judge found that the appellant "accepted the routing" of the aircraft and that, alternatively, he recognized the risk when he filled out the E311. With respect, I do not find the latter persuasive of the original intention of the appellant as he was in the air when he was asked to fill in form E311.

84 Nevertheless, the appellant cannot deny that from that point forward he knew his flight would land in Canada, and he took no steps to avoid the consequences of his self-inflicted circumstances. It may be that he was powerless to retrieve the drugs and dispose of them on the aircraft. Theoretically, however, he could have surrendered himself to Canadian authorities upon arriving here and disclaimed any intention to import these drugs into Canada. It is a moot question whether, on those facts alone, he would be guilty of the offence of importing. Cases such as *R. v. Tolson* (1989), 23 Q.B.D. 168 (U.K.) and *Beaver v. The Queen* (1957), 118 C.C.C. 129, [1957] S.C.R. 531, 26 C.R. 193, and other authorities, and the principle of abandonment, might provide a defence. He chose, however, with full knowledge that he had brought narcotics into Canada, to maintain control over those drugs until he was caught out.

85 However, I do not consider it necessary to decide this case on such theoretical grounds because it was not argued and, in any event, I am satisfied that the intention of the appellant to import these drugs into Canada or wherever the aircraft took him, may be inferred from the circumstances.

86 Counsel for the appellant argued that there is no direct evidence which indicates the appellant knew the flight would be stopping in Canada. His ticket did not disclose that this flight included a scheduled stop here. While I might take notice that flights are posted and announced, I cannot assume the latter would be in the English language.

87 With respect, I do not agree that there is no evidence from which an inference may be drawn that the appellant knew his flight would stop in Canada. As the appellant did not give evidence, his state of mind may be inferred from the known facts. The appellant's passport indicated that he was an experienced international traveller. It is common for long-distance flights to make scheduled stops. The appellant deliberately swallowed the drugs knowing and expecting they would be taken wherever he went. Is it reasonable to infer that the appellant, an experienced air traveller, who was carrying within his person a large amount of a dangerous and illegal substance, would be oblivious to the routing of his aircraft?

88 Absent any evidence to the contrary, the facts of this case are such that it is permissible to infer that the appellant actually did know that his flight would make a scheduled stop in Vancouver. If he did not actually know of this stop, it is my view that it would be sufficient to support a conviction if the evidence establishes that the appellant was wilfully blind or reckless as to that fact.

2. *Mens Rea:* Recklessness and Wilful Blindness

(a) IS WILFUL BLINDNESS AS TO WHETHER THE PLANE WOULD STOP IN CANADA SUFFICIENT TO ESTABLISH *MENS REA* FOR THE OFFENCE OF "IMPORTING INTO CANADA"?

90 In *Sansregret v. The Queen* (1985), 18 C.C.C. (3d) 223 at p. 235, 17 D.L.R. (4th) 577, [1985] 1 S.C.R. 570, the court contrasted wilful blindness and recklessness:

> Wilful blindness is distinct from recklessness because, while recklessness involves knowledge of a danger or risk and persistence in a course of conduct which creates a risk that the prohibited result will occur, wilful blindness arises where a person who has become aware of the need for some inquiry declines to make the inquiry because he does not wish to know the truth.

91 I wish to observe that proof of the last clause in the above quote, "because he does not wish to know the truth," cannot be a part of the Crown's burden. The reasons for the failure of the appellant to inquire, if such was the case, are so subjective that they could seldom be proven, and wilful blindness is usually an alternative position that assumes the appellant did not actually know some notorious fact which he probably knew anyway but of which proof cannot be given. These words, in my view, are merely a characterization the law places upon the failure of someone to learn or recognize what should have been known if it was not known.

93 In *Sansregret*, a sexual assault case, the accused said he did not know the victim was not consenting, and both the victim and the trial judge accepted the honesty of his belief that the victim was freely consenting. In spite of this, the Supreme Court of Canada applied the wilful blindness principle to find that the accused must have known the victim was not consenting. As McIntyre, J., said at p. 237, there was self-deception to the point of wilful blindness.

94 The concept of wilful blindness cannot be considered in a factual vacuum, in isolation from the reasonable inferences to be drawn from known facts. In this case, with respect, I cannot conclude other than that the appellant, if he did not know his flight would stop in Canada, which seems inconceivable, was wilfully blind to that fact. His lack of knowledge, if any, resulted from his wilful failure to obtain information which was readily available and which was of significant importance to him. Because of his wilful blindness, the law attributes such knowledge to him.

(b) IS RECKLESSNESS AS TO WHETHER THE PLANE WOULD BE STOPPING IN CANADA SUFFICIENT TO SATISFY THE *MENS REA* ELEMENT OF "IMPORTING INTO CANADA"?

97 In this case, we are concerned with whether the appellant intended to come to Canada. In order to prove recklessness, the Crown must show that he was aware that there was a risk that his plane would stop in Canada, and that he proceeded in the face of that risk. For the reasons stated above, it is my view that the appellant was, at the very least, aware that there was a risk that the airplane would land in a place other than his final destination, and that he proceeded to board the plane, carrying illegal narcotics within his person, despite his knowledge of that risk.

98 I agree with the trial judge that the appellant accepted the routing of the aircraft, and that it is permissible to infer that he accepted the corresponding risk that the plane might take him to somewhere like Canada, where his illegal activities might be discovered. His recklessness in continuing to pursue his plan of couriering narcotics in the face of that risk brings this case within the authority of *Sansregret* at p. 231, where McIntyre, J., said that the conduct of the accused in that case, with his then state of knowledge, "constitutes recklessness sufficient to sustain a charge of rape . . . ." The conduct of the appellant in this case, knowing what he must have known, at the very least constitutes recklessness sufficient to sustain this indictment for importing.

D. Conclusion and Disposition

99 I would accordingly conclude that the *mens rea* of the offence of importing has been established. The evidence demonstrates that the appellant either had actual knowledge that the plane would be stopping in Canada, or that he was wilfully blind or reckless to that fact. I also conclude that recklessness alone is a sufficient answer in this case to the absence of specific evidence that the appellant knew the aircraft would be stopping in Canada.

100 For these reasons I would dismiss the appeal against the conviction for importing.

Appeal dismissed.

Regina v. Martineau

SUPREME COURT OF CANADA   SEPTEMBER 13, 1990

BACKGROUND

Martineau was convicted at his trial on two counts of second degree murder. His appeal to the Alberta Court of Appeal was allowed and a new trial was ordered. The Crown subsequently appealed to the Supreme Court of Canada against the judgment of the Court of Appeal.

MAIN ISSUES

(1) Was section 213(a) [now section 230(a)] of the Criminal Code invalid under the Charter? (2) Does the Charter require that the minimum form of *mens rea* required for conviction of murder be the *subjective* foreseeability of death? (3) To what extent (if any) does section 212(c)[now section 229(c)] infringe sections 7 and 11(d) of the Charter?

JUDGMENTS

The *majority* judgment was delivered by Chief Justice Lamer (with whom Chief Justice Dickson and Justices Wilson, Gonthier, and Cory agreed). (Lamer C.J.C. was Chief Justice at the time of the judgment, while Dickson C.J.C. had been Chief Justice at the time of the original hearing before the Supreme Court of Canada.) The *concurring* judgment of Justice Sopinka and the *dissenting*

judgment of Justice L'Heureux-Dubé have been omitted.

....

LAMER C.J.C.: — This is the first of a series of appeals that raises the constitutionality of s. 213(a) of the Criminal Code, R.S.C. 1970, c. C-34, (now s. 230(a) of the Criminal Code, R.S.C., 1985, c. C-46). The appeal arises as a result of the application to s. 213(a) by the Alberta Court of Appeal of this court's decision in *R. v. Vaillancourt* (1987), 39 C.C.C. (3d) 118, 47 D.L.R. (4th) 399, [1987] 2 S.C.R. 636, in which s. 213(d) of the Criminal Code was declared of no force or effect because it infringed ss. 7 and 11(d) of the Canadian Charter of Rights and Freedoms, and could not be saved by s. 1 of the Charter.

Facts

The facts of this case are not central to the disposition of this appeal, and therefore, may be briefly summarized as follows. On February 7, 1985, the bodies of James McLean and Ann McLean were found in the bathroom of their home, a trailer, in Valleyview, Alberta. A police investigation led to Martineau and one Patrick Tremblay. Martineau, who was fifteen at the time, was charged with both murders and was transferred to adult court.

Martineau was tried by a judge and jury starting on September 12, 1985. Thirty witnesses gave evidence including the accused. The evidence revealed that Martineau and his friend, Tremblay, had set out one evening armed with a pellet pistol and rifle respectively. Martineau testified that he knew that they were going to commit a crime, but that he thought it would only be a "b and e." After robbing the trailer and its occupants, Martineau's friend Tremblay shot and killed the McLeans.

As they left the trailer, Martineau asked Tremblay why he killed them and Tremblay answered, "they saw our faces." Martineau responded, "But they couldn't see mine 'cause I had a mask on." They drove James McLean's car to Grande Prairie where they abandoned it. The respondent was convicted of second degree murder. The trial judge charged the jury on s. 213(a) and (d) of the Criminal Code and on s. 21(1) and (2) of the Criminal Code.

Issues

The following constitutional questions were stated by Chief Justice Dickson:

1. Does s. 213(a) of the Criminal Code infringe or deny the rights or freedoms guaranteed by s. 7 and/or s. 11(d) of the Canadian Charter of Rights and Freedoms?
2. If the answer to question 1 is affirmative, is s. 213(a) justified by s. 1 of the Canadian Charter of Rights and Freedoms, and therefore not inconsistent with the Constitution Act, 1982?

Analysis

Parliament, of course, decides what a crime is to be, and has the power to define the elements of a crime. With the advent of the Charter in 1982, Parliament also has, however, directed the courts to review those definitions to ensure that they are in accordance with the principles of fundamental justice. We, as a court, would be remiss not to heed this command of Parliament. This is an unassailable proposition since the decision of Parliament to entrench into our constitutional framework a Charter of Rights and Freedoms and also the principle that the Constitution is the supreme law of the land. Since 1982, this court has consistently assumed its duty to measure the content of legislation against the guarantees in our Charter designed to protect individual rights and freedoms.

In *R. v. Vaillancourt* (1987), 39 C.C.C. (3d) 118, 47 D.L.R. (4th) 399, [1987] 2 S.C.R. 636, s. 213(d) of the Criminal Code was declared of no force or effect because it violated ss. 7 and 11(d) of the Charter. The *ratio* of *Vaillancourt*, strictly speaking, was that it is a principle of fundamental justice that, before a person could be convicted of murder, there must be proof beyond a reasonable doubt of at least objective foreseeability of death. The impugned section in that case did not accord with this principle because it would be possible for a conviction for murder to occur under s. 213(d) despite the jury's having a reasonable doubt as to whether the accused ought to have known that death was likely to ensue.

In *Vaillancourt*, I analyzed a number of matters, including s. 213 of the Code in the context of the other murder provisions, the historical development of s. 213, felony murder provisions in other jurisdictions, the essential elements of certain crimes at common law, and the principles of fundamental justice under the Charter and their application to s. 213 of the Code. As a result of this analysis I concluded that objective foreseeability of death was the minimum threshold test before a conviction for murder could be sustained. I went on to state, however, that it was my view that the principles of fundamental justice require more; they demand that a conviction for murder requires proof beyond a reasonable doubt of subjective foresight of death. The Chief Justice, Estey and Wilson JJ. agreed with that position. I am still of that view today, and indeed, while I agree with the Alberta Court of Appeal and could dispose of this appeal on the basis of objective foreseeability, it is on the basis of the principle of subjective foresight of death that I choose to dispose of this appeal. I choose this route because I would not want this case, a very serious matter, to return to this court once again on the grounds that there is some doubt as to the validity of the portion of s. 212(d) of the Code that allows for a conviction for murder if the accused "ought to know" that death is likely to result. I need not, therefore, repeat the analysis from *Vaillancourt* here, except to add some brief observations as regards s. 213(a) and the principle of fundamental justice that subjective foresight of death is required before a conviction for murder can be sustained.

Section 213(a) of the Code defines culpable homicide as murder where a person causes the death of a human being while committing or attempting to commit a range of listed offences, whether or not the person means to cause death or whether or not he or she knows that death is likely to ensue if that person means to cause bodily harm for the purpose of facilitating the commission of the offence or flight after committing or attempting to commit the offence. The introductory paragraph of the section, therefore, expressly removes from the Crown the burden of proving beyond a reasonable doubt that the accused had subjective foresight of death. This section stands as an anomaly as regards the other murder provisions, especially in light of the common law presumption against convicting a person of a true crime without proof of intent or recklessness.

A conviction for murder carries with it the most severe stigma and punishment of any crime in our society. The principles of fundamental justice require, because of the special nature of the stigma attached to a conviction for murder, and the available penalties, a *mens rea* reflecting the particular nature of that crime. The effect of s. 213 is to violate the principle that punishment must be proportionate to the moral blameworthiness of the offender, or as Professor Hart puts it in *Punishment and Responsibility* (1968), at p. 162, the fundamental principle of a morally based system of law is that those causing harm intentionally be punished more severely than those causing harm unintentionally.

The rationale underlying the principle that subjective foresight of death is required before a person is labelled and punished as a murderer is linked to the more general principle that criminal liability for a particular result is not justified except where the actor possesses a culpable mental state in respect of that result. In my view, in a free and democratic society that values the autonomy and free will of the individual, the stigma and punishment attaching to the most serious of crimes, murder, should be reserved for those who choose to intentionally cause death or who choose to inflict bodily harm that they know is likely to cause death. The essential role of requiring subjective foresight of death in the context of murder is to maintain a proportionality between the stigma and punishment attached to a murder conviction and the moral blameworthiness of the offender. Murder has long been recognized as the "worst" and most heinous of peace-time crimes. It is, therefore, essential that to satisfy the principles of fundamental justice, the stigma and punishment attaching to a murder conviction must be reserved for those who either intend to cause death or who intend to cause bodily harm that they know will likely cause death.

In sum then, I am of the view that a special mental element with respect to death is necessary before a culpable homicide can be treated as murder. That special mental element gives rise to the moral blameworthiness that justifies the stigma and punishment attaching to a murder conviction. For all the foregoing reasons, and for the reasons stated in *Vaillancourt*, I conclude that it is a principle of fundamental justice that a conviction for murder cannot rest on anything less than proof beyond a reasonable doubt of subjective foresight of death. That was my position when *Vaillancourt* was decided, and that is my position today. Therefore, since s. 213 of the Code expressly eliminates the requirement for proof of subjective foresight, it infringes ss. 7 and 11(d) of the Charter.

As regards s. 1 of the Charter, there is no doubt that the objective of deterring the infliction of bodily harm during the commission of certain offences because of the increased risk of death is of sufficient importance to warrant overriding a Charter right. Further, indiscriminately punishing for murder all those who cause death irrespective of whether they intended to cause death might well be thought to discourage the infliction of bodily harm during the commission of certain offences because of the increased risk of death. But it is not necessary in order to achieve this objective to convict of murder persons who do not intend or foresee the death. In this regard, the section unduly impairs the Charter rights. If Parliament wishes to deter persons from causing bodily harm during certain offences, then it should punish persons for causing the bodily harm. Indeed, the conviction for manslaughter that would result instead of a conviction for murder is punishable by one day in jail to confinement for life. Very stiff sentences for the infliction of bodily harm leading to death in appropriate cases would sufficiently meet any deterrence objective that Parliament might have in mind. The more flexible sentencing scheme under a conviction for manslaughter is in accord with the principle that punishment be meted out with regard to the level of moral blameworthiness of the offender. To label and punish a person as a murderer who did not intend or foresee death unnecessarily stigmatizes and punishes those whose moral blameworthiness is not that of a murderer, and thereby unnecessarily impairs the rights guaranteed by ss. 7 and 11(d) of the Charter. In my view then, s. 213(a), indeed all of s. 213, cannot be saved by s. 1 of the Charter.

The fact that I have based my reasons on the principle of subjective foresight casts serious if not fatal doubt on the constitutionality of part of s. 212(c) of the Code, specifically the words "ought to know is likely to cause death." The validity of s. 212(c) of the Code has not been directly attacked in this appeal, but the court has had the benefit of hearing argument from the Attorney-General of Canada and from the Attorney-Generals for Alberta, British Columbia, Ontario, Québec, and Manitoba, who chose to intervene on the issue of whether subjective foresight or objective foreseeability of death is the constitutionally required minimum *mens rea* for murder. In my view, subjective foresight of death must be proven beyond a reasonable doubt before a conviction for murder can be sustained, and as a result, it is obvious the part of s. 212(c) of the Code allowing for a conviction upon proof that the accused ought to have known that death was likely to result violates ss. 7 and 11(d) of the Charter.

Although it would be open to save that part of s. 212(c) under s. 1 of the Charter, it seems to me that the attempt would fail for the reasons I have given in respect of the attempt to similarly save s. 213 of the Code. I would therefore answer the constitutional questions as follows:

Question: Does s. 213(a) of the Criminal Code infringe or deny the rights or freedoms guaranteed by s. 7 and/or s. 11(d) of the Canadian Charter of Rights and Freedoms?

Answer: Yes, the section infringes both ss. 7 and 11(d) of the Charter.

Question: If the answer to question 1 is affirmative, is s. 213(a) justified by s. 1 of the Canadian Charter of Rights and Freedoms, and therefore not inconsistent with the Constitution Act, 1982?

Answer: No.

In the present case, the respondent was convicted pursuant to a combination of ss. 213 and 21 of the Code. Since in this case the jury was left only with s. 213, which has been declared to be inoperative, a new trial must be ordered. Accordingly, the Court of Appeal's decision quashing the convictions and directing a new trial is affirmed. The appeal is, therefore, dismissed.

Appeal dismissed.

The Mental Element in Criminal Law: Objective Liability

INTRODUCTION

This chapter presents five cases that illustrate the imposition of a form of *objective mens rea* in relation to a variety of serious criminal offences under the Criminal Code. Objective liability does not take into account what was actually going on in the head of the accused at the time of the alleged offence; rather, it is concerned with what the reasonable person *would have known* if placed in exactly the same circumstances as the accused.

The Supreme Court of Canada has held that the courts must apply a *modified* objective test of responsibility to those Criminal Code offences which impose objective *mens rea* requirements. Essentially, this means that, when courts impose objective liability, they must first take into account the particular circumstances that faced the accused and then apply the "reasonable person test" in light of what the accused actually knew about those circumstances. In other words, the courts must ask "What would a reasonable person have done, knowing what the accused knew of the surrounding circumstances?"

In *DeSousa* (1992), the Supreme Court of Canada ruled that section 269 of the Criminal Code, which defines the offence of unlawfully causing harm, imposes objective *mens rea* requirements. The Court also held that objective *mens rea* does not infringe the Charter unless the crime concerned is one of those very few serious offences, such as murder, that requires a minimal degree of subjective *mens rea* in order to meet the require-

ments of the Charter. In the extremely important case of *Creighton* (1993), the Supreme Court of Canada undertook a comprehensive examination of the nature of objective liability and ruled that the imposition of objective *mens rea* requirements for the serious offence of (unlawful act) manslaughter did not violate the Charter.

In *Hundal* (1993), the Supreme Court of Canada held that the *mens rea* requirements of the offence of dangerous driving were objective in nature. The Supreme Court articulated the basic elements of the modified objective test of liability that should be applied by the courts in the context of dangerous driving. In all cases involving the imposition of objective liability, the courts have emphasized that it is not enough that the accused is considered to have been merely careless; the Charter requires that there be "morally blameworthy" conduct on the part of the accused if he or she is to be convicted of a Criminal Code offence. In order to meet this requirement of moral blameworthiness, the Crown must, therefore, prove that the accused's conduct represents a marked and substantial departure from the standard of care to be expected of a reasonable person placed in the circumstances that faced the accused.

The final two cases involve the interpretation of section 219 of the Code, which defines "criminal negligence." In *Tutton and Tutton* (1989) and *Waite* (1989), the Justices of the Supreme Court of Canada were evenly split (3-3) as to whether criminal negligence imported an objective or a subjective form of *mens rea*. Realistically, in the vast majority of cases, the application of either an objective or a subjective test will ultimately lead to exactly the same result. Nevertheless, it is unfortunate that the Supreme Court of Canada has not resolved the issue beyond doubt. In light of the objective test of liability subsequently imposed by the Supreme Court in relation to (unlawful act) manslaughter (Creighton) and in relation to other serious offences, such as dangerous driving (Hundal), it is most likely that the Supreme Court of Canada will, in the future, extend this objective approach to those offences that are based on criminal negligence [e.g., (criminal negligence) manslaughter and causing death or bodily harm by criminal negligence].

Regina v. DeSousa

SUPREME COURT OF CANADA   SEPTEMBER 24, 1992

BACKGROUND

Prior to his trial on a charge of unlawfully causing bodily harm (section 269 of the Criminal Code), DeSousa brought a motion to have section 269 declared invalid on the basis that it contravened the fundamental principles of justice guaranteed by section 7 of the Charter. The trial judge ruled that section 269 of the Code *did* violate section 7 of the Charter and quashed the indictment. The Crown's appeal to the Ontario Court of Appeal was allowed and the case was sent back for trial. DeSousa appealed to the Supreme Court of Canada against the judgment of the Court of Appeal.

MAIN ISSUES

(1) Does the Crown have to prove *subjective* or *objective* foresight of bodily harm in order to obtain a conviction under section 269? (2) If it is sufficient for the Crown to prove that the accused's act was *objectively* dangerous (in the sense of creating a risk of non-trivial bodily harm), does section 269 infringe the fundamental principles of justice enshrined in section 7 of the Charter?

JUDGMENT

The judgment of the Supreme Court of Canada was delivered by Justice Sopinka. The other mem-

bers of the Court were Justices Gonthier, Cory, McLachlin, and Iacobucci.

SOPINKA J.: — This appeal concerns a constitutional challenge to s. 269 (unlawfully causing bodily harm) of the Criminal Code, R.S.C. 1985, c. C-46 (formerly s. 245.3). The appellant was involved in a fight in which a bystander was injured when a bottle allegedly thrown by the appellant broke against a wall and a glass fragment from the bottle struck the bystander.

Prior to trial, the appellant brought a motion to have s. 269 declared of no force or effect as contrary to s. 7 of the Canadian Charter of Rights and Freedoms. The appellant argued that the offence of unlawfully causing bodily harm was contrary to fundamental justice as it put an accused at risk of imprisonment without the requirement of a blameworthy state of mind. Additionally, the appellant argued that the provision allows a conviction despite an accused's lack of intent to cause the consequence of bodily harm. The motion succeeded and the indictment under which the appellant stood charged was quashed. On appeal, the motion judgment was overturned and the order quashing the indictment was set aside.

The Facts

As no trial has yet been held in this matter, the facts have been taken from the evidence at the preliminary inquiry. The transcript of the preliminary inquiry was filed with the Court of Appeal and with this court as the factual basis for the appeals.

On December 31, 1987, Teresa Santos attended a New Year's Eve party in Toronto. Shortly after midnight, a fight broke out at the party. As she was attempting to gather her belongings, which were located at a table in the vicinity of the fight, Ms. Santos was struck on the arm by a piece of glass. The glass fragment produced a large gash on her left forearm which required seven stitches to mend the underlying pronator muscle in her arm and a further seven stitches to mend the skin above the muscle. Eight months later, the feeling and movement in the victim's forearm was still restricted.

The victim's husband, Fernando Santos, was standing near his wife while the fight was in progress. He noticed that the appellant and a number of others were involved in the altercation. The appellant and the Santos were standing approximately eight feet away from a wall on opposite sides of the same table. Some of the men who were fighting began throwing bottles. Mr. Santos then noticed the appellant throw a bottle which hit the wall beside Ms. Santos and shattered. A piece of glass from the bottle thrown by the appellant ricocheted off the wall and struck the victim on the arm causing her injury. As a result of this incident, the appellant was charged with unlawfully causing bodily harm contrary to s. 245.3 of the Criminal Code, R.S.C. 1970, c. C-34 (now s. 269). He was committed for trial after a preliminary inquiry held on October 31, 1988.

At the outset of the trial and before any evidence was heard, the accused made a motion to have s. 269 declared of no force or effect on the ground that it contravened s. 7 of the Charter. The motion was granted and the indictment was quashed. On appeal to the Court of Appeal for Ontario, the motion judgment was overturned and the order quashing the indictment was set aside. This appeal comes before the court as of right.

Points in Issue

The following constitutional questions were stated for this appeal:

1. Does s. 269 of the Criminal Code violate s. 7 or 11(d) of the Canadian Charter of Rights and Freedoms?
2. If the answer to question 1 is "yes", then is s. 269 of the Code a reasonable limit justified by s. 1 of the Charter?

Analysis

B. Section 269 of the Criminal Code

To be brought within the ambit of s. 269, an accused must have committed an underlying unlawful offence (otherwise referred to as the predicate offence) and have caused bodily harm to another person as a result of committing that underlying offence. For liability to be imposed for unlawfully causing bodily harm, the harm caused must have sufficient causal connection to the underlying offence committed. The requirement of an underlying "unlawful" offence includes at its most general, and subject to the restrictions discussed below, only offences prohibited by federal or provincial legislation.

(1) THE MENTAL ELEMENT REQUIREMENT OF S. 269

The major issue raised in this appeal concerns the mental element required by s. 269 of the Code. After delineating the statutorily required mental element, the question of the constitutional sufficiency of this element will then be addressed to determine whether it passes constitutional muster.

It is axiomatic that in criminal law there should be no responsibility without personal fault. A fault requirement was asserted to be a fundamental aspect of our common law by this court in *R. v. Sault Ste. Marie (City)* (1978), 40 C.C.C. (2d) 353, 85 D.L.R. (3d) 161, [1978] 2 S.C.R. 1299, and as a matter of constitutional law under s. 7 of the

Charter in *Reference re: s. 94(2) of Motor Vehicle Act* (1985), 23 C.C.C. (3d) 289, 24 D.L.R. (4th) 536, [1985] 2 S.C.R. 486. As a matter of statutory interpretation, a provision should not be interpreted to lack any element of personal fault unless the statutory language mandates such an interpretation in clear and unambiguous terms. Unlike most offences, the mental element of s. 269 is composed of two separate requirements. The first requirement is that the mental element of the underlying offence of s. 269 be satisfied. The second requirement is that the additional fault requirement supplied by the wording of s. 269, discussed more fully *infra*, also be satisfied.

(a) THE MENTAL ELEMENT OF THE UNDERLYING OFFENCE

To be convicted under s. 269, the prosecution must first satisfy the mental element requirement of the underlying offence. In interpreting the ambit of the underlying offences covered by s. 269, it is important to recognize the abhorrence of the criminal law for offences of absolute liability. The criminal law is based on proof of personal fault, and this concept is jealously guarded when a court is asked to interpret criminal provisions, especially those with potentially serious penal consequences. This statutory conclusion is mandated by the general presumption in the interpretation of criminal statutes against absolute liability and the absence of clear words to the contrary to rebut this presumption. Thus, the concept of "unlawful" as it is used in s. 269 does not include any underlying offence of absolute liability. The inclusion of such offences would be contrary to the general canons of criminal interpretation quite apart from any Charter considerations. Although not relying on constitutional requirements in foreclosing the possibility of absolute liability offences forming the predicate offences of s. 269, certainly principles of fundamental justice require no less.

In addition to satisfying the statutorily required mental element of the underlying offence, the mental element of the underlying offence must also be constitutionally sufficient in its own right. If the underlying offence contains a constitutionally insufficient mental element, it is of no force or effect and thus cannot form the basis for a prosecution under s. 269. The underlying offence must be valid in law on its own before it can be used to support a charge under s. 269.

(b) THE MEANING OF "UNLAWFUL" IN S. 269

In addition to the mental element required by the underlying offence, the wording of s. 269, and particularly the case law interpreting the term "unlawfully," imports an additional aspect to the mental element of s. 269. The case law interpreting the use of this term in similar provisions has focused on the offence most commonly known as unlawful act manslaughter. While manslaughter is not the offence at issue in this appeal, the case law which seeks to interpret the term "unlawful" in that context is instructive.

English authority has consistently held that the underlying unlawful act required by its manslaughter offence requires proof that the unlawful act was "likely to injure another person" or, in other words, put the bodily integrity of others at risk.

In accordance with the English law and in furtherance of the developing Canadian case law, the most principled approach to the meaning of "unlawful" in the context of s. 269 is to require that the unlawful act be at least objectively dangerous. This conclusion is supported by the meaning given to the words "unlawful act" by virtually all of the lower courts and is also in accord with the emerging jurisprudence of this Court in regard to personal fault.

The test is one of objective foresight of bodily harm for all underlying offences. The act must be both unlawful, as described above, *and* one that is likely to subject another person to danger of harm or injury. This bodily harm must be more than merely trivial or transitory in nature and will in most cases involve an act of violence done deliberately to another person. In interpreting what constitutes an objectively dangerous act, the courts should strive to avoid attaching penal sanctions to mere inadvertence.

(2) CONSTITUTIONAL SUFFICIENCY

The mental element of s. 269 has two separate aspects. The first aspect is the requirement that an underlying offence with a constitutionally sufficient mental element has been committed. Additionally, s. 269 requires that the prosecution prove that the bodily harm caused by the underlying unlawful act was objectively foreseeable. This latter requirement insures that all prosecutions under s. 269 contain *at least* a fault requirement based on an objective standard. As this court has not indicated that fundamental justice requires fault based on a subjective standard for all offences, the mental element required by s. 269 passes constitutional muster unless s. 269 is one of those few offences which, due to its stigma and penalty, require fault based on a subjective standard. I agree with the respondent and interveners that s. 269 has neither the stigma nor criminal sanction to require a more demanding mental element than it already has. The criminal sanction is flexible and thus can be tailored to suit the circumstances of the case. The stigma associated with conviction will generally reflect the degree of opprobrium which the underlying offence attracts. The stigma attached to the underlying offence will in turn influence the minimum mental requirement for that offence.

Unless a minimum mind state of subjective intention in regard to consequences is constitutionally required, the test discussed above satisfies the dictates of s. 7 of the Charter. I will now consider that issue.

C. Foresight of Consequences

Although I have concluded by means of statutory interpretation that s. 269 requires objective foresight of the consequences of an accused's unlawful act, the appellant argues that s. 7 of the Charter requires subjective foresight of all consequences which comprise part of the *actus reus* of an offence.

Lamer C.J.C. stated in *Martineau* that "[i]f Parliament wishes to deter persons from causing bodily harm during certain offences, then it should punish persons for causing the bodily harm." This is exactly what s. 269 attempts to do. In this particular provision, the mental element requirement is composed of both the mental element of the underlying unlawful act and the additional requirement of objective foresight of bodily harm. There is, however, no constitutional requirement that intention, either on an objective or a subjective basis, extend to the consequences of unlawful acts in general.

In many offences, such as assault or dangerous driving, the offence is made out regardless of the consequences of the act, but the consequences can be used to aggravate liability for the offence. For example, both assault and assault causing bodily harm have identical *mens rea* requirements; the element of causing bodily harm is merely used to classify the offence. No principle of fundamental justice prevents Parliament from treating crimes with certain consequences as more serious than crimes which lack those consequences.

Conduct may fortuitously result in more or less serious consequences depending on the circumstances in which the consequences arise. The same act of assault may injure one person but not another. The implicit rationale of the law in this area is that it is acceptable to distinguish between criminal responsibility for equally reprehensible acts on the basis of the harm that is actually caused. This is reflected in the creation of higher maximum penalties for offences with more serious consequences. Courts and legislators acknowledge the harm actually caused by concluding that in otherwise equal cases a more serious consequence will dictate a more serious response.

There appears to be a general principle in Canada and elsewhere that, in the absence of an express legislative direction, the mental element of an offence attaches only to the underlying offence and not to the aggravating circumstances: E. Colvin, *Principles of Criminal Law*, 2nd ed. (1991), p. 57. This has been confirmed by this court in a number of cases including those which have held that sexual assault requires intention simply in relation to the assault and not any aggravating circumstance: see *R. v. Chase* (1987), 37 C.C.C. (3d) 97,

45 D.L.R. (4th) 98, [1987] 2 S.C.R. 293, and *R. v. Bernard* (1988), 45 C.C.C. (3d) 1 at pp. 42–4, [1988] 2 S.C.R. 833, 67 C.R. (3d) 113. To require fault in regard to each consequence of an action in order to establish liability for causing that consequence would substantially restructure current notions of criminal responsibility. Such a result cannot be founded on the constitutional aversion to punishing the morally innocent. One is not morally innocent simply because a particular consequence of an unlawful act was unforeseen by that actor. In punishing for unforeseen consequences, the law is not punishing the morally innocent but those who cause injury through avoidable unlawful action. Neither basic principles of criminal law nor the dictates of fundamental justice require, by necessity, intention in relation to the consequences of an otherwise blameworthy act.

Disposition

On a proper interpretation of s. 269 of the Code, the concept of an unlawful act as it is used in that section includes only federal and provincial offences. Excluded from this general category of offences are any offences which are based on absolute liability and which have constitutionally insufficient mental elements on their own. Additionally, the term "unlawfully," as it is used in this section, requires an act which is at least objectively dangerous. Interpreted in this way, s. 269 complies with the requirements of s. 7 of the Charter. In the absence of a violation of s. 7, there is no violation of s. 11(d). I would answer the constitutional questions as follows:

Question 1: Does s. 269 of the Criminal Code violate ss. 7 or 11(d) of the Canadian Charter of Rights and Freedoms?

Answer: No.

Question 2: If the answer to question 1 is "yes," then is s. 269 of the Code a reasonable limit justified by s. 1 of the Charter?

Answer: It is not necessary to answer this question.

Accordingly, the appeal is dismissed.

Appeal dismissed.

Regina v. Creighton

SUPREME COURT OF CANADA

SEPTEMBER 9, 1993

BACKGROUND

Creighton was convicted at his trial of the offence of (unlawful act) manslaughter. He appealed against his conviction to the Ontario Court of Appeal which dismissed his appeal. Creighton subsequently appealed to the Supreme Court of Canada against the judgment of the Court of Appeal.

MAIN ISSUES

(1) What is the *mens rea* that must be proved by the Crown in a case of (unlawful act) manslaughter? (2) If *objective* foreseeability of the risk of bodily harm is the necessary *mens rea* for conviction of (unlawful act) manslaughter, does this infringe the "fundamental principles of justice" guaranteed by section 7 of the Charter?

JUDGMENTS

The *majority* judgment was delivered by Justice McLachlin (with whom Justices La Forest, L'Heureux-Dubé, Gonthier, and Cory agreed). Chief Justice Lamer (with whom Justices Sopinka, Iacobucci, and Major agreed) delivered a judgment that *concurred* with the dismissal of Creighton's appeal; however, his reasoning differed, in some

important respects, from that of Justice McLachlin. The brief judgment of Justice La Forest has been omitted.

....

LAMER C.J.C.: —

Facts

The events giving rise to this appeal took place over an 18-hour period beginning on the evening of October 26, 1989. A group including the appellant, Marc Creighton, and the deceased, Ms. Martin, consumed a large quantity of alcohol and cocaine that night. In the afternoon of the following day, the appellant, a companion (Frank Caddedu) and the deceased planned to share a quantity of cocaine at the deceased's apartment. The evidence indicates that all of the parties involved were experienced cocaine users.

The appellant obtained an "eight-ball" (3.5 gr.) of cocaine. He did not seek to determine the quality or potency of the cocaine before injecting the drug intravenously into himself and Frank Caddedu. With the consent of the deceased, the appellant then injected a quantity of cocaine into the deceased's right forearm. She immediately began to convulse violently and appeared to cease breathing. Subsequent expert testimony confirmed

Adapted from *R. v. Creighton* (1993), 83 C.C.C. (3d), pp. 350–394. Copyright © 1993 by *Canada Law Book*. Reprinted with permission.

that, as a result of the injection, she had experienced a cardiac arrest, and later asphyxiated on the contents of her stomach.

Both the appellant and Mr. Caddedu attempted unsuccessfully to resuscitate Ms. Martin. Mr. Caddedu indicated he wanted to call for emergency assistance, but the appellant, by verbal intimidation, convinced Mr. Caddedu not to call 911. The appellant placed the deceased, who was still convulsing, on her bed. The appellant then proceeded to clean the apartment of any possible fingerprints. The two men then left the apartment. Mr. Caddedu returned unaccompanied to the deceased's apartment six or seven hours later and called for emergency assistance. Ms. Martin was thereupon pronounced dead.

The appellant was charged with manslaughter. Defence counsel conceded at trial that the injection into the deceased's body constituted "trafficking" within the meaning of s. 4(1) of the Narcotic Control Act, R.S.C. 1985, c. N-1. The Crown argued that the appellant was guilty of manslaughter as Ms. Martin's death was the direct consequence of an unlawful act, contrary to s. 222(5)(a) of the Criminal Code.

The appellant was convicted of manslaughter on May 18, 1990, and sentenced to four years' imprisonment. The appellant appealed to the Ontario Court of Appeal, which affirmed the conviction.

Analysis

A. Constitutionality of s. 222(5)(a) of the Criminal Code

In *R. v. Vaillancourt* (1987), 39 C.C.C. (3d) 118, 47 D.L.R. (4th) 399, [1987] 2 S.C.R. 636, I emphasized that the guiding principle underlying the constitutional analysis of fault in criminal law is that the state cannot punish a person as morally blameworthy unless such blameworthiness has been established.

In *Vaillancourt*, I emphasized that the hallmark of murder is that there must be some special mental element with respect to death which gives rise to the moral blameworthiness which justifies the stigma and sentence attached to a murder conviction. As I said:

> . . . murder is distinguished from manslaughter only by the mental element with respect to the death. *It is thus clear that there must be some special mental element with respect to the death before a culpable homicide can be treated as a murder.* That special mental element gives rise to the moral blameworthiness which justifies the stigma and sentence attached to a murder conviction. I am presently of the view that it is a principle of fundamental justice that a conviction for murder cannot rest on anything less than proof beyond a reasonable doubt of subjective foresight.

(Emphasis added.)

In my view, the stigma which attaches to a conviction for unlawful act manslaughter is significant, but does not approach the opprobrium reserved in our society for those who *knowingly* or *intentionally* take the life of another. It is for this reason that manslaughter developed as a separate offence from murder at common law.

Thus, as I stated, unlawful act manslaughter falls into the class of offences where a mental element in relation to the consequence must be established, but in any event, I find the stigma attached to a conviction for culpable homicide, albeit culpable homicide which is not murder, to be significant enough to require, at a minimum, objective foresight of the risk of death in order for the offence to comply with s. 7 of the Charter.

Therefore, in accordance with the requirements of s. 7 of the Charter, the proper interpretation of unlawful act manslaughter under s. 222(5)(a) of the Code requires the Crown to prove beyond reasonable doubt: (a) that the accused has committed an unlawful act which caused the death of the deceased; (b) that the unlawful act must be one that is objectively dangerous (i.e., in the sense that a reasonable person would realize that it gives rise to a risk of harm); (c) that the fault requirement of the predicate offence, which cannot extend to offences of absolute liability, was in existence; and (d) that a reasonable person in the circumstances of the accused would foresee the unlawful act giving rise to a risk of death.

The second element of unlawful act manslaughter involves a determination, as a question of law, of whether the predicate unlawful act is objectively dangerous. The fourth element, however, asks the trier of fact to place the reasonable person in the circumstances of the accused in order to determine whether the risk of death created by the unlawful act was objectively foreseeable by the accused.

B. The Objective Test

An accused can only be held to the standard of a reasonable person if the accused was capable, in the circumstances of the offence, of attaining that standard. Consequently, in determining whether a reasonable person in the circumstances of the accused would have foreseen the risk of death arising from the unlawful act, the trier of fact must pay particular attention to any human frailties which might have rendered the accused incapable of having foreseen what the reasonable person would have foreseen. If the criminal law were to judge every accused by the inflexible standard of the monolithic "reasonable person," even where the accused could not possibly have attained that standard, the result, as Stuart notes, would be "absolute responsibility" for such persons: *Canadian Criminal Law: A Treatise*, 2nd ed. (1987), p. 192.

The objective test can be best understood when stated as a "checklist" for the trier of fact to apply to the accused's conduct in a particular case. Where the accused is charged with the offence of unlawful act manslaughter, the trier of fact must ask:

(1) Would a reasonable person in the same circumstances have been aware that the likely consequences of his or her unlawful conduct would create the risk of death?

This question provides the threshold to the objective test. If the answer to this question is No, then the accused must be acquitted. If the answer is Yes, however, the trier must then ask:

(2) Was the accused unaware
(a) because he or she did not turn his or her mind to the consequences of the conduct and thus to the risk of death likely to result; or
(b) because he or she lacked the capacity to turn his or her mind to the consequences of the conduct and thus to the risk of death likely to result, due to human frailties?

If the answer is (a), the accused must be convicted, since the criminal law cannot allow the absence of actual awareness to be an excuse to criminal liability. An important distinction must be maintained within the objective test between the capacity to decide to turn one's mind to a risk, and the decision not to turn one's mind to it. A key element of the objective test is that of the control an accused could have exercised over the frailty which rendered him or her incapable of acting as the reasonable person would in the same circumstances. The notion of control is related to that of moral responsibility; if one is able to act prudently and not endanger the life of others, one will be held liable for failing to do so. One must be morally — and criminally — responsible to act according to his or her capacities not to inflict harm, even unintentional harm. By contrast, the inability to control a particular frailty which resulted in the creation of the risk may offer a moral excuse for having brought about that risk. Therefore, if the answer to the second branch of the objective test is (b), the third and final stage of the inquiry is required:

(3) In the context of the particular offence, would the reasonable person with the capacities of the accused have made him or herself aware of the likely consequences of the unlawful conduct and the resulting risk of death?

In this inquiry, the accused's behaviour is still measured against the standard of the reasonable person, but the reasonable person is constructed to account for the accused's particular capacities and resulting inability to perceive and address certain risks. It must be emphasized that this is *not* a subjective test: if a reasonable person with the frailties of the accused would nevertheless have appreciated the risk, and the accused did not in fact appreciate the risk, the accused must be convicted.

Human frailties encompass personal characteristics habitually affecting an accused's awareness of the circumstances which create risk. Such characteristics must be relevant to the ability to perceive the particular risk. For example, while illiteracy may excuse the failure to take care with a hazardous substance identifiable only by a label, as the accused may be unable, in this case, to apprehend the relevant facts, illiteracy may not be relevant to the failure to take care with a firearm.

It should be emphasized that the relevant characteristics must be traits which the accused could not control or otherwise manage in the circumstances. For example, while a person with cataracts cannot be faulted for having reduced vision, he or she may be expected to avoid activity in which that limitation will either create risk or render him or her unable to manage risk which is inherent in an activity (driving, for example). The reasonable person is expected to compensate for his or her frailties, to the extent he or she is conscious of them and able to do so.

C. The Application of the Objective Test

Applied to the facts of this case, therefore, one must ask whether the reasonable individual in the circumstances of the offence and with Mr. Creighton's experience in drug use would have been aware of the risk of death arising from the injection of the deceased with the cocaine. Given the lethal nature of the narcotic in question and the fashion in which it was administered, the familiarity of the accused with the drug and its dangerous properties, the trial judge concluded that the accused foresaw

the risk of death or serious bodily harm in injecting the deceased with cocaine. Indeed, when first informed of the charges against him, the appellant was apprised of the death of Ms. Martin as a result of a cocaine overdose, to which he responded the following: "You know better than I that that stuff kills a lot of people. I hear lots of things about people dying of drug overdoses but I don't know them so I don't care." Since the accused was aware of the risk of death resulting from the unlawful act of trafficking, it is not necessary to proceed to the second or third branch of the objective test.

VI. Disposition

I would answer the constitutional question as follows:

Question: Does the common law definition of unlawful act manslaughter contravene s. 7 of the Canadian Charter of Rights and Freedoms?

Answer: No.

McLACHLIN J.: — I respectfully disagree with the Chief Justice on two points. The first is his conclusion that the common law offence of manslaughter is unconstitutional because it does not require foreseeability of death. The Chief Justice concludes that the offence of manslaughter must be "read up" to include this requirement in order to bring it into line with the principles of fundamental justice enshrined in s. 7 of the Canadian Charter of Rights and Freedoms, and in particular with the principle that the moral fault required for conviction be commensurate with the gravity and the stigma of the offence. In my view, the offence of unlawful act manslaughter, as defined by our courts and those in other jurisdictions for many centuries, is entirely consistent with the principles of fundamental justice. There is no need to read up its requirements; as it stands, it conforms to the Charter.

The second point on which I respectfully diverge is the Chief Justice's conclusion that the standard of care on the objective test in manslaughter and in crimes of negligence varies with the degree of experience, education, and other personal characteristics of the accused. This leads the Chief Justice to hold Mr. Creighton to a higher standard of care than that of the reasonable person in determining if he would have foreseen the risk in question, because of Creighton's long experience as a drug user. For the reasons set out below, I believe the appropriate standard to be that of the reasonable person in all the circumstances of the case. The criminal law is concerned with setting minimum standards of conduct; the standards are not to be altered because the accused possesses more or less experience than the hypothetical average reasonable person.

A. Constitutionality of the Requirement of Foreseeability of Bodily Injury in Manslaughter

1. THE *MENS REA* OF MANSLAUGHTER

Manslaughter is a crime of venerable lineage. It covers a wide variety of circumstances. Two requirements are constant: (1) conduct causing the death of another person, and (2) fault short of intention to kill. That fault may consist either in committing another unlawful act which causes the death, or in criminal negligence. The common law classification of manslaughter is reflected in the definition of culpable homicide in s. 222(5) of the Criminal Code:

> 222(5) A person commits culpable homicide when he causes the death of a human being
>> (a) by means of an unlawful act;
>> (b) by means of criminal negligence;

The structure of the offence of manslaughter depends on a predicate offence of an unlawful act or criminal negligence, coupled with a homicide. It is now settled that the fact that an offence depends upon a predicate offence does not render it unconstitutional, provided that the predicate offence involves a dangerous act, is not an offence of absolute liability, and is not unconstitutional: *R. v. DeSousa* (1992), 76 C.C.C. (3d) 124, 95 D.L.R. (4th) 595, [1992] 2 S.C.R. 944. But a further

objection is raised in this case. It is said that the offence of manslaughter is unconstitutional because it requires only foreseeability of the risk of bodily harm and not foreseeability of death, and that the trial judge erred in requiring only foreseeability of bodily harm.

The cases establish that in addition to the *actus reus* and *mens rea* associated with the underlying act, all that is required to support a manslaughter conviction is reasonable foreseeability of the risk of bodily harm. While s. 222(5)(a) does not expressly require foreseeable bodily harm, it has been so interpreted: see *R. v. DeSousa, supra*. The unlawful act must be objectively dangerous, that is, likely to injure another person. The law of unlawful act manslaughter has not, however, gone so far as to require foreseeability of death. The same is true for manslaughter predicated on criminal negligence; while criminal negligence, *infra*, requires a marked departure from the standards of a reasonable person in all the circumstances, it does not require foreseeability of death.

The test set out by Sopinka J. for the unlawful act required by s. 269 of the Criminal Code is equally applicable to manslaughter:

> . . . the test is one of objective foresight of bodily harm for all underlying offences. The act must be both unlawful, as described above, *and* one that is likely to subject another person to danger of harm or injury. This bodily harm must be more than merely trivial or transitory in nature and will in most cases involve an act of violence done deliberately to another person. In interpreting what constitutes an objectively dangerous act, the courts should strive to avoid attaching penal sanctions to mere inadvertence. The contention that no dangerousness requirement is required if the unlawful act is criminal should be rejected.

(Emphasis in original.)

So the test for the *mens rea* of unlawful act manslaughter in Canada, as in the United Kingdom, is (in addition to the *mens rea* of the underlying offence) objective foreseeability of the risk of bodily harm which is neither trivial nor transitory, in the context of a dangerous act. Foreseeability of the risk of death is not required. The question is whether this test violates the principles of fundamental justice under s. 7 of the Charter.

2. CONSTITUTIONALITY OF THE "FORESIGHT OF BODILY HARM" TEST FOR MANSLAUGHTER

As I read the reasons of the Chief Justice, his conclusion that the offence of manslaughter as it stands is unconstitutional rests on two main concerns. First, it is his view that the gravity or seriousness of the offence of manslaughter, and in particular the stigma that attaches to it, requires a minimum *mens rea* of foreseeability of death. Second, considerations of symmetry between the element of mental fault and the consequences of the offence mandate this conclusion.

(a) GRAVITY OF THE OFFENCE
A number of concepts fall under this head. Three of them figure among the four factors relevant to determining the constitutionality of a *mens rea* requirement, as set out by this court in *R. v. Martineau* (1990), 58 C.C.C. (3d) 353, [1990] 2 S.C.R. 633, 79 C.R. (3d) 129:

1. the stigma attached to the offence, and the available penalties requiring a *mens rea* reflecting the particular nature of the crime;
2. whether the punishment is proportionate to the moral blameworthiness of the offender; and
3. the idea that those causing harm intentionally must be punished more severely than those causing harm unintentionally.

To the extent that stigma is relied on as requiring foreseeability of the risk of death in the offence of manslaughter, I find it unconvincing. The most important feature of the stigma of manslaughter is the stigma which is *not* attached to it. The Criminal Code confines manslaughter to non-intentional homicide. A person convicted of manslaughter is *not* a murderer. He or she did *not* intend to kill someone. A person has been killed through the fault of another, and that is always serious. But by the very act of calling the killing *manslaughter*, the law indicates that the killing is less blameworthy than murder.

To put it another way, the stigma attached to manslaughter is an appropriate stigma. The stigma associated with manslaughter is arguably exactly what it should be for an unintentional killing in circumstances where risk of bodily harm was foreseeable.

It would shock the public's conscience to think that a person could be convicted of manslaughter absent any moral fault based on foreseeability of harm. Conversely, it might well shock the public's conscience to convict a person who has killed another only of aggravated assault — the result of requiring foreseeability of death — on the sole basis that the risk of death was not reasonably foreseeable. The terrible consequence of death demands more. In short, the *mens rea* requirement which the common law has adopted — foreseeability of harm — is entirely appropriate to the stigma associated with the offence of manslaughter. To change the *mens rea* requirement would be to risk the very disparity between *mens rea* and stigma of which the appellant complains.

I come then to the second factor mentioned in *Martineau*, the relationship between the punishment for the offence and the *mens rea* requirement. Here again, the offence of manslaughter stands in sharp contrast to the offence of murder. Murder entails a mandatory life sentence; manslaughter carries with it no minimum sentence. This is appropriate. Because manslaughter can occur in a wide variety of circumstances, the penalties must be flexible. The point is, the sentence can be and is tailored to suit the degree of moral fault of the offender. It follows that the sentence attached to manslaughter does not require elevation of the degree of *mens rea* for the offence.

This brings me to the third factor relating to the gravity of the offence set out in *Martineau*, the principle that those causing harm intentionally must be punished more severely than those causing harm unintentionally. As noted, this principle is strictly observed in the case of manslaughter. It is by definition an unintentional crime. Accordingly, the penalties imposed are typically less than for its intentional counterpart, murder.

I conclude that the standard of *mens rea* required for manslaughter is appropriately tailored to the seriousness of the offence.

(b) SYMMETRY BETWEEN THE ELEMENT OF FAULT AND THE CONSEQUENCES OF THE OFFENCE

The Chief Justice correctly observes that the criminal law has traditionally aimed at symmetry between the *mens rea* and the prohibited consequences of the offence. The *actus reus* generally consists of an act bringing about a prohibited consequence, e.g. death. Criminal law theory suggests that the accompanying *mens rea* must go to the prohibited consequence. The moral fault of the accused lies in the act of bringing about that consequence. The Chief Justice reasons from this proposition that since manslaughter is an offence involving the prohibited act of killing another, a *mens rea* of foreseeability of harm is insufficient; what is required is foreseeability of death.

I turn first to the distinction between appreciation of the risk of bodily harm and the risk of death in the context of manslaughter. In my view, when the risk of bodily harm is combined with the established rule that a wrongdoer must take his victim as he finds him and the fact that death did in fact occur, the distinction disappears. The accused who asserts that the risk of death was not foreseeable is in effect asserting that a normal person would not have died in these circumstances, and that he could not foresee the peculiar vulnerability of the victim. Therefore, he says, he should be convicted only of assault causing bodily harm or some lesser offence. This is to abrogate the thin-skull rule that requires that the wrongdoer take his victim as he finds him. Conversely, to combine the test of reasonable foreseeability of bodily harm with the thin-skull rule is to mandate that in some cases, foreseeability of the risk of bodily harm alone will properly result in a conviction for manslaughter.

What the appellant asks us to do, then, is to abandon the "thin-skull" rule. It is this rule which, on analysis, is alleged to be unjust. Such a conclusion I cannot accept. The law has consistently set its face against such a policy. It decrees that the aggressor must take his victim as he finds him.

The thin-skull rule is a good and useful principle. It requires aggressors, once embarked on their dangerous course of conduct which may foreseeably injure others, to take responsibility for all the consequences that ensue, even to death. That is not, in my view, contrary to fundamental justice. Yet the consequence of adopting the amendment proposed by the Chief Justice would be to abrogate this principle in cases of manslaughter.

In fact, when manslaughter is viewed in the context of the thin-skull principle, the disparity diminishes between the *mens rea* of the offence and its consequence. The law does not posit the average victim. It says the aggressor must take the victim as he finds him. Wherever there is a risk of harm, there is also a practical risk that some victims may die as a result of the harm. At this point, the test of harm and death merge.

The second assumption inherent in the argument based on symmetry between *mens rea* and each consequence of the offence is that this is not only a general rule of criminal law, but a principle of fundamental justice — a basic constitutional requirement. I agree that as a general rule the *mens rea* of an offence relates to the consequences prohibited by the offence. Yet our criminal law contains important exceptions to this ideal of perfect symmetry. The presence of these exceptions suggests that the rule of symmetry is just that — a rule — to which there are exceptions. If this is so, then the rule cannot be elevated to the status of a principle of fundamental justice, which must, by definition, have universal application.

Thus it cannot be said that the law in all circumstances insists on absolute symmetry between the *mens rea* and the consequences of the offence. Sometimes it does not insist on the consequences at all, as in crimes of attempts. Sometimes, as in unlawful act manslaughter, it elevates the crime by reason of its serious consequences while leaving the mental element the same.

Just as it would offend fundamental justice to punish a person who did not intend to kill for murder, so it would equally offend common notions of justice to acquit a person who has killed another of manslaughter and find him guilty instead of aggravated assault on the ground that death, as opposed to harm, was not foreseeable. Consequences can be important.

Thus when considering the constitutionality of the requirement of foreseeability of bodily harm, the question is not whether the general rule of symmetry between *mens rea* and the consequences prohibited by the offence is met, but rather whether the fundamental principle of justice is satisfied that the gravity and blameworthiness of an offence must be commensurate with the moral fault engaged by that offence. Fundamental justice does not require absolute symmetry between moral fault and the prohibited consequences. Consequences, or the absence of consequences, can properly affect the seriousness with which Parliament treats specified conduct.

3. POLICY CONSIDERATIONS

First, the need to deter dangerous conduct which may injure others and in fact may kill the peculiarly vulnerable supports the view that death need not be objectively foreseeable, only bodily injury. Given the finality of death and the absolute unacceptability of killing another human being, it is not amiss to preserve the test which promises the greatest measure of deterrence, provided the penal consequences of the offence are not disproportionate. This is achieved by retaining the test of foreseeability of bodily harm in the offence of manslaughter.

Secondly, retention of the test based on foreseeability of bodily harm accords best with our sense of justice. The criminal law must reflect not only the concerns of the accused, but the concerns of the victim and, where the victim is killed, the concerns of society for the victim's fate. Both go into the equation of justice.

Finally, the traditional test founded on foreseeability of the risk of bodily harm provides, in my belief, a workable test which avoids troubling judges and juries about the fine distinction between foreseeability of the risk of bodily injury and foreseeability of the risk of death. The traditional common law test permits a principled approach to the offence which meets the concerns of society, provides fairness to the accused, and facilitates a just and workable trial process.

4. SUMMARY ON THE CONSTITUTIONALITY OF THE TEST OF FORESIGHT OF BODILY HARM FOR MANSLAUGHTER

The foregoing considerations lead me to conclude that the fact that the *mens rea* of manslaughter requires foreseeable risk of harm rather than foreseeable risk of death does not violate the principles of fundamental justice. In the final analysis, the moral fault required for manslaughter is commensurate with the gravity of the offence and the penalties which it entails, and offends no principle of fundamental justice.

B. The Nature of the Objective Test

I respectfully differ from the Chief Justice on the nature of the objective test used to determine the *mens rea* for crimes of negligence. In my view, the approach advocated by the Chief Justice personalizes the objective test to the point where it devolves into a subjective test, thus eroding the minimum standard of care which Parliament has laid down by the enactment of offences of manslaughter and penal negligence.

The *mens rea* of a criminal offence may be either subjective or objective, subject to the principle of fundamental justice that the moral fault of the offence must be proportionate to its gravity and penalty. Subjective *mens rea* requires that the accused have intended the consequences of his or her acts, or that knowing of the probable consequences of those acts, the accused have proceeded recklessly in the face of the risk. The requisite intent or knowledge may be inferred directly from what the accused said or says about his or her mental state, or indirectly from the act and its circumstances.

Objective *mens rea*, on the other hand, is not concerned with what the accused intended or knew. Rather, the mental fault lies in failure to direct the mind to a risk which the reasonable person would have appreciated. Objective *mens rea* is not concerned with what was actually in the accused's mind, but with what should have been there, had the accused proceeded reasonably.

It is now established that a person may be held criminally responsible for negligent conduct on the objective test, and that this alone does not violate the principle of fundamental justice that the moral fault of the accused must be commensurate with the gravity of the offence and its penalty: *R. v. Hundal* (1993), 79 C.C.C. (3d) 97, [1993] 1 S.C.R. 867, 19 C.R. (4th) 169.

However, as stated in *Martineau*, it is appropriate that those who cause harm intentionally should be punished more severely than those who cause harm inadvertently. Moreover, the constitutionality of crimes of negligence is also subject to the caveat that acts of ordinary negligence may not suffice to justify imprisonment. To put it in the terms used in *Hundal*, the negligence must constitute a "marked departure" from the standard of the reasonable person. The law does not lightly brand a person as a criminal.

UNDERLYING PRINCIPLES

I agree with the Chief Justice that the rule that the morally innocent not be punished in the context of the objective test requires that the law refrain from holding a person criminally responsible if he or she is not capable of appreciating the risk. Where I differ from the Chief Justice is in his designation of the sort of educational, experiential, and so-called "habitual" factors personal to the accused which can be taken into account. The Chief Justice, while in principle advocating a uniform standard of care for all, in the result seems to contemplate a standard of care which varies with the background and predis-

position of each accused. Thus an inexperienced, uneducated, young person, like the accused in *R. v. Naglik*, S.C.C. Nos. 22490 and 22636, could be acquitted even though she does not meet the standard of the reasonable person. On the other hand, a person with special experience, like Mr. Creighton in this case, or the appellant police officer in *R. v. Gosset*, S.C.C. No. 22523, will be held to a higher standard than the ordinary reasonable person.

I must respectfully dissent from this extension of the objective test for criminal fault. In my view, considerations of principle and policy dictate the maintenance of a single, uniform legal standard of care for such offences, subject to one exception: incapacity to appreciate the nature of the risk which the activity in question entails.

This principle that the criminal law will not convict the morally innocent does not, in my view, require consideration of personal factors short of incapacity. The criminal law, while requiring mental fault as an element of a conviction, has steadfastly rejected the idea that a person's personal characteristics can (short of incapacity) excuse the person from meeting the standard of conduct imposed by the law.

In summary, I can find no support in criminal theory for the conclusion that protection of the morally innocent requires a general consideration of individual-excusing conditions. The principle comes into play only at the point where the person is shown to lack the capacity to appreciate the nature and quality or the consequences of his or her acts. Apart from this, we are all, rich and poor, wise and naive, held to the minimum standards of conduct prescribed by the criminal law.

To the principle of a uniform minimum standard for crimes having an objective test, there is but one exception — incapacity to appreciate the risk.

Consistent with these principles, this court has rejected experiential, educational, and psychological defences falling short of incapacity.

This test I believe to flow from the fundamental premises of our system of criminal justice. But drawing the line of criminal responsibility for negligent conduct at incapacity is also socially justifiable. In a society which licenses people, expressly or implied, to engage in a wide range of dangerous activities posing risk to the safety of others, it is reasonable to require that those choosing to undertake such activities and possessing the basic capacity to understand their danger take the trouble to exercise that capacity: see *R. v. Hundal, supra*. Not only does the absence of such care connote moral fault, but the sanction of the criminal law is justifiably invoked to deter others who choose to undertake such activities from proceeding without the requisite caution. Even those who lack the advantages of age, experience, and education may properly be held to this standard as a condition of choosing to engage in activities which may maim or kill other innocent people.

The criminal law, as noted, is concerned with setting minimum standards of behaviour in defined circumstances. If this goal is to be achieved, the minimum cannot be lowered because of the frailties or inexperience of the accused, short of incapacity.

But the social justification for a uniform standard of care stops at the point of incapacity. Convicting and punishing a person who lacks the capacity to do what the law says he or she should have done serves no useful purpose. The purpose of Parliament in creating an offence of objective foresight, as in manslaughter, is to stipulate a minimum standard which people engaged in the activity in question are expected to meet. If the standard is lowered by reason of the lack of experience, education, or the presence of some other "personal characteristic" of the accused, the minimum standard which the law imposes on those engaging in the activity in question will be eroded. The objective test inevitably is transformed into a subjective test, violating the wise admonition in *R. v. Hundal, supra*, that there should be a clear distinction in the law between subjective and objective standards, and negating the legislative goal of a minimum standard of care for all those who choose to engage in criminally dangerous conduct.

It may be that, in some cases, educational deficiencies, such as illiteracy on the part of a person

handling a marked bottle of nitroglycerine in the Chief Justice's example, may preclude a person from being able to appreciate the risk entailed by his or her conduct. Problems of perception may have the same effect; regardless of the care taken, the person would have been incapable of assessing the risk, and hence been acquitted. But, in practice, such cases will arise only exceptionally. The question of *mens rea* will arise only where it has been shown that the accused's conduct (the *actus reus*) constitutes a dangerous and unlawful act (as in unlawful act manslaughter), or a marked departure from the standard of care of a reasonably prudent person (as in manslaughter by criminal negligence, or penal negligence offences). This established, conflict with the prohibition against punishing the morally innocent will arise only rarely. In unregulated activities, ordinary common sense is usually sufficient to permit anyone who directs his or her mind to the risk of the danger inherent in an activity to appreciate that risk and act accordingly — be the activity bottle throwing (as in *R. v. DeSousa*) or a bar-room brawl. In many licensed activities, such as driving motor vehicles, there must be a basic amount of knowledge and experience before permission to engage in that activity will be granted (see *R. v. Hundal*). Where individuals engage in activities for which they lack sufficient knowledge, experience, or physical ability, they may be properly found to be at fault, not so much for their inability to properly carry out the activity, but for their decision to attempt the activity without having accounted for their deficiencies. The law expects people embarking on hazardous activities to ask questions or seek help before they venture beyond their depth. Thus even the inexperienced defendant may be properly found to be morally blameworthy for having embarked on a dangerous venture without taking the trouble to properly inform himself or herself. The criminal law imposes a single minimum standard which must be met by all people engaging in the activity in question, provided that they enjoy the requisite capacity to appreciate the danger, and judged in all the circumstances of the case, including unforeseen events and reasonably accepted misinformation. Without a constant minimum standard, the duty imposed by the law would be eroded and the criminal sanction trivialized.

Mental disabilities short of incapacity generally do not suffice to negative criminal liability for criminal negligence. The explanations for why a person fails to advert to the risk inherent in the activity he or she is undertaking are legion. They range from simple absent-mindedness to attributes related to age, education, and culture. To permit such a subjective assessment would be "co-extensive with the judgment of each individual, which would be as variable as the length of the foot of each individual" leaving "so vague a line as to afford no rule at all, the degree of judgment belonging to each individual being infinitely various." Provided the capacity to appreciate the risk is present, lack of education and psychological predispositions serve as no excuse for criminal conduct, although they may be important factors to consider in sentencing.

This is not to say that the question of guilt is determined in a factual vacuum. While the legal duty of the accused is not particularized by his or her personal characteristics short of incapacity, it is particularized in application by the nature of the activity and the circumstances surrounding the accused's failure to take the requisite care. The question is what the reasonably prudent person would have done in all the circumstances. Thus a welder who lights a torch causing an explosion may be excused if he has made an enquiry and been given advice upon which he was reasonably entitled to rely, that there was no explosive gas in the area.

The matter may be looked at in this way. The legal standard of care is always the same — what a reasonable person would have done in all the circumstances. The *de facto* or applied standard of care, however, may vary with the activity in question and the circumstances in the particular case.

We see then that the care required by some activities is greater than the care required by others. For example, under s. 216 of the Criminal Code, it has been held that persons administering medical treatment will be held to the special standard appropriate to that activity. Such a standard has long been recognized by the common law, which made no distinction on the basis of the actor, only on the basis of the activity. The standard flows from the circumstances of the activity. It does not vary with the experience or ability of the actual accused.

A person may fail to meet an elevated *de facto* standard of care in either of two ways. First, the person may undertake an activity requiring special care when he or she is not qualified to give that care. Absent special excuses like necessity, this may constitute culpable negligence. An untrained person undertaking brain surgery might violate the standard in this way. Second, a person who is qualified may negligently fail to exercise the special care required by the activity. A brain surgeon performing surgery in a grossly negligent way might violate the standard in this second way. The standard is the same, although the means by which it is breached may differ.

Just as the adoption of a uniform standard of care which is blind to personal characteristics of the accused short of incapacity precludes lowering the standard for deficiencies of experience and temperament, so it precludes raising the standard for special experience or training. Since the criminal law is concerned with setting minimum standards for human conduct, it would be inappropriate to hold accused persons to a higher standard of care by reason of the fact that they may be better informed or better qualified than the person of reasonable prudence.

The foregoing analysis suggests the following line of inquiry in cases of penal negligence. The first question is whether *actus reus* is established. This requires that the negligence constitute a marked departure from the standards of the reasonable person in all the circumstances of the case. This may consist in carrying out the activity in a dangerous fashion, or in embarking on the activity when in all the circumstances it is dangerous to do so.

The next question is whether the *mens rea* is established. As is the case with crimes of subjective *mens rea*, the *mens rea* for objective foresight of risking harm is normally inferred from the facts. The standard is that of the reasonable person in the circumstances of the accused. If a person has committed a manifestly dangerous act, it is reasonable, absent indications to the contrary, to infer that he or she failed to direct his or her mind to the risk and the need to take care. However, the normal inference may be negated by evidence raising a reasonable doubt as to lack of capacity to appreciate the risk.

I conclude that the legal standard of care for all crimes of negligence is that of the reasonable person. Personal factors are not relevant, except on the question of whether the accused possessed the necessary capacity to appreciate the risk.

C. Application of the Law to This Appeal

The trial judge properly found that Mr. Creighton committed the unlawful act of trafficking in cocaine. He also found that he was guilty of criminal negligence, using the standard which I view as correct, the standard of the reasonable person. The only remaining question, on the view I take of the law, was whether the reasonable person in all the circumstances would have foreseen the risk of bodily harm. I am satisfied that the answer to this question must be affirmative. At the very least, a person administering a dangerous drug like cocaine to another has a duty to inform himself as to the precise risk the injection entails and to refrain from administering it unless reasonably satisfied that there was no risk of harm. That was not the case here, as the trial judge found.

The conviction was properly entered and should not be disturbed. I would answer the constitutional question in the negative and dismiss the appeal.

Appeal dismissed.

Regina v. Hundal

SUPREME COURT OF CANADA   MARCH 11, 1993

BACKGROUND

Hundal was convicted at his trial of dangerous driving causing death. His subsequent appeals to the B.C. Court of Appeal and the Supreme Court of Canada were dismissed.

MAIN ISSUE

What is the nature of the *mens rea* in relation to the offence of dangerous driving? Should the *mens rea* be objective or subjective in nature?

JUDGMENTS

The leading judgment in the Supreme Court of Canada was delivered by Justice Cory (with whom Justices L'Heureux-Dubé, Sopinka, Gonthier, and Iacobucci agreed). Justice McLachlin (with whom Chief Justice Lamer agreed) delivered a judgment that *concurred* with the dismissal of Hundal's appeal. The brief, *concurring* judgment of Justice La Forest has been omitted.

....

CORY J.: — At issue on this appeal is whether there is a subjective element in the requisite *mens rea* which must be established by the Crown in order to prove the offence of dangerous driving described in s. 233 of the Criminal Code, R.S.C. 1970, c. C-34, as amended by 1985, c. 19, s. 36 (now R.S.C. 1985, c. C-46, s. 249).

Factual Background

The accident occurred at about 3:40 in the afternoon in downtown Vancouver. The streets were wet at the time, a situation not uncommon to that city. The downtown traffic was heavy. The appellant was driving his dump truck eastbound on Nelson Street, a four-lane road, approaching its intersection with Cambie Street. At the time, his truck was overloaded. It exceeded by 1160 kg the maximum gross weight permitted for the vehicle. He was travelling in the passing lane for eastbound traffic. The deceased was travelling southbound on Cambie Street. He had stopped for a red light at the intersection with Nelson Street. When the light turned green, the deceased proceeded into the intersection through a cross-walk, continued south across the two lanes for westbound traffic on Nelson Street and reached the passing lane for eastbound traffic. At that moment, his car was struck on the right side by the dump truck, killing him instantly.

The appellant stated that when he approached the intersection of Nelson and Cambie Streets he observed that the light had turned amber. He

....

thought that he could not stop in time so he simply honked his horn and continued through the intersection when the impact occurred. Several witnesses observed the collision. They testified that the appellant's truck entered the intersection after the Nelson Street traffic light had turned red. It was estimated that at least one second had passed between the end of the amber light and the time when the dump truck first entered the intersection. A Vancouver police officer gave evidence that the red light for Nelson at this intersection is preceded by a three-second amber light and there is a further one-half-second delay before the Cambie light turned green. One witness observed that the deceased's vehicle had travelled almost the entire width of the intersection before it was struck by the truck. Another witness, Mr. Mumford, had been travelling close to the appellant's truck through some twelve intersections. He testified that on an earlier occasion, the appellant went through an intersection as the light turned red. He estimated the speed of the truck at the time of the collision was between 50 and 60 km/h.

The trial judge rejected the evidence of the appellant and accepted that of the other witnesses. In his view, the Crown was required to establish "that the accused did not exercise the care of a prudent driver having regard to all the circumstances that were in existence at the time that this collision occurred." He reviewed all the surrounding conditions and found that the appellant's actions represented a gross departure from the standard of care to be expected from a prudent driver. He therefore found the appellant guilty of dangerous driving causing death.

The Constitutional Requirement of *Mens Rea*

The appellant contends that the prison sentence which may be imposed for a breach of s. 233 (now s. 249) makes it evident that an accused cannot be convicted without proof beyond a reasonable doubt of a subjective mental element of an intention to drive dangerously. Certainly every crime requires proof of an act or failure to act, coupled with an ele-

ment of fault, which is termed the *mens rea*. This court has made it clear that s. 7 of the Canadian Charter of Rights and Freedoms prohibits the imposition of imprisonment in the absence of proof of that element of fault: see *Reference re: s. 94(2) of Motor Vehicle Act* (1985), 23 C.C.C. (3d) 289, 24 D.L.R. (4th) 536, [1985] 2 S.C.R. 486, and *R. v. Vaillancourt* (1987), 39 C.C.C. (3d) 118, 47 D.L.R. (4th) 399, [1987] 2 S.C.R. 636.

Depending on the provisions of the particular section and the context in which it appears, the constitutional requirement of *mens rea* may be satisfied in different ways. The offence can require proof of a positive state of mind such as intent, recklessness, or wilful blindness. Alternatively, the *mens rea* or element of fault can be satisfied by proof of negligence whereby the conduct of the accused is measured on the basis of an objective standard without establishing the subjective mental state of the particular accused. In the appropriate context, negligence can be an acceptable basis of liability which meets the fault requirement of s. 7 of the Charter: see *R. v. Wholesale Travel Group Inc.* (1991), 67 C.C.C. (3d) 193, 84 D.L.R. (4th) 161, [1991] 3 S.C.R. 154. Thus, the intent required for a particular offence may be either subjective or objective.

A truly subjective test seeks to determine what was actually in the mind of the particular accused at the moment the offence is alleged to have been committed. On the other hand, the test for negligence is an objective one requiring a marked departure from the standard of care of a reasonable person. There is no need to establish the intention of the particular accused. The question to be answered under the objective test concerns what the accused "should" have known. The potential harshness of the objective standard may be lessened by the consideration of certain personal factors as well as the consideration of a defence of mistake of fact. Nevertheless, there should be a clear distinction in the law between one who was aware (pure subjective intent) and one who should have taken care irrespective of awareness (pure objective intent).

What is the *Mens Rea* Required to Prove the Offence of Dangerous Driving?

The nature of driving offences suggests that an objective test, or more specifically a modified objective test, is particularly appropriate to apply to dangerous driving. I say that for a number of reasons.

(a) THE LICENSING REQUIREMENT

First, driving can only be undertaken by those who have a licence. The effect of the licensing requirement is to demonstrate that those who drive are mentally and physically capable of doing so. Moreover, it serves to confirm that those who drive are familiar with the standards of care which must be maintained by all drivers. There is a further aspect that must be taken into consideration in light of the licensing requirement for drivers. Licensed drivers choose to engage in the regulated activity of driving. They place themselves in a position of responsibility to other members of the public who use the roads.

As a result, it is unnecessary for a court to establish that the particular accused intended or was aware of the consequences of his or her driving. The minimum standard of physical and mental well-being coupled with the basic knowledge of the standard of care required of licensed drivers obviate that requirement. As a general rule, a consideration of the personal factors, so essential in determining subjective intent, is simply not necessary in light of the fixed standards that must be met by licensed drivers.

(b) THE AUTOMATIC AND REFLEXIVE NATURE OF DRIVING

Secondly, the nature of driving itself is often so routine, so automatic that it is almost impossible to determine a particular state of mind of a driver at any given moment. Driving motor vehicles is something that is familiar to most adult Canadians. It cannot be denied that a great deal of driving is done with little conscious thought. It is an activity that is primarily reactive and not contemplative. It is every bit as routine and familiar as taking a shower or going to work. Often it is impossible for a driver to say what his or her specific intent was at any moment during a drive other than the desire to go from A to B.

It would be a denial of common sense for a driver, whose conduct was objectively dangerous, to be acquitted on the ground that he was not thinking of his manner of driving at the time of the accident.

(c) THE WORDING OF S. 233 (NOW S. 249)

Thirdly, the wording of the section itself which refers to the operation of a motor vehicle "in a manner that is dangerous to the public, having regard to all the circumstances," suggests that an objective standard is required. The "manner of driving" can only be compared to a standard of reasonable conduct. That standard can be readily judged and assessed by all who would be members of juries.

Thus, it is clear that the basis of liability for dangerous driving is negligence. The question to be asked is not what the accused subjectively intended but rather whether, viewed objectively, the accused exercised the appropriate standard of care. It is not overly difficult to determine when a driver has fallen markedly below the acceptable standard of care. There can be no doubt that the concept of negligence is well understood and readily recognized by most Canadians. Negligent driving can be thought of as a continuum that progresses, or regresses, from momentary lack of attention, giving rise to civil responsibility through careless driving under a provincial Highway Traffic Act, to dangerous driving under the Criminal Code.

(d) STATISTICS

Fourthly, the statistics, which demonstrate that all too many tragic deaths and disabling injuries flow from the operation of motor vehicles, indicate the need to control the conduct of drivers. The need is obvious and urgent. Section 233 (now s. 249) seeks to curb conduct which is exceedingly dangerous to the public. The statistics on car accidents in Canada indicate with chilling clarity the extent of the problem. The number of people killed and injured each year in traffic accidents is staggering. Data from Transport Canada shows that, in 1991, the number of deaths related to traffic accidents in Canada was 3654. In 1990, there were 178 423 personal injury traffic accidents, 630 000 property damage accidents and 3442 fatal accidents. These figures highlight the tragic social cost which can and does arise from the operation of motor vehicles. There is therefore a compelling need for effective legislation which strives to regulate the manner of driving vehicles and thereby lessen the carnage on our highways. It is not only appropriate but essential in the control of dangerous driving that an objective standard be applied.

In my view, to insist on a subjective mental element in connection with driving offences would be to deny reality. It cannot be forgotten that the operation of a motor vehicle is, as I have said so very often, automatic and with little conscious thought. It is simply inappropriate to apply a subjective test in determining whether an accused is guilty of dangerous driving.

(e) MODIFIED OBJECTIVE TEST

Although an objective test must be applied to the offence of dangerous driving, it will remain open to the accused to raise a reasonable doubt that a reasonable person would have been aware of the risks in the accused's conduct. The test must be applied with some measure of flexibility. That is to say, the objective test should not be applied in a vacuum but rather in the context of the events surrounding the incident.

There will be occasions when the manner of driving viewed objectively will clearly be dangerous, yet the accused should not be convicted. Take for example a driver who, without prior warning, suffers a totally unexpected heart attack, epileptic seizure, or detached retina. As a result of the sudden onset of a disease or physical disability, the manner of driving would be dangerous, yet those

circumstances could provide a complete defence despite the objective demonstration of dangerous driving. Similarly, a driver who, in the absence of any warning or knowledge of its possible effects, takes a prescribed medication which suddenly and unexpectedly affects the driver in such a way that the manner of driving was dangerous to the public, could still establish a good defence to the charge although it had been objectively established. These examples, and there may well be others, serve to illustrate the aim and purpose of the modified objective test. It is to enable a court to take into account the sudden and unexpected onset of disease and similar human frailties as well as the objective demonstration of dangerous driving.

In summary, the *mens rea* for the offence of dangerous driving should be assessed objectively but in the context of all the events surrounding the incident. That approach will satisfy the dictates both of common sense and fairness. As a general rule, personal factors need not be taken into account. This flows from the licensing requirement for driving, which assures that all who drive have a reasonable standard of physical health and capability, mental health, and a knowledge of the reasonable standard required of all licensed drivers.

In light of the licensing requirement and the nature of driving offences, a modified objective test satisfies the constitutional minimum fault requirement for s. 233 (now s. 249) of the Criminal Code and is eminently well-suited to that offence.

It follows then that a trier of fact may convict if satisfied beyond a reasonable doubt that, viewed objectively, the accused was, in the words of the section, driving in a manner that was "dangerous to the public, having regard to all the circumstances, including the nature, condition and use of such place and the amount of traffic that at the time is or might reasonably be expected to be on such place." In making the assessment, the trier of fact should be satisfied that the conduct amounted to a marked departure from the standard of care that a reasonable person would observe in the accused's situation.

Next, if an explanation is offered by the accused, such as a sudden and unexpected onset of illness, then in order to convict, the trier of fact must be satisfied that a reasonable person in similar circumstances ought to have been aware of the risk and of the danger involved in the conduct manifested by the accused. If a jury is determining the facts, they may be instructed with regard to dangerous driving along the lines set out above. There is no necessity for a long or complex charge. Neither the section nor the offence requires it. Certainly the instructions should not be unnecessarily confused by any references to advertent or inadvertent negligence. The offence can be readily assessed by jurors who can arrive at a conclusion based on common sense and their own everyday experiences.

Application of These Principles to the Facts

Let us now consider whether the modified objective test was properly applied in this case. The trial judge carefully examined the circumstances of the accident. He took into account the busy downtown traffic, the weather conditions, and the mechanical conditions of the accused vehicle. He concluded, in my view very properly, that the appellant's manner of driving represented a gross departure from the standard of a reasonably prudent driver. No explanation was offered by the accused that could excuse his conduct. There is no reason for interfering with the trial judge's finding of fact and application of the law.

In the result, the appeal must be dismissed.

McLACHLIN J.: — I agree with the reasons and disposition proposed by Justice Cory, but wish to add certain observations on the concept of fault and the "modified objective test."

The label "modified objective test" might be taken to suggest an amalgam of objective and subjective factors; a test that looks at what ought to have been in the accused's mind, but goes on to consider what was actually there or not there. If this is what it means, it runs afoul of Professor Stuart's sensible admonition that jurists should be very clear about whether they are convicting on the basis of the subjective test or the objective test. On the objective test, the Crown is not required to establish what was in the accused's mind as a matter of fact.

Consideration of the context in which the term has been used suggests that the phrase "modified objective test" was introduced in an effort to ensure that jurists applying the objective test take into account all relevant circumstances in the events surrounding the alleged offence and give the accused an opportunity to raise a reasonable doubt as to what a reasonable person would have thought in the particular situation in which the accused found himself or herself. Thus, Cory J. in discussing the modified objective test stresses that "personal factors" may be raised, and affirms that "it will remain open to the accused to raise a reasonable doubt that a reasonable person would have been aware of the risks in the accused's conduct." He goes on to say: "The test must be applied with some measure of flexibility. That is to say, the objective test should not be applied in a vacuum but rather in the context of the events surrounding the incident."

If, as my colleague suggests, McIntyre J. was describing a modified objective test in *R. v. Tutton* (1989), 48 C.C.C. (3d) 129 at p. 140, [1989] 1 S.C.R. 1392, 69 C.R. (3d) 289, the language and example used indicate that his concern too was to ensure that in applying the objective test all relevant circumstances, including those personal to the accused, be considered. He reaffirms the objective test by asserting that only "an honest and reasonably held belief" can exonerate the accused. In other words, it is no defence to say, on the subjective level, "I was being careful," or "I believed I could do what I did without undue risk." The defence arises only if that belief was reasonably held. McIntyre J. goes on to offer the example of a welder who is engaged to work in a confined space believing, on the assurance of the owner of the premises, that no combustible or explosive material is nearby. The welder charged in connection with a subsequent explosion, McIntyre J. asserts, should be allowed to introduce evidence that he believed there were no combustible or explosive materials on the premises. This is an objective test; the fact that the welder had been told there were no combustible or explosive materials on the site is one of the circumstances which a jury should take into account in determining what a reasonable person would have thought and done. Was it reasonable for the welder in these circumstances to turn his torch on in the enclosed space? The answer, on the objective test, is "of course."

Nor does Cory J.'s example of "a totally unexpected heart attack, epileptic seizure, or detached retina," which renders an accused unable to control his or her motor vehicle, require the introduction of an element of subjectivity. The better analysis, in my view, is that the onset of a "disease or disability" makes the act of losing control of the motor vehicle involuntary, with the result that there is no *actus reus*. Thus, we do not reach the question of what a reasonable person would have been thinking or adverting to as the car goes off the road, much less what the accused was in fact thinking or not thinking. Alternatively, if the *actus reus* were taken as established in these examples, the heart attack or epileptic seizure might be viewed as a circumstance which negates the ordinary inference of want of care which flows from the fact of having lost control of a motor vehicle.

I would dispose of the appeal as proposed by Cory J.

Appeal dismissed.

Regina v. Tutton and Tutton

SUPREME COURT OF CANADA   JUNE 8, 1989

BACKGROUND

The two co-accused, who were husband and wife, were charged with the manslaughter of their five-year-old son. The indictment specified that they had been criminally negligent* insofar as they had failed, without lawful excuse, to provide the necessities of life to their child (in this case, insulin injections), as they were required to do by the provisions of section 197 (now section 215) of the Criminal Code. The accused were convicted by a jury at their trial. They appealed to the Ontario Court of Appeal, which allowed their appeal and ordered new trials. The Crown then appealed to the Supreme Court of Canada against the judgment of the Court of Appeal.

MAIN ISSUE

Is the *mens rea* for criminal negligence to be determined by an *objective* or a *subjective* test?

JUDGMENTS

While all the members of the Supreme Court agreed that the Crown's appeal should be dismissed, they were evenly divided (3-3) on the question of whether the *mens rea* for criminal negligence was *objective* or *subjective*. Justice McIntyre (with whom Justice L'Heureux-Dubé agreed) ruled that the test was *objective*. Justice Lamer concurred with the judgment of Justice McIntyre, although his reasoning was somewhat different (this judgment has been omitted). Justice Wilson (with whom Chief Justice Dickson and Justice La Forest agreed) ruled that the test was *subjective* in nature.

....

MCINTYRE J.: — This appeal raises again the question of criminal negligence, as defined in s. 202 of the Criminal Code, R.S.C. 1970, c. C-34, and the test to be applied by a jury in its application to a given case.

The respondents, Carol Anne Tutton and Arthur Thomas Tutton, were the parents of a five-year-old child, Christopher Tutton, who died on October 17, 1981.

The Tuttons, according to the evidence, which was unquestioned on this point, had a good reputation in their community for honesty and integrity and, as well, they were loving and responsible parents. They were also deeply religious and they belonged to a religious sect which believes in faith healing. Their religious convictions did not prevent

---

* Criminal negligence was defined by section 202 (now section 219) of the Criminal Code.

---

them from seeking and acting on medical advice nor from taking medicines, but they believed that divine intervention could miraculously effect cures for illnesses and ailments beyond the power of modern medical science.

In April of 1979, their family physician, a general practitioner named Dr. Love, diagnosed the child, Christopher, as a diabetic and admitted him to hospital where he remained for some weeks. While the child was in hospital, his mother attended classes at a diabetic education centre where she received instruction regarding insulin injections and the impact of diet and exercise on diabetes and diabetics. She also attended in July, 1979, a full week of seminars at a juvenile diabetic clinic to gain an understanding of her son's condition and to learn how to deal with it. There was then evidence upon which the jury could conclude that Mrs. Tutton had made herself competent to deal with her child's illness under general supervision from the family physician.

Throughout the son's illness, the Tuttons main concern was to find a cure for the boy. They both believed that there would be a spiritual cure. They discussed this possibility with Dr. Love who considered that there was no possibility of a miraculous cure, and in November, 1979, a diabetic specialist from the Sick Children's Hospital in Toronto advised the respondents that their son would never be able to discontinue his insulin injections. He told the respondents not to discontinue the insulin treatments. However, on October 2, 1980, Mrs. Tutton stopped giving the child insulin in the belief that he was being healed by the power of the Holy Spirit. In two days, the child became quite ill and was taken to a hospital emergency unit. The physician who attended the child said that on admission to hospital the child was dangerously ill, suffering from diabetic acidosis, a potentially fatal disorder, which was due to the absence of insulin. The doctor admonished the parents when he learned that they had consciously withheld the insulin. He told the parents that insulin would be required by their son for life, and after this incident Mr. Tutton assured the family physician that insulin would not

be withheld in future without consulting a doctor. A year later, however, insulin was again stopped. Mrs. Tutton believed that she had a vision of God in which she was told that Christopher was cured, that no more insulin was needed, and that God would take care of her son. The insulin injections were stopped on October 14, 1981. Mr. Tutton did not know of the withdrawal of insulin until October 15 but on learning of it he approved. The child sickened quickly. On October 17, he was taken to the hospital where he was pronounced dead on arrival. The forensic pathologist who conducted a postmortem examination gave his opinion that death was caused by complications of diabetic hyperglycemia. The respondents were jointly charged with manslaughter in an indictment which provided:

ARTHUR TUTTON AND CAROL TUTTON stand charged that between the period of the 14th day of October, 1981, and the 17th day of October, 1981, both dates inclusive, at the Township of Wilmot, in the Judicial District of Waterloo, being the parents of Christopher Tutton, they did cause the death of Christopher Tutton, age five years, by criminal negligence, to wit, they did, without lawful excuse, omit to provide necessaries of life to Christopher Tutton, which was their duty to provide, thereby showing wanton or reckless disregard for the life or safety of the said Christopher Tutton, and did thereby commit manslaughter, contrary to the Criminal Code.

Particulars were given in these terms:

It is further particularized that the said Arthur Tutton and Carol Tutton failed, without lawful excuse, while their said son, Christopher, was in necessitous circumstances,

(1) to provide insulin to him
(2) to obtain timely medical assistance for him.

At trial, the defence was that, as far as the Crown's case rested on the failure to provide insulin, the Tuttons honestly believed that Christopher had been cured by divine intervention and, therefore, no further insulin was necessary. This would raise the defence of an honest though mistaken belief in the existence of a circumstance or circumstances which, if present, would render their conduct non-culpable. It was also argued that, as far as the Crown's case depended upon a failure to provide timely medical assistance for their son, the parents were unaware of the fact that he was seriously ill as a result of the withdrawal of the insulin and, accordingly, their conduct in this regard could not be said to exhibit a wanton or reckless disregard for the life or safety of their son.

The Crown has alleged that the appellants have caused the death of their son by criminal negligence and did thereby commit manslaughter. It has particularized its allegation in the indictment and also in the particulars, alleging that the appellants without lawful excuse did omit to provide necessaries of life to their son which it was their duty to provide. This failure is the basis of the allegation of wanton or reckless disregard for the life or safety of their son and it is the sole basis on which the charge of manslaughter may be supported. It is therefore clear that while the appellants are charged with the commission of one specific offence, manslaughter, the Crown may only succeed in its proof by establishing the commission of a different offence, provided for in s. 197(2) of the Criminal Code, and one in which a burden of proof relating to the question of lawful excuse is imposed on the accused.

The task of a trial judge charging a jury in these circumstances would be difficult and, in my view, it would be necessary to keep clearly separate the two offences or the elements of the two offences that must be dealt with. This could be achieved by approaching the charge in two steps. The first step, I suggest, would be to deal with the underlying offence in s. 197(2) of the Code, for under this indictment, until this question is settled, no approach can be made to the crime of manslaughter actually charged. The jury should be instructed on the elements of the offence under s. 197 and told that for a conviction under that section they must

be satisfied beyond a reasonable doubt that the appellants were under a duty to provide necessaries of life to their son, and that they failed to do so without lawful excuse. If they were not so satisfied, they would acquit the accused and go no further, for the sole basis of the manslaughter allegation would be gone. If, however, they were to find that the accused had failed to provide the necessaries without lawful excuse, then it would be necessary for them to go further and consider whether in such failure they had shown a wanton and reckless disregard for the life and safety of their son. If the jury were satisfied beyond a reasonable doubt that such conduct had been shown and that it had caused the death of the child, they would be obligated to convict of manslaughter, and on this indictment, that is the only way a conviction of manslaughter could be reached. If, on the other hand, the jury were not so satisfied, they would be required to acquit the accused of the crime of manslaughter. If, however, they were satisfied that the necessaries of life had been withheld but in doubt as to whether the deprivation was the cause of the son's death, they could in that case convict of the included offence under s. 197; otherwise they would acquit. The advantage, in my view, of putting the matter to the jury in this manner is that it would clarify the separate issues and make it clear that, in reaching a conclusion on the offence of manslaughter, it is the conduct of the parents in relation to the provision of necessaries and medical assistance which must be considered in deciding if wanton and reckless disregard has been shown.

Our concept of criminal culpability relies primarily upon a consideration of the mental state which accompanies or initiates the wrongful act, and the attribution of criminal liability without proof of such a blameworthy mental state raises serious concerns. Nonetheless, negligence has become accepted as a factor which may lead to criminal liability and strong arguments can be raised in its favour. Section 202 of the Criminal Code affords an example of its adoption. In choosing the test to be applied in assessing conduct under s. 202 of the Criminal Code, it must be observed at once that what is made criminal is negligence. Negligence connotes the opposite of thought-directed action. In other words, its existence precludes the element of positive intent to achieve a given result. This leads to the conclusion that what is sought to be restrained by punishment under s. 202 of the Code is conduct and its results. What is punished, in other words, is not the state of mind but the consequence of mindless action. This is apparent, I suggest, from the words of the section, which make criminal, conduct that *shows* wanton or reckless disregard. It may be observed as well that the words "wanton or reckless" support this construction, denying as they do the existence of a directing mental state. Nor can it be said that criminal negligence, as defined in s. 202, imports in its terms some element of malice or intention.

In my view, then, an objective standard must be applied in determining this question because of the difference between the ordinary criminal offence, which requires proof of a subjective state of mind, and that of criminal negligence. In criminal cases, generally, the act coupled with the mental state or intent is punished. In criminal negligence, the act which exhibits the requisite degree of negligence is punished. If this distinction is not kept clear, the dividing line between the traditional *mens rea* offence and the offence of criminal negligence becomes blurred. The difference, for example, between murder and manslaughter, both unlawful killings, is merely one of intent. If the question of an accused's intent had to be considered and separately proved in offences under s. 202 of the Criminal Code, the purpose of the section would be defeated because intentional conduct would perforce be considered under other sections of the Code, and s. 202, aimed at mindless but socially dangerous conduct, would have no function. For these reasons, the objective test should be employed and, in my view, the Court of Appeal was in error in concluding in this case that a subjective test would be required. The test is that of reasonableness, and proof of conduct, which reveals a marked and significant departure from the standard that could be expected of a reasonably prudent person in the circumstances, will justify a conviction of criminal negligence.

The application of an objective test under s. 202 of the Criminal Code, however, may not be made in a vacuum. Events occur within the framework of other events and actions, and when deciding on the nature of the questioned conduct, surrounding circumstances must be considered. The decision must be made on a consideration of the facts existing at the time and in relation to the accused's perception of those facts. Since the test is objective, the accused's perception of the facts is not to be considered for the purpose of assessing malice or intention on the accused's part, but only to form a basis for a conclusion as to whether or not the accused's conduct, in view of his perception of the facts, was reasonable. This is particularly true where, as here, the accused have raised the defence of mistake of fact. If an accused under s. 202 has an honest and reasonably held belief in the existence of certain facts, it may be a relevant consideration in assessing the reasonableness of his conduct. For example, a welder, who is engaged to work in a confined space, believing, on the assurance of the owner of the premises, that no combustible or explosive material is stored nearby, should be entitled to have his perception, as to the presence or absence of dangerous materials, before the jury on a charge of manslaughter when his welding torch causes an explosion and a consequent death.

As noted earlier, the Tuttons raised the defence of mistake of fact at trial. They argued that the failure to supply insulin was based upon the belief that the child had been cured by divine intervention and that the failure to provide medical care in timely fashion was based upon the belief that the child was not seriously ill, so medical assistance was not necessary. The trial judge, it was argued, was in error in telling the jury that for any such belief to be effective as a defence it must have been reasonably held. It was held in this court in *Pappajohn v. The Queen* (1980), 52 C.C.C. (2d 481, 111 D.L.R. (3d) 1, [1980] 2 S.C.R. 120 (S.C.C.), that an honest, though mistaken, belief in the existence of circumstances which, if present, would make the questioned conduct non-culpable would entitle an accused to an acquittal. It was also held in *Pappajohn* that the honest belief need not be reasonable, because its effect would be to deny the existence of the requisite *mens rea*. The situation would be different, however, where the offence charged rests upon the concept of negligence, as opposed to that of the guilty mind or blameworthy mental state. In such a case, an unreasonable, though honest, belief on the part of the accused would be negligently held. The holding of such a belief could not afford a defence when culpability is based on negligent conduct. I would therefore conclude that the trial judge made no error in charging the jury to the effect that any mistaken belief which could afford a defence in a charge of criminal negligence would have to be reasonable.

In the case at bar, then, the assertion of the Tuttons that they believed a cure had been effected by divine intervention and that insulin was not necessary for the preservation of the child's life would have to be considered by the jury. The jury would have to consider whether such belief was honest and whether it was reasonable. In this, they would be required to consider the whole background of the case. They would have to take into account the experience of the Tuttons with the child's illness; the fact that they had seen the result of the withdrawal of insulin on one occasion and that they had been informed of its necessity for the continued care of the child; and that Mrs. Tutton had received some formal instruction or training in dealing with diabetes and diabetics. They would, as well, have to consider whether the belief in a miraculous cure leading to the conclusion that insulin and medical care were not required, though honest, was reasonable. Upon these facts and all others concerning the matter which were revealed in the evidence, the jury would be required to decide whether the refusal of insulin and medical attention represented a marked and significant departure from the standard to be observed by reasonably prudent parents.

I would dismiss the appeal and confirm the direction for a new trial.

WILSON J.: — I have had the benefit of the reasons of my colleagues McIntyre and Lamer JJ. and I agree with them that the appeal should be dismissed and a new trial ordered because the trial judge's charge failed to make clear to the jury that the Crown had the burden to prove all the elements of the offence of manslaughter by criminal negligence. I do not, however, agree with my colleagues' conclusion that criminal negligence under [s. 219] of the Criminal Code consists only of conduct in breach of an objective standard and does not require the Crown to prove that the accused had any degree of guilty knowledge. I also have reservations concerning the approach my colleagues suggest is available in order to relieve against the harshness of the objective standard of liability which they find in [s. 219], and to ensure that the morally innocent are not punished for the commission of serious criminal offences committed through criminal negligence.

I wish to deal first with the implications of my colleagues' approach in this case. By concluding that [s. 219] of the Criminal Code prohibits conduct and the consequences of mindless action absent any blameworthy state of mind, they have, in effect, held that the crime of criminal negligence is an absolute liability offence. Conviction follows upon proof of conduct which reveals a marked and substantial departure from the standard expected of a reasonably prudent person in the circumstances regardless of what was actually in the accused's mind at the time the act was committed.

This court made clear in *R. v. Sault Ste. Marie* (1978), 40 C.C.C. (2d) 353, 85 D.L.R. (3d) 161, [1978] 2 S.C.R. 1299 (S.C.C.), and other cases that the imposition of criminal liability in the absence of proof of a blameworthy state of mind, either as an inference from the nature of the act committed or by other evidence, is an anomaly which does not sit comfortably with the principles of penal liability and fundamental justice. This is particularly so in the case of offences carrying a substantial term of imprisonment which, by their nature, severity and attendant stigma, are true criminal offences aimed at punishing culpable behaviour as opposed to securing the public welfare. In the absence of clear statutory language and purpose to the contrary, this court should, in my view, be most reluctant to interpret a serious criminal offence as an absolute liability offence.

In this case there can be no doubt that we are dealing with a serious criminal offence. The appellants are charged with committing manslaughter by criminal negligence. Under [s. 236] of the Criminal Code they are liable to imprisonment for life. Other offences committed by means of criminal negligence are also serious.

Section [219] of the Criminal Code is, in my view, notorious in its ambiguity. Since its enactment in its present form in the 1955 amendments to the Criminal Code, it has bedevilled both courts and commentators who have sought out its meaning. The interpretation put upon it usually depends upon which words are emphasized. On the one hand, my colleague's judgment demonstrates that emphasizing the use of the words "shows" and "negligence" can lead to the conclusion that an objective standard of liability was intended and that proof of unreasonable conduct alone will suffice. On the other hand, if the words "wanton or reckless disregard for the lives or safety of other persons" are stressed along with the fact that what is prohibited is not negligence *simpliciter* but "criminal" negligence, one might conclude that Parliament intended some degree of advertence to the risk to the lives or safety of others to be an essential element of the offence. When faced with such fundamental ambiguity, it would be my view that the court should give the provision the interpretation most consonant, not only with the text and purpose of the provision, but also, where possible, with the broader concepts and principles of the law.

It is my view that the phrase "reckless disregard for the lives or safety of other persons" found in [s. 219], when read in the context of Canadian criminal law jurisprudence, requires the Crown to prove advertence or awareness of the risk that the prohibited consequences will come to pass.

The expression "wanton disregard for the lives and safety of others" is perhaps less clear. The word

"wanton" taken in its acontextual sense could signal an element of randomness or arbitrariness more akin to an objective standard but, given the context in which it appears, coupled with the adjective "reckless," and its clear use to accentuate and make more heinous the already serious matter of disregard for the lives or safety of others, I would think that the preferable interpretation is that the word "wanton" was intended to connote wilful blindness to the prohibited risk.

In short, the phrase "wanton or reckless disregard for the lives or safety of other persons" signifies more than gross negligence in the objective sense. It requires some degree of awareness or advertence to the threat to the lives or safety of others, or, alternatively, a wilful blindness to the threat which is culpable in light of the gravity of the risk that is prohibited.

Conduct that displays a wanton or reckless disregard for the lives or safety of others will constitute the *actus reus* of the offence under [s. 219] and the *prima facie* evidence of the accused's blameworthy state of mind. It can be assumed that a person functioning with normal faculties of awareness and engaging in conduct which represents such a grave departure from the norm is either aware of the risk or is wilfully blind to the risk. Proof of the conduct will, in other words, cast an evidential burden on the accused to explain why the normal inference of conscious awareness or wilful blindness should not be drawn. The inference will arise in most cases because the intent requirement under [s. 219] is the minimal intent requirement of awareness or advertence or wilful blindness to the prohibited risk.

I agree with my colleague McIntyre J. that malice or intent in the sense of a mind directed to a purpose is not an element of [s. 219]. Moreover, the fact that the accused may desire or calculate that his purpose can be achieved without the realization of the risk does not relieve the accused of liability under [s. 219] if he either adverted to or became aware of the risk to the lives or safety of others or wilfully closed his eyes to the reality of that risk.

The words of the section can reasonably bear an interpretation which leaves room for the mental element of awareness or advertence to a risk to the lives or safety of others or wilful blindness to such risk. Conduct which shows a wanton or reckless disregard for the lives and safety of others will by its nature constitute *prima facie* evidence of the mental element, and, in the absence of some evidence that casts doubt on the normal degree of mental awareness, proof of the act and reference to what a reasonable person in the circumstances must have realized will lead to a conclusion that the accused was aware of the risk or wilfully blind to the risk.

I would add that the importance of what the reasonable person would have foreseen to the determination of whether a particular accused would have become aware or wilfully blind to the prohibited risk will vary with the context. For example, in the case of a licensed driver engaging in high-risk motoring, I am in general agreement with Morden J.A. in *R. v. Sharp* (1984), 12 C.C.C. (3d) 428 at pp. 434–5, 39 C.R. (3d) 367, 26 M.V.R. 279 (Ont. C.A.), that it is open to the jury to find the accused's blameworthy state of mind from driving that shows wanton or reckless disregard for the lives or safety of others subject to an explanation in the evidence which would account for the deviant conduct, such as a sudden mechanical malfunction or a bee sting or other accident beyond the accused's control. I would think that in the driving context, where risks to the lives and safety of others present themselves in a habitual and obvious fashion, the accused's claim that he or she gave no thought to the risk or has simply a negative state of mind would in most, if not all, cases amount to the culpable positive mental state of wilful blindness to the prohibited risk.

The minimal nature of the requirement of a blameworthy state of mind and the relevance of the objective standard as a refutable mode of proof suggests to me that a holding that [s. 219] requires proof of the mental element of advertence to the risk or wilful blindness to the risk will not undermine the policy objectives of the provision. The loss in terms of deterrence and social protection would seem to be negligible when the retention of a subjective standard would at most offer protection for those who, due to some peculiarity or unexpected accident, commit conduct which, although it shows a reckless or wanton disregard for the lives or safety of others, can be explained as inconsistent with any degree of awareness of or wilful blindness to such a risk. Should social protection require the adoption of an objective standard, it is open to Parliament to enact a law which clearly adopts such a standard. In my respectful view, this court should not do it for them.

To sum up, although I agree with my colleagues as to the proper disposition of this appeal, I am unable to agree with their conclusion that the offence of manslaughter by criminal negligence consists of conduct in breach of an objective standard.

Appeal dismissed.

Waite v. The Queen

SUPREME COURT OF CANADA   JUNE 8, 1989

BACKGROUND

Waite was charged with four counts of criminal negligence causing death, contrary to section 203 [now section 220] of the Criminal Code, and one count of criminal negligence causing bodily harm, contrary to section 204 [now section 221]. At his trial, the jury returned verdicts of not guilty in relation to all of the criminal negligence charges but convicted him instead of dangerous driving on all charges. The Crown's appeal to the Ontario Court of Appeal was allowed and a new trial was ordered. Waite appealed to the Supreme Court of Canada against the judgment of the Court of Appeal.

MAIN ISSUE

Is the *mens rea* for criminal negligence, as defined by section 202 [now section 219] of the Criminal Code, to be determined by an *objective* or a *subjective* test?

JUDGMENTS

While all the members of the Supreme Court agreed that the accused's appeal should be dismissed, they were evenly divided (3-3) on the question of whether the *mens rea* for criminal negligence was *objective* or *subjective*. Justice McIntyre (with

whom Justice L'Heureux-Dubé agreed) ruled that the test was *objective*. The *concurring* judgment of Justice Lamer has been omitted. Justice Wilson (with whom Chief Justice Dickson and Justice La Forest agreed) ruled that the test was *subjective* in nature.

....

McINTYRE J.: — The events giving rise to this appeal occurred on September 8, 1984. Between approximately 3:15 P.M. and 6:00 P.M. on that day the appellant consumed about five bottles or tins of beer at a fall fair in the arena at Drayton, Ontario. At about 7:00 P.M. he consumed two more bottles of beer. At about 8:20 P.M. on the same day the Bethel Mennonite Church hayride commenced. The hayride was made up of three tractors, each of which towed one wagon containing bales of hay. The wagons proceeded along the public road, one after the other, and some forty or fifty people, mostly young, rode in the wagons. The accused, accompanied by two friends, followed the wagons in his car. He had a bottle or tin of beer in his hand while driving. Evidence was given by certain witnesses that some of the hayride participants, four or five in number, were walking or running along the road beside the wagons and moving from the second wagon to the first wagon. The appellant drove past the wagons and he and his passengers testified that in passing the vehicles they did not observe anyone on the roadway. Having passed the hayride, the appellant proceeded some distance down the highway and there turned his car around and drove back along the road towards the now oncoming hayride. The appellant gave evidence that at this time he said to his companions: "Let's see how close we can get." One of the passengers testified that the accused had said: "Let's play chicken." The accused drove toward the hayride on the left side of the road. He was thus heading directly for the hayride vehicles and travelling on their side of the road. The posted speed on the road was 50 m.p.h. The accused testified that he was travelling at approximately 70 m.p.h. Other estimates of the speed, drawn from the evidence given at trial, vary from 50 to 90 m.p.h. The appellant at this time was driving without his headlights. He was using only fog lights, though the state of light was such that headlights would ordinarily have been required. He continued in the left lane, approaching the hayride until he was, according to the evidence, some 150 feet from the leading tractor, at which time he swerved into the right lane to pass the hayride. As he passed the wagons, he struck five members of the hayride party who were on the roadway running along beside the wagons. Four were struck by the car and killed; one was injured, suffering a fractured leg. After the impact, the appellant brought his vehicle to a halt and removed a cooler of beer from the trunk and threw it into the adjacent field.

Evidence was given at trial of blood alcohol readings taken after the accident. They showed that the appellant's blood alcohol level was something in excess of 80 milligrams of alcohol per 100 millilitres of blood, and expert evidence was to the effect that the appellant's blood alcohol would have been approximately 110 to 112 milligrams of alcohol per 100 millilitres of blood at the time of the accident. The appellant and his passengers testified that they had not expected to find any of the hayride party on the road, and the appellant testified to the effect that he was not aware of the presence of anyone on the road until the accident occurred.

The Code has defined the concept of criminal negligence, and the issue raised in this appeal is how the Code definition should be applied. More particularly, how should a jury be instructed when it must consider a case involving a charge of criminal negligence?

The crime of criminal negligence is a crime that, like other criminal offences, requires proof by the Crown of a *mens rea*. In instructing the jury on this question, the trial judge set out the following test. He said:

> On all the evidence, after considering all the circumstances, are you satisfied that the accused's conduct was such as to amount to a wanton or reckless disregard for the safety of other persons?
>
> The driver of a motor vehicle on a public highway is under a duty to take care in its operation so as to avoid injury to persons or property of others, and if he fails in that duty and his acts or omissions are of such a character as to show this wanton or reckless disregard for the lives and safety of others, then, according to the law, that conduct amounts to criminal negligence.
>
> The lack of intention to cause harm is not an answer to a charge of criminal negligence. What you are concerned with is the conduct of the accused at the time of the accident or immediately prior thereto, and if that conduct, when you view it objectively, shows a wanton and reckless disregard for the lives and safety of others, then that is criminal negligence as defined in the Criminal Code.

And he added later:

> If the evidence satisfies you beyond a reasonable doubt that the driving behaviour of the accused was a flagrant departure from normal driving standards, in the absence of some explanation, some rational explanation, then the driving conduct is properly characterized as criminal negligence. Dangerous driving, to give you a distinction between them, is conduct of a lesser nature and it lacks that high degree of moral fault required for criminal negligence.

In this, it is my opinion that the trial judge correctly dealt with the question. He was telling the jury that the *mens rea* required for proof of the commission of the offence could be found in the conduct of the accused. He did not mention specifically the test that has become accepted in this and most appellate courts in Canada, to the effect that criminal negligence is shown where the Crown proves conduct on the part of the accused which shows a marked and substantial departure from the standard of behaviour expected of a reasonably prudent person in the circumstances, but in my view he conveyed in the quoted words an adequate instruction.

After about two hours of deliberation the jury returned for further instructions and put the following question to the trial judge: "What is the moral difference between dangerous driving and criminal negligence. We want a clearer definition." The trial judge heard submissions from counsel on the question of the test for determining the *mens rea* of criminal negligence and then gave the jury a further direction in these terms:

> The position is that in dangerous driving the intention or the state of mind, if you wish, of the driver is not important. You look objectively at the manner of driving. You just look at the manner of driving.
>
> Now, when you go over to criminal negligence, you have to look at two things, the objective driving, as you do for dangerous driving, and you also have to look at the subjective element, that is the attitude, or what is in the mind of the accused. That is whether there is a deliberate and wilful assumption of the risk involved in driving in the manner in which he was driving. So that you have in one, the dangerous driving, there is simply an objective standard, as compared to what the prudent driver would do. In the criminal negligence you have that, plus the subjective element of assumption and deliberate assumption of the risk.

The jury then returned a verdict of not guilty on all the criminal negligence charges but guilty of dangerous driving on all charges.

In the Court of Appeal, the Crown's appeal was allowed and a new trial was ordered. Cory J.A. considered that the requisite *mens rea* for criminal negligence may be objectively determined from the action or conduct of an accused. He considered that the trial judge in responding to the question from the jury was in error in telling the jury that criminal negligence involves a subjective element and requires the deliberate assumption of risk by an accused. He was also of the view that the trial judge's final instructions placed too high an onus on the Crown, in requiring the application by the jury of a subjective test for the determination of the required *mens rea*. He said, at p. 344:

> This placed too high an onus on the Crown. It would have been sufficient had the trial judge simply read [s. 219] of the Code to the jury together with the instruction that the driving had to amount to a marked and substantial departure from the standard of a reasonable driver.

The appellant argued in this court that the Court of Appeal erred in adopting an objective test in determining the *mens rea* of criminal negligence. It was argued that such a test was not in accord with the authorities, and that a subjective test inquiring into the mind and mental state of the accused was required. It was also argued that the Court of Appeal had erred in arriving at the conclusion that the Crown had satisfied the onus that the verdict would not necessarily have been the same in the absence of the error found in the charge to the jury. In my view, neither of these arguments can succeed.

In limiting the application of the objective test to cases involving acts of commission and in holding that an objective test will not suffice for cases involving acts of omission, it is my view that Cory J.A. was in error. An objective test must be applied in cases based on an allegation of criminal negligence, whether by acts of commission or omission. In all other respects I would, as I have said, adopt as my own the reasons for judgment of Cory J.A., dismiss the appeal, and confirm the order for a new trial.

WILSON J.: — Although I find myself in respectful disagreement for the reasons I gave in *R. v. Tutton and Tutton,* [1989] 1 S.C.R. 1392, 48 C.C.C. (3d) 129, 69 C.R. (3d) 289, 98 N.R. 19, 13 M.V.R. (2d) 161 (S.C.C.), with my colleague McIntyre J. insofar as he adopts an objective test for criminal negligence, I agree with him that this appeal should be dismissed and the Court of Appeal's order for a new trial affirmed.

In my view, the trial judge's final instruction to the jury was in error as to the degree of *mens rea* required under [s. 219] of the Criminal Code, R.S.C. 1970, c. C-34. When the jury asked the trial judge to explain the moral difference between dangerous driving and causing death by criminal negligence, the trial judge instructed the jury that the subjective element in criminal negligence was "a deliberate and wilful assumption of the risk involved in driving in the manner in which he was driving." Later in his reply to the jury he repeated that the subjective element in criminal negligence was "assumption and deliberate assumption of the risk." Although I believe there is a subjective element to criminal negligence, the judge in this case placed much too high an onus on the Crown to prove elements of deliberation and wilfulness. For the reasons I gave in *Tutton,* I am of the view that the mental element in criminal negligence is the minimal intent of awareness of the prohibited risk or wilful blindness to the risk.

The trial judge's erroneous instructions to the jury were given near the close of the trial and they were crucial because they were in response to a question from the jury. The facts of the case also suggest that, had the jury been instructed as to the minimal intent requirements of awareness or wilful blindness to the prohibited risk, they would not necessarily have returned the verdict of acquittal on the charges of causing death by criminal negligence.

Appeal dismissed.

The Special Case of Regulatory Offences: Strict and Absolute Liability in Canada

INTRODUCTION

The three cases excerpted in this chapter illustrate the nature of criminal responsibility that may be imposed in relation to *regulatory offences* (as distinguished from the "true crimes" created primarily by the Criminal Code.

The landmark case of *Sault Ste. Marie* (1978) established, for the first time, that there are three different categories of offence in Canadian criminal law: (i) true crimes that require proof of *mens rea* by the Crown; (ii) strict liability offences that do not require the Crown to prove *mens rea* but permit the accused to prove that he or she was not negligent (the "due diligence" defence); and (iii) absolute liability offences that neither require the Crown to prove *mens rea* nor permit the accused to raise a defence of "due diligence." The Supreme Court of Canada held that most regulatory offences impose strict liability. It articulated various principles for the guidance of judges who are required to determine whether a regulatory offence is one of strict, as opposed to absolute, liability.

The Charter was enacted in 1982, four years after *Sault Ste. Marie* was decided, and it did not take long for the Supreme Court of Canada to seize the opportunity to resolve the question of whether absolute liability offences were invalid under the provisions of sections 7 and 11(d) of the Charter. In the important case *Reference re: Section 94(2) of the Motor Vehicle Act* (1985), the Supreme Court held that absolute liability did indeed infringe the Charter whenever it is coupled with potential imprisonment.

In the *Wholesale Travel Group Inc.* case (1991), the Supreme Court of Canada comprehensively re-examined the whole rationale underlying the manner in which regulatory offences are dealt with under Canadian criminal law and ultimately ruled that strict liability offences are not invalid under the Charter. The case also provides a practical example of the manner in which the Supreme Court draws the critical distinction between strict and absolute liability.

CASE

20

Regina v. City of Sault Ste. Marie

SUPREME COURT OF CANADA   MAY 1, 1978

BACKGROUND

The City of Sault Ste. Marie was charged with the offence of "discharging, causing to be discharged, or permitting to be discharged or deposited materials into a body of water or on the shore or bank thereof, or in such place that might impair the quality of the water," contrary to the provisions of section 32(1) of the Ontario Water Resources Act, R.S.O. 1970, c. 332. At trial, the City was acquitted in the (Ontario) Provincial Court (Criminal Division) but the Crown appealed and, after a trial *de novo*, the City was convicted of the offence. The City appealed to the Divisional Court, which allowed the appeal and quashed the conviction. However, the Crown made another appeal to the Ontario Court of Appeal which ordered a new trial for the City. Both the Crown and the City appealed to the Supreme Court of Canada against the judgment of the Ontario Court of Appeal (technically, the accused's appeal was designated a cross-appeal).

MAIN ISSUES

Did the specific offence charged — a public welfare offence — impose *absolute* or *strict* liability on the accused? In other words, could the City escape conviction by establishing that it had acted without

negligence (viz., "*with due diligence*") in all of the circumstances of the case?

JUDGMENTS

The judgment of the Supreme Court of Canada was delivered by Justice Dickson. The other members of the Court were Chief Justice Laskin and Justices Martland, Ritchie, Spence, Pigeon, Beetz, Estey, and Pratte.

....

DICKSON, J.: — In the present appeal, the Court is concerned with offences variously referred to as "statutory," "public welfare," "regulatory," "absolute liability," or "strict responsibility," which are not criminal in any real sense, but are prohibited in the public interest: *Sherras v. De Rutzen*, [1895] 1 Q.B. 918. Although enforced as penal laws through the utilization of the machinery of the criminal law, the offences are in substance of a civil nature and might well be regarded as a branch of administrative law to which traditional principles of criminal law have but limited application. They relate to such everyday matters as traffic infractions, sales of impure food, violations of liquor laws, and the like. In this appeal we are concerned with pollution.

The doctrine of the guilty mind expressed in terms of intention or recklessness, but not negli-

Adapted from *R. v. City of Sault Ste. Marie* (1978), 40 C.C.C. (2d), pp. 357–359, 362–366, 373–378. Copyright © 1978 by *Canada Law Book*. Reprinted with permission.

gence, is at the foundation of the law of crimes. In the case of true crimes there is a presumption that a person should not be held liable for the wrongfulness of his act if that act is without *mens rea*. Blackstone made the point over two hundred years ago in words still apt: ". . . to constitute a crime against human laws, there must be, first, a vicious will; and secondly, an unlawful act consequent upon such vicious will . . .": see *Commentaries on the Laws of England* (1809), Book IV, 15th ed., c. 15, p. 21. I would emphasize at the outset that nothing in the discussion which follows is intended to dilute or erode that basic principle.

The City of Sault Ste. Marie was charged that it did discharge or cause to be discharged, or permitted to be discharged, or deposited materials into Cannon Creek and Root River, or on the shore or bank thereof, or in such place along the side that might impair the quality of the water in Cannon Creek and Root River, between March 13, 1972, and September 11, 1972. The charge was laid under s. 32(1) of the Ontario Water Resources Act, R.S.O. 1970, c. 332, [formerly Ontario Water Resources Commission Act, renamed by 1972, c. 1, s. 70(1)] which provides, so far as relevant, that every municipality or person that discharges, or deposits, or causes, or permits the discharge or deposit of any material of any kind into any water course, or on any shore or bank thereof, or in any place that may impair the quality of water, is guilty of an offence and, on summary conviction, is liable on first conviction to a fine of not more than $5000 and on each subsequent conviction to a fine of not more than $10 000, or to imprisonment for a term of not more than one year, or to both fine and imprisonment.

To relate briefly the facts, the City on November 18, 1970, entered into an agreement with Cherokee Disposal and Construction Co. Ltd., for the disposal of all refuse originating in the City. Under the terms of the agreement, Cherokee became obligated to furnish a site and adequate labour, material, and equipment. The site selected bordered Cannon Creek, which, it would appear, runs into the Root River. The method of disposal adopted is known as the "area" or "continuous slope" method of sanitary land fill, whereby garbage is compacted in layers which are covered each day by natural sand or gravel.

Prior to 1970, the site had been covered with a number of freshwater springs that flowed into Cannon Creek. Cherokee dumped material to cover and submerge these springs and then placed garbage and wastes over such material. The garbage and wastes in due course formed a high mound sloping steeply toward, and within 20 ft. of, the creek. Pollution resulted. Cherokee was convicted of a breach of s. 32(1) of the Ontario Water Resources Act, the section under which the City has been charged. The question now before the Court is whether the City is also guilty of an offence under that section.

The *Mens Rea* Point

The distinction between the true criminal offence and the public welfare offence is one of prime importance. Where the offence is criminal, the Crown must establish a mental element, namely, that the accused who committed the prohibited act did so intentionally or recklessly, with knowledge of the facts constituting the offence, or with wilful blindness toward them. Mere negligence is excluded from the concept of the mental element required for conviction. Within the context of a criminal prosecution, a person who fails to make such inquiries as a reasonable and prudent person would make, or who fails to know facts he should have known, is innocent in the eyes of the law.

In sharp contrast, "absolute liability" entails conviction on proof merely that the defendant committed the prohibited act constituting the *actus reus* of the offence. There is no relevant mental element. It is no defence that the accused was entirely without fault. He may be morally innocent in every sense, yet be branded as a malefactor and punished as such.

Public welfare offences obviously lie in a field of conflicting values. It is essential for society to maintain, through effective enforcement, high standards of public health and safety. Potential victims of those who carry on latently pernicious activities have a strong claim to consideration. On the other hand, there is a generally held revulsion against punishment of the morally innocent.

Public welfare offences evolved in mid-19th century Britain as a means of doing away with the requirement of *mens rea* for petty police offences. The concept was a judicial creation, founded on expediency. That concept is now firmly embedded in the concrete of Anglo-American and Canadian jurisprudence, its importance heightened by the ever-increasing complexities of modern society.

Various arguments are advanced in justification of absolute liability in public welfare offences. Two predominate. Firstly, it is argued that the protection of social interests requires a high standard of care and attention on the part of those who follow certain pursuits, and such persons are more likely to be stimulated to maintain those standards if they know that ignorance or mistake will excuse them. The removal of any possible loophole acts, it is said, as an incentive to take precautionary measures beyond what would otherwise be taken, in order that mistakes and mishaps be avoided. The second main argument is one based on administrative efficiency. Having regard to both the difficulty of proving mental culpability and the number of petty cases which daily come before the Courts, proof of fault is just too great a burden in time and money to place upon the prosecution. To require proof of each person's individual intent would allow almost every violator to escape. This, together with the glut of work entailed in proving *mens rea* in every case would clutter the docket and impede adequate enforcement as virtually to nullify the regulatory statutes. In short, absolute liability, it is contended, is the most efficient and effective way of ensuring compliance with minor regulatory legislation, and the social ends to be achieved are of such importance as to override the unfortunate by-product of punishing those who may be free of moral turpitude. In further justification, it is urged that slight penalties are usually imposed and that conviction for breach of a public welfare offence does not carry

the stigma associated with conviction for a criminal offence.

Arguments of greater force are advanced against absolute liability. The most telling is that it violates fundamental principles of penal liability. It also rests upon assumptions which have not been, and cannot be, empirically established. There is no evidence that a higher standard of care results from absolute liability. If a person is already taking every reasonable precautionary measure, is he likely to take additional measures, knowing that however much care he takes, it will not serve as a defence in the event of breach? If he has exercised care and skill, will conviction have a deterrent effect upon him or others? Will the injustice of conviction lead to cynicism and disrespect for the law, on his part and on the part of others? These are among the questions asked. The argument that no stigma attaches does not withstand analysis, for the accused will have suffered loss of time, legal costs, exposure to the processes of the criminal law at trial, and, however one may downplay it, the opprobrium of conviction. It is not sufficient to say that the public interest is engaged and, therefore, liability may be imposed without fault. In serious crimes, the public interest is involved and *mens rea* must be proven. The administrative argument has little force. In sentencing, evidence of due diligence is admissible and therefore the evidence might just as well be heard when considering guilt. Additionally, it may be noted that s. 198 of the Alberta Highway Traffic Act, R.S.A. 1970, c. 169, provides that upon a person being charged with an offence under this Act, if the Judge trying the case is of the opinion that the offence (a) was committed wholly by accident or misadventure and without negligence, and (b) could not by the exercise of reasonable care or precaution have been avoided, the Judge may dismiss the case. See also s. 230(2) [am. 1976, c. 62, s. 48] of the Manitoba Highway Traffic Act, R.S.M. 1970, c. H60, which has a similar effect. In these instances at least, the Legislature has indicated that administrative efficiency does not foreclose inquiry as to fault. It is also worthy of note that historically the penalty for breach of statutes enacted for the regulation of individual conduct in the interests of health and safety was minor, $20 or $25; today, it may amount to thousands of dollars and entail the possibility of imprisonment for a second conviction. The present case is an example.

Public welfare offences involve a shift of emphasis from the protection of individual interests to the protection of public and social interests. The unfortunate tendency in many past cases has been to see the choice as between two stark alternatives: (i) full *mens rea*; or (ii) absolute liability. In respect of public welfare offences (within which category pollution offences fall) where full *mens rea* is not required, absolute liability has often been imposed. English jurisprudence has consistently maintained this dichotomy. There has, however, been an attempt in Australia, in many Canadian Courts, and indeed in England, to seek a middle position, fulfilling the goals of public welfare offences while still not punishing the entirely blameless. There is an increasing and impressive stream of authority which holds that where an offence does not require full *mens rea*, it is nevertheless a good defence for the defendant to prove that he was not negligent.

Dr. Glanville Williams has written: "There is a half-way house between *mens rea* and strict responsibility for negligence" (*Criminal Law: General Part*, 2nd ed. (1961), p. 262). Morris and Howard, in *Studies in Criminal Law* (1964), p. 200, suggest that strict responsibility might with advantage be replaced by a doctrine of responsibility for negligence strengthened by a shift in the burden of proof. The defendant would be allowed to exculpate himself by proving affirmatively that he was not negligent. The doctrine proceeds on the assumption that the defendant could have avoided the *prima facie* offence through the exercise of reasonable care and he is given the opportunity of establishing, if he can, that he did in fact exercise such care.

The case which gave the lead in this branch of the law is the Australian case of *Proudman v. Dayman* (1941), 67 C.L.R. 536, where Dixon, J., said, at p. 540:

It is one thing to deny that a necessary ingredient of the offence is positive knowledge of the fact that the driver holds no subsisting licence. It is another to say that an honest belief founded on reasonable grounds that he is licensed cannot exculpate a person who permits him to drive. As a general rule an honest and reasonable belief in a state of facts which, if they existed, would make the defendant's act innocent affords an excuse for doing what would otherwise be an offence.

This case, and several others like it, speak of the defence as being that of reasonable mistake of fact. The reason is that the offences in question have generally turned on the possession by a person or place of an unlawful status, and the accused's defence was that he reasonably did not know of this status: e.g., permitting an unlicensed person to drive, or lacking a valid licence oneself, or being the owner of property in a dangerous condition. In such cases, negligence consists of an unreasonable failure to know the facts which constitute the offence. It is clear, however, that in principle the defence is that all reasonable care was taken. In other circumstances, the issue will be whether the accused's behaviour was negligent in bringing about the forbidden event when he knew the relevant facts. Once the defence of reasonable mistake of fact is accepted, there is no barrier to acceptance of the other constituent part of a defence of due diligence.

We have the situation therefore in which many Courts of this country, at all levels, dealing with public welfare offences favour (i) *not* requiring the Crown to prove *mens rea*, (ii) rejecting the notion that liability inexorably follows upon mere proof of the *actus reus*, excluding any possible defence. The Courts are following the lead set in Australia many years ago and tentatively broached by several English Courts in recent years.

It may be suggested that the introduction of a defence based on due diligence and the shifting of the burden of proof might better be implemented by legislative act. In answer, it should be recalled that the concept of absolute liability and the creation of a jural category of public welfare offences are both the product of the judiciary and not of the Legislature. The development to date of this defence, in the numerous decisions I have referred to, of Courts in this country as well as in Australia and New Zealand, has also been the work of Judges. The present case offers the opportunity of consolidating and clarifying the doctrine.

The correct approach, in my opinion, is to relieve the Crown of the burden of proving *mens rea*, having regard to the virtual impossibility in most regulatory cases of proving wrongful intention. In a normal case, the accused alone will have knowledge of what he has done to avoid the breach and it is not improper to expect him to come forward with the evidence of due diligence. This is particularly so when it is alleged, for example, that pollution was caused by the activities of a large and complex corporation. Equally, there is nothing wrong with rejecting absolute liability and admitting the defence of reasonable care.

In this doctrine it is not up to the prosecution to prove negligence. Instead, it is open to the defendant to prove that all due care has been taken. This burden falls upon the defendant as he is the only one who will generally have the means of proof. This would not seem unfair as the alternative is absolute liability, which denies an accused any defence whatsoever. While the prosecution must prove beyond a reasonable doubt that the defendant committed the prohibited act, the defendant must only establish on the balance of probabilities that he has a defence of reasonable care.

I conclude, for the reasons which I have sought to express, that there are compelling grounds for the recognition of three categories of offences rather than the traditional two:

1. Offences in which *mens rea*, consisting of some positive state of mind such as intent, knowledge, or recklessness, must be proved by the prosecution either as an inference from the nature of the act committed, or by additional evidence.

2. Offences in which there is no necessity for the prosecution to prove the existence of *mens rea*; the doing of the prohibited act *prima facie* imports the offence, leaving it open to the accused to avoid liability by proving that he took all reasonable care. This involves consideration of what a reasonable man would have done in the circumstances. The defence will be available if the accused reasonably believed in a mistaken set of facts which, if true, would render the act or omission innocent, or if he took all reasonable steps to avoid the particular event. These events may properly be called offences of strict liability. Mr. Justice Estey so referred to them in *R. v. Hickey* (1976), 29 C.C.C. (2d) 23.

3. Offences of absolute liability where it is not open to the accused to exculpate himself by showing that he was free of fault.

Offences which are criminal in the true sense fall in the first category. Public welfare offences would, *prima facie*, be in the second category. They are not subject to the presumption of full *mens rea*. An offence of this type would fall in the first category only if such words as "wilfully," "with intent," "knowingly," or "intentionally" are contained in the statutory provision creating the offence. On the other hand, the principle that punishment should in general not be inflicted on those without fault applies. Offences of absolute liability would be those in respect of which the Legislature had made it clear that guilt would follow proof merely of the proscribed act. The overall regulatory pattern adopted by the Legislature, the subject-matter of the legislation, the importance of the penalty, and the precision of the language used will be primary considerations in determining whether the offence falls into the third category.

Ontario Water Resources Act, s. 32(1)

Turning to the subject-matter of s. 32(1) — the prevention of pollution of lakes, rivers, and streams — it is patent that this is of great public concern.

Pollution has always been unlawful and, in itself, a nuisance. Natural streams which formerly afforded "pure and healthy" water for drinking or swimming purposes become little more than cesspools when riparian factory owners and municipal corporations discharge into them filth of all descriptions. Pollution offences are undoubtedly public welfare offences enacted in the interests of public health. There is thus no presumption of a full *mens rea*.

There is another reason, however, why this offence is not subject to a presumption of *mens rea*. The presumption applies only to offences which are "criminal in the true sense." The Ontario Water Resources Act is a provincial statute. If it is valid provincial legislation (and no suggestion was made to the contrary), then it cannot possibly create an offence which is criminal in the true sense.

The present case concerns the interpretation of two troublesome words frequently found in public welfare statutes: "cause" and "permit." These two words are troublesome because neither denotes clearly either full *mens rea* or absolute liability.

In themselves, the words "cause" and "permit" fit much better into an offence of strict liability than either full *mens rea* or absolute liability. Since s. 32(1) creates a public welfare offence, without a clear indication that liability is absolute, and without any words such as "knowingly" or "wilfully" expressly to import *mens rea*, application of the criteria which I have outlined above undoubtedly places the offence in the category of strict liability.

Proof of the prohibited act *prima facie* imports the offence, but the accused may avoid liability by proving that he took reasonable care.

The Present Case

As I am of the view that a new trial is necessary, it would be inappropriate to discuss at this time the facts of the present case. It may be helpful, however, to consider in a general way the principles to be applied in determining whether a person or municipality has committed the *actus reus* of discharging, causing, or permitting pollution within the terms of s. 32(1), in particular in connection with pollution from garbage disposal. The prohibited act would, in my opinion, be committed by those who undertake the collection and disposal of garbage, who are in a position to exercise continued control of this activity and prevent the pollution from occurring, but fail to do so. The "discharging" aspect of the offence centres on direct acts of pollution. The "causing" aspect centres on the defendant's active undertaking of something which it is in a position to control and which results in pollution. The "permitting" aspect of the offence centres on the defendant's passive lack of interference or, in other words, its failure to prevent an occurrence which it ought to have foreseen. The close interweaving of the meanings of these terms emphasizes again that s. 32(1) deals with only one generic offence.

Nor does liability rest solely on the terms of any agreement by which a defendant arranges for eventual disposal. The test is a factual one, based on an assessment of the defendant's position with respect to the activity which it undertakes and which causes pollution. If it can and should control the activity at the point where pollution occurs, then it is responsible for the pollution. Whether it "discharges," "causes," or "permits" the pollution will be a question of degree, depending on whether it is actively involved at the point where pollution occurs, or whether it merely passively fails to prevent the pollution. In some cases the contract may expressly provide the defendant with the power and authority to control the activity. In such a case the factual assessment will be straightforward. *Prima facie*, liability will be incurred where the defendant could have prevented the impairment by intervening pursuant to its right to do so under the contract, but failed to do so. Where there is no such express provision in the contract, other factors will come into greater prominence. In every instance the question will depend on an assessment of all the circumstances of the case.

It must be recognized, however, that a municipality is in a somewhat different position by virtue of the legislative power which it possesses and which others lack. This is important in the assessment of whether the defendant was in a position to control the activity which it undertook and which caused the pollution. A municipality cannot slough off responsibility by contracting out the work. It is in a position to control those whom it hires to carry out garbage disposal operations, and to supervise the activity, either through the provisions of the contract or by municipal by-laws. It fails to do so at its peril.

The majority of the Ontario Court of Appeal directed a new trial as, in the opinion of that Court, the findings of the trial Judge were not sufficient to establish actual knowledge on the part of the City. I share the view that there should be a new trial, but for a different reason. The City did not lead evidence directed to a defence of due diligence, nor did the trial Judge address himself to the availability of such a defence. In these circumstances, it would not be fair for this Court to determine, upon findings of fact directed toward other ends, whether the City was without fault.

I would dismiss the appeal and direct a new trial. I would dismiss the cross-appeal. There should be no costs.

Appeal dismissed; cross-appeal dismissed.

Reference re: Section 94(2) of the Motor Vehicle Act

SUPREME COURT OF CANADA　　　　　　　　DECEMBER 17, 1985

BACKGROUND

The Lieutenant-Governor in Council of British Columbia submitted a reference to the B.C. Court of Appeal. The reference concerned the question of whether section 94(2) of the Motor Vehicle Act, R.S.B.C. 1979, c. 288, was invalid under section 7 of the Charter and, if so, was it saved by the application of section 1 of the Charter? The Court of Appeal ruled that section 94(2) did infringe section 7 of the Charter and that it was not saved by section 1 of the Charter. The Attorney-General of B.C. appealed against the judgment of the Court of Appeal to the Supreme Court of Canada.

MAIN ISSUE

Does the imposition of absolute liability in the context of regulatory legislation infringe the Charter and, if so, can it be saved by the application of section 1 of the Charter?

JUDGMENTS

The *majority* judgment was delivered by Justice Lamer (with whom Chief Justice Dickson and Justices Beetz, Chouinard, and Le Dain agreed). The *concurring* judgments of Justices McIntyre and Wilson have been omitted.

LAMER J.: — A law that has the potential to convict a person who has not really done anything wrong offends the principles of fundamental justice and, if imprisonment is available as a penalty, such a law then violates a person's right to liberty under s. 7 of the Canadian Charter of Rights and Freedoms (Part I of the Constitution Act, 1982, as enacted by the Canada Act, 1982, as enacted by the Canada Act, 1982 (U.K.), c. 11).

In other words, absolute liability and imprisonment cannot be combined.

The Facts

On August 16, 1982, the Lieutenant-Governor in Council of British Columbia referred the following question to the Court of Appeal of that province, by virtue of s. 1 of the Constitutional Question Act, R.S.B.C. 1979, c. 63:

> Is s. 94(2) of the Motor Vehicle Act, R.S.B.C. 1979, as amended by the Motor Vehicle Amendment Act, 1982, consistent with the Canadian Charter of Rights and Freedoms?

On February 3, 1983, the Court of Appeal handed down reasons in answer to the question in which it stated that s. 94(2) of the Act is inconsistent with the Canadian Charter of Rights and Freedoms. The Attorney-General for British Columbia launched an appeal to this Court.

The Legislation

Motor Vehicle Act, R.S.B.C. 1979, c. 288, s. 94, as amended by the Motor Vehicle Amendment Act, 1982, c. 36, s. 19:

> 94(1) A person who drives a motor vehicle on a highway or industrial road while
>
> > (a) he is prohibited from driving a motor vehicle under section 90, 91, 92, 92.1, or
> > (b) his driver's licence or his right to apply for or obtain a driver's licence is suspended under section 82 or 92 as it was before its repeal and replacement came into force pursuant to the Motor Vehicle Amendment Act, 1982,
>
> commits an offence and is liable,
>
> > (c) on a first conviction, to a fine of not less than $300 and not more than $2000 and to imprisonment for not less than 7 days and not more than 6 months, and
> > (d) on a subsequent conviction, regardless of when the contravention occurred, to a fine of not less than $300 and not more than $2000 and to imprisonment for not less than 14 days and not more than one year.
>
> (2) Subsection (1) creates an absolute liability offence in which guilt is established by proof of driving, whether or not the defendant knew of the prohibition or suspension.

Absolute Liability and Fundamental Justice in Penal Law

It has from time immemorial been part of our system of laws that the innocent not be punished. This principle has long been recognized as an essential element of a system for the administration of justice which is founded upon a belief in the dignity and worth of the human person and on the rule of law. It is so old that its first enunciation was in Latin *actus non facit reum nisi mens sit rea.*

In my view, it is because absolute liability offends the principles of fundamental justice that this Court created presumptions against Legislatures having intended to enact offences of a regulatory nature falling within that category. This is not to say, however, and to that extent I am in agreement with the Court of Appeal, that, as a result, absolute liability *per se* offends s. 7 of the Charter.

A law enacting an absolute liability offence will violate s. 7 of the Charter only if and to the extent that it has the potential of depriving of life, liberty, or security of the person.

Obviously, imprisonment (including probation orders) deprives persons of their liberty. An offence has that potential as of the moment it is open to the judge to impose imprisonment. There is no need that imprisonment, as in s. 94(2), be made mandatory.

I am therefore of the view that the combination of imprisonment and of absolute liability violates s. 7 of the Charter and can only be salvaged if the authorities demonstrate under s. 1 that such a deprivation of liberty in breach of those principles of fundamental justice is, in a free and democratic society, under the circumstances, a justified reasonable limit to one's rights under s. 7.

As no one has addressed imprisonment as an alternative to the non-payment of a fine, I prefer not to express any views in relation to s. 7 as regards that eventuality as a result of a conviction for an absolute liability offence; nor do I need to address here, given the scope of my finding and the nature of this appeal, minimum imprisonment, whether it offends the Charter *per se* or whether such violation, if any, is dependent upon whether it be for a *mens rea* or strict liability offence. Those issues were not addressed by the court below and it would be unwise to attempt to address them here. It is sufficient and desirable for this appeal to make the findings I have and no more, that is, that no imprisonment may be imposed for an absolute liability offence, and, consequently, given the question put to us, an offence punishable by imprisonment cannot be an absolute liability offence.

Indeed, as I said, in penal law, absolute liability always offends the principles of fundamental justice irrespective of the nature of the offence; it offends s. 7 of the Charter if, as a result, anyone is deprived of his life, liberty, or security of the person, irrespective of the requirement of public interest. In such cases it might only be salvaged for reasons of public interest under s. 1.

In this latter regard, something might be added.

Administrative expediency, absolute liability's main supportive argument, will undoubtedly under s. 1 be invoked and occasionally succeed. Indeed, administrative expediency certainly has its place in administrative law. But when administrative law chooses to call in aid imprisonment through penal law, indeed sometimes criminal law and the added stigma attached to a conviction, exceptional, in my view, will be the case where the liberty or even the security of the person guaranteed under s. 7 should be sacrificed to administrative expediency. Section 1 may, for reasons of administrative expediency, successfully come to the rescue of an otherwise violation of s. 7, but only in cases arising out of exceptional conditions, such as natural disasters, the outbreak of war, epidemics, and the like.

Of course, I understand the concern of many as regards corporate offences, specially, as was mentioned by the Court of Appeal, in certain sensitive areas such as the preservation of our vital environment and our natural resources. This concern might well be dispelled were it to be decided, given the proper case, that s. 7 affords protection to human persons only and does not extend to corporations.

Even if it be decided that s. 7 does extend to corporations, I think the balancing under s. 1 of the public interest against the financial interests of a corporation would give very different results from that of balancing public interest and the liberty or security of the person of a human being.

Indeed, the public interest as regards "air and water pollution offences" requires that the guilty be dealt with firmly, but the seriousness of the offence does not, in my respectful view, support the proposition that the innocent *human* person be open to conviction; quite the contrary.

Section 94(2)

No doubt s. 94(2) enacts in the clearest of terms an absolute liability offence, the conviction for which a person will be deprived of his or her liberty, and little more, if anything, need be added.

In the final analysis, it seems that both the appellant and the respondent agree that s. 94 will impact upon the right to liberty of a limited number of morally innocent persons. It creates an absolute liability offence which effects a deprivation of liberty for a limited number of persons. To me, that is sufficient for it to be in violation of s. 7.

Section 1

Having found that s. 94(2) offends s. 7 of the Charter, there remains the question as to whether the appellants have demonstrated that the section is salvaged by the operation of s. 1 of the Charter. No evidence was adduced in the Court of Appeal or in this Court.

I do not take issue with the fact that it is highly desirable that "bad drivers" be kept off the road. I do not take issue either with the desirability of punishing severely bad drivers who are in contempt of prohibitions against driving. The bottom line of the question to be addressed here is whether the Government of British Columbia has demonstrated as justifiable that the risk of imprisonment of a few innocent is, given the desirability of ridding the roads of British Columbia of bad drivers, a reasonable limit in a free and democratic society. That result is to be measured against the offence being one of strict liability open to a defence of due diligence, the success of which does nothing more than let those few who did nothing wrong remain free.

As did the Court of Appeal, I find that this demonstration has not been satisfied, indeed, not in the least.

In the result, I would dismiss the appeal and answer the question in the negative, as did the Court of Appeal, albeit for somewhat different reasons, and declare s. 94(2) of the Motor Vehicle Act, as amended by the Motor Vehicle Amendment Act,

1982, inconsistent with s. 7 of the Canadian Charter of Rights and Freedoms.

Having come to this conclusion, I choose, as did the Court of Appeal, not to address whether the section violates the rights guaranteed under ss.11(d) and 12 of the Charter.

Appeal dismissed.

Wholesale Travel Group Inc. v. The Queen

SUPREME COURT OF CANADA   OCTOBER 24, 1991

BACKGROUND

The corporation, known as Wholesale Travel Group Inc., was charged with five counts of false or misleading advertising, contrary to section 36(1)(a) of (what is now) the Competition Act, R.S.C. 1985, c. C-34. The trial judge dismissed the charges after ruling that section 36 of the Competition Act, as well as section 37.3(2) (which established a statutory defence of "due diligence" in relation to the offence under section 36), infringed sections 7 and 11(d) of the Charter and could not be saved by the application of section 1 of the Charter. The Crown's subsequent appeal to the Supreme Court of Ontario was allowed: Justice Montgomery ruled that the relevant provisions of the Competition Act did not violate the Charter and sent the case back to the Provincial Court for a new trial.

Wholesale Travel appealed the decision of the Supreme Court of Ontario to the Ontario Court of Appeal, which upheld the order to return the case to the Provincial Court for a new trial. However, the Court of Appeal also allowed part of Wholesale Travel's appeal insofar as it ruled that subsections (c) and (d) of section 37.3(2) should be severed from the rest of the section and declared them to be of no force or effect because they infringed section 7 of the Charter and could not be saved by section 1 of the Charter. Furthermore, the Court of Appeal held that the words "he establishes that," in section 37.3(2) of the Competition Act, could be severed from the rest of the section. The Court of Appeal declared that these words were of no force or effect because they infringed the presumption of innocence, guaranteed by section 11(d) of the Charter, and could not be saved by the application of section 1 of the Charter.

In essence, the Ontario Court of Appeal ruled that section 36, read in the light of subsections (c) and (d) of section 37.3(2), infringed section 7 of the Charter because it imposed a régime of *absolute liability* along with a penalty of potential imprisonment. The Court of Appeal also ruled that the "due diligence" defence articulated in section 37.3(2) infringed section 11(d) of the Charter because it placed the onus on the accused to establish that he or she was not negligent. Both Wholesale Travel and the Crown appealed to the Supreme Court of Canada which dismissed the accused corporation's appeal and allowed the Crown's appeal *in part*.

MAIN ISSUES

(1) Are subsections (c) and (d) of section 37.3(2) of the Competition Act invalid in light of section 7 of the Charter? (2) Are the words "he establishes that," in section 37.3(2), invalid in light of section 11(d) of the Charter?

Adapted from *R. v. Wholesale Travel Group Inc.* (1991), 67 C.C.C. (3d), pp. 201–202, 211–220, 236–266. Copyright © 1991 by *Canada Law Book*. Reprinted with permission.

JUDGMENTS

On the first issue, all nine Justices *agreed* that subsections (c) and (d) of section 37.3(2) of the Competition Act infringed section 7 of the Charter and could not be saved by the application of section 1 of the Charter. Chief Justice Lamer delivered an opinion with which Justices La Forest, Sopinka, and McLachlin agreed. Justice Cory (with whom Justice L'Heureux-Dubé agreed) wrote a separate judgment which *concurred* with the Court's decision on the first issue but reflected somewhat different reasoning. A separate judgment by Justice Iacobucci (with whom Justices Gonthier and Stevenson agreed) *concurred* with the Court's decision on the first issue; however, this judgment has been omitted.

As to the second issue, the Court split in a 5-4 vote. The *majority* of the court ruled that the words "he establishes that," in Section 37.3(2) of the Competition Act, were not invalid under the Charter. Justice Iacobucci (with whom Justices Gonthier and Stevenson agreed) delivered a judgment which held that while section 37.3(2) of the Competition Act did infringe the presumption of innocence guaranteed by section 11(d) of the Charter, it nevertheless constituted a reasonable limit under section 1 of the Charter. This judgment has been omitted. Justice Cory (with whom Justice L'Heureux-Dubé agreed) wrote a judgment in which he held that section 37.3(2) did not infringe section 11(d) of the Charter but that, even if it did so, it would be saved by section 1 of the Charter. The *minority* of the Court took the view that section 37.3(2) did infringe section 11(d) of the Charter and that it could not be saved by the application of section 1 of the Charter. The *dissenting* judgments of Chief Justice Lamer (with whom Justice Sopinka agreed), Justice La Forest, and Justice McLachlin have all been omitted.

....

LAMER C.J.C.: — This case involves a constitutional challenge, under ss. 7 and 11(d) of the Canadian Charter of Rights and Freedoms, to the false or misleading advertising provisions of the Compe-

tition Act, R.S.C. 1970, c. C-23 (as amended), ss. 36(1)(a), 36(5) and 37.3(2):

> 36(1) No person shall, for the purpose of promoting, directly or indirectly, the supply or use of a product or for the purpose of promoting, directly or indirectly, any business interest, by any means whatever,
>
> > (a) make a representation to the public that is false or misleading in a material respect;
>
> ....
>
> (5) Any person who violates subsection (1) is guilty of an offence and is liable
>
> > (a) on conviction on indictment, to a fine in the discretion of the court or to imprisonment for five years or to both; or
> > (b) on summary conviction, to a fine of twenty-five thousand dollars or to imprisonment for one year or to both.
>
> ....
>
> 37.3(2) No person shall be convicted of an offence under section 36 or 36.1, if he establishes that,
>
> > (a) the act or omission giving rise to the offence with which he is charged was the result of error;
> > (b) he took reasonable precautions and exercised due diligence to prevent the occurrence of such error;
> > (c) he, or another person, took reasonable measures to bring the error to the attention of the class of persons likely to have been reached by the representation or testimonial; and
> > (d) the measures referred to in paragraph (c), except where the representation or testimonial related to a security, were taken forthwith after the representation was made or the testimonial was published.

The Facts

Wholesale Travel Group Inc. (a travel agency) and Mr. Colin Chedore were jointly charged with five counts of false or misleading advertising, contrary to s. 36(1)(a) of the Competition Act. The Crown elected to proceed by way of summary conviction and the accused pleaded not guilty. The advertisements in question referred to vacations at "wholesale prices." Apparently, the Crown intended to argue at trial that "wholesale price" refers to the price at which Wholesale Travel acquired its travel packages and that the advertisements were therefore false or misleading. This argument was never made because, at the outset of the trial, the accused brought a motion pursuant to s. 52(1) of the Constitution Act, 1982, for a declaration that ss. 36(1) and 37.3(2) of the Competition Act were inconsistent with ss. 7 and 11(d) of the Charter and were, therefore, of no force or effect.

Do ss. 36(1)(a) and 37.3(2) of the Competition Act Violate the Charter?

SECTION 7

In *Reference re: s. 94(2) of Motor Vehicle Act* (1985), 23 C.C.C. (3d) 289, 24 D.L.R. (4th) 536, [1985] 2 S.C.R. 486, this court held that the combination of absolute liability and possible imprisonment violates s. 7 of the Charter and will rarely be upheld under s. 1. This is because an absolute liability offence has the potential of convicting a person who really has done nothing wrong (i.e., has acted neither intentionally nor negligently). *Reference re: s. 94(2) of Motor Vehicle Act* inferentially decided that even for a mere provincial regulatory offence *at least* negligence is required, in that at least a defence of due diligence must always be open to an accused *who risks imprisonment* upon conviction. It is a principle of fundamental justice that the penalty imposed on an accused and the stigma which attaches to that penalty and/or to the conviction itself necessitate a level of fault which reflects the particular nature of the crime.

Thus, the question to be addressed under s. 7 in this case is whether the offence of false/misleading advertising is missing any "elements" (i.e., level of fault) which are constitutionally required by s. 7 of the Charter.

Given that the offence of false/misleading advertising is punishable by up to five years' imprisonment, it is clear from the developing jurisprudence of this court that the offence must not be one of absolute liability and that it commands a minimum fault requirement of negligence, in that at least a defence of due diligence must always be open to an accused in order for the provision to conform to the requirements of s. 7 of the Charter. Therefore, it will be necessary to examine the components of s. 37.3(2) ((a) through (d)) in order to determine whether they, in fact, provide a defence of due diligence to an accused.

Section 37.3(2), (a) through (d), sets out the only defence, under the Act, to false/misleading advertising, once it has been established that the advertisement is objectively false or misleading (i.e., once the *actus reus* is established). It is clear from the inclusion of the word "and" after s. 37.3(2)(c) that *all four components* of s. 37.3(2) must be established in order for the accused to be acquitted.

Thus, the question becomes whether a situation could arise where an accused would be unable to establish all four components of s. 37.3(2) but would nonetheless be duly diligent (i.e., not negligent). If the answer to this question is yes, it means that the constitutionally required element of negligence is not fulfilled by the statutory defence contained in s. 37.3(2).

Paras. (a) and (b) operate so as to provide a defence to an accused who has taken reasonable precautions to prevent false/misleading advertising and who has been duly diligent in ensuring that advertising is not false or misleading in nature. However, the additional requirement of "timely retraction" embodied in paras. (c) and (d) means that the statutory defence is considerably more narrow than the common law defence of due diligence.

An accused who did not realize, and could not reasonably have been expected to realize, that the representation in question was false or misleading until it was too late to comply with paras. (c) and (d) or who was, for some reason, unable to comply with paras. (c) and (d), but who had nonetheless taken reasonable precautions and who had exercised due diligence in preventing false/misleading advertising, would not fall within the statutory defence and would be convicted of false/misleading advertising. Paras. (c) and (d) of s. 37.3(2) could have the effect of depriving an accused of the defence of due diligence and could therefore require the conviction of an accused who was not negligent. Paragraphs (c) and (d) make the failure to undertake corrective advertising (a component of the offence of false/misleading advertising) an "offence" of absolute liability. Consequently, the constitutionally required fault level is not present in the false/misleading advertising provisions.

It is the presence of paras. (c) and (d) alone which offends s. 7 of the Charter. Thus, unless the limitation on s. 7 can be upheld under s. 1 of the Charter, these two paragraphs must be held to be of no force or effect, pursuant to s. 52(1) of the Constitution Act, 1982.

SECTION 1

The procedure to be followed when the state is attempting to justify a limit on a right or freedom under s. 1 was set out by this Court in *R. v. Oakes, supra*, (1986), 24 C.C.C. (3d) 321 (S.C.C.), and was summarized in *R. v. Chaulk* (1990), 62 C.C.C. (3d) 193 at pp. 216–7, [1990] 3 S.C.R. 1303, 2 C.R. (4th) 1, as follows:

1. The objective of the impugned provision must be of sufficient importance to warrant overriding a constitutionally protected right or freedom; it must relate to concerns which are pressing and substantial in a free and democratic society before it can be characterized as sufficiently important.

2. Assuming that a sufficiently important objective has been established, the means chosen to achieve the objective must pass a proportionality test; that is to say they must:

    (a) be "rationally connected" to the objective and not be arbitrary, unfair or based on irrational considerations;

    (b) impair the right or freedom in question as "little as possible"; and

    (c) be such that their effects on the limitation of rights and freedoms are proportional to the objective.

Objective

I am prepared to accept that preventing false/misleading advertisers from benefiting from false/misleading advertising and protecting consumers from the detrimental effects of false/misleading advertising is sufficiently important to warrant overriding constitutionally protected rights and freedoms. It remains to be seen, however, whether the means chosen by Parliament to achieve this objective pass the "proportionality test" set out in *R. v. Oakes, supra*.

The means chosen by Parliament to achieve the dual objectives was to make the "failure to undertake corrective advertising" component of the offence one of *absolute liability*, thereby facilitating proof of the offence.

Proportionality Test

1. RATIONAL CONNECTION

Requiring an accused to make a "timely retraction" of the representation in question, in order to avail itself of the only statutory defence to the offence of false/misleading advertising, will surely encourage advertisers to undertake "corrective advertising" *as soon as they discover there may be a problem with the advertisement*. This, in turn, will lessen the detrimental effects on consumers and will reduce the gains to advertisers from false/misleading advertisements. Of course, these means will not encourage those who do not know that there is a problem to undertake corrective advertising. A person who doesn't think that an advertisement is false or misleading or who is not aware of an error will not contemplate the statutory defence nor will that person contemplate taking corrective measures. Thus, the means are a rational way of achieving these objectives with respect to some accused, but not with respect to others.

These means will, however, clearly facilitate proof of the offence of false/misleading advertising. Assuming that part of Parliament's objective in enacting paras. (c) and (d) was to facilitate convictions of false/misleading advertising, the means chosen are rationally connected to this objective.

Taking all of the above into account, there is, in my view, a rational connection between the objectives and the means chosen to attain the objectives, and paras. (c) and (d) therefore pass the first part of the proportionality test in *R. v. Oakes.*

2. AS LITTLE AS POSSIBLE

The question under this part of the proportionality test is whether the impugned law (in this case, the modified due diligence defence embodied in paras. (c) and (d) of s. 37.3(2)) violates Charter rights as little as possible in order to achieve the "pressing and substantial" objectives. In other words, while the means chosen may be rationally connected to the objectives, they may, at the same time, be unnecessarily intrusive on constitutional rights in light of alternative means.

It is not necessary to convict of false/misleading advertising those who did not undertake corrective advertising because they did not realize (and ought not to have realized) that the advertisement was false/misleading, in order to achieve the objectives set out above. Parliament could have retained the absolute liability component and, at the same time, infringed Charter rights to a much lesser extent, *had it not combined this absolute liability with the possibility of imprisonment.* In this sense, removing the possibility of imprisonment and leaving paras. (c) and (d) unchanged was a further less intrusive means which was available to Parliament.

In summary, it is my view that the modified due diligence defence embodied in paras. (c) and (d) limits an accused's rights under s. 7 of the Charter and cannot be upheld as a reasonable limit under s. 1. Consequently, paras. (c) and (d) of s. 37.3(2) of the Competition Act must be held to be of no force or effect, pursuant to s. 52(1) of the Constitution Act, 1982.

CORY J.: —

I. Regulatory Offences and Strict Liability

A. THE DISTINCTION BETWEEN CRIMES AND REGULATORY OFFENCES

The common law has long acknowledged a distinction between truly criminal conduct and conduct, otherwise lawful, which is prohibited in the public interest. Earlier, the designations *mala in se* and *mala prohibita* were utilized; today prohibited acts are generally classified as either crimes or regulatory offences.

While some regulatory legislation, such as that pertaining to the content of food and drink, dates back to the Middle Ages, the number and significance of regulatory offences increased greatly with the onset of the Industrial Revolution. Unfettered industrialization had led to abuses. Regulations were therefore enacted to protect the vulnerable — particularly the children, men, and women who laboured long hours in dangerous and unhealthy surroundings. Without these regulations, many would have died. It later became necessary to regulate the manufactured products themselves and, still later, the discharge of effluent resulting from the manufacturing process. There is no doubt that regulatory offences were originally and still are designed to protect those who are unable to protect themselves.

R. v. Sault Ste. Marie (City) (1978), 40 C.C.C. (2d) 353, 85 D.L.R. (3d) 161, [1978] 2 S.C.R. 1299, affirmed the distinction between regulatory offences and true crimes. There, on behalf of a unanimous court, Justice Dickson (as he then was) recognized public welfare offences as a distinct class.

The *Sault Ste. Marie* case recognized strict liability as a middle ground between full *mens rea* and absolute liability. Where the offence is one of strict liability, the Crown is required to prove neither *mens rea* nor negligence; conviction may follow merely upon proof beyond a reasonable doubt of the proscribed act. However, it is open to the defendant to avoid liability by proving on a balance of probabilities that all due care was taken. This is the hallmark of the strict liability offence: the defence of due diligence.

THE RATIONALE FOR THE DISTINCTION

It has always been thought that there is a rational basis for distinguishing between crimes and regulatory offences. Acts or actions are criminal when they constitute conduct that is, in itself, so abhorrent to the basic values of human society that it ought to be prohibited completely. Murder, sexual assault, fraud, robbery, and theft are all so repugnant to society that they are universally recognized as crimes. At the same time, some conduct is prohibited, not because it is inherently wrongful, but because unregulated activity would result in dangerous conditions being imposed upon members of society, especially those who are particularly vulnerable.

The objective of regulatory legislation is to protect the public or broad segments of the public (such as employees, consumers, and motorists, to name but a few) from the potentially adverse effects of otherwise lawful activity. Regulatory legislation involves a shift of emphasis from the protection of individual interests and the deterrence and punishment of acts involving moral fault to the protection of public and societal interests. While criminal offences are usually designed to condemn and punish past, inherently wrongful conduct, regulatory measures are generally directed to the prevention of future harm through the enforcement of minimum standards of conduct and care.

It follows that regulatory offences and crimes embody different concepts of fault. Since regulatory offences are directed primarily not to conduct itself, but to the consequences of conduct, conviction of a regulatory offence may be thought to import a significantly lesser degree of culpability than conviction of a true crime. The concept of fault in regulatory offences is based upon a reasonable care standard and, as such, does not imply moral blameworthiness in the same manner as criminal fault. Conviction for breach of a regulatory offence suggests nothing more than that the defendant has failed to meet a prescribed standard of care.

B. THE FUNDAMENTAL IMPORTANCE OF REGULATORY OFFENCES IN CANADIAN SOCIETY

Regulatory measures are the primary mechanisms employed by governments in Canada to implement public policy objectives. What is ultimately at stake in this appeal is the ability of federal and provincial governments to pursue social ends through the enactment and enforcement of public welfare legislation.

It is difficult to think of an aspect of our lives that is not regulated for our benefit and for the protection of society as a whole. From cradle to grave, we are protected by regulations; they apply to the doctors attending our entry into this world and to the morticians present at our departure. Every day, from waking to sleeping, we profit from regulatory measures, which we often take for granted. On rising, we use various forms of energy whose safe distribution and use are governed by regulation. The trains, buses, and other vehicles that get us to work are regulated for our safety. The food we eat and the beverages we drink are subject to regulation for the protection of our health.

In short, regulation is absolutely essential for our protection and well-being as individuals, and for the effective functioning of society. It is properly present throughout our lives. The more complex the activity, the greater the need for and the greater our reliance upon regulation and its enforcement.

II. The Offence in the Present Case

COMPETITION LEGISLATION GENERALLY

The offence of misleading advertising with which Wholesale Travel is charged is found in the Competition Act (the "Act"). This Act, like its predecessor, the Combines Investigation Act, is aimed at regulating unacceptable business activity. The Competition Act in all its aspects is regulatory in character.

THE OFFENCE OF FALSE OR MISLEADING
ADVERTISING

Is the offence of false or misleading advertising regulatory in nature? It seems to me that the fact that
the provision is located within a comprehensive
regulatory framework would ordinarily be sufficient to demonstrate its regulatory nature. Several
other considerations point to the same conclusion.

The offence does not focus on dishonesty, but
rather on the harmful consequences of otherwise
lawful conduct. Conviction suggests only that the
defendant has made a representation to the public
which was in fact misleading and that the defendant was unable to establish the exercise of due diligence in preventing the error. This connotes a fault
element of negligence rather than one involving
moral turpitude. Thus, any stigma that might flow
from a conviction is very considerably diminished.

In summary, the offence of false advertising possesses the essential characteristics which distinguish
regulatory offences from those which are truly
criminal. Accordingly, it should be considered to be
a regulatory offence rather than a crime in the ordinary sense.

III. A Contextual Approach to Charter Interpretation

A. THE IMPORTANCE OF CONSIDERING CHARTER
RIGHTS IN CONTEXT

It is now clear that the Charter is to be interpreted
in light of the context in which the claim arises.

A contextual approach is particularly appropriate in the present case to take account of the regulatory nature of the offence and its place within a
larger scheme of public welfare legislation. This
approach requires that the rights asserted by the
appellant be considered in light of the regulatory
context in which the claim is situated, acknowledging that a Charter right may have different scope
and implications in a regulatory context than in a
truly criminal one.

Under the contextual approach, constitutional
standards developed in the criminal context cannot

be applied automatically to regulatory offences.
Rather, the content of the Charter right must be
determined only after an examination of all relevant factors and in light of the essential differences
between the two classes of prohibited activity.

The contextual approach further requires that
the appellant's claim be considered and weighed in
light of the realities of a modern industrial society,
where the regulation of innumerable activities is
essential for the benefit of all. It is vital that the
fundamentally important role of regulatory legislation in the protection of individuals and groups in
Canadian society today be recognized and
accepted. Canadians rely on and expect their governments to regulate and control activities which
may be dangerous to others.

B. THE BASIS FOR THE DIFFERENTIAL TREATMENT
OF REGULATORY OFFENCES

In the present case, the contextual approach
requires that regulatory and criminal offences be
treated differently for the purposes of Charter
review.

1. THE LICENSING JUSTIFICATION

Criminal law is rooted in the concepts of individual
autonomy and free will and the corollary that each
individual is responsible for his or her conduct. It
assumes that all persons are free actors, at liberty to
choose how to regulate their own actions in relation to others. The criminal law fixes the outer limits of acceptable conduct, constraining individual
freedom to a limited degree in order to preserve the
freedom of others. Thus, the basis of criminal
responsibility is that the accused person has made a
deliberate and conscious choice to engage in activity prohibited by the Criminal Code. The accused
person who is convicted of an offence will be held
responsible for his or her actions, with the result
that the opprobrium of society will attach to those
acts and any punishment imposed will be considered to be deserved.

The licensing argument is directed to this question of choice. Thus, while in the criminal context,

the essential question to be determined is whether the accused has made the choice to act in the manner alleged in the indictment, the regulated defendant is, by virtue of the licensing argument, assumed to have made the choice to engage in the regulated activity. The question then becomes not whether the defendant chose to enter the regulated sphere, but whether, having done so, the defendant has fulfilled the responsibilities attending that decision.

The licensing concept rests on the view that those who choose to participate in regulated activities have, in doing so, placed themselves in a responsible relationship to the public generally and must accept the consequences of that responsibility. Therefore, it is said, those who engage in regulated activity should, as part of the burden of responsible conduct attending participation in the regulated field, be deemed to have accepted certain terms and conditions applicable to those who act within the regulated sphere. Foremost among these implied terms is an undertaking that the conduct of the regulated actor will comply with and maintain a certain minimum standard of care.

The licensing justification is based not only on the idea of a conscious choice being made to enter a regulated field but also on the concept of control. The concept is that those persons who enter a regulated field are in the best position to control the harm which may result, and that they should therefore be held responsible for it.

The nature of the regulated conduct will itself go far to determining whether the licensing argument applies. It is useful to distinguish between conduct which, by virtue of its inherent danger or the risk it engenders for others, would generally alert a reasonable person to the probability that the conduct would be regulated, from that conduct which is so mundane and apparently harmless that no thought would ordinarily be given to its potentially regulated nature. In the latter circumstances, the licensing argument would not apply.

These considerations do not, however, apply in the present case. The appellant, having chosen to enter a regulated sphere of business activity, the

regulation of which had received wide publicity, should have known that there would be regulations governing its conduct.

By virtue of the decision to enter the regulated field, the regulated person (here the appellant) can be taken to have accepted certain terms and conditions of entry. The procedural and substantive protections a person can reasonably expect may vary depending upon the activity that brings that person into contact with the state. Thus the extent of Charter protection may differ depending upon whether the activity in question is regulatory or criminal in nature.

2. THE VULNERABILITY JUSTIFICATION

Regulatory legislation is essential to the operation of our complex industrial society; it plays a legitimate and vital role in protecting those who are most vulnerable and least able to protect themselves. It was regulatory legislation, with its enforcement provisions, which brought to an end the shameful situation that existed in mines, factories, and workshops in the nineteenth century. The differential treatment of regulatory offences is justified by their common goal of protecting the vulnerable.

It follows that a contextual approach is required in the present case in order that the distinctive nature of regulatory offences and their fundamental importance in Canadian society may be considered. Both licensing and vulnerability considerations justify differential treatment, for the purposes of Charter interpretation, of crimes and regulatory offences.

IV. The Constitutionality of Strict Liability

A. SECTION 7: THE *MENS REA* ISSUE

Wholesale Travel contends that, wherever imprisonment is available as a penalty for breach of a regulatory statute, the failure to require the Crown to prove guilty intent as an essential element of the offence violates s. 7 of the Charter. It is constitutionally impermissible, it is argued, to impose liability solely on the basis of lack of reasonable care.

Thus, it is the appellant's position that strict liability as defined in *Sault Ste. Marie* has been superseded and rendered invalid by the Charter. The appellant's argument, if accepted, would eliminate any distinction between criminal and regulatory offences.

Does s. 7 require in all cases that the Crown prove *mens rea* as an essential element of the offence? The resolution of this question requires that a contextual approach be taken to the meaning and scope of the s. 7 right. Certainly, there can be no doubt that s. 7 requires proof of some degree of fault. That fault may be demonstrated by proof of intent, whether subjective or objective, or by proof of negligent conduct, depending on the nature of the offence. I am of the view that, with respect to regulatory offences, proof of negligence satisfies the requirement of fault demanded by s. 7. Although the element of fault may not be removed completely, the demands of s. 7 will be met in the regulatory context where liability is imposed for conduct which breaches the standard of reasonable care required of those operating in the regulated field.

Where negligence is the basis of liability, the question is not what the accused intended, but rather whether the accused exercised reasonable care. The application of the contextual approach suggests that negligence is an acceptable basis of liability in the regulatory context which fully meets the fault requirement in s. 7 of the Charter.

It must be remembered that regulatory offences were historically developed and recognized as a distinct category precisely for the purpose of relieving the Crown of the burden of proving *mens rea*. This is their hallmark. The tremendous importance of regulatory legislation in modern Canadian industrial society requires that courts be wary of interfering unduly with the regulatory role of government through the application of inflexible standards. Under the contextual approach, negligence is properly acceptable as the minimum fault standard required of regulatory legislation by s. 7.

What some writers have referred to as "licensing" considerations lead to the same conclusion.

The regulated actor is allowed to engage in activity which potentially may cause harm to the public. That permission is granted on the understanding that the actor accept, as a condition of entering the regulated field, the responsibility to exercise reasonable care to ensure that the proscribed harm does not come about. As a result of choosing to enter a field of activity known to be regulated, the regulated actor is taken to be aware of and to have accepted the imposition of a certain objective standard of conduct as a precondition to being allowed to engage in the regulated activity. In these circumstances, it misses the mark to speak in terms of the "unfairness" of an attenuated fault requirement because the standard of reasonable care has been accepted by the regulated actor upon entering the regulated sphere.

Further, from a practical point of view, it is simply impossible for the government to monitor adequately every industry so as to be able to prove actual intent or *mens rea* in each case. In order to do so, governments would have to employ armies of experts in every conceivable field.

In our complex society, the government can, as a practical matter, do no more than to demonstrate that it has set reasonable standards to be met by persons in the regulated sphere, and to prove beyond a reasonable doubt that there has been a breach of those standards by the regulated defendant. The whole governmental regulatory scheme would be rendered meaningless if the appellant's *mens rea* argument were to succeed.

For these reasons, I conclude that the appellant's claim that strict liability offences violate s. 7 of the Charter cannot succeed. The requirements of s. 7 are met in the regulatory context by the imposition of liability based on a negligence standard. Therefore, no violation of s. 7 results from the imposition of strict liability.

B. SECTION 11(d): ONUS AND THE DUE DILIGENCE DEFENCE

Wholesale Travel argues that the placing of a persuasive burden on the accused to establish due diligence on a balance of probabilities violates the presumption of innocence as guaranteed by s. 11(d) of the Charter. As the due diligence defence is the essential characteristic of strict liability offences as defined in *Sault Ste. Marie*, the appellant's s. 11(d) claim represents a fundamental challenge to the entire regime of regulatory offences in Canada.

THE CONTENT OF THE PRESUMPTION IN THE REGULATORY CONTEXT

The importance of regulatory legislation and its enforcement strongly support the use of a contextual approach in the interpretation of the s. 11(d) right as applied to regulatory offences.

The reasons for ascribing a different content to the presumption of innocence in the regulatory context are persuasive and compelling. As with the *mens rea* issue, if regulatory mechanisms are to operate effectively, the Crown cannot be required to disprove due diligence beyond a reasonable doubt. Such a requirement would make it virtually impossible for the Crown to prove regulatory offences, and would effectively prevent governments from seeking to implement public policy through regulatory means.

Criminal offences have always required proof of guilt beyond a reasonable doubt; the accused cannot, therefore, be convicted where there is a reasonable doubt as to guilt. This is not so with regulatory offences, where a conviction will lie if the accused has failed to meet the standard of care required. Thus, the question is not whether the accused has exercised *some* care, but whether the degree of care exercised was sufficient to meet the standard imposed. If the false advertiser, the corporate polluter, and the manufacturer of noxious goods are to be effectively controlled, it is necessary to require them to show, on a balance of probabilities, that they took reasonable precautions to avoid the harm which actually resulted. In the regulatory context, there is nothing unfair about imposing that onus; indeed, it is essential for the protection of our vulnerable society.

Quite simply, the enforcement of regulatory offences would be rendered virtually impossible if the Crown were required to prove negligence beyond a reasonable doubt. The means of proof of reasonable care will be peculiarly within the knowledge and ability of the regulated accused. Only the accused will be in a position to bring forward evidence relevant to the question of due diligence.

Nor can it be argued that other solutions would be satisfactory; there is simply no other practical solution. Both with respect to the consumption of government resources and the intrusiveness of regulatory measures, the consequences of a finding that the due diligence defence violates s. 11(d) of the Charter would be extremely severe. Governments would be forced to devote tremendous expenditure, in terms of monetary and human resources, to regulatory enforcement mechanisms. Armies of investigators and experts would be required in order to garner sufficient evidence to establish negligence or disprove due diligence beyond a reasonable doubt.

Further, a marked expansion in enforcement mechanisms by definition implies an escalation in the intrusiveness of regulatory measures. The greater the burden of proof on the Crown, the greater the likelihood that those charged with the enforcement of regulatory measures would have to resort to legislation authorizing search and surveillance in order to gather sufficient evidence to discharge that onus.

As with the s. 7 challenge, licensing considerations support the conclusion that strict liability does not violate s. 11(d) of the Charter. The licensing argument attributes to the regulated actor knowledge and acceptance, not only of the standard of reasonable care itself, but also of the responsibility to establish, on a balance of probabilities, the exercise of reasonable care. Acceptance of this burden is an implied term and a precondition of being allowed to engage in activity falling within the regulated sphere. Regulated actors are taken to understand that, should they be unable to discharge this burden, an inference of negligence will be drawn from the fact that the proscribed result has occurred.

For these reasons, I conclude that the presumption of innocence as guaranteed in s. 11(d) of the

Charter is not violated by strict liability offences as defined in *Sault Ste. Marie*. The imposition of a reverse persuasive onus on the accused to establish due diligence on a balance of probabilities does not run counter to the presumption of innocence, notwithstanding the fact that the same reversal of onus would violate s. 11(d) in the criminal context.

C. THE IMPRISONMENT CONCERN

The ultimate question is whether the imposition of imprisonment on the basis of strict liability comports with the principles of fundamental justice. For the reasons set out earlier concerning the underlying rationale of regulatory offences, I am of the opinion that it does.

Regulatory schemes can only be effective if they provide for significant penalties in the event of their breach. Indeed, although it may be rare that imprisonment is sought, it must be available as a sanction if there is to be effective enforcement of the regulatory measure. Nor is the imposition of imprisonment unreasonable in light of the danger that can accrue to the public from breaches of regulatory statutes. The spectre of tragedy evoked by such names as Thalidomide, Bhopal, Chernobyl, and the *Exxon Valdez* can leave no doubt as to the potential human and environmental devastation which can result from the violation of regulatory measures. Strong sanctions including imprisonment are vital to the prevention of similar catastrophes. The potential for serious harm flowing from the breach of regulatory measures is too great for it to be said that imprisonment can never be imposed as a sanction.

E. SECTION 1

In light of my conclusion regarding the appellant's ss. 7 and 11(d) claims, there is no need to proceed to s. 1. However, had it been necessary to consider the matter, the same reasons I have set forth in finding that neither ss. 7 nor s. 11(d) are necessarily infringed by strict liability offences would have led me to conclude that strict liability offences can be justified under s. 1 of the Charter.

V. Application to s. 36(1)(a) and s. 37.3(2)

Section 36(1)(a) of the Competition Act creates the offence of false or misleading advertising. Section 37.3(2) provides a statutory defence to that charge. The defence will only lie where all four conditions set out in paras. (a) through (d) are met.

THE VALIDITY OF PARAS. (c) AND (d) OF S. 37.3(2)

Paragraph (c) of s. 37.3(2) requires an accused who has made a misleading representation to take positive steps to bring the error to the attention of those likely to be affected by it. Paragraph (d) requires this to be done promptly. The effect of these provisions is to impose an obligation on the accused to make a prompt retraction as a precondition to relying on the defence of due diligence.

Even where an accused can establish the absence of negligence in the making of misleading representations, paras. (c) and (d) nonetheless require conviction if the accused has failed to make a prompt correction or retraction. In these circumstances, the accused would be deprived of the defence of due diligence and the offence would be tantamount to absolute liability, since liability could be imposed in the absence of fault on the part of the accused.

Such a result clearly violates s. 7 of the Charter. Nor do I think that paras. (c) and (d) can be justified under s. 1 of the Charter.

THE VALIDITY OF PARAS. (a) AND (b)

These paragraphs in essence put forward the common law defence of due diligence. In the regulatory context, it is appropriate that fault should be imposed on the basis of negligence. There is therefore no violation of s. 7 resulting from the removal of the *mens rea* requirement in strict liability offences. It follows that paras. (a) and (b) of s. 37.3(2) do not violate s. 7 of the Charter.

It has been noted earlier that the s. 11(d) presumption of innocence has a different scope and meaning in relation to regulatory, as opposed to criminal, offences. In my view, the imposition in strict liability offences of a reverse persuasive onus on the accused to establish due diligence is proper and permissible and does not constitute a violation of the s. 11(d) presumption of innocence. I therefore conclude that paras. (a) and (b) of s. 37.3(2) do not violate s. 11(d) of the Charter.

VI. Conclusion

Strict liability offences, as exemplified in this case by the combination of s. 36(1)(a) and s. 37.3(2)(a) and (b) of the Competition Act, do not violate either ss. 7 or 11(d) of the Charter. Neither the absence of a *mens rea* requirement nor the imposition of an onus on the accused to establish due diligence on a balance of probabilities offends the Charter rights of those accused of regulatory offences.

Regulatory legislation is essential to the functioning of our society and to the protection of the public. It responds to the compelling need to protect the health and safety of the members of our society and to preserve our fragile environment. The imposition of strict liability is both reasonable and essential to the operation of regulatory schemes.

VII. Disposition

Since paragraphs (c) and (d) of s. 37.3(2) of the Competition Act violate s. 7 of the Charter and cannot be justified under s. 1, they must be struck down and declared to be of no force or effect. What remains in s. 36(1)(a) and s. 37.3(2)(a) and (b) is a strict liability regulatory offence. These provisions are valid and enforceable. In the result, I would dismiss the appeal and allow the Crown's Appeal to the extent required to reflect this disposition.

Appeal by accused dismissed; appeal by Crown allowed in part.

Modes of Participation in Crime

INTRODUCTION

The five cases excerpted in this chapter address two major issues in Canadian criminal law: (i) the various ways in which one may become a party to a criminal offence; and (ii) the nature and scope of criminal liability in relation to inchoate offences (counselling, attempt, and conspiracy).

In the *Greyeyes* case (1997), the Supreme Court of Canada explored the extent to which the courts should give a broad interpretation to the concepts of aiding and abetting in the context of dealing in illicit drugs.

In the *Logan* case (1990), the Supreme Court of Canada considered the nature of criminal liability that arises by virtue of "common intention" under the provisions of section 21(2) of the Criminal Code. The case establishes that the objective component of section 21(2) (viz., the words "ought to have known") is invalid under the Charter when the Crown is seeking to prove that the accused was a party to the offences of murder or attempted murder.

Ancio (1984), *Dynar* (1997) and *Gladstone* (1996) are all cases that illustrate various dimensions of the nature of inchoate offences. In the *Ancio* case, the Supreme Court of Canada held that the *mens rea* for an attempt always consists of *the intent to commit the complete offence* in question. In *Dynar*, the Supreme Court of Canada reaffirmed the principle that an accused person may be legitimately convicted of either attempt or conspiracy even if it would have been impossible for him or her to have completed the offence. In *Dynar*, the Supreme Court also provided a valuable overview of the essential elements of the offences of attempt and conspiracy. Finally, the *Gladstone* case examines the difficult question of where courts should draw the line between acts that are sufficiently "proximate" to the completed offence to merit the imposition of criminal liability upon the accused, and acts that are too "remote" from the completed offence to justify punishment under the criminal law.

Greyeyes v. The Queen

SUPREME COURT OF CANADA   JULY 10, 1997

BACKGROUND

Greyeyes was charged with trafficking in cocaine. He was acquitted at his trial. The Crown appealed to the Saskatchewan Court of Appeal, which allowed the Crown's appeal and convicted the accused. Greyeyes appealed against his conviction to the Supreme Court of Canada.

MAIN ISSUE

Can an accused person who acts as an agent for a purchaser of narcotics, or who provides assistance to a purchaser to buy narcotics, be considered a party to the offence of trafficking by virtue of section 21(1)(b) and (c) of the Criminal Code (aiding and/or abetting)?

JUDGMENTS

The *majority* judgment was delivered by Justice L'Heureux-Dubé (with whom Justices La Forest, Sopinka, and Gonthier agreed). Justice Cory delivered a *concurring* judgment (with which Justices McLachlin and Major agreed).

....

1 L'HEUREUX-DUBÉ J.: — I have had the advantage of reading the reasons of my colleague Justice Cory. While I agree with much of his analysis as well as the conclusion he reaches, I have difficulty with one aspect of his reasons. Specifically, I believe that his interpretation of s. 21 of the Criminal Code, R.S.C. 1985, c. C-46, and the manner in which it applies to the offence of drug trafficking under s. 4(1) of the Narcotic Control Act, R.S.C. 1985, c. N-1, leads to a broad scope of liability which is unwarranted.

2 The thrust of my colleague's reasons (at para. 32) is that "one who assists a purchaser to buy narcotics . . . come[s] within the definition of 'aiding' or 'abetting' under s. 21(1) of the Code." By assisting the purchaser, this person makes the sale of narcotics possible, and thus is a party to the offence of trafficking. My colleague recognizes, however, that a purchaser, through the act of buying alone, cannot be convicted of trafficking, but feels that *any* act of the person offering assistance to the purchaser, no matter how trivial, can lead (assuming the requisite knowledge and intent are also present) to a finding of guilt for this offence.

3 This reasoning is based, in part, upon the idea that Parliament has specifically excluded purchasers from the offence of trafficking, yet never intended to extend that immunity to persons assisting the purchase. I do not share my colleague's view of Parliament's intent in this regard. Moreover, I am deeply concerned that the adoption of his

Adapted from *R. v. Greyeyes* (1997), 116 C.C.C. (3d), pp. 338–350. Copyright © 1997 by *Canada Law Book*. Reprinted with permission.

approach would lead to convictions for trafficking in situations that were never intended to come within that definition.

4   Merely as an example of the breadth of my colleague's approach, I offer the following scenario. Ms. A wishes to buy drugs and warns her boyfriend, Mr. B, that she will walk over, through a dangerous neighbourhood, unless he drives her there. He agrees, and upon arrival, she enters and makes the purchase alone. Despite his minimal participation, Mr. B has assisted the sale because he has conveyed the purchaser to the designated sale location. As a result, while Ms. A, as a purchaser, will receive the lesser possession conviction, Mr. B. will be guilty of trafficking.

5   In my view, such a result is unacceptable. In this regard, while I express no opinion about the particular situation to which he was referring, I agree with the general sentiment expressed by Seaton J.A. in *R. v. Eccleston* (1975), 24 C.C.C. (2d) 564 (B.C.C.A.) at p. 568, who observed that extending "the definition of trafficking so as to encompass conduct that right-minded people would say is not trafficking is damaging and to be avoided."

6   It should not be forgotten that the offence of trafficking is taken extremely seriously by both the courts and the public, and a conviction brings along with it a great deal of social stigma. It goes without saying that someone branded as a "trafficker" is held in extremely low regard by the public. Additionally, sentencing for these offences tends to be quite high. I am reluctant to sanction an approach which encourages convictions in cases where the assistance rendered is *solely* to the purchaser.

7   Moreover, I am of the view that in such a case, a charge of trafficking would actually be the incorrect legal result. As my colleague points out [*post*, paras. 29–31]:

> . . . Martin J.A. [in *R. v. Meston* (1975), 28 C.C.C. (2d) 497 (Ont. C.A.)] then went on to consider this Court's decision in *Poitras v. The Queen*, [1974] S.C.R. 649. The reasons in that case per-

suaded him that a purchaser should not, by reason of the purchase alone, be found to be a party to the offence of trafficking. . . . I agree with that conclusion.

....

Certainly there can be no doubt that someone who purchases a narcotic must assist the vendor in completing the sale. Without a purchaser, there could be no sale of the narcotic. However, Parliament has chosen to address the culpability of purchasers in a different fashion. As soon as someone obtains possession of a narcotic, he or she may be charged with possession or possession for the purpose of trafficking. Yet it is clear that that person does not come within the definition of trafficking. *Nor can he or she be found guilty of aiding or abetting the offence of trafficking on the basis of the purchase alone. Parliament has created other offences under which a purchaser may be charged as a result of the purchase.* [Emphasis added.]

8   In my view, this excerpt clearly demonstrates the important distinction between vendor and purchaser. I agree that, despite his or her crucial assistance in helping to complete the sale of narcotics, the purchaser cannot *by this action alone* be found guilty of the offence of aiding or abetting the offence of trafficking. Frankly, I see no reason why this reasoning should not be extended to third parties as well. In situations where the facts reveal no more than incidental assistance of the sale through rendering aid to the purchaser, it stands to reason that these persons should be treated as purchasers, and not as traffickers. The proper charge in these circumstances would be aiding or abetting the possession of a narcotic, and not trafficking.

9   The offence of aiding or abetting possession of a narcotic is a permissible legal result and has occurred on many occasions.

10   In my view, this approach also offers a number of advantages. First, I believe it accords with the general notion that the "punishment" should be in accord with the crime. A trafficking conviction, in the circumstances indicated above, is

quite harsh, carries with it considerable stigma, and has negative consequences for the repute of justice. In this regard, it is also worth noting that the sentencing structure for these offences is rather disparate. A trafficking conviction is punishable by up to life imprisonment, while a possession conviction carries a maximum seven-year sentence.

11 Perhaps more importantly, I believe this approach benefits from a certain symmetry. It is clear that someone whose acts are designed to aid a purchaser, yet incidentally benefit the seller, has assisted much more in the purchase of the narcotic than in the sale. As such, it is only fitting that this person share the culpability and stigma of the purchaser rather than that of the vendor.

12 Moreover, it addresses the concern set out at para. 32 by Cory J. that "[i]f the same exception which applies to purchasers were extended to agents for the purchaser, then the agents could escape culpability entirely." In my view, this is a valid concern, which is certainly not ignored by this approach; where the facts warrant it, agents or people assisting a purchaser could well face a conviction for aiding or abetting possession of a narcotic.

13 In the case at bar, however, I have no difficulty concluding that the appellant did far more than act as a purchaser. My colleague has described the nature of the appellant's participation in the sale in detail, and these facts demonstrate a concerted effort on his part to effect the transfer of narcotics. The appellant located the seller, brought the buyer to the site, and introduced the parties. It is clear that without this assistance, the purchase would never have taken place. Moreover, he acted as a spokesperson, negotiated the price of the drugs, and passed the money over to the seller. He also accepted money for having facilitated the deal. As my colleague points out, without the appellant's assistance, the buyer would never have been able to enter the apartment building and contact the seller. These are not the acts of a mere purchaser, and as a result it is clear that the appellant aided the traffic of narcotics.

14 With respect to the required intention to commit such an offence under s. 21(1)(b) of the Code, and whether it was established in this case, I am in complete agreement with the approach taken by my colleague.

15 I would dispose of the appeal as proposed by Cory J.

16 CORY J.: — A purchaser of narcotics can be found guilty of possession of drugs or possession of drugs for the purposes of trafficking. As a result of this exposure to criminal prosecution for these offences, it has been determined that a purchaser of drugs cannot be convicted of aiding or abetting a vendor of drugs. Courts have differed as to the culpability of one who assists the purchaser. In some cases it has been held that, since the purchaser could not be found guilty of aiding and abetting, someone assisting the purchaser must also be found not guilty. Other decisions appear to come to a different conclusion. The question which must be addressed on this appeal is whether a person who aids or abets a purchaser of drugs should be found guilty as a party to the illegal drug transaction.

Factual Background

17 In August of 1994, Constable Morgan, an undercover RCMP officer, bought five "joints" of marijuana from the appellant, Ernest Richard Greyeyes. The following day, Morgan asked the appellant if he knew where he could get some cocaine. The appellant stated that he knew a source, and if Morgan would drive him, he would attempt to get some. The appellant directed Morgan to an apartment building. Greyeyes went inside alone and returned to say that the people he was hoping to talk to were out but would be back later that evening.

18 Morgan and the appellant returned to the apartment building that evening and entered together. Greyeyes identified himself over the intercom and they both went up to the apartment door. Greyeyes again identified himself. A voice from inside asked what they wanted. The appellant said "cocaine." The voice asked how much, and the appellant looked at Morgan, who indicated "one." The appellant replied "one." Morgan asked the appellant how much it would cost, and the appellant told him it would be $40. At this point the people in the apartment encountered difficulty opening the door, and after a few minutes the person inside said to slide the money under the door, which the appellant did. Immediately a small pink flap containing two-tenths of a gram of cocaine was passed back under the door. The appellant picked it up, handed it to Morgan and then started walking towards the exit. When they left the building, Morgan drove the appellant home and gave him $10 for helping him obtain the cocaine.

Analysis

25 Can someone either acting as an agent for a purchaser of narcotics or assisting a purchaser to buy narcotics be found to be a party to the offence of trafficking under s. 21(1) of the Code, by aiding or abetting in the sale of narcotics? In my view, the response to the question must be that such a person can indeed be found to be a party to the offence.

Aiding and Abetting

26 The terms "aiding" and "abetting" are often used together in the context of determining whether persons are parties to an offence. Although the meanings of these terms are similar, they are separate concepts. To aid, under s. 21(1)(b), means to assist or help the actor. To abet, within the meaning of s. 21(1)(c), includes encouraging, instigating, promoting, or procuring the crime to be committed.

Liability of an Agent for the Purchaser

27 The appellant claims that he cannot be a party to the offence of trafficking since he was acting exclusively on behalf of the purchaser of the drugs and not the seller. He contends that since a purchaser of a narcotic cannot be convicted of aiding and abetting the seller's offence of trafficking, then someone who extends assistance only to the purchaser should not be found to be a party either.

30 The provisions of the Narcotic Control Act, which deal with the possession of a narcotic, support the contention that a purchaser is in a unique situation and should not be found to be a party to the offence of trafficking simply by reason of the purchase. The definition of trafficking in s. 2 of the Act includes the manufacture, sale, transportation, delivery, and distribution, but *not* the purchase, of a narcotic. However, s. 3(1) of the Act makes it an offence to possess a narcotic. Further, although the reverse onus provision has been found to infringe s. 11(d) of the Charter (see *R. v. Oakes*, [1986] 1 S.C.R. 103, 24 C.C.C. (3d) 321, 26 D.L.R. (4th) 200), it is of historical interest as to the intent of Parliament in that s. 8(2) did go so far as to provide that an accused found to be in possession of a narcotic bears the onus of establishing that he did not have the drugs for the purpose of trafficking. Parliament has established a clear legislative scheme which addresses the culpability of those involved in the purchase of narcotics. As Martin J.A. concluded at p. 507 of *Meston*, *supra*:

> If the purchaser who has encouraged the sale of a narcotic drug to himself cannot be convicted of trafficking, it must be because the Narcotic Control Act manifests a legislative intention that a mere purchaser does not incur liability in respect of the offence of trafficking committed by the seller.

A similar observation is made in the helpful text *Criminal Pleadings & Practice in Canada*, 2nd ed. (Aurora, Ont.: Canada Law Book, 1996 (looseleaf)), at p. 15–9, para. 12:2090 (release May 1997):

> It seems that a purchaser of drugs, although factually aiding or abetting the seller, does *not* legally aid or abet the seller, i.e., the trafficker of drugs, since the purchaser commits the separate offence (when purchasing the drugs) of simple possession of the drugs or possession of the drugs for the purpose of trafficking. [Emphasis in original.]

31 Certainly there can be no doubt that someone who purchases a narcotic must assist the vendor in completing the sale. Without a purchaser, there could be no sale of the narcotic. However, Parliament has chosen to address the culpability of purchasers in a different fashion. As soon as someone obtains possession of a narcotic, he or she may be charged with possession or possession for the purpose of trafficking. Yet it is clear that that person does not come within the definition of trafficking. Nor can he or she be found guilty of aiding or abetting the offence of trafficking on the basis of the purchase alone. Parliament has created other offences under which a purchaser may be charged as a result of the purchase.

32 It must be emphasized that there is no legislative intention similar to that which exists for purchasers to be found for those who assist or act as agents for a purchaser. Drug trafficking by its very nature is a business which involves and is dependent upon many "middle men." If the same exception that applies to purchasers were extended to agents for the purchaser, then the agents could escape culpability entirely. They should not. Quite simply, there is no reason to extend the exception for purchasers to those who assist or encourage purchasers in an illegal sale. The activities of an agent for a purchaser, or one who assists a purchaser to buy narcotics, certainly come within the definition of "aiding" or "abetting" under s. 21(1) of the Code. By bringing together the source of supply and the prospective purchaser, these persons obviously assist in the sale of narcotics. Acting as a spokesperson for a purchaser has the effect of assisting both the purchaser and the vendor to complete the transaction. It follows that an agent for a purchaser or one who assists the purchaser to buy the drugs can properly be found guilty as a party to the offence of trafficking under s. 21(1) of the Code.

35 In summary, someone who acts on behalf of a purchaser of narcotics can be found to be a party to the offence of trafficking under s. 21(1) of the Code. This is so because such a person assists in the commission of the offence by bringing the purchaser to the seller. Without that intervention or assistance, the sale would never occur. There is nothing in the provisions of the Narcotic Control Act, in any applicable principles of criminal law, or in reasons of policy, which indicates that any special status should be granted to those assisting purchasers of drugs so as to exempt them from the clear provisions of s. 21 of the Code.

Application of the Principle to the Case at Bar

36 Let us apply that principle to the facts of this case. It must be determined whether the accused actually aided or abetted the sale of narcotics. There is no doubt in my mind that he did. The trial judge found as a fact that the appellant acted as a spokesperson for the purchaser. He was the one who brought the customer to the seller. He was the connection between the buyer and the seller. He escorted the buyer to the seller's apartment, negotiated with the seller to purchase the drug, and accepted $10 from the buyer for facilitating the deal. The buyer had tried to purchase drugs from the very same apartment earlier in the week, but was denied access, apparently because he was unknown to the seller. It was only as a result of the appellant's assistance that the prospective buyer was able to get into the apartment building. These facts are sufficient to establish that the appellant aided in the sale of narcotics within the meaning of s. 21(1)(b) of the Code, and encouraged the sale within the meaning of s. 21(1)(c) of the Code.

37 Next it must be determined whether the appellant had the requisite *mens rea* or guilty mind to satisfy s. 21(b). That section provides that any person who does anything *for the purpose of aiding* a person to commit an offence is a party to the offence. In order to satisfy the purpose requirement under s. 21(1)(b), the Crown is required to prove only that the accused intended the consequences that flowed from his or her aid to the principal offender, and need not show that he or she desired or approved of the consequences.

38 Section 21(1)(c) simply provides that any person who abets any person in committing an offence is a party to that offence. In order to secure a conviction, the Crown must prove not only that the accused encouraged the principal with his or her words or acts, but also that the accused intended to do so: *R. v. Curran* (1977), 38 C.C.C. (2d) 151 (Alta. C.A.); *R. v. Jones* (1977), 65 Cr. App. R. 250 (C.A.). It is the establishment by the Crown of that intention which satisfies the *mens rea* or guilty mind requirement of s. 21(1)(c).

39 Did the appellant intend to assist or encourage the sale? There can be no doubt that the appellant knew he was assisting in the illegal sale of narcotics, and that he intended to do so. His words and actions demonstrate that he deliberately set out to bring together the parties to the transaction and acted as the conduit for delivering the drugs from the seller to the buyer. The appellant may have been *motivated* solely by a desire to help the buyer, but what he *intended* to do was to facilitate the sale of narcotics, and this is a culpable intention. Since the appellant actually encouraged and assisted in the illegal sale of narcotics, and since he had the intention of doing so, he was guilty of trafficking as a party pursuant to s. 21(1)(b) and (c) of the Code.

Disposition

42 I would dismiss this appeal and uphold the conviction imposed by the Court of Appeal.

Appeal dismissed.

Regina v. Logan et al.

SUPREME COURT OF CANADA   SEPTEMBER 13, 1990

BACKGROUND

Logan and Leroy were charged with a number of offences, including attempted murder and robbery. During the robbery of a convenience store, Logan's brother shot and severely injured a clerk. The trial judge instructed the members of the jury that they could convict Logan and Leroy of attempted murder on the basis of section 21(2) of the Code, if the accused either knew or "ought to have known" that one of the members of their gang would probably shoot someone with the intent of killing him or her.

Logan and Leroy were convicted of attempted murder. Their appeal to the Ontario Court of Appeal against their conviction was dismissed, but the Court substituted convictions of robbery for the convictions of attempted murder. The Crown subsequently appealed to the Supreme Court of Canada.

MAIN ISSUE

Does section 21(2) of the Criminal Code contravene sections 7 and/or 11(d) of the Charter and, if so, is it saved by section 1 of the Charter?

JUDGMENTS

The *majority* judgment was delivered by Chief Justice Lamer (with whom Chief Justice Dickson and Justices Wilson, Gonthier, and Cory agreed). *Concurring* judgments were delivered by Justices Sopinka and L'Heureux-Dubé.

....

LAMER C.J.C.: —

Facts

The two respondents, Sutcliffe Logan Jr. and Warren Leroy Johnson, together with two other co-accused, Hugh Logan (the brother of respondent Logan) and Clive Brown, were all charged with a number of offences arising from a series of robberies in the Toronto area. This appeal pertains only to the charges against the two respondents for attempted murder which resulted from an incident during one of the robberies.

The facts surrounding the incident are as follows. At around 11:00 P.M. on September 23, 1983, Hugh Logan, Clive Brown, and the respondent Warren Johnson entered a convenience store wearing masks and armed with revolvers. Hugh Logan shot the lone clerk, Barbara Turnbull, in the neck, causing severe injuries. The cash register was robbed and the men fled.

In his charge to the jury with respect to the respondent Warren Johnson, the trial judge said that "you may well have considerable doubt whether he knew or should have known that one of his group would probably shoot somebody with the intention to kill." With respect to the respondent Sutcliffe Logan, he stated that "you would then have to consider whether he knew or should have known that one of the group would probably, in the course of the robbery, shoot someone with intent to kill." In his explanation of s. 21 of the Criminal Code, R.S.C. 1970, c. C-34, the trial judge instructed the jury that "[i]t must be established beyond a reasonable doubt that the accused knew or ought to have known that someone would probably shoot with the intention of killing."

Hugh Logan was found by the jury to have been the one who shot the victim. The respondents were convicted by the jury of a number offences, including the attempted murder of Barbara Turnbull. The respondents appealed their convictions to the Court of Appeal for Ontario. The Court of Appeal allowed their appeals with respect to the convictions for attempted murder, and substituted convictions for armed robbery in their stead. The only issue before this court is the constitutionality of s. 21(2) of the Criminal Code.

Analysis

Requisite *Mens Rea* for Conviction Pursuant to s. 21(2)

The question whether a party to an offence had the requisite *mens rea* to found a conviction pursuant to s. 21(2) must be answered in two steps. First, is there a minimum degree of *mens rea* which is required as a principle of fundamental justice before one can be convicted as a principal for this particular offence? This is an important initial step because, if there is no such constitutional requirement for the offence, the objective component of s. 21(2) can operate without restricting the constitutional rights of the party to the offence. Secondly, if the principles of fundamental justice do require a certain minimum degree of *mens rea* in order to convict for this offence, then that minimum degree of *mens rea* is constitutionally required to convict a party to that offence as well.

STEP ONE: S. 7 AND ATTEMPTED MURDER

With respect to the case at bar, then, the first question which must be answered is whether the principles of fundamental justice require a minimum degree of *mens rea* in order to convict an accused of attempted murder. *Ancio* (1984), 10 C.C.C. (3d) 385 (S.C.C.), established that a specific intent to kill is the *mens rea* required for a principal on the charge of attempted murder. However, as the constitutional question was not raised or argued in that case, it did not decide whether that requisite *mens rea* was a *constitutional* requirement. The case simply interpreted the offence as currently legislated.

In *R. v. Martineau* (1990), 58 C.C.C. (3d) 353 (S.C.C.), a judgment handed down this day, this court has decided, as a constitutional requirement, that no one can be convicted of murder unless the Crown proves beyond a reasonable doubt that the person had *subjective* foresight of the fact that the death of the victim was likely to ensue. Because of both the stigma and the severe penal consequences which result from a conviction for murder, the Constitution Act, 1982 requires at least that degree of intent.

As defined in *Ancio*, the elements of *mens rea* for attempted murder are identical to those for the most severe form of murder, murder under s. 212(a)(i). For each, the accused must have had the specific intent to kill. All that differs is the "consequences" component of the *actus reus*. Quite simply, an attempted murderer is, if caught and convicted, a "lucky murderer." Therefore, it would seem logical that the requisite *mens rea* for a murder conviction, as described in *Martineau*, must be the same for a conviction of attempted murder. However, logic is not sufficient reason to label something a "constitutional requirement." As I have stated in *Vaillancourt* (1987), 39 C.C.C. (3d) 118 (S.C.C.), the principles of fundamental justice require a minimum degree of *mens rea* for only a very few offences. The criteria by which these offences can be identified are, primarily, the stigma associated with a conviction and, as a secondary consideration, the penalties available.

The stigma associated with a conviction for attempted murder is the same as it is for murder. Such a conviction reveals that, although no death ensued from the actions of the accused, the intent to kill was still present in his or her mind. The attempted murderer is no less a killer than a murderer: he may be lucky — the ambulance arrived early, or some other fortuitous circumstance — but he still has the same killer instinct. Secondly, while a conviction for attempted murder does not automatically result in a life sentence, the offence is punishable by life and the usual penalty is very severe.

It should be noted that, as a basis for a constitutionally required minimum degree of *mens rea*, the social stigma associated with a conviction is the most important consideration, not the sentence. Few offences have a high minimum sentence such as that for murder. For some offences, there is a high maximum and a low minimum penalty available; for other offences, the maximum penalty is much reduced and there is no minimum imposed whatsoever. In either situation, the fact that a lesser sentence is available or imposed, by statute or through the exercise of judicial discretion, in no way ends the inquiry. The sentencing range available to the judge is not conclusive of the level of *mens rea* constitutionally required. Instead, the crucial consideration is whether there is a continuing serious social stigma which will be imposed on the accused upon conviction.

For these reasons, the *mens rea* for attempted murder cannot, without restricting s. 7 of the Charter, require of the accused less of a mental element than that required of a murderer under s. 212(a)(i), that is, *subjective* foresight of the consequences. While Parliament, as I have already implied, could well extend our definition of attempted murder in *Ancio* to include the unsuccessful murderers of s. 212(a)(ii), it cannot go further and include objective foreseeability as being sufficient for a conviction without restricting s. 7 of the Charter.

STEP TWO: *MENS REA* FOR ATTEMPTED MURDER PURSUANT TO S. 21(2)

Having completed the initial step of the inquiry, one can proceed to the second step in determining the requisite *mens rea* for the conviction of a party pursuant to s. 21(2) on a charge of attempted murder. When the principles of fundamental justice require *subjective* foresight in order to convict a principal of attempted murder, that same minimum degree of *mens rea* is constitutionally required to convict a party to the offence of attempted murder. Any conviction for attempted murder, whether of the principal directly or of a party pursuant to s. 21(2), will carry enough stigma to trigger the constitutional requirement. To the extent that s. 21(2) would allow for the conviction of a party to the offence of attempted murder on the basis of objective foreseeability, its operation restricts s. 7 of the Charter.

Section 1 Analysis

Given the finding that s. 7 is restricted in the present case, can that restriction be found to be a reasonable limit demonstrably justified in a free and democratic society? The section 1 analysis to be followed in answering this question has been set out in the decision of this court in *R. v. Oakes* (1986), 24 C.C.C. (3d) 321, 26 D.L.R. (4th) 200, [1986] 1 S.C.R. 103.

In determining the importance of the legislative objective, it is necessary to focus on what exactly needs to be justified in each particular case. At this stage, the finding that the offence of attempted murder requires, as a principle of fundamental justice, a minimum degree of *mens rea* is not in issue, but merely triggers the restriction under s. 21(2). The requisite *mens rea* for attempted murder is not the issue undergoing the s. 1 test because the current legislation for attempted murder, as interpreted by this court in *Ancio*, meets the constitutional requirement of subjective foresight, i.e., a specific intent to kill.

Given that a minimum degree of *mens rea* (subjective foresight) is constitutionally required to convict a principal of the offence of attempted murder, the restriction of s. 7 in this case is in convicting, through the operation of s. 21(2), a nonprincipal who does not have that same degree of *mens rea*. It is not the legislative objective of s. 21(2) as a whole which this court must scrutinize, but only the legislative objective of that portion of s. 21(2) that restricts the accused's rights under s. 7 of the Charter in issue in the present case. This differential treatment of parties and principals charged with *attempted murder* is the restriction which must undergo the s. 1 test.

In this case, the objective of such a differentiation is to deter joint criminal enterprises and to encourage persons who do participate to ensure that their accomplices do not commit offences beyond the planned unlawful purpose. This is a legislative objective of sufficient importance to justify overriding the rights of an accused under s. 7 of the Charter.

The next question to be addressed is whether the means by which Parliament has chosen to achieve that purpose are reasonable and justified, that is, if they are proportional to the objective they are meant to achieve.

First, a rational connection must be shown between the legislative objective and the restriction. By operation of s. 21(2) with respect to attempted murder, any person involved with others in an unlawful purpose is held responsible for the acts of all accomplices, whether or not that person actually foresaw that the accomplice would try to kill someone in furtherance of the unlawful purpose. The objective of the legislation is that this possibility of conviction through s. 21(2) will make parties more responsible for the actions of their accomplices. Clearly, then, there is a rational connection between the restriction and the legislative objective.

However, even though Parliament has sought to achieve an important legislative objective by enacting the restriction in issue in this appeal and even though such restriction is rationally connected to that objective, I am of the view that it does not satisfy the proportionality test because it unduly impairs an accused's rights under s. 7 of the Charter.

The objective component of s. 21(2) unduly impairs rights under s. 7 of the Charter when it operates with respect to an offence for which a conviction carries severe stigma and for which, therefore, there is a constitutionally required minimum degree of *mens rea*. The words "ought to know" allow for the possibility that while a party may not have considered and accepted the risk that an accomplice may do something with the intent to kill in furtherance of the common purpose, the party, through this negligence, could still be found guilty of attempted murder. In other words, parties could be held to be criminally negligent with respect to the behaviour of someone else. For most offences under the Criminal Code, a person is only convicted for criminal negligence if consequences have ensued from their actions. While a person may be convicted, absent consequences, for criminal negligence (e.g., dangerous operation of a motor vehicle), none of these forms of criminal negligence carry with them the stigma of being labelled a "killer." In a situation where s. 21(2) is operating in relation to the offence of attempted murder, no consequences have resulted from the actions of the party and yet the party could be convicted of this offence and suffer severe accompanying stigma and penalty.

Because of the importance of the legislative purpose, the objective component of s. 21(2) can be justified with respect to most offences. However, with respect to the few offences for which the Constitution requires subjective intent, the stigma renders the infringement too serious and outweighs the legislative objective which, therefore, cannot be justified under s. 1.

Conclusion

I would, therefore, as did the Court of Appeal, declare inoperative the words "or ought to have known" when considering under s. 21(2) whether a person is a party to any offence where it is a constitutional requirement for a conviction that foresight of the consequences be subjective, which is the case for attempted murder. Once these words are deleted, the remaining section requires, in the context of attempted murder, that the party to the common venture know that it is probable that his accomplice would do something with the intent to kill in carrying out the common purpose.

I would dismiss the appeal. I would restrict my answers to the constitutional questions as follows:

Question 1: Does s. 21(2) of the Criminal Code contravene the rights and freedoms guaranteed by s. 7 and/or s. 11(d) of the Canadian Charter of Rights and Freedoms?

Answer: Yes, on charges where subjective foresight is a constitutional requirement, to the extent that a party may be convicted if that person objectively "ought to have known" that the commission of the offence would be a probable consequence of carrying out the common purpose.

Question 2: If the answer to question 1 is in the affirmative, is s. 21(2) of the Criminal Code justified under s. 1 of the Canadian Charter of Rights and Freedoms, and therefore not inconsistent with the Constitution Act, 1982?

Answer: No.

Appeal dismissed.

Regina v. Ancio

SUPREME COURT OF CANADA   APRIL 2, 1984

BACKGROUND

At his trial, Ancio was convicted by the trial judge on a charge of attempted murder. Ancio subsequently appealed to the Ontario Court of Appeal which allowed his appeal and ordered a new trial. The Crown appealed against this decision to the Supreme Court of Canada.

MAIN ISSUE

Does the Crown have to prove an actual intent to kill in order to obtain a conviction on a charge of attempted murder?

JUDGMENTS

The *majority* judgment of the Supreme Court of Canada was delivered by Justice McIntyre (with whom Justices Dickson, Beetz, Estey, Chouinard, Lamer, and Wilson agreed). The *dissenting* judgment of Justice Ritchie has been omitted. Note that the Supreme Court Justices refer to the numbering in the 1970 edition of the Criminal Code. Section 222 is now section 239, section 213(d) has been repealed, and section 212 is now section 229.

McINTYRE J.: — This appeal involves consideration of the mental element required for proof of the crime of attempted murder, the subject of this Court's earlier judgment in *Lajoie v. The Queen* (1973), 10 C.C.C. (2d) 313, 33 D.L.R. (3d) 618, [1974] S.C.R. 399.

At the date of the events which give rise to this appeal, the respondent had been married some 25 years. His wife had left the matrimonial home and was living with one Kurely. The respondent was depressed and had been drinking to excess on the date in question. He telephoned his wife at Kurely's residence and told her he was afraid that their 23-year-old son was about to commit suicide and asked her to meet him. She refused to co-operate. Later the same evening, the respondent broke into a friend's home while its owners were absent and took away three shot-guns. He sawed off the barrel of one, loaded it, and, taking some extra ammunition with him, went to Kurely's apartment building and gained entry by breaking the glass in the front door. On hearing the noise caused by the breaking glass, Kurely came from his bedroom to investigate, carrying a chair with a jacket hanging on it. He saw the respondent, carrying the shot-gun, ascending the stairs to the second floor. He threw the chair and jacket, hitting the respondent. The gun went off. The blast missed Kurely by some three feet but put a hole in the jacket which had been on the chair. A struggle followed in which Kurely appears to have wrestled the gun from the respondent. When the police arrived, having been called during the course of the fight between the two men, Kurely was on the floor with his head partly under a bed and with the respondent upon him, striking him weakly.

According to the respondent's account of events, the gun was discharged accidentally, although, under tests conducted by the police, the weapon was not found to be prone to accidental discharge.

The respondent was charged with a number of offences arising out of this affair but only one, that of attempted murder, is involved in this appeal. He elected trial by judge alone and was convicted. The conviction was quashed in the Court of Appeal and a new trial directed [63 C.C.C. (2d) 309, 34 O.R. (2d) 437]. This appeal is taken by leave of this Court.

The trial judge disposed of the other charges against the respondent and made a finding that he had broken into Kurley's apartment building with intent to use the shot-gun to force his wife to leave. He said:

> I turn now to the very real point of the charge of attempted murder, and having made the finding I have of the break and enter at the house at 108 6th Street, with intent to commit an indictable offence, wither [*sic*] forceable confinement or worse. Forceable confinement if you accept the evidence of the accused. I feel probably worse than that.

He then referred to s. 213(d) of the Criminal Code which is in these terms:

> 213. Culpable homicide is murder where a person causes the death of a human being while committing or attempting to commit . . . (kidnapping and forcible confinement) . . . (breaking and entering) . . . whether or not the person means to cause death to any human being and whether or not he knows that death is likely to be caused to any human being, if
>
> (a) . . .
>
> (b) . . .
>
> (c) . . .

> (d) he uses a weapon or has it upon his person
>> (i) during or at the time he commits or attempts to commit the offence, or
>> (ii) during or at the time of his flight after committing or attempting to commit the offence,
>
> and the death ensues as a consequence.

Noting that breaking and entering with intent to commit an indictable offence is one of the offences named in the section, he convicted the respondent of attempted murder on the basis that the respondent had carried and used a weapon in the course of a breaking and entry with intent to effect forceable confinement of his wife.

The Crown contended in this Court that the Court of Appeal was in error in holding that the *mens rea* in attempted murder was limited to an intention to cause death (s. 212(a)(i)), or an intention to cause bodily harm knowing it to be likely to cause death and being reckless whether death ensues (s. 212(a)(ii)). The Crown's position was stated in its factum in these words:

> . . . the intention for attempted murder is not restricted to an actual intention to kill or an intention to cause grievous bodily harm that one knows is likely to cause death and is reckless whether death ensues or not, but *extends to an intention to do that which constitutes the commission of the offence of murder as defined in ss. 212 and 213 of the Criminal Code. It is the Crown's position that s. 24 and s. 213(d) in combination can form the basis for a conviction of attempted murder.*

(Emphasis added.)

The respondent supported the judgment of the Court of Appeal, which followed the judgment of this Court in *Lajoie v. The Queen*. In that case it was held that a conviction for attempted murder could be sustained where the Crown had shown on the part of the accused either an intent to kill the potential victim or an intent to cause bodily harm which he knows is likely to cause death and is reckless whether death ensues or not. The respondent submitted that the Crown's position, that s. 213(d) coupled with s. 24(1) described a further intent sufficient to warrant a conviction for attempted murder, should not be accepted because there was no authority to extend the concept of a constructive intent further than *Lajoie* had taken it. While contending on the facts of this case that he was not obliged to go further, he argued that in reason and logic a specific intent to kill should be the only intent sufficient to ground a conviction for attempted murder. It was said that the effect of the Crown's argument in extending the concept of an attempt to s. 213(d) of the Criminal Code would be to justify a conviction for attempted murder in the absence of any mental element with respect to the causing of death, which would be to ignore the words of s. 24(1) specifically requiring an intent to commit the offence in question.

Lying at the heart of the controversy which arises in this case is the judgment of this Court in *Lajoie*, *supra*. In that case the appellant shot a taxi-driver while attempting a robbery. The victim was struck by a bullet while fleeing the scene but did not die. The appellant was charged with various offences, one of which was attempted murder. At trial the judge instructed the jury that in order to convict the appellant upon the attempted murder charge, they had to be satisfied beyond a reasonable doubt that, in shooting at the victim, the accused had the intent to kill him. He declined to act on the Crown's request to charge the jury to the effect that, if they were not satisfied on the question of the intent to kill, a conviction of attempted murder could also rest upon proof of an intent to cause the appellant bodily harm, knowing it to be likely to cause death and being reckless whether death ensued or not. The appellant was found guilty of the lesser offence of discharging a firearm with intent to endanger life.

On appeal the Crown succeeded and a new trial was ordered. The majority, Branca J.A. and Nemetz J.A. (as he then was), were of the view that the mental element or intent required for attempted murder was not limited to the intent to kill but included as well those mental elements described in s. 212(a)(i) and (ii).

In the Supreme Court of Canada the appeal was dismissed. Martland J. wrote the judgment of the Court. He recognized that there was conflicting authority upon the question, but he expressed agreement with the majority of the Court of Appeal and he said:

> Section 210 [now s. 239] of the Criminal Code provides that every one who attempts by any means to commit murder is guilty of an indictable offence and is liable to imprisonment for life. Murder may be committed if the accused means to cause death, but it may also be committed if he means to cause bodily harm knowing that it is likely to cause death and is reckless whether death ensues or not. If it can be established that the accused tried to cause bodily harm to another of a kind which he knew was likely to cause death, and that he was reckless as to whether or not death would ensue then, under the wording of s. 210, if death did not ensue, an attempt to commit murder has been proved.

A great deal of the confusion surrounding the nature of the intent required to found a conviction for attempted murder may well stem from an assumption that murder and attempted murder are related offences which must share the same mental elements. A brief review of the historical development of the law relating to the two offences demonstrates that the crime of attempt developed as a separate and distinct offence from the offence of murder.

In very early times murder was simply the killing of a human being. The law was concerned with the injury done to the family of the deceased and the compensation which should follow. The consequence of the killing was the important feature and the intent or *mens rea* was of little if any significance. Special mental elements were recognized in statutes as early as the 13th century, and by the 14th century the concept of malice aforethought had developed (see 13 Richard II Stat. 2, c. 1). Thus two elements came to be recognized in murder: the killing, and the malice aforethought, which in modern times has come to mean the necessary intent or intents.

As the common law developed, the mental element required for the commission of murder expanded to include both constructive intent and knowledge of the likelihood of death as a result of a person's acts, with recklessness as to whether death ensued or not.

I would first observe that ss. 212 and 213 of the present Criminal Code prescribe the various mental elements which, if accompanied by a killing, may amount to murder. It is trite to say then that murder may be a killing with intent to kill and it may also be a killing with a variety of other intents which involve no intent to kill.

The offence of attempts developed much later than the offence of murder. In early times an attempt to commit an offence was not itself a crime. It was considered that in the absence of a guilty act, intention alone was not punishable. The modern offence of attempting the commission of a crime is said to have its origins in the Court of Star Chamber.

The practice of the Court of Star Chamber in this respect became firmly established in that court and was in time adopted in the Court of King's Bench. It has been said that the origin of the doctrine of criminal attempt as it is known in the common law was Lord Mansfield's judgment in *R. v. Scofield* (1784), Cald. Mag. Rep. 397. Any doubt remaining regarding the existence of the offence of attempted murder in England was set to rest by the enactment in 1861 (U.K.), c. 100, ss. 11 to 15. These sections made it a felony to attempt the commission of murder in the various ways described.

In Canada the common law offence of attempt was codified in the 1892 Criminal Code as s. 64. A minor amendment in the Criminal Code 1953–54 (Can.), c. 51, changed the section to its present form in s. 24:

> 24(1) Every one who, having an intent to commit an offence, does or omits to do anything for the purpose of carrying out his intention is

guilty of an attempt to commit the offence whether or not it was possible under the circumstances to commit the offence.

> (2) The question whether an act or omission by a person who has an intent to commit an offence is or is not mere preparation to commit the offence, and too remote to constitute an attempt to commit the offence, is a question of law.

The section has therefore covered the law of attempt in general since the codification of the law in 1892. In addition, particular provision has been made in the Criminal Code for the offence of attempted murder.

In the 1953–54 Code, s. 210 dealt with the matter in these words:

> 210. Everyone who attempts by any means to commit murder is guilty of an indictable offence and is liable to imprisonment for life.

This section appears as s. 222 [now s. 239] in the present Code.

It is clear from the foregoing that in common law and under the criminal law of Canada, criminal attempt is itself an offence separate and distinct from the crime alleged to be attempted. As with any other crime, the Crown must prove a *mens rea*, that is, the intent to commit the offence in question, and the *actus reus*, that is, some step towards the commission of the offence attempted going beyond mere acts of preparation. Of the two elements the more significant is the *mens rea*. In *R. v. Cline* (1956), 115 C.C.C. 18 at p. 27, 4 D.L.R. (2d) 480 at p. 488, [1956] O.R. 539, Laidlaw, J.A., speaking for the Ontario Court of Appeal, said:

> Criminal intention alone is insufficient to establish a criminal attempt. There must be *mens rea* and also an *actus reus*. But it is to be observed that whereas in most crimes it is the *actus reus* which the law endeavours to prevent, and the *mens rea* is only a necessary element of the offence, in a criminal attempt the *mens rea* is of

primary importance and the *actus reus* is the necessary element.

The common law recognition of the fundamental importance of intent in the crime of attempt is carried forward into the Criminal Code. A reading of s. 24 of the Code and all its predecessors since the enactment of the first Code in 1892 confirms that the intent to commit the desired offence is a basic element of the offence of attempt. Indeed, because the crime of attempt may be complete without the actual commission of any other offence and even without the performance of any act unlawful in itself, it is abundantly clear that the criminal element of the offence of attempt may lie solely in the intent. The question now arises: What is the intent required for an attempt to commit murder?

While it is clear from ss. 212 and 213 of the Criminal Code that an unintentional killing can be murder, it is equally clear that, whatever mental elements may be involved and whatever means may be employed, there cannot be a murder without a killing. Section 24 of the Code defines, in part, the offence of attempt as "having an intent to commit an offence." The completed offence of murder involves a killing. The intention to commit the complete offence of murder must therefore include an intention to kill. I find it impossible to conclude that a person may intend to commit the unintentional killings described in ss. 212 and 213 of the Code. I am then of the view that the *mens rea* for an attempted murder cannot be less than the specific intent to kill.

It was argued, and it has been suggested in some of the cases and academic writings on the question, that it is illogical to insist upon a higher degree of *mens rea* for attempted murder, while accepting a lower degree amounting to recklessness for murder. I see no merit in this argument. The intent to kill is the highest intent in murder and there is no reason in logic why an attempt to murder, aimed at the completion of the full crime of murder, should have any lesser intent. If there is any illogic in this matter, it is in the statutory characterization of unintentional killing as murder. The *mens rea* for attempted murder is, in my view, the specific intent to kill. A mental state falling short of that level may well lead to conviction for other offences, for example, one or other of the various aggravated assaults, but not a conviction for an attempt at murder. For these reasons, it is my view that *Lajoie* should no longer be followed.

I would accordingly dismiss the Crown's appeal and confirm the Court of Appeal's order for a new trial.

Appeal dismissed.

United States of America and Minister of Justice v. Dynar

SUPREME COURT OF CANADA   JUNE 26, 1997

BACKGROUND

Dynar, a Canadian citizen, was the subject of an abortive "sting" operation conducted by the FBI in the United States. He was charged in the U.S. District Court of Nevada with one count of attempting to launder money. The U.S. government requested the extradition of Dynar. A judge of the Ontario Court (General Division) committed Dynar for extradition. He appealed his committal to the Ontario Court of Appeal, which allowed the appeal on the basis that Dynar's conduct would not have constituted a criminal offence in Canada. The United States of America and the Minister of Justice of Canada appealed to the Supreme Court of Canada. Dynar also brought a cross-appeal.

MAIN ISSUE

Even though Dynar could not have been convicted in Canada of the completed offence of "money laundering" under the (Canadian) Criminal Code and Narcotic Control Act, could he nevertheless have been convicted of criminal attempt or criminal conspiracy to do so?

JUDGMENTS

The *majority* judgment was delivered by Justices Cory and Iacobucci (with whom Chief Justice Lamer and Justices La Forest, L'Heureux-Dubé, and Gonthier agreed). The *concurring* judgment of Justice Major (with whom Justices Sopinka and McLachlin agreed) has been omitted.

....

1   CORY AND IACOBUCCI JJ.: — The issue in this appeal is whether the respondent's conduct in the United States would constitute a crime if carried out in this country, thereby meeting the requirement of "double criminality," which is the precondition for the surrender of a Canadian fugitive for trial in a foreign jurisdiction. This issue requires the Court to consider the scope of the liability for attempted offences and conspiracy under Canadian criminal law, specifically, whether impossibility constitutes a defence to a charge of attempt or conspiracy in Canada.

I. Facts

3   Mr. Dynar was indicted together with Maurice Cohen, who is also a Canadian citizen, in the United States District Court of Nevada. The United States indictment charged both Mr. Dynar and Mr. Cohen with one count of attempting to launder money in violation of Title 18, United States Code, § 1956(a)(3), and one count of conspiracy to violate Title 18, United States Code, § 1956(a)(3), contrary to Title 18, United States

....

Code, § 371. The Government of the United States requested their extradition by Diplomatic Note dated November 30, 1992.

4 The events that formed the basis of the indictment began with a telephone call placed on January 2, 1990, from Canada, by Mr. Dynar to a former associate, Lucky Simone, who was living in Nevada. The call was apparently made to seek investors for a business operation in the United States. Lucky Simone had, unbeknownst to Mr. Dynar, become a confidential informant working for FBI agent William Matthews.

5 During the 1980s, Mr. Dynar was the subject of investigations in the United States pertaining to the laundering of substantial amounts of money originating in the State of Nevada. When Mr. Dynar made contact with Lucky Simone in 1990, Agent Matthews deposed that he decided to determine whether or not Mr. Dynar was still involved in laundering money that was the proceeds of crime. He had Mr. Simone introduce a second confidential informant, known as "Anthony," to Mr. Dynar. Anthony was instructed to ask if Mr. Dynar would be willing to launder large sums obtained as a result of illegal trafficking. When asked, Mr. Dynar agreed with alacrity to launder money for Anthony.

6 A great many conversations between the two men were recorded over the course of some months. On all of these occasions, Anthony was in Las Vegas, Nevada, and Mr. Dynar was in Canada. Eventually, Mr. Dynar and Anthony arranged an initial meeting. The meeting was purportedly to allow Anthony to give money to Mr. Dynar for laundering as a first step towards developing a relationship in which Mr. Dynar would regularly launder money for him. During several of the conversations, it was made clear that the money to be laundered was "drug money." Mr. Dynar insisted more than once that the amounts had to be large in order to make his efforts worthwhile. The conversations also disclosed that Mr. Dynar had an associate named "Moe," who was subsequently identified as Maurice Cohen.

8 In Buffalo, Mr. Cohen met with Special Agent Dennis McCarthy of the IRS, who was posing as Anthony's associate. The conversations that

took place between them in preparation for the transfer of funds were recorded by Agent McCarthy. They contain several statements to the effect that Mr. Cohen was working for Mr. Dynar, as well as some explanations of the logistics of the laundering scheme. In the end, however, the money was not transferred to Mr. Cohen. The FBI aborted the operation by pretending to arrest Agent McCarthy just prior to the transfer of the money. Mr. Cohen was allowed to return to Canada.

9 A committal hearing under s. 13 of the Extradition Act, R.S.C. 1985, c. E-23, was held before Keenan J. of the Ontario Court (General Division). In support of the request for extradition of Mr. Dynar and Mr. Cohen, the United States as the Requesting State relied upon affidavits from the investigating officers and transcripts of the recorded telephone conversations. This evidence formed the basis for the decision to commit Mr. Dynar for extradition.

12 Mr. Dynar appealed to the Ontario Court of Appeal from Keenan J.'s committal decision, and sought judicial review of the Minister's decision to order his surrender. Galligan J.A., for a unanimous Court, allowed the appeal and the application for judicial review on the basis that the activities of Mr. Dynar would not constitute a criminal offence in Canada, even though they did constitute an offence under the applicable United States law. Mr. Dynar was therefore discharged.

13 The Minister of Justice and the United States have appealed Mr. Dynar's discharge and Mr. Dynar has brought a cross-appeal.

II. Applicable Legislation

14 The relevant statutory provisions are not the United States provisions under which Mr. Dynar has been indicted, but the provisions of the Canadian Criminal Code, R.S.C. 1985, c. C-46, and the Narcotic Control Act, R.S.C. 1985, c. N-1. It is these enactments which will determine whether the conduct of Mr. Dynar in the United States would constitute offences in this country.

15 The Criminal Code provision that establishes the substantive "money laundering" offence is:

462.31 (1) Every one commits an offence who uses, transfers the possession of, sends or delivers to any person or place, transports, transmits, alters, disposes of or otherwise deals with, in any manner and by any means, any property or any proceeds of any property with intent to conceal or convert that property or those proceeds and knowing that all or a part of that property or of those proceeds was obtained or derived directly or indirectly as a result of

(a) the commission in Canada of an enterprise crime offence or a designated drug offence; or

(b) an act or omission anywhere that, if it had occurred in Canada, would have constituted an enterprise crime offence or a designated drug offence.

16 A similar offence is contained in the Narcotic Control Act:

19.2 (1) No person shall use, transfer the possession of, send or deliver to any person or place, transport, transmit, alter, dispose of or otherwise deal with, in any manner and by any means, any property or any proceeds of any property with intent to conceal or convert that property or those proceeds and knowing that all or a part of that property or of those proceeds was obtained or derived directly or indirectly as a result of

(a) the commission in Canada of an offence under section 4, 5 or 6; or

(b) an act or omission anywhere that, if it had occurred in Canada, would have constituted an offence under section 4, 5, or 6.

IV. Issues

35 The major issue which arises on the appeal is whether Mr. Dynar's conduct would have amounted to an offence under Canadian law if it had occurred in Canada. This question in turn has two parts: whether an accused who attempts to do the "impossible" may be guilty of attempt and whether an accused who conspires with another to do the impossible may be guilty of conspiracy.

V. Analysis

A. The Criminality of Mr. Dynar's Conduct under Canadian Law

(1) INTRODUCTION

37 In our view, Mr. Dynar's conduct would have amounted to a criminal attempt and a criminal conspiracy under Canadian law.

39 It is clear that, if Mr. Dynar had successfully consummated in Canada a scheme like the one that he embarked upon in the United States, he would not have been guilty of any completed offence known to the law of Canada. The conversion of monies that are believed to be the proceeds of crime but that are not in fact the proceeds of crime was, at the relevant time in the history of this proceeding, not an offence in Canada.

40 There were two statutory provisions (s. 462.31(1) of the Criminal Code and s. 19.2(1) of the Narcotic Control Act) under which Canadian authorities might have prosecuted money-laundering schemes like the one that Mr. Dynar attempted to consummate. However, both required that an accused, if he was to be convicted, should have known that the money he converted was the proceeds of crime:

462.31(1) Every one commits an offence who uses, transfers the possession of, sends or delivers to any person or place, transports, transmits, alters, disposes of or otherwise deals with, in any manner and by any means, any property or any proceeds of any property with intent to conceal or convert that property or those proceeds and *knowing* that all or a part of that property or of those proceeds was obtained or derived directly or indirectly as a result of [the commission of a designated offence].

....

19.2(1) No person shall use, transfer the possession of, send or deliver to any person or place, transport, transmit, alter, dispose of or otherwise deal with, in any manner and by any means, any property or any proceeds of any property with intent to conceal or convert that property or those proceeds and *knowing* that all or a part of that property or of those proceeds was obtained or derived directly or indirectly as a result of [the commission of a designated offence]. [Emphasis added.]

41 Because it is not possible to know what is false, no one who converts money that is not in fact the proceeds of crime commits these offences. This is clear from the meaning of the word "know." In the Western legal tradition, knowledge is defined as *true* belief: "The word 'know' refers exclusively to true knowledge; we are not said to 'know' something that is not so" (Glanville Williams, *Textbook of Criminal Law,* 2nd ed. (London: Stevens & Sons, 1983), at p. 160).

42 Consistently with Professor Williams' definition of "knowledge," this Court has said previously that proof of knowledge requires proof of truth. For example, in *R. v. Zundel,* [1992] 2 S.C.R. 731, 75 C.C.C. (3d) 449, 95 D.L.R. (4th) 202, the Court had to consider the validity of a provision that criminalized the wilful publication of a statement that the publisher knows to be false. The Court interpreted this provision to require a showing by the Crown that the accused published a statement that was in fact false (at p. 747).

47 Because the money that the U.S. undercover agents asked Mr. Dynar to launder was not in fact the proceeds of crime, Mr. Dynar could not possibly have known that it was the proceeds of crime. Therefore, even if he had brought his plan to fruition, he would not have been guilty of any completed offence known to Canadian law. But this is not the end of the story.

48 We conclude that the steps that Mr. Dynar took towards the realization of his plan to launder money would have amounted to a criminal attempt and a criminal conspiracy under Canadian law if the conduct in question had taken place entirely within Canada. We reach our conclusion on the basis of the wording in the applicable provisions of the Criminal Code interpreted in the light of the

underlying theory of impossible attempts and conspiracies.

(2) THE LAW OF ATTEMPT

49 The Criminal Code creates the crime of attempt to commit an offence:

> 24(1) Every one who, having an intent to commit an offence, does or omits to do anything for the purpose of carrying out the intention is guilty of an attempt to commit the offence *whether or not it was possible under the circumstances to commit the offence.* [Emphasis added.]

On its face, the statute is indifferent about whether or not the attempt might possibly have succeeded. Therefore it would seem, at first blush, not to matter that Mr. Dynar could not possibly have succeeded in laundering money known to be the proceeds of crime. So long as he attempted to do so, he is guilty of a crime.

50 In our view, s. 24(1) is clear: the crime of attempt consists of an intent to commit the completed offence together with some act more than merely preparatory taken in furtherance of the attempt. In this case, sufficient evidence was produced to show that Mr. Dynar intended to commit the money-laundering offences, and that he took steps more than merely preparatory in order to realize his intention. That is enough to establish that he attempted to launder money contrary to s. 24(1) of the Criminal Code.

51 However, the respondent argues that Parliament did not intend by s. 24(1) to criminalize all attempts to do the impossible, but only those attempts that the common law has classified as "factually impossible." An attempt to do the factually impossible, according to the respondent, is an attempt that runs up against some intervening obstacle and for that reason cannot be completed. The classic example involves a pickpocket who puts his hand into a man's pocket intending to remove the wallet, only to find that there is no wallet to remove.

52 Traditionally, this sort of impossibility has been contrasted with "legal impossibility." An attempt to do the legally impossible is, according to those who draw the distinction, an attempt that must fail because, even if it were completed, no crime would have been committed.

53 According to the respondent, the Criminal Code criminalizes only attempts to do the factually impossible. An attempt to do the legally impossible, in the absence of an express legislative reference to that variety of impossibility, is not a crime.

59 The conventional distinction between factual and legal impossibility is not tenable. The only relevant distinction for purposes of s. 24(1) of the Criminal Code is between imaginary crimes and attempts to do the factually impossible. The criminal law of Canada recognizes no middle category called "legal impossibility." Because Mr. Dynar attempted to do the impossible but did not attempt to commit an imaginary crime, he can only have attempted to do the "factually impossible." For this reason, Mr. Dynar's proposal that s. 24(1) criminalizes only attempts to do the factually impossible does not help him.

60 As we have already indicated, an attempt to do the factually impossible is considered to be one whose completion is thwarted by mere happenstance. In theory at least, an accused who attempts to do the factually impossible could succeed but for the intervention of some fortuity. A legally impossible attempt, by contrast, is considered to be one which, even if it were completed, still would not be a crime.

65 There is, however, a relevant difference between a failed attempt to do something that is a crime and an imaginary crime. It is one thing to attempt to steal a wallet, believing such thievery to be a crime, and quite another thing to bring sugar into Canada, believing the importation of sugar to be a crime. In the former case, the would-be thief has the *mens rea* associated with thievery. In the latter case, the would-be smuggler has no *mens rea* known to law. Because s. 24(1) clearly provides that it is an element of the offence of attempt to have "an intent to commit an offence," the latter sort of attempt is not a crime.

66 Nor should it be. A major purpose of the law of attempt is to discourage the commission of subsequent offences. But one who attempts to do something that is not a crime or even one who actually does something that is not a crime, believing that what he has done or has attempted to do is a crime, has not displayed any propensity to commit crimes in the future, unless perhaps he has betrayed a vague willingness to break the law. Probably all he has shown is that he might be inclined to do the same sort of thing in the future; and from a societal point of view, that is not a very worrisome prospect, because, by hypothesis, what he attempted to do is perfectly legal.

67 Therefore, we conclude that s. 24(1) draws no distinction between attempts to do the possible but by inadequate means, attempts to do the physically impossible, and attempts to do something that turns out to be impossible "following completion." All are varieties of attempts to do the "factually impossible" and all are crimes. Only attempts to commit imaginary crimes fall outside the scope of the provision. Because what Mr. Dynar attempted to do falls squarely into the category of the factually impossible — he attempted to commit crimes known to law and was thwarted only by chance — it was a criminal attempt within the meaning of s. 24(1). The evidence suggests that Mr. Dynar is a criminal within the contemplation of the Canadian law, and so the double criminality rule should be no bar to his extradition to the United States.

68 Notwithstanding the difficulties associated with the conventional distinction between factual and legal impossibility, a certain reluctance to embrace our conclusion persists in some quarters. It seems to us that this is in part due to a misunderstanding of the elements of the money-laundering offences. Both s. 462.31(1) of the Criminal Code and s. 19.2(1) of the Narcotic Control Act require knowledge that the property being laundered is the proceeds of crime. It is tempting to think that knowledge is therefore the *mens rea* of these offences. But "*mens rea*" denotes a mental state. *Mens rea* is the subjective element of a crime.

Knowledge is not subjective, or, more accurately, it is not entirely subjective.

69 As we have already said, knowledge, for legal purposes, is true belief. Knowledge therefore has two components — truth and belief — and of these, only belief is mental or subjective. Truth is objective, or at least consists in the correspondence of a proposition or mental state to objective reality. Accordingly, truth, which is a state of affairs in the external world that does not vary with the intention of the accused, cannot be a part of *mens rea*. Knowledge as such is not then the *mens rea* of the money-laundering offences. Belief is.

70 The truth of an actor's belief that certain monies are the proceeds of crime is something different from the belief itself. That the belief be true is one of the attendant circumstances that is required if the *actus reus* is to be completed. In other words, the act of converting the proceeds of crime presupposes the existence of some money that is in truth the proceeds of crime.

71 In this, the money-laundering offences are no different from other offences. Murder is the intentional killing of a person. Because a person cannot be killed who is not alive, and because a killing, if is to be murder, must be intentional, it follows that a successful murderer must believe that his victim is alive. An insane man who kills another, believing that the one he kills is a manikin, does not have the *mens rea* needed for murder. Thus, the successful commission of the offence of murder presupposes both a belief that the victim is alive just before the deadly act occurs and the actual vitality of the victim at that moment. Both truth and belief are required. Therefore, knowledge is required. But this does not mean that the vitality of the victim is part of the *mens rea* of the offence of murder. Instead, it is an attendant circumstance that makes possible the completion of the *actus reus*, which is the killing of a person.

72 In general, the successful commission of any offence presupposes a certain coincidence of circumstances. But these circumstances do not enter into the *mens rea* of the offence.

73 The absence of an attendant circumstance is irrelevant from the point of view of the law of attempt. An accused is guilty of an attempt if he intends to commit a crime and takes legally sufficient steps towards its commission. Because an attempt is, in its very nature, an incomplete substantive offence, it will always be the case that the *actus reus* of the completed offence will be deficient, and sometimes this will be because an attendant circumstance is lacking.

74 So it should not be troubling that what Mr. Dynar did does not constitute the *actus reus* of the money-laundering offences. If his actions did constitute the *actus reus*, then he would be guilty of the completed offences described in s. 462.31 of the Criminal Code and s. 19.2 of the Narcotic Control Act. There would be no need even to consider the law of attempt. The law of attempt is engaged only when, as in this case, the *mens rea* of the completed offence is present entirely and the *actus reus* of it is present in an incomplete but more-than-merely-preparatory way.

81 Looking to intent rather than motive accords with the purpose of the criminal law in general and of the law of attempt in particular. Society imposes criminal sanctions in order to punish and deter undesirable conduct. It does not matter to society, in its efforts to secure social peace and order, what an accused's motive was, but only what the accused intended to do. It is no consolation to one whose car has been stolen that the thief stole the car intending to sell it to purchase food for a food bank. Similarly, the purpose of the law of attempt is universally acknowledged to be the deterrence of subsequent attempts. A person who has intended to do something that the law forbids and who has actually taken steps towards the completion of an offence is apt to try the same sort of thing in the future; and there is no assurance that next time his attempt will fail.

82 Applying this rationale to impossible attempts, we conclude that such attempts are no less menacing than are other attempts. After all, the only difference between an attempt to do the possible and an attempt to do the impossible is chance.

A person who enters a bedroom and stabs a corpse thinking that he is stabbing a living person has the same intention as a person who enters a bedroom and stabs someone who is alive. In the former instance, by some chance, the intended victim expired in his sleep perhaps only moments before the would-be assassin acted. It is difficult to see why this circumstance, of which the tardy killer has no knowledge and over which he has no control, should in any way mitigate his culpability. Next time, the intended victim might be alive. Similarly, even if Mr. Dynar could not actually have laundered the proceeds of crime this time around, there is hardly any guarantee that his next customer might not be someone other than an agent of the United States Government.

83 The import of all of this is that Mr. Dynar committed the crime of attempt; and for having done so he should be extradited to the United States. The facts disclose an intent to launder money and acts taken in furtherance of that design. Section 24(1) of the Criminal Code requires no more.

(3) COULD MR. DYNAR'S CONDUCT JUSTIFY HIS SURRENDER ON THE CONSPIRACY CHARGE?

84 Mr. Dynar's extradition has also been requested on a charge of conspiracy. Thus it is necessary to determine whether Mr. Dynar's conduct in combination with Mr. Cohen's could also constitute the crime of conspiracy in this country. The applicability of the defence of "impossibility" under Canadian criminal law is as much an issue with respect to the conspiracy charge as it is with regard to the attempt charge.

85 Section 465(1)(c) of the Criminal Code makes it an offence to conspire with another person to commit any indictable offence, other than murder or false prosecution, which are governed by paragraphs (a) and (b) of the same subsection. There is no doubt that laundering proceeds of crime is an indictable offence in Canada. The question that must be decided, however, is whether a conspiracy can exist even where all the elements of the full indictable offence are not present because the circumstances are not as the accused believed them to be.

(a) WHAT IS A CRIMINAL CONSPIRACY?

85 Conspiracy is in fact a more "preliminary" crime than attempt, since the offence is considered to be complete before any acts are taken that go beyond mere preparation to put the common design into effect. The Crown is simply required to prove a meeting of the minds with regard to a common design to do something unlawful, specifically the commission of an indictable offence. See s. 465(1)(c) of the Criminal Code.

88 A conspiracy must involve more than one person, even though all the conspirators may not either be identified or be capable of being convicted. Further, each of the conspirators must have a genuine intention to participate in the agreement. A person cannot be a conspirator if he or she merely pretends to agree. Where one member of a so-called conspiracy is a police informant who never intends to carry out the common design, there can be no conspiracy involving that person. Nonetheless, a conspiracy can still exist between other parties to the same agreement. It is for this reason that the conspiracy in this case is alleged to involve Mr. Dynar and Mr. Cohen, and not the confidential informant "Anthony."

89 There can be no doubt that a criminal conspiracy constitutes a serious offence that is properly extraditable. Society is properly concerned with conspiracies since two or more persons working together can achieve evil results that would be impossible for an individual working alone. For example, it usually takes two or more conspirators to manufacture and secrete explosives or to arrange for the purchase, importation, and sale of heroin. The very fact that several persons in combination agree to do something has for many years been considered to constitute "a menace to society": *R. v. O'Brien*, [1954] S.C.R. 666 at p. 669, 110 C.C.C. 1, [1955] 2 D.L.R. 311. In fact, the scale of injury that might be caused to the fabric of society can be far greater when two or more persons conspire to commit a crime than when an individual sets out alone to do an unlawful act.

90 As a result, it is obvious that the reason for punishing conspiracy before any steps are taken towards attaining the object of the agreement is to prevent the unlawful object from being attained, and therefore to prevent this serious harm from occurring. It is also desirable to deter similar conduct in the future. Those who conspire to do something that turns out to be impossible betray by their actions a propensity and aptitude to commit criminal acts; and there is no reason to believe that schemers who are thwarted on one occasion will not be successful on the next. Thus, the rationale for punishing conspirators coincides with the rationale for punishing persons for attempted crimes. Not only is the offence itself seen to be harmful to society, but it is clearly in society's best interests to make it possible for law enforcement officials to intervene before the harm occurs that would be occasioned by a successful conspiracy or, if the conspiracy is incapable of completion, by a subsequent and more successful conspiracy to commit a similar offence.

(b) IS IMPOSSIBILITY A DEFENCE TO CONSPIRACY?

91 By virtue of the "preliminary" nature of the offence of criminal conspiracy, the mere fact that money was not transferred to Mr. Cohen for laundering by Mr. Dynar would not preclude a finding that a conspiracy existed between them. Criminal liability will still ensue, as long as the agreement and the common intention can be proved. Does it make any difference to the potential liability of the conspirators that they could not have committed the substantive offence even if they had done everything that they set out to do? Put another way, should conspirators escape liability because, owing to matters entirely outside their control, they are mistaken with regard to an attendant circumstance that must exist for their plan to be successful? Such a result would defy logic and could not be justified.

102 From a purely conceptual perspective, the distinction between factual and legal impossibility is as unsound in the law of conspiracy as it is in the law of attempt. As we concluded in discussing impossible attempts, cases of so-called "legal" impossibility turn out to be cases of factual impossibility and the distinction collapses, except in cases of "imaginary crimes." Conspiracy to commit such fanciful offences of course cannot give rise to criminal liability.

103 Furthermore, like attempt, conspiracy is a crime of intention. The factual element — or *actus reus* — of the offence is satisfied by the establishment of the agreement to commit the predicate offence. This factual element does not have to correspond with the factual elements of the substantive offence. The goal of the agreement, namely the commission of the substantive offence, is part of the mental element — or *mens rea* — of the offence of conspiracy.

104 The conspiracy alleged in the case at bar involves the commission of an offence that requires knowledge of a circumstance as one of its essential elements. When a substantive offence requires knowledge of a particular circumstance, the Crown is required to prove a subjective element, which is best described as belief that the particular circumstance exists. The Crown is also required to prove an objective element, namely the truth of the circumstance. It is the presence of the objective circumstance that translates the subjective belief into knowledge or "true belief."

105 However, since the offence of conspiracy only requires an *intention* to commit the substantive offence, and not the commission of the offence itself, it does not matter that, from an objective point of view, commission of the offence may be impossible. It is the subjective point of view that is important, and from a subjective perspective, conspirators who intend to commit an indictable offence intend to do everything necessary to satisfy the conditions of the offence. The fact that they cannot do so because an objective circumstance is not as they believe it to be does not in any way affect this intention. The intention of the conspirators remains the same, regardless of the absence of the circumstance that would make the realization of that intention possible. It is only in retrospect that the impossibility of accomplishing the common design becomes apparent.

106 If the failure of a conspiracy as a result of some defect in the attendant circumstances were to be considered to constitute "legal" impossibility, and as such a defence to a charge of conspiracy, the fact that the conspirators are not culpable becomes a matter of pure luck, divorced from their true intentions. This result is unacceptable. Rather, it would be consistent with the law of conspiracy to hold that the absence of the attendant circumstance has no bearing on the intention of the parties, and therefore no bearing on their liability.

107 It has long been accepted that conspirators can be punished for their agreement (*actus reus*) and their intention to commit the offence (*mens rea*). This is true even though the police intervene to prevent the conspirators from committing the substantive offence which was the aim of the conspiracy. By the same token, it should make no difference to the culpability of the conspirators if the police intervene in a way that makes the offence impossible to commit because, for example, the money to be laundered is not derived from crime. The conspirators could still be properly convicted on the basis that the agreement to do the unlawful object is considered dangerous to society and reprehensible in itself.

109 It follows from all that has been said above that a conspiracy to commit a crime which cannot be carried out because an objective circumstance is not as the conspirators believed it to be is still capable of giving rise to criminal liability in Canada. Legal impossibility cannot be invoked as a defence to the charge.

(c) APPLICATION OF THESE PRINCIPLES TO THIS CASE

110 The only reason that the conspiracy alleged to exist between Mr. Dynar and Mr. Cohen was considered "impossible" was because one external circumstance — the existence of actual proceeds of crime — was absent. Yet, the absence of this circumstance is not a defence to a charge of conspiracy.

111 There is evidence that Mr. Dynar was a member of a conspiracy that included Mr. Cohen. On several occasions in the wiretapped conversations between Anthony and Mr. Dynar, Maurice Cohen was implicated as the intimate associate of Mr. Dynar in his money-laundering operations. In the recorded conversations that took place between Mr. Cohen and Agent McCarthy in Buffalo, Mr. Cohen clearly indicated that he was working for Mr. Dynar and demonstrated a basic knowledge of the exchanges that took place between Mr. Dynar and Anthony. The very fact that Mr. Cohen showed up in Buffalo as arranged between Mr. Dynar and Anthony supports an inference that he and Mr. Dynar were acting in concert.

112 At a minimum, the evidence clearly supports the existence of an agreement to launder what the conspirators believed were the proceeds of crime. Furthermore, there is evidence that the agreement extended beyond the scheme that was being discussed in the "sting" operation. Mr. Dynar spoke of his operations as well-established, with worldwide affiliates, and of his ability to launder large sums of illicit money very quickly. Mr. Cohen demonstrated an intimate knowledge of the logistics of money laundering in Canada, which he indicated was a function of his association with Mr. Dynar. Finally, the appearance of Mr. Cohen in Buffalo, as arranged between Anthony and Mr. Dynar, was an overt act that suggested that Mr. Dynar's claims about his abilities, and about his association with Mr. Cohen, were not mere "puff" and exaggeration. It is reasonable to infer that Dynar's claims, pursuant to the agreement between Dynar and Cohen, were intended to be translated into action.

114 It is clear that the evidence presented demonstrated a *prima facie* case for extradition purposes, since it would warrant committing Mr. Dynar and Mr. Cohen for trial for conspiracy in Canada if their conduct had taken place here. Keenan J. was therefore correct in holding that Mr. Dynar was extraditable on both the charge of attempt to launder money and conspiracy to launder money.

VI. Conclusion

148 In the result, therefore, the appeal is allowed, the judgment of the Court of Appeal is set aside, and the cross-appeal is dismissed. The order of Keenan J. committing the fugitive for extradition and the Minister of Justice's decision to surrender the fugitive are reinstated.

Note

As a result of the legal difficulties caused in the *Dynar* case by the wording of the relevant sections of the Criminal Code [section 462.31(1)] and the Narcotic Control Act [section 19.2(1)], the Parliament of Canada amended them in order to ensure that accused persons may now be convicted of the respective laundering offences if they either know *or believe* that the funds in question constitute the proceeds of crime. This means, of course, that a defendant in Dynar's situation, who deals in any way with funds that he or she *believes* constitute the proceeds of crime, will now be found guilty of having committed a laundering offence and it will be irrelevant that the funds are not, in fact, derived from criminal sources.

Section 462.31 of the Code was amended in 1997 to reflect this change in the law. The entire Narcotic Control Act was repealed in 1997 and replaced by the Controlled Drugs and Substances Act. The equivalent provision to the "old" section 19.2(1) of the N.C.A. is section 9(1) of the Controlled Drugs and Substances Act (which now contains similar wording to that in section 462.31 of the Criminal Code).

Under the "new" law, accused persons such as Dynar would no longer be able to claim that they were attempting or conspiring to do something that was legally "impossible." The significance of the *Dynar* case, however, is that the Supreme Court of Canada indicated that, *even if it were "impossible" for Dynar to have committed the complete offence of laundering the proceeds of crime*, he would still be liable to conviction for an attempt or conspiracy to do so.

Gladstone et al. v. The Queen

SUPREME COURT OF CANADA   AUGUST 21, 1996

BACKGROUND

Donald and William Gladstone, members of the Heiltsuk Band in British Columbia, were convicted at their trial in the Provincial Court of attempting to sell herring spawn on kelp [contrary to section 20(3) of the Pacific Herring Fishery Regulations (Can.)] and offering to sell herring spawn on kelp [contrary to section 27(5) of the British Columbia Fishery (General) Regulations]. The accused appealed against their convictions to the B.C. Supreme Court, which allowed their appeal against their conviction of *offering* to sell herring spawn on kelp but upheld their conviction of *attempting* to sell herring spawn on kelp. The accused then appealed against the judgment of the B.C. Supreme Court to the B.C. Court of Appeal, which dismissed their appeal. Finally, Donald and William Gladstone appealed to the Supreme Court of Canada against the judgment of the Court of Appeal.

MAIN ISSUES

The main issue in the case turned on the constitutional validity of the Pacific Herring Fishery Regulations under which the accused were convicted of *attempting* to sell herring spawn on kelp. The validity of the regulation was questioned in light of the provisions of section 35(1) of the Constitution Act,

1982, which recognizes and affirms the "existing aboriginal and treaty rights of the aboriginal peoples of Canada." However, the issue that is dealt with in the following extract concerns the question of whether the two accused persons had committed acts that were sufficiently *proximate* to the complete offence of selling herring spawn on kelp to justify convicting them of an *attempt* to sell herring spawn on kelp.

JUDGMENTS

The *majority* judgment was delivered by Chief Justice Lamer (with whom Justices Sopinka, Gonthier, Cory, Iacobucci, and Major agreed). The *concurring* judgments of Justices L'Heureux-Dubé and McLachlin and the *dissenting* judgment of Justice La Forest have been omitted.

....

LAMER C.J.C.: —

I. Facts

1   Donald and William Gladstone, the appellants, are members of the Heiltsuk Band. The appellants were charged under s. 61(1) of the Fisheries Act, R.S.C. 1970, c. F-14, with the offences of offering to sell herring spawn on kelp caught under the

....

authority of an Indian food fish licence, contrary to s. 27(5) of the British Columbia Fishery (General) Regulations, SOR/84-248, and of attempting to sell herring spawn on kelp not caught under the authority of a Category J herring spawn on kelp licence, contrary to s. 20(3) of the Pacific Herring Fishery Regulations, SOR/84-324. Only the charges arising under s. 20(3) of the Pacific Herring Fishery Regulations are still at issue in this appeal.

2   The charges arose out of events taking place in April of 1988. On approximately April 27, 1988, the appellants shipped 4200 pounds of herring spawn on kelp from Bella Bella to Richmond, a suburb of Vancouver. On April 28, 1988, the appellants took a pail containing approximately 35 pounds of herring spawn on kelp to Seaborn Enterprises Ltd., a fish store in Vancouver. At Seaborn Enterprises Ltd. the appellants had a conversation with Mr. Katsu Hirose, the owner of the store, in which they asked Mr. Hirose if he was "interested" in herring spawn on kelp. Mr. Hirose informed the appellants that he did not purchase herring spawn on kelp from Native Indians. Upon leaving Seaborn Enterprises Ltd. the appellants, who had been under surveillance by fisheries officers throughout these events, were arrested and the entire 4200 pounds of herring spawn on kelp were seized. Upon arrest, the appellant William Gladstone produced an Indian food fish licence permitting him to harvest 500 pounds of herring spawn on kelp.

3   At the time at which the appellants were charged, s. 20(3) of the Pacific Herring Fishery Regulations read:

> 20(3) No person shall buy, sell, barter or attempt to buy, sell, or barter herring spawn on kelp other than herring spawn on kelp taken or collected under the authority of a Category J licence.

4   The appellants have not disputed the essential facts of the case. The essence of the appellants' defence is that, in these circumstances, the regulations violated the appellants' aboriginal rights as recognized and affirmed by s. 35(1) of the Consti-

tution Act, 1982, with the result that, by operation of s. 52 of the Constitution Act, 1982, the regulations are of no force or effect with respect to the appellants. The appellants also take the position that the facts related to the shipment of the herring spawn on kelp, and the conversation with Mr. Hirose, are insufficient to constitute an "attempt to sell" in law.

IV. Analysis

Attempt to Sell

18   The basis of the appellants' position is that because the Crown only provided evidence to show that the appellants asked Mr. Hirose if he was "interested" in herring spawn on kelp, without providing any evidence that the appellants had discussed the quantity, quality, price, or delivery date of the herring spawn on kelp with Mr. Hirose, the Crown only demonstrated that the appellants had engaged in preparation for an attempt to sell; the Crown did not demonstrate that the appellants had actually attempted to sell herring spawn on kelp to Mr. Hirose.

19   This argument is without merit. In *R. v. Deutsch*, [1986] 2 S.C.R. 2, 30 D.L.R. (4th) 435, 27 C.C.C. (3d) 385 (S.C.C.), Le Dain J., writing for a unanimous Court on this issue, discussed the distinction between an attempt and mere preparation at pp. 22–23:

> It has been frequently observed that no satisfactory general criterion has been, or can be, formulated for drawing the line between preparation and attempt, and that the application of this distinction to the facts of a particular case must be left to common sense judgment. . . Despite academic appeals for greater clarity and certainty in this area of the law, I find myself in essential agreement with this conclusion.

> In my opinion the distinction between preparation and attempt is essentially a qualitative one, involving the relationship between the nature and quality of the act in question and the nature of the

complete offence, although consideration must necessarily be given, in making that qualitative distinction, to the relative proximity of the act in question to what would have been the completed offence, in terms of time, location and acts under the control of the accused remaining to be accomplished.

In this case the facts as found by the trial judge clearly demonstrate that the appellants attempted to sell herring spawn on kelp to Mr. Hirose. The appellants arranged for the shipment of the herring spawn on kelp to Vancouver, they took a sample of the herring spawn on kelp to Mr. Hirose's store, and they specifically asked Mr. Hirose if he was "interested" in herring spawn on kelp. The appellants' actions have sufficient proximity to the acts necessary to complete the offence of selling herring spawn on kelp to move those actions beyond mere preparation to an actual attempt. I would note here that the appellants have not disputed the facts as found by the trial judge and that the courts below were unanimous in finding that the actions of the appellants were sufficient to amount to an attempt to sell.

V. Disposition

85 In the result, the appeal is allowed and a new trial directed on the issue of guilt or innocence and, with regards to the constitutionality of s. 20(3), on the issue of the justifiability of the government's allocation of herring.

86 For the reasons given above, the constitutional question must be answered as follows:

Question: Is s. 20(3) of the Pacific Herring Fishery Regulations, SOR/84-324, as it read on April 28, 1988, of no force or effect with respect to the appellants in the circumstances of these proceedings, in virtue of s. 52 of the Constitution Act, 1982, by reason of the aboriginal rights within the meaning of s. 35 of the Constitution Act, 1982, invoked by the appellants?

Answer: This question will have to be sent back to trial to be answered in accordance with the analysis set out in these reasons.

Mental Disorder as a Defence: The Verdict of Not Criminally Responsible on Account of Mental Disorder (NCRMD)

INTRODUCTION

In this chapter, the special defence of "not criminally responsible on account of mental disorder" (NCRMD) is examined in the light of four significant cases. In the *Chaulk* case (1990), the Supreme Court of Canada interpreted the word "wrong" in section 16(1) of the Criminal Code (which articulates the criteria for the NCRMD defence) as meaning "wrong according to the ordinary moral standards of reasonable members of society": by so doing, the Supreme Court significantly expanded the scope of the NCRMD defence in Canada. In addition, the Supreme Court ruled in *Chaulk* that the presumption against mental disorder, enshrined in section 16(2) of the Code, is not invalid under the Charter.

The *Swain* case (1991) is one of the most important decisions that the Supreme Court of Canada has made in the field of criminal law during the past twenty years. The Court struck down the so-called "Lieutenant-Governor's warrant" system that dictated that all those acquitted under section 16 of the Code must be automatically confined for an indefinite period at the discretion

of the relevant provincial or territorial government. As a consequence of the *Swain* decision, Parliament made sweeping amendments to the Criminal Code provisions concerning the disposition and treatment of mentally disordered defendants in Canada. The *Swain* case is also important because it established a new common law rule to regulate the circumstances in which the Crown is entitled to introduce evidence of mental disorder over the objections of the accused. In the *LePage* case (1997), the Ontario Court of Appeal firmly rejected a Charter challenge to the Criminal Code provisions that were introduced by Parliament in response to the decision in the *Swain* case.

In the *Jacquard* case (1997), the Supreme Court of Canada explicitly recognized that, even if accused persons charged with murder do not qualify for an NCRMD acquittal under section 16 of the Criminal Code, their mental disorder may still be eminently relevant to the questions of whether they had the specific intent for murder and whether their conduct reflected the elements of planning and deliberation required for conviction of first, as opposed to second, degree murder under section 231(2) of the Code.

Chaulk v. The Queen

SUPREME COURT OF CANADA   DECEMBER 20, 1990

BACKGROUND

At their trial before a judge and jury in the Manitoba Court of Queen's Bench, Chaulk and Morrissette were convicted of first degree murder. Both accused appealed against their conviction to the Manitoba Court of Appeal, which dismissed their appeal. The accused subsequently appealed to the Supreme Court of Canada against the judgment of the Court of Appeal.

MAIN ISSUES

(1) Does section 16(4) [now section 16(2)] of the Criminal Code infringe section 11(d) of the Charter and, if so, can it be saved by the application of section 1 of the Charter? (2) What is the meaning of the word "wrong" in section 16(2) [now section 16(1)] of the Code: in particular, does it mean "legally wrong" or "morally wrong"?

JUDGMENTS

The *majority* judgment was delivered by Chief Justice Lamer.* On the issue of the validity of section 16(4) of the Code, Chief Justice Dickson** and Justices La Forest, Sopinka, and Cory *concurred* with

Chief Justice Lamer. On the issue of the meaning of the word "wrong" in section 16(2), Chief Justice Dickson and Justices Wilson, La Forest, Gonthier, and Cory *concurred* with Chief Justice Lamer.

Justice McLachlin delivered a judgment in which she *concurred* with the ruling made by Chief Justice Lamer in relation to the question of the validity of section 16(4), but *dissented* in relation to the Chief Justice's interpretation of the meaning of the word "wrong" in section 16(2). [Justices L'Heureux-Dubé and Gonthier concurred with Justice McLachlin in relation to the section 16(4) issue and Justices L'Heureux-Dubé and Sopinka concurred with Justice McLachlin with respect to the meaning of the word "wrong."] Justice McLachlin's judgment has been omitted, as has a judgment delivered by Justice Wilson who agreed with Chief Justice Lamer's disposition of both the section 16(4) and 16(2) issues.

LAMER C.J.C.: —

Facts

On September 3, 1985, the appellants Chaulk and Morrissette entered a home in Winnipeg, plundered it for valuables, and then stabbed and blud-

---

* Chief Justice at the time that judgment was delivered by the Supreme Court of Canada.
** Chief Justice at the time that the case was originally heard by the Supreme Court of Canada.

Adapted from *R. v. Chaulk* (1990), 62 C.C.C. (3d), pp. 200, 203–204, 207–233, 239. Copyright © 1990 by *Canada Law Book*. Reprinted with permission.

geoned its sole occupant to death. A week later they turned themselves in, making full confessions.

After a transfer proceeding in the Youth Court (Chaulk and Morrissette were 15 and 16 years of age, respectively), the appellants were tried and convicted of first degree murder by a jury in the Manitoba Court of Queen's Bench. The only defence raised was insanity within the meaning of s. 16 of the Code. Expert evidence was given at trial that the appellants suffered from a paranoid psychosis which made them believe that they had the power to rule the world and that the killing was a necessary means to that end. They knew the laws of Canada existed, but believed that they were above the ordinary law; they thought the law was irrelevant to them. They thought they had a right to kill the victim because he was "a loser."

Analysis

Is s. 16(4) of the Code Inconsistent with s. 11(d) of the Charter?

Section 16(4) of the Code sets out a presumption of sanity. This presumption can be rebutted if "the contrary is proved." In *Smythe v. The King* (1941), 74 C.C.C. 273, [1941] 1 D.L.R. 497, [1941] S.C.R. 17, this Court held that when insanity is raised by the defence, the accused must prove that he or she was insane, at the time of the offence, on a balance of probabilities.

The appellant Morrissette argues that the words "until the contrary is proved" in s. 16(4) should be interpreted, based on common law, so as to require an accused to merely raise a reasonable doubt as to his insanity. He assumes that if the words were given this interpretation, s. 16(4) would not violate the presumption of innocence and it would not be necessary to address the Charter arguments in this case.

In my view, the words "until the contrary is proved" cannot be interpreted as requiring an accused merely to discharge an evidentiary burden (i.e., raise a reasonable doubt as to insanity); the words in s. 16(4) clearly impose a persuasive burden on the accused.

Accordingly, it is necessary, in this case, to measure s. 16(4) against s. 11(d) of the Charter.

The appellants argue that the requirement that an accused person prove his or her insanity on a balance of probabilities is contrary to the presumption of innocence, guaranteed by s. 11(d) of the Charter.

The Nature of the Insanity Provisions

The insanity defence can be raised in a number of different ways, depending on the mental condition of the accused. All of these examples have one thing in common however. Each is based on an underlying claim that the accused has no capacity for criminal intent because his or her mental condition has brought about a skewed frame of reference. When a person claims insanity, he or she may well be denying the existence of *mens rea* in the particular case or putting forward an excuse which would preclude criminal liability in the particular case; but he is also making a more basic claim which goes beyond *mens rea* or *actus reus* in the particular case — he is claiming that he does not fit within the normal assumptions of our criminal law model because he does not have the capacity for criminal intent. Such a claim may or may not be successful. If the incapacity is such that it fits into the defence of insanity encompassed in s. 16, it will preclude a conviction.

Based on the foregoing, I prefer to characterize the insanity defence as an exemption to criminal liability which is based on an incapacity from criminal intent. I note, however, that this basic claim for an exemption will usually be manifested under s. 16 either as a denial of *mens rea* in the particular case or as an excuse for what would otherwise be a criminal offence; this is because of the way that s. 16 is worded.

In *R. v. Abbey* (1982), 68 C.C.C. (2d) 394, 138 D.L.R. (3d) 202, [1982] 2 S.C.R. 24, this court held (*per* Dickson J., as he then was) that "appreciate the nature and quality of an act or omission" refers to an accused's ability to perceive the consequences, impact, and results of a physical act and *not* to an accused's ability to appreciate that the *legal* consequences of an act are applicable to him or her. Dickson J. stated, in coming to this conclusion, that a delusion falling under the "first branch" of the insanity defence negatives the element of *mens rea*, with respect to either the circumstances or consequences which form part of the *actus reus*. Given the wording of the "first branch" of s. 16(2), this is true in the vast majority of cases. A claim of insanity under the "first branch" will be manifested as a denial of *mens rea* in the particular case. It is possible, however, that such a claim could also manifest itself as a denial of voluntary *actus reus* in the particular case.

This court also held in *Abbey* that the "second branch" of s. 16(2) "is concerned with cognitive capabilities, with knowledge, and not with appreciation of consequences." This provision is also based on *incapacity for criminal intent*. Such incapacity arises because the accused, due to his mental condition, is incapable of distinguishing between right and wrong. This claim of incapacity does not manifest itself as a denial of *mens rea* in the particular case. The criminal law is not concerned with whether a sane accused *knew* that his act was wrong. Knowledge of wrongness is not part of the requirement of *mens rea*. This is because sane people are presumed to have the capacity to distinguish between right and wrong — if a sane person is of the opinion that murder is not wrong, his opinion makes him "bad" (as opposed to "sick") *because he has the capacity to distinguish right from wrong.* However, if an accused makes a claim of insanity under the "second branch" of s. 16(2), he is challenging the assumption that he is capable of distinguishing between right and wrong. If it is proved that his mental condition brought about such incapacity, he will be excused from criminal liability *despite* the elements of *actus reus* and *mens rea* being established in the particular case. Thus, while a claim of insanity under the "second branch" is based on the same basic denial of criminal capacity upon which a claim under the "first branch" is based, it is manifested not as a denial of *actus reus* or *mens rea*, but rather as a claim to be excused for what would otherwise be criminal behaviour.

Does the Nature of s. 16 Determine the Charter Issue?

The Crown has argued that sanity is not an essential element of an offence (as is *mens rea*) and, therefore, does not engage the presumption of innocence.

The Crown argues that insanity does not "disprove" an offence (nor, I assume, an essential element of an offence) and that the presumption of innocence is therefore inapplicable to s. 16. The Crown submits that the insanity claim is a means of escaping criminal liability "above and beyond" the presumption of innocence which applies in respect of the specific offence. The Crown is essentially arguing that the presumption of innocence only operates with respect to essential elements of the offence and with respect to common law defences. A claim of insanity under s. 16 raises a claim for an *exemption* to criminal liability; it neither negates an essential element of the offence nor raises a common law defence (justification or excuse). Therefore, the requirement embodied in s. 16(4) that the accused prove insanity on a balance of probabilities does not violate the presumption of innocence.

In my view, this argument does not accord with the principles enunciated by this court in *R. v. Whyte* (1988), 42 C.C.C. (3d) 97, 51 D.L.R. (4th) 481, [1988] 2 S.C.R. 3. In *Whyte*, the constitutionality of s. 237(1)(a) of the Code was in issue. Section 237(1)(a) raised a presumption of care or control of an automobile upon a finding of occupancy of the driver's seat, with respect to the offence of impaired driving. Dickson C.J.C. stated (at pp. 109–10):

> The real concern is not whether the accused must disprove an element or prove an excuse, but that an accused may be convicted while a reasonable doubt exists. When that possibility exists, there is a breach of the presumption of innocence.
>
> The exact characterization of a factor as an essential element, a collateral factor, an excuse, or a defence should not affect the analysis of the pre-

sumption of innocence. *It is the final effect of a provision on the verdict that is decisive. If an accused is required to prove some fact on the balance of probabilities to avoid conviction, the provision violates the presumption of innocence because it permits a conviction in spite of a reasonable doubt in the mind of the trier of fact as to the guilt of the accused.* The trial of an accused in a criminal matter cannot be divided neatly into stages, with the onus of proof on the accused at an intermediate stage and the ultimate onus on the Crown. Section 237(1)(a) requires the accused to prove lack of intent on a balance of probabilities. If an accused does not meet this requirement, the trier of fact is required by law to accept that the accused had care or control and to convict. But of course it does not follow that the trier of fact is convinced beyond a reasonable doubt that the accused had care or control of the vehicle.

(Emphasis added.) In my view, the principles enunciated in *Whyte* are applicable to this case and establish that the presumption of sanity embodied in s. 16(4) violates the presumption of innocence. If an accused is found to have been insane at the time of the offence, he will *not* be found guilty; thus the "fact" of insanity precludes a verdict of guilty. Whether the claim of insanity is characterized as a denial of *mens rea*, an excusing defence or, more generally, as an exemption based on criminal incapacity, the fact remains that sanity is essential for guilt. Section 16(4) allows a factor which is essential for guilt to be *presumed*, rather than proven by the Crown beyond a reasonable doubt. Moreover, it requires an accused to disprove sanity (or prove insanity) on a balance of probabilities; it therefore violates the presumption of innocence because it permits a conviction in spite of a reasonable doubt in the mind of the trier of fact as to the guilt of the accused.

The presumption of sanity is not an *inference* drawn from the existence or proof of an underlying fact (such as being found in the driver's seat of a motor vehicle). Rather, sanity is something which is assumed from the outset. Thus, in enacting s. 16(4), Parliament has not designated any basic "fact" which, when established, removes all possibility of reasonable doubt as to lack of insanity (and therefore removes all reasonable doubt as to guilt). Parliament has simply reversed the onus on a factor which is essential for guilt. If an accused cannot discharge the persuasive burden with respect to his insanity, the trier of fact may well be obliged to convict the accused despite the existence of a reasonable doubt as to sanity, and therefore, as to guilt.

In summary, I find that the presumption of sanity embodied in s. 16(4) of the Code limits the presumption of innocence guaranteed by s. 11(d) of the Charter.

Is s. 16(4) a Reasonable Limit under s. 1 of the Charter?

There is no question that the presumption of innocence, guaranteed by s. 11(d) of the Charter, is a fundamental legal right which plays a very important role in our criminal justice system. It has been referred to as "the golden thread" of English criminal law: *Woolmington v. Director of Public Prosecutions*, [1935] A.C. 462 at pp. 481–2. However, like the other rights and freedoms guaranteed by the Charter, it is subject to limitations under s. 1 of the Charter. The procedure to be followed when the state is attempting to justify a limit on a right or freedom under s. 1 was set out by this Court in *R. v. Oakes* (1986), 24 C.C.C. (3d) 321, 26 D.L.R. (4th) 200, [1986] 1 S.C.R. 103:

1. The objective of the impugned provision must be of sufficient importance to warrant overriding a constitutionally protected right or freedom; it must relate to concerns which are pressing and substantial in a free and democratic society before it can be characterized as sufficiently important.

2. Assuming that a sufficiently important objective has been established, the means chosen to achieve the objective must pass a proportionality test; that is to say they must:

(a) be "rationally connected" to the objective and not be arbitrary, unfair or based on irrational considerations;

(b) impair the right or freedom in question as "little as possible"; and

(c) be such that their effects on the limitation of rights and freedoms are proportional to the objective.

Objective

Before characterizing the relevant objective, I feel that it is necessary to focus on what it is about s. 16(4) which violates s. 11(d). The problem with s. 16(4) is twofold. First, the provision allows sanity (something which is essential to guilt) to be *presumed*. This violates the basic principle (set out in *Oakes*) that the state bears the burden of proving guilt beyond a reasonable doubt. Secondly, the provision requires an accused to *prove* his or her insanity, on a balance of probabilities, in order to rebut the presumption of sanity. This gives rise to a reversal of the burden of proof such that an accused could be found guilty of a criminal offence despite a reasonable doubt in the mind of the trier of fact about the accused's insanity.

It is therefore necessary to focus on the presumption and on the reversal of the burden of proof and ask: what was Parliament's specific objective in forcing an accused who raises s. 16 to prove his or her insanity on a balance of probabilities? The answer can only be that Parliament wished to avoid placing on the Crown the impossibly onerous burden of disproving insanity and to thereby secure the conviction of the guilty (who are not "sick") by defeating acquittals based on a doubt as regards insanity. Section 16(4) is a purely evidentiary section whose objective is to relieve the prosecution of the tremendous difficulty of proving an accused's sanity in order to secure a conviction.

The Code provides no method of forcing an accused to submit to psychiatric examinations unless fitness to stand trial is in issue. The Attorney-General of Canada has described, in detail, the difficulties involved in obtaining a conclusive psychiatric opinion as to an accused's sanity, and characterizes the objective of s. 16(4) as "to allocate the burden of proof on the issue of insanity in a *workable* fashion." A further difficulty arises because the Crown would be required to prove sanity not as of the time of trial, but *as of the time of the offence*. Given that the Crown will often not know that insanity is going to be raised until some time *after* the offence takes place, the difficulties mentioned above are compounded.

Accordingly, the objective of s. 16(4) is to avoid placing an impossible burden of proof on the Crown and to thereby secure the conviction of the guilty. In my view, this objective is sufficiently important to warrant limiting constitutionally protected rights and s. 16(4) passes the first branch of the *Oakes* test.

Proportionality Test

1. RATIONAL CONNECTION

The question to be addressed at this stage of the *Oakes* analysis is whether there is a rational connection between the objective, which was identified above under the first branch of the test, and the means which have been chosen to attain this objective — namely, the reverse onus provision embodied in s. 16(4).

Placing a burden on an accused who raises s. 16 to prove his or her insanity on a balance of probabilities certainly furthers the objective of not putting a burden on the Crown which is virtually impossible to meet. Thus, the presumption of sanity and the reverse onus embodied in s. 16(4) are rationally connected to the objective.

Therefore, it is necessary to turn to the next part of the proportionality branch of the *Oakes* test: does s. 16(4) impair s. 11(d) "as little as possible"?

2. AS LITTLE AS POSSIBLE

The appellants have argued that s. 16(4) does *not* impair the presumption of innocence as little as possible because the objective of the provision could be obtained in a manner which is *less* intrusive on Charter rights. For example, Parliament could have enacted a provision which merely requires an accused alleging insanity to meet an evidentiary burden (i.e., raise a reasonable doubt), at which point the burden would shift to the Crown to disprove insanity (or prove sanity) beyond a reasonable doubt.

The Attorney-Generals of Québec and Ontario both argue that an evidentiary burden would be ineffective because it is very easy for an accused to "fake" insanity and to raise a reasonable doubt. Thus, lowering the burden on the accused to a mere evidentiary burden would defeat the very purpose of the presumption of sanity.

If insanity were easier for an accused to establish, the defence would be successfully invoked *more* often (even if, statistically, it is still infrequently raised). Thus, putting a lesser burden on the accused would *not* have achieved the objective which is achieved by s. 16(4).

In enacting s. 16(4), Parliament may not have chosen the absolutely *least* intrusive means of meeting its objective, but it has chosen from a range of means which impair s. 11(d) as little as is reasonably possible. Within this range of means, it is virtually impossible to know, let alone be sure, which means violate Charter rights the *least*.

In summary, I conclude that s. 16(4) violates s. 11(d) as little as possible in achieving its objective. It is therefore necessary to address the last part of the proportionality test: are the detrimental effects of s. 16(4) on the presumption of innocence proportional to the objective?

3. PROPORTIONALITY BETWEEN EFFECTS AND OBJECTIVE

The presumption of sanity and the reversal of onus embodied in s. 16(4) exist in order to avoid placing a virtually impossible burden on the Crown. The burden on the accused is not the full criminal burden; rather, the accused is required to prove his or her insanity on a balance of probabilities. If an accused were able to rebut the presumption merely by raising a reasonable doubt as to his or her insan-

ity, the very purpose of the presumption of sanity would be defeated and the objective would not be achieved. Any other means of achieving the objective could also give rise to violations of other Charter rights.

While the effect of s. 16(4) on the presumption of innocence is clearly detrimental, given the importance of the objective that the Crown not be encumbered with an unworkable burden and given that I have concluded above that s. 16(4) limits s. 11(d) as little as is reasonably possible, it is my view that there is proportionality between the effects of the measure and the objective.

Accordingly, s. 16(4) is a reasonable limit on the presumption of innocence which can be upheld under s. 1 of the Charter.

The Meaning of "Wrong" in s. 16(2)

The appellants submit that the trial judge erred in his direction to the jury in stating that the word "wrong" as used in s. 16(2) means contrary to the laws of Canada, and that the Court of Appeal erred in holding that the trial judge had made no mistake in this regard. It is argued that the word "wrong" in s. 16(2) of the Code should be interpreted by this Court to mean "morally wrong" and not simply "legally wrong." Section 16(2) reads as follows:

> 16(2) For the purposes of this section, a person is insane when the person is in a state of natural imbecility or has disease of the mind to an extent that renders the person incapable of appreciating the nature and quality of an act or omission or of knowing that an act or omission is wrong.

The meaning of the term "wrong" for the purposes of s. 16(2) was determined by this court in *Schwartz v. The Queen* (1976), 29 C.C.C. (2d) 1, 67 D.L.R. (3d) 716, [1977] 1 S.C.R. 673. Speaking for the majority, Martland J. held that the capacity to know that an act is wrong in this context means no more than the capacity to know that what one is doing is against the law of the land.

The majority in *Schwartz* considered the judgment of the High Court of Australia in *Stapleton v. The Queen* (1952), 86 C.L.R. 358. In *Stapleton*, Dixon C.J. for the court held that the capacity of the accused to make moral judgments must be examined and that "wrong" was not to be defined narrowly as a legal wrong (at p. 367):

> The question is whether he was able to appreciate the wrongness of the particular act he was doing at the particular time. Could this man be said to know in this sense whether his act was wrong if, through a disease or defect or disorder of the mind, he could not think rationally of the reasons which to ordinary people make that act right or wrong? If, through the disordered condition of the mind, he could not reason about the matter with a moderate degree of sense and composure, it may be said that he could not know that what he was doing was wrong.

The majority in *Schwartz* rejected the application of the *M'Naghten* rules by Dixon C.J. in *Stapleton*. In their view, the effect of s. 16(2) is to make the defence of insanity available to an accused who, because he suffered from a disease of the mind, did not know that he was committing a crime. The majority did not believe that Dixon C.J.'s test differed from the "legally wrong" test since, "according to the ordinary principles of reasonable men, it is wrong to commit a crime." Even if there was a difference between the two tests, they could not accept that an insane person, committing an act that he knows to be a crime, could be acquitted if he believed that the act was acceptable according to the standards of reasonable men when a sane person believing such would not be acquitted. Furthermore, the majority rejected Dixon C.J.'s interpretation on the ground that it articulated a subjective approach by examining the individual capacity of an accused to reason as to the wrongfulness of an act (at p.12):

> In my opinion the test provided in s. 16(2) is not as to whether the accused, by reason of mental

disease, could or could not calmly consider whether or not the crime which he committed was morally wrong. He is not to be considered as insane within s. 16(2) if he knew what he was doing and also knew that he was committing a criminal act.

Dickson J., as he then was, dissented in *Schwartz*. He noted that the word "wrong" as used in s. 16(2) is ambiguous and is capable of meaning either "legally" or "morally" wrong.

In order to resolve this question, Dickson J. first examined the internal structure of the Code in order to determine the meaning that Parliament intended to give the term. It would have been internally coherent, he submitted, for Parliament to use the word "unlawful" if it had intended "wrong" to mean "contrary to law." Furthermore, the use of the word "*mauvais*" in the French version of s. 16(2) suggests that Parliament intended the term to have a meaning broader than merely "unlawful."

Dickson J. then considered jurisprudential and doctrinal authorities antedating *M'Naghten's Case* (1843), 10 Cl. & Fin. 200, 8 E.R. 718, and concluded that the historical common law test to determine the criminal responsibility of insane persons was whether the particular accused had the capacity to distinguish between conduct that was good or evil, right or wrong. *M'Naghten's Case*, in his view, did not depart from this standard. In fact, the case drew a clear line between knowledge that an act is illegal and knowledge that the act is one that a person ought not do; this distinction is revealed in the following passage in *M'Naghten's Case*, at p. 210, p. 723 E.R.: "If the accused was conscious that the act was one which he ought not to do, and if that act was at the same time contrary to the law of the land, he is punishable." This passage indicates clearly that an accused will only be convicted if he commits an act which he knows he ought not do and which, at the same time, is contrary to law.

More fundamentally, Dickson J. concluded that a reading of s. 16(2) as a whole leads to the conclusion that "wrong" must mean contrary to the ordinary moral standards of reasonable men and women (at p. 22):

> Section 16(2) must be read *in toto*. One looks at capacity to reason and to reach rational decisions as to whether the act is morally wrong. If wrong simply means "illegal," this virtually forecloses any inquiry as to capacity. The question for the jury is whether mental illness so obstructed the thought processes of the accused as to make him incapable of knowing that his acts were morally wrong. The argument is sometimes advanced that a moral test favours the amoral offender and that the most favoured will be he who had rid himself of all moral compunction. This argument overlooks the factor of disease of the mind. If, as a result of disease of the mind, the offender has lost completely the ability to make moral distinctions and acts under an insane delusion, it can well be said that he should not be criminally accountable.

The interpretation of "wrong" as meaning "morally wrong" would not, in his opinion, have the effect of opening up the insanity defence to a far greater number of accused persons. First, what is illegal and what breaches society's moral standards do not often differ. Secondly, "'[m]oral wrong' is not to be judged by the personal standards of the offender but by his awareness that society regards the act as wrong" (p. 13). He concluded that an accused is not therefore free, as a result of such interpretation, to substitute at will his own sense of morality for that of society, but is to be acquitted by reason of insanity if, by reason of disease of the mind, he is incapable of knowing that society generally considers a particular act to be immoral.

With respect for contrary views, it is my opinion that *Schwartz* was wrongly decided by this court and that the dissenting opinion of Dickson J. (concurred in by Laskin C.J.C., Spence and Beetz JJ.) is to be preferred. The majority judgment fails, in my respectful view, to appreciate the manner in

which insanity renders our normal principles of criminal responsibility inapplicable to an individual as well as the particular objectives of s. 16 of the Code.

The rationale underlying the defence of insanity in Canada, as discussed above under the rubric "The Nature of the Insanity Provisions," rests on the belief that persons suffering from insanity should not be subject to standard criminal culpability with its resulting punishment and stigmatization. This belief, in turn, flows from the principle that individuals are held responsible for the commission of criminal offences because they possess the capacity to distinguish between what is right and what is wrong.

Section 16(2) of the Code embodies this conception of criminal responsibility by providing that no person shall be convicted of an offence who, at the time of committing the act in question, is in a state of "natural imbecility" or has disease of the mind to such a degree as to render him incapable of "knowing that an act or omission is wrong." The principal issue in this regard is the *capacity* of the accused person to know that a particular act or omission is wrong. As such, to ask simply what is the meaning of the word "wrong" for the purposes of s. 16(2) is to frame the question too narrowly. To paraphrase the words of the House of Lords in *M'Naghten's Case*, the courts must determine in any particular case *whether an accused was rendered incapable, by the fact of his mental disorder, of knowing that the act committed was one that he ought not have done.*

Viewed from this perspective, it is plain to me that the term "wrong" as used in s. 16(2) must mean more than simply legally wrong. In considering the capacity of a person to know whether an act is one that he ought or ought not to do, the inquiry cannot terminate with the discovery that the accused knew that the act was contrary to the formal law. A person may well be aware that an act is contrary to law but, by reason of "natural imbecility" or disease of the mind, is at the same time incapable of knowing that the act is morally wrong in the circumstances according to the moral standards of society. This would be the case, for example, if the person suffered from a disease of the mind to such a degree as to know that it is legally wrong to kill but, as described by Dickson J. in *Schwartz*, kills "in the belief that it is in response to a divine order and therefore not morally wrong" (p. 13).

In applying s. 16(2) to a particular set of facts, it may be established that the accused who attempts to invoke the insanity defence is capable of knowing that he ought not do the act because he knows, first, that the act is contrary to the formal law *or*, secondly, that the act breaches the standard of moral conduct that society expects of its members. The insanity defence should not be made unavailable simply on the basis that an accused knows that a particular act is contrary to law and that he knows, generally, that he should not commit an act that is a crime. It is possible that a person may be aware that it is ordinarily wrong to commit a crime but, by reason of a disease of the mind, believes that it would be "right" according to the ordinary morals of his society to commit the crime in a particular context. In this situation, the accused would be entitled to be acquitted by reason of insanity.

An interpretation of s. 16(2) that makes the defence available to an accused who knew that he or she was committing a crime but was unable to comprehend that the act was a moral wrong will not open the floodgates to amoral offenders or to offenders who relieve themselves of all moral considerations. First, the incapacity to make moral judgments must be causally linked to a disease of the mind; if the presence of a serious mental disorder is not established, criminal responsibility cannot be avoided. Secondly, as was pointed out by Dickson J. in *Schwartz, supra,* "'[m]oral wrong' is not to be judged by the personal standards of the offender but by his awareness that society regards

the act as wrong" (p. 13). The accused will not benefit from substituting his own moral code for that of society. Instead, he will be protected by s. 16(2) if he is incapable of understanding that the act is wrong according to the ordinary moral standards of reasonable members of society.

In the case at bar, the trial judge directed the jury that the insanity defence was not available to the appellants pursuant to the second branch of the test set out in s. 16(2) if it reached the conclusion that the appellants knew, at the time of committing the offence, that the act was contrary to the laws of Canada. Of course, he cannot be faulted for having followed the decision of this court in *Schwartz*. Nevertheless, for the reasons discussed above, our interpretation of s. 16(2) in *Schwartz* was not correct. As a result, I would order a new trial.

Disposition

I would answer the constitutional questions as follows:

Question 1: Is s. 16(4) of the Criminal Code of Canada inconsistent with s. 11(d) of the Canadian Charter of Rights and Freedoms?

Answer: Yes.

Question 2: If the answer to question 1 is yes, is s. 16(4) justified by s. 1 of the Canadian Charter of Rights and Freedoms and therefore not inconsistent with the Constitution Act, 1982?

Answer: Yes.

Given the interpretation that I have given to the word "wrong" in s. 16(2), I would allow the appeal and order a new trial.

Appeal allowed; new trial ordered.

Regina v. Swain

SUPREME COURT OF CANADA   MAY 2, 1991

BACKGROUND

At his trial, Swain was found not guilty by reason of insanity on charges of assault and aggravated assault. It was Crown Counsel, rather than Swain himself, who raised the issue of insanity at the trial. Swain was ordered to be kept in strict custody until the pleasure of the Lieutenant-Governor was known [section 614(2) of the Criminal Code]. Swain appealed to the Ontario Court of Appeal against both his acquittal by reason of insanity and the order for strict custody, claiming that section 614(2) should be declared invalid under the Charter. The Ontario Court of Appeal dismissed Swain's appeals. Swain then appealed to the Supreme Court of Canada.

MAIN ISSUES

(1) Were the Criminal Code provisions relating to the disposition of "insanity acquittees" within the scope of Parliament's power to enact criminal law? (2) If so, were these provisions valid under the Charter? (3) Was the common law rule that permitted the Crown to introduce evidence of mental disorder at trial, despite the accused's objections, invalid under the Charter?

JUDGMENTS

The *majority* judgment was delivered by Chief Justice Lamer (with whom Justices La Forest, Sopinka, Gonthier, and Cory agreed). The *concurring* judgment of Justice Wilson and the *dissenting* judgment of Justice L'Heureux-Dubé have been omitted.

....

LAMER C.J.C.: —

The Facts

In October of 1983, Owen Swain was arrested and charged with assault and aggravated assault, contrary to ss. 245 and 245.2(2) of the Criminal Code (now R.S.C. 1985, c. C-46, ss. 266 and 268). These charges arose from an incident in which the appellant, Mr. Swain, attacked his wife and two infant children in a bizarre manner. Fortunately, Mrs. Swain and the children sustained only superficial physical injuries. At trial, the appellant's wife testified that during the incident Swain appeared to be fighting with the air and talking about spirits. At the time of his arrest, the appellant was very excited and spoke in a "dialect" about religious themes. Mr. Swain testified at trial that, during the incident, he

....

felt his family was being attacked by devils and that he had to protect them by carrying out certain acts.

On November 1, 1983, the appellant was transferred from the Toronto Jail to the Penetanguishene Mental Health Centre pursuant to a Form 1 application under the Mental Health Act, R.S.O. 1980, c. 262. While at the centre, Swain behaved in a bizarre and regressive manner. Two anti-psychotic drugs were prescribed and administered to him and his condition improved rapidly. By December 19, 1983, the appellant was released into the community (on the condition that he would continue to see a psychiatrist) on the recommendation of Dr. Fleming, the Director of the forensic unit at the Penetanguishene Mental Health Centre. Mr. Swain returned briefly to jail and was granted bail on conditions shortly thereafter. The appellant remained on bail until June 10, 1985, and continued to take medication and to see a psychiatrist.

On May 3, 1985, Mr. Swain's trial took place in the District Court of Ontario before O'Connell D.C.J. At trial, the Crown sought to adduce evidence with respect to insanity at the time of the offence, to which the appellant objected. After conducting a *voir dire*, the trial judge ruled that the Crown could adduce such evidence. At the conclusion of the trial, Mr. Swain was found not guilty by reason of insanity on all counts. Defence counsel then moved to have s. 542(2) of the Code (now s. 614), which provides for the automatic detention at the pleasure of the Lieutenant-Governor of an insanity acquittee, declared inoperative on the basis that it violated the Charter. O'Connell D.C.J. reserved judgment and on June 10, 1985, held that Mr. Swain's constitutional rights were not infringed by s. 542(2) and ordered that the appellant be kept in strict custody at the Queen Street Mental Health Centre in Toronto until the Lieutenant-Governor's pleasure was known. Mr. Swain filed a notice of appeal in the Ontario Court of Appeal. On June 12, 1985, the Lieutenant-Governor issued a warrant further detaining the appellant in safe custody in a mental hospital for assessment and report to the Advisory Review Board within 30 days. Pursuant to the above-mentioned warrant, Mr.

Swain was sent for psychiatric examination and assessment to the Clarke Institute of Psychiatry, where he remained a patient in the forensic unit until July 12, 1985. The Advisory Review Board held a review hearing on July 26, 1985, pursuant to the provisions of s. 547 of the Code (now s. 619). The appellant and his counsel were present at this hearing. On August 6, 1985, the Advisory Review Board recommended to the Lieutenant-Governor that Mr. Swain should remain in safe custody at the Queen Street Mental Health Centre. Shortly thereafter, the Lieutenant-Governor issued a warrant for the further detention of Mr. Swain. The Lieutenant-Governor accepted the recommendations of the Board, which provided, *inter alia*, that the administrator of the Queen Street Mental Health Centre have the discretion to permit the appellant to re-enter the community with conditions as to supervision and follow-up treatment.

The appeal to the Ontario Court of Appeal was heard in early September, 1985. A majority of the Court of Appeal dismissed the appeal. The appellant sought leave to appeal to this court, which application was granted on March 26, 1987. At the time that the application for leave to appeal was filed, the appellant was in safe custody. However, on September 4, 1986, the Lieutenant-Governor of Ontario ordered that his warrant detaining the appellant be vacated and that the appellant be discharged absolutely.

Issues

The following constitutional questions were stated by former Dickson C.J. on September 25, 1987:

1. Is s. 542(2) of the Criminal Code of Canada *intra vires* the Parliament of Canada?
2. Do the common law criteria, enunciated by the Ontario Court of Appeal, permitting the Crown to adduce evidence of an accused's insanity, violate ss. 7, 9, and 15 of the Canadian Charter of Rights and Freedoms?
3. If the answer to question 2 is affirmative, are the common law criteria, enunciated by the

Ontario Court of Appeal, permitting the Crown to adduce evidence of an accused's insanity, justified by s. 1 of the Canadian Charter of Rights and Freedoms and therefore not inconsistent with the Constitution Act, 1982?

4. Does the statutory power to detain a person found not guilty by reason of insanity, pursuant to s. 542(2) of the Criminal Code of Canada violate ss. 7 and 9 of the Canadian Charter of Rights and Freedoms?

5. If the answer to question 4 is affirmative, is the statutory power to detain a person found not guilty by reason of insanity, pursuant to s. 542(2) of the Criminal Code of Canada, justified by s. 1 of the Canadian Charter of Rights and Freedoms and therefore not inconsistent with the Constitution Act, 1982?

Analysis

1. Does It Violate the Charter for the Crown to Raise Evidence of Insanity over and above the Wishes of the Accused?

The appellant argues that the common law rule for permitting the Crown to adduce evidence of insanity over and above the accused's wishes, which was enunciated by the Ontario Court of Appeal in *R. v. Simpson, supra,* (1997), 35 C.C.C. (2d) 337, and *R. v. Saxell, supra,* (1980), 59 C.C.C. (2d) 176, violates s. 7 of the Charter.

If a common law rule is inconsistent with the provisions of the Constitution, it is, to the extent of the inconsistency, of no force or effect (s. 52(1)). Having said that, I will begin by considering the appellant's argument under s. 7.

SECTION 7

For ease of reference, I have reproduced the text of s. 7 below:

7. Everyone has the right to life, liberty and security of the person and the right not to be deprived thereof except in accordance with the principles of fundamental justice.

It is therefore necessary to consider whether it is inconsistent with the basic tenets of our legal system for the Crown to be able to adduce evidence of insanity over and above the wishes of the accused.

The appellant argues that it is a principle of fundamental justice that an accused person be able to participate in a meaningful way in his or her defence and to make fundamental decisions about the conduct of his or her defence — such as waiving the defence of insanity. It is argued that the functioning of the adversarial system is premised on the autonomy of an accused to make fundamental decisions about his or her defence that require certain consequences and risks to be weighed.

This court has, on numerous occasions, acknowledged that the basic principles underlying our legal system are built on respect for the autonomy and intrinsic value of all individuals. This court has also recognized the constructs of the adversarial system as a fundamental part of our legal system.

Given that the principles of fundamental justice contemplate an accusatorial and adversarial system of criminal justice which is founded on respect for the autonomy and dignity of human beings, it seems clear to me that the principles of fundamental justice must also require that an accused person have the right to control his or her own defence. The appellant has properly pointed out that an accused will not be in the position of choosing whether to raise the defence of insanity at his or her trial unless he or she is fit to stand trial. Thus, an accused who has not been found unfit to stand trial must be considered capable of conducting his or her own defence.

An accused person has control over the decision of whether to have counsel, whether to testify on his or her own behalf, and what witnesses to call. This is a reflection of our society's traditional respect for individual autonomy within an adversarial system.

The question remains, does the ability of the Crown to raise evidence of insanity over and above the accused's wishes interfere with the accused's control over the conduct of his or her defence?

The mere fact that the Crown is able to raise a defence which the accused does not wish to raise, and thereby to trigger a special verdict which the accused does not wish to trigger, means that the accused has lost a degree of control over the conduct of his or her defence. In my view, this in itself is sufficient to answer the question posed above.

It is not difficult to see that the Crown's ability to raise independently the issue of insanity could very well interfere with other defences being advanced by the accused. For example, an accused who wishes to defend on the basis of alibi could very well be thwarted in this approach by the Crown's raising the inconsistent defence of insanity. It is also apparent that the Crown's ability to raise insanity could undermine an accused's credibility with the jury and could give rise to the inference that the accused is someone who would likely commit a crime. The mentally ill have historically been the subjects of abuse, neglect, and discrimination in our society. The stigma of mental illness can be very damaging. While I have a very high regard for the intelligence and good faith of Canadian juries, it is none the less apparent that an accused's credibility could be irreversibly damaged by the Crown's raising evidence of insanity.

In my view, the ability of the Crown to raise evidence of insanity over and above the accused's wishes, under the existing common law rule, does interfere with the accused's control over the conduct of his or her defence. However, this is not to say that if an accused chooses to raise evidence which tends to put his or her mental capacity for criminal intent into question but falls short of raising the defence of insanity (within s. 16), the Crown will be unable to raise its own evidence of insanity. In circumstances where the accused's own evidence tends to put his or her mental capacity for criminal intent into question, the Crown will be entitled to put forward its own evidence of insanity and the trial judge will be entitled to charge the jury on s. 16. Whether the accused's evidence does, in fact, put mental capacity for criminal intent in issue will be a matter for the trial judge to determine in the particular circumstances of each case. The Crown's ability to raise evidence of insanity in these circumstances is necessary because, otherwise,

the jury could well be left with an incomplete picture of the accused's mental capacity. If an accused were able to raise some evidence of mental incapacity (short of an insanity defence) and, at the same time, able to preclude the Crown from raising any evidence of insanity that it may have in its possession, the possibility would arise that the accused could be acquitted by a jury which was deprived of the "full story" surrounding the accused's mental incapacity. Such a result is clearly undesirable. Furthermore, the Crown's ability to raise evidence of insanity only after an accused has put his or her mental capacity for criminal intent in issue does not raise the problem, discussed above, of the Crown's being able to place an accused in a position where inconsistent defences must be advanced.

The common law rule which was enunciated in *R. v. Simpson, supra,* and *R. v. Saxell, supra,* does not limit the Crown to raising insanity only in circumstances where an accused's own defence puts his or her mental capacity for criminal intent into issue. Thus, the existing common law rule which allows the Crown to raise evidence of insanity over and above the wishes of the accused does violate a principle of fundamental justice.

If a new common law rule could be enunciated which would not interfere with an accused person's right to have control over the conduct of his or her defence, I can see no conceptual problem with the court's simply enunciating such a rule to take the place of the old rule, without considering whether the old rule could nonetheless be upheld under s. 1 of the Charter. Given that the common law rule was fashioned by judges and not by Parliament or a legislature, judicial deference to elected bodies is not an issue. If it is possible to reformulate a common law rule so that it will not conflict with the principles of fundamental justice, such a reformulation should be undertaken. Of course, if it were not possible to reformulate the common law rule so as to avoid an infringement of a constitutionally protected right or freedom, it would be necessary for the court to consider whether the common law rule could be upheld as a reasonable limit under s. 1 of the Charter. As was noted at the outset of this analysis, this court has stated that a limit "prescribed by law" within the meaning of s. 1 may arise from the application of a common law rule as well as from a statute or regulation. Thus, I do not wish to be taken as having held that s. 1 can never have application when a common law rule is challenged under the Charter.

For the reasons given above, I will now consider whether the existing common law rule can be upheld as a reasonable limit under s. 1 of the Charter.

SECTION 1

Like the other rights and freedoms set out in the Charter, s. 7 is subject to limitations under s. 1 of the Charter. The procedure to be followed when the state is attempting to justify a limit on a right or freedom under s. 1 was set out by this court in *R. v. Oakes* (1986), 24 C.C.C. (3d) 321, 26 D.C.R. (4th) 200, [1986] 1 S.C.R. 103:

1. The objective of the impugned provision must be of sufficient importance to warrant overriding a constitutionally protected right or freedom; it must relate to concerns which are pressing and substantial in a free and democratic society before it can be characterized as sufficiently important.
2. Assuming that a sufficiently important objective has been established, the means chosen to achieve the objective must pass a proportionality test; that is to say they must:
   (a) be "rationally connected" to the objective and not be arbitrary, unfair or based on irrational considerations;
   (b) impair the right or freedom in question as "little as possible"; and
   (c) be such that their effects on the limitation of rights and freedoms are proportional to the objective.

(i) OBJECTIVE

In my view, the objective of the common law rule, which allows the Crown, in some cases, to raise evidence of insanity over and above the accused's

wishes, is twofold. One of the objectives was identified by Martin J.A. in *Simpson, supra*, at p. 362: ". . . to avoid the conviction of an accused who may not be responsible on account of insanity, but who refuses to adduce cogent evidence that he was insane." The common law rule is aimed not only at avoiding the unfair treatment of the accused but also at maintaining the integrity of the criminal justice system itself. The accused is not the only person who has an interest in the outcome of the trial; society itself has an interest in ensuring that the system does not incorrectly label insane people as criminals.

The second objective was aptly characterized by the appellant as the protection of the public from presently dangerous persons requiring hospitalization. This objective arises from the fact that the Crown's option to simply discontinue the prosecution of an accused, whom it suspects was insane at the time of the offence, does not address the concern that such a person may well be presently dangerous and may therefore bring him or herself into contact with the criminal justice system once again.

In my view, the dual objectives outlined above relate to pressing and substantial concerns in our society and are of sufficient importance to warrant overriding a constitutionally protected right or freedom. Accordingly, I turn now to consider whether the common law rule passes the proportionality test set out in *Oakes*.

(ii) PROPORTIONALITY TEST

1. RATIONAL CONNECTION ◆ Allowing the Crown to raise evidence of insanity in cases where the accused has chosen not to do so is one way of avoiding the conviction of individuals who were insane at the time the offence was committed, but who do not wish to raise the issue of insanity. While this method of achieving the first objective may raise certain problems and may not be the preferred method of achieving the objective, it is nonetheless a logical means of achieving the desired objective.

Similarly, allowing the Crown to raise insanity in cases where the accused has chosen not to do so is one way of protecting the public from people who may be presently dangerous.

Thus, in my view, there is a rational connection between the objectives and the means chosen to attain the objectives, and the common law rule therefore passes the first part of the proportionality test in *Oakes*.

2. AS LITTLE AS POSSIBLE ◆ The question under this part of the proportionality test is whether the impugned law (in this case, the common law rule and criteria enunciated by the Ontario Court of Appeal) violates Charter rights as little as possible in order to achieve the "pressing and substantial" objective. In other words, while the means chosen may be rationally connected to the objective, they may, at the same time, be unnecessarily intrusive on constitutional rights in light of alternative means. This court has stated on a number of occasions that the absolutely least intrusive means need not be chosen in order for a law to pass the "as little as possible" test. However, as I have indicated above, it is my view that the *Oakes* analysis requires somewhat different considerations when, as here, a judge-made rule is being challenged under the Charter.

The least intrusive common law rule which will attain the objectives without disproportionately affecting rights must be adopted by the court.

It is necessary to consider whether a new common law rule can be fashioned which does not limit constitutionally protected rights and freedoms; in my view it is possible to do so.

The dual objectives discussed above could be met without unnecessarily limiting Charter rights if the existing common law rule were replaced with a rule which would allow the Crown to raise independently the issue of insanity only after the trier of fact had concluded that the accused was otherwise guilty of the offence charged. Under this scheme, the issue of insanity would be tried after a verdict of guilty had been reached, but prior to a conviction being entered. If the trier of fact then subsequently found that the accused was insane at the time of the offence, the verdict of not guilty by reason of insan-

ity would be entered. Conversely, if the trier of fact found that the accused was not insane within the meaning of s. 16 at the time of the offence, a conviction would then be entered.

Such a rule would safeguard an accused's right to control his or her defence and would achieve both the objective of avoiding the conviction of a person who was insane at the time of the offence and the objective of protecting the public from a person who may be presently dangerous. While the Crown would be limited to raising evidence of insanity only after the trier of fact was satisfied that the full burden of proof on *actus reus* and *mens rea* had been discharged or after the accused's own defence has somehow put his or her mental capacity for criminal intent in issue, the accused would have the option of raising evidence of insanity at any time during the trial. This new common law rule would give an accused the option of waiting until the Crown has discharged its full burden of proof to raise the issue of insanity, without removing the existing right of an accused to raise evidence of his or her mental condition during the course of the trial.

In my view, the new common law rule achieves the dual objectives enunciated above without limiting an accused's rights under s. 7 of the Charter. Under the new common law rule, there will only be two instances in which the Crown will be entitled to lead evidence of insanity. First, the Crown may raise evidence of insanity after the trier of fact has concluded that the accused is otherwise guilty of the offence charged. In these circumstances the Crown's ability to raise evidence of insanity cannot interfere with the conduct of the accused's defence because the Crown's ability to do so will not be triggered until after the accused has concluded his or her defence. Second, the Crown may raise evidence of insanity if the accused's own defence has (in the view of the trial judge) put the accused's capacity for criminal intent in issue. In these circumstances the Crown's ability to raise evidence of insanity is not inconsistent with the accused's right to control the conduct of his or her defence because the very issue has been raised by the accused's conduct of his or her defence. Furthermore, as was stated above, the Crown's ability to raise evidence of insanity only after an accused has put his or her mental capacity for criminal intent in issue does not raise the problem of the Crown's being able to place an accused in a position where inconsistent defences must be advanced.

In light of the reasons given above, it can be seen that it is indeed possible to fashion a new common law rule which does not limit s. 7 of the Charter. Surely, if it is possible to fashion a common law rule which attains the original objectives but does not limit s. 7, it follows that the existing rule cannot be said to infringe rights "as little as possible." The existing common law rule does not meet the proportionality test enunciated in *Oakes* and cannot be upheld as a reasonable limit which is demonstrably justified in a free and democratic society.

Given the findings reached above, it is my view that the common law rule is inconsistent with the provisions of the Constitution and, pursuant to s. 52(1), is of no force or effect.

SECTION 15

For ease of reference, I have reproduced the text of s. 15(1) below:

> 15(1) Every individual is equal before and under the law and has the right to the equal protection and equal benefit of the law without discrimination and, in particular, without discrimination based on race, national or ethnic origin, colour, religion, sex, age or mental or physical disability.

I cannot see how a rule which allows the Crown to move an individual from the category of those who will surely be convicted and sentenced to those who may be acquitted, albeit on the grounds of insanity, can be said to impose a burden or a disadvantage on that individual. In my view, to say otherwise is tantamount to saying that an accused has a right to be convicted and punished even though

he or she does not have the mental capacity for criminal intent. This cannot be the case.

In light of the above reasoning, it is my view that while one aspect of the new common law rule gives rise to differential treatment under the law based on a personal characteristic, it does not result in "discrimination." Accordingly, in my view, the new common law rule does not infringe s. 15(1) of the Charter.

CONCLUSION

In the case at bar, the accused was acquitted on the basis of insanity after the Crown raised evidence of insanity, during the trial, over and above his wishes. It is impossible to say whether Mr. Swain would have been convicted or acquitted had evidence of insanity not been raised by the Crown in this manner. In these circumstances, I would normally be of the view that a new trial is in order. However, in this case, Mr. Swain has been through the trial process, has been acquitted on account of insanity, has been detained on a warrant of the Lieutenant-Governor, and has subsequently been absolutely discharged by order of the Lieutenant-Governor. To order a new trial now on the basis that his constitutional rights were violated at the first trial would, in my view, be unfair. At the same time, it would be inappropriate to enter an acquittal in these circumstances. In my view, the proper disposition in these circumstances is a judicial stay of proceedings. Consequently, I would allow the appeal and enter a stay of proceedings.

2. Is s. 542(2) of the Criminal Code of Canada *Intra Vires* the Parliament of Canada?

The appellant submits that s. 542(2) and the surrounding legislative scheme, including ss. 545 and 547, are *ultra vires* Parliament's criminal law power. These provisions are set out above.

Whenever an issue of federalism arises, the first step in the analysis must be to characterize the "pith and substance" of the impugned legislation. In order to determine the pith and substance of any particular legislative provision, it is necessary to examine that provision in its overall legislative context. The "pith and substance" of the legislative scheme dealing with individuals acquitted by reason of insanity is the protection of society from dangerous people who have engaged in conduct proscribed by the Criminal Code through the prevention of such acts in the future. While treatment may be incidentally involved in the process, it is not the dominant objective of the legislation.

A statute that includes a prohibition and a penalty and is enacted to serve a public purpose commonly recognized as being criminal in nature, will fall within the scope of Parliament's criminal law power.

It is true that the insanity provisions do not include a "penalty," in that individuals acquitted by reason of insanity are not held responsible for their actions and are not punished. Nevertheless, it has long been recognized that there also exists a preventative branch of the criminal law power.

Since the insanity provisions only relate to persons whose actions are proscribed by the Criminal Code, the required connection with criminal law is present. The system of Lieutenant-Governor warrants, through the supervision of persons acquitted by reason of insanity, serves to prevent further dangerous conduct proscribed by the Criminal Code and thereby protects society. The protection of society is clearly one of the aims of the criminal law.

The Criminal Code provisions do not speak directly of the administration of medical treatment. They simply stipulate the procedures for a criminal committal, procedures designed to protect society, not to treat the individual. Parliament has developed a scheme by which to protect society through the neutralization of potentially dangerous persons who have brought themselves within the criminal sphere by committing acts proscribed by the criminal law. The removal of these persons from society, in the interest of protecting society, flows from the federal power. For humanitarian reasons, Parliament has determined that these individuals will be transferred into the hands of the provincial authorities for treatment. However, the impugned provisions themselves deal primarily with the removal of these people from society and only relate to treatment in a secondary, ancillary way. Rather than prescribing "treatment," the provisions provide for an alternative to simple incarceration, based on a humanitarian concern for persons acquitted by reason of insanity.

The provisions providing for confinement, and the criteria for the decision to release or not, therefore, do not focus on treatment as much as on the protection of society. Of course, Parliament is sympathetic to persons suffering from psychological illnesses and it will not hold them responsible for their actions or punish them. However, it is not Parliament's responsibility to treat these people; Parliament must concern itself with the consequences for society if these individuals are released while dangerous. The fact that the Code provisions themselves do not focus on treatment is not callousness on the part of Parliament, but simply a recognition of the responsibilities and priorities assigned to it by the division of powers provisions in the Constitution.

3. Does the Automatic Detention of a Person Found Not Guilty by Reason of Insanity Required by s. 542(2) of the Criminal Code of Canada Violate the Canadian Charter of Rights and Freedoms?

Following a verdict of not guilty by reason of insanity, s. 542(2) requires that the trial judge automatically order the acquittee into strict custody until the pleasure of the Lieutenant-Governor of the province is known. The appellant submits that this provision of the Criminal Code restricts his rights under ss. 7 and 9 of the Canadian Charter of Rights and Freedoms and cannot be saved under s. 1. First, he submits that s. 542(2) of the Criminal Code restricts his procedural rights under s. 7 because there is no opportunity for a hearing before the trial judge orders the insanity acquittee into "strict custody." Since any evidence of insanity adduced during the trial only relates to insanity at the time of the offence, there is no evidence before the trial judge as to whether such detention is necessary because the patient is dangerous.

Additionally, the appellant submits that s. 542(2) infringes his substantive rights under s. 7 and his right to be free from arbitrary detention under s. 9, because it imposes a duty on the trial judge to order "strict custody" automatically and arbitrarily, without providing any standards for the exercise of this power. The provision substitutes an overly inclusive assumption that all accused persons acquitted by reason of insanity are presently dangerous, and require hospitalization, for an actual determination on the facts of each case as to whether or not that assumption is valid.

SECTION 7

The automatic detention required under s. 542(2) clearly deprives the appellant of his right to liberty. However, if this deprivation is in accordance with the principles of fundamental justice, there will be no limitation of his rights under s. 7 of the Charter. Because s. 542(2) provides for no hearing or other procedural safeguards whatsoever, I need not proceed any further to conclude that the deprivation of liberty is not in accordance with the principles of fundamental justice.

Because the wording of s. 542(2) is precise and requires the trial judge to order the insanity acquitee into strict custody immediately following the trial, this is not a situation in which this court can simply "read in" procedural safeguards to make the legislation accord with constitutional requirements.

SECTION 9

The detention order is automatic, without any rational standard for determining which individual insanity acquittees should be detained and which should be released. I need not determine at this point what standard would be required by s. 9 in order to detain an insanity acquittee. The duty of the trial judge to detain is unqualified by any standards whatsoever. I cannot imagine a detention being ordered on a more arbitrary basis.

In conclusion, because s. 542(2) *requires* a trial judge to automatically order strict custody based on no criteria or standards, and before any kind of

hearing can be conducted on the issue of present mental condition, this provision infringes the appellant's rights under ss. 7 and 9 of the Canadian Charter of Rights and Freedoms. I turn now to the issue of whether the provision can be saved under s. 1.

SECTION 1

OBJECTIVE

All of the parties to this appeal seem to agree that the objective of s. 542(2) — the protection of the public and the prevention of crime through the detention of those insanity acquittees who are dangerous because still insane, pending the decision of the Lieutenant-Governor — is indeed "pressing and substantial."

PROPORTIONALITY TEST

Before embarking on the proportionality test of the s. 1 inquiry, it is necessary to specify which particular aspect of the impugned legislation has limited the Charter rights in question and therefore must be balanced against the importance of the objective. In the case at bar, the lack of a hearing in s. 542(2) deprives the appellant of his right to liberty in a way that is not in accordance with the principles of fundamental justice, thereby infringing his rights under s. 7 of the Charter. His right under s. 9 of the Charter not to be detained arbitrarily is also restricted in that there are no criteria for the exercise of the trial judge's power to detain.

1. RATIONAL CONNECTION ♦ In order to satisfy the first part of the proportionality test, there must be a rational connection between the *objective* of protecting the public and preventing crime through the detention of dangerous insanity acquittees, pending the decision of the Lieutenant-Governor, and the *means* chosen to obtain this objective, which has been found to limit the appellant's right. The means chosen by Parliament in s. 542(2) which infringes ss. 7 and 9 is the automatic and arbitrary order of detention, issued in the absence of any procedural safeguards and without any governing standards.

I accept the submissions of the respondent and of the Attorney-General of Canada that there is a rational connection between the objective and the means because it is reasonable to assume that some insanity acquittees will continue to represent a danger to the public. While I recognize that not every individual will pose a continued threat to society, I do agree that this assumption, while certainly not irrefutable, is *reasonable.*

Of course, while the assumption that persons found not guilty by reason of insanity pose a threat to society may well be *rational,* I hasten to add that I recognize that it is not *always* valid. While past violent conduct and previous mental disorder may indicate a greater possibility of future dangerous conduct, this will not necessarily be so. Furthermore, not every individual found not guilty by reason of insanity will have such a personal history. Nevertheless, the connection between the objective and means is a rational one. By ordering the detention of *all* insane acquittees pending the decision of the Lieutenant-Governor, Parliament is ensuring that society will be protected from the ones who *are* dangerous.

2. MINIMAL IMPAIRMENT ◆ Because s. 542(2) affects the appellant's rights under ss. 7 and 9 differently, I will deal with each separately, beginning with his right to liberty under s. 7.

The order of strict custody required by s. 542(2) remains in effect until the pleasure of the Lieutenant-Governor of the province is known. The pleasure of the Lieutenant-Governor is "known" once the patient is released or an L.G.W. is issued imposing either a conditional release or detention. There is no time requirement within which the Lieutenant-Governor must act: no time limit is placed on the order under s. 542(2), and the language of s. 545, pursuant to which the L.G.W. is issued, is discretionary. In fact, the wording of the legislation does not require the Lieutenant-Governor to ever make an order.

Whatever the actual length of time between court judgment and the issuance of an L.G.W. in any particular case, s. 542(2) does not meet the minimal impairment component of the proportionality test. Parliament could easily employ a means which would still meet its objective and yet not limit the appellant's liberty under s. 7 to such a great extent.

Given that the determination of present mental condition and dangerousness must be made prior to release, and given the nature of the issues to be determined, there will necessarily be a gap in time between the acquittal by reason of insanity and the decision whether to release or detain under an L.G.W. The delay in making the dangerousness determination is inevitable because evidence adduced at trial with respect to the s. 16 defence only relates to mental condition at the time of the offence. Automatic detention following an acquittal by reason of insanity is to some extent, then, a codification of practical reality.

In the long term, then, crime is prevented and society protected as dangerous individuals in need of treatment will be held in custody under an L.G.W.

Therefore, the means chosen by Parliament, automatic detention, furthers the objective in two important ways. First, if individuals acquitted by reason of insanity are immediately ordered into custody, they cannot pose a threat to society in the short term. Secondly, if observation of the individual on an in-patient basis results in more accurate predictions of recurring mental illness, crime is prevented and society protected in the future.

However, the minimal impairment component of the *Oakes, supra,* test requires that insanity acquittees be detained no longer than necessary to determine whether they are currently dangerous due to their insanity.

In conclusion, s. 542(2) cannot be justified as a reasonable limit on the appellant's rights under s. 7 and is accordingly of no force or effect, pursuant to s. 52(1) of the Constitution Act, 1982.

The fact that the means chosen by Parliament in s. 542(2) is a period of *indeterminate* detention tips the balance, in my opinion, and renders the *effect* of the limitation disproportionate to the objective. Therefore, s. 542(2) cannot satisfy the *Oakes* test and therefore cannot be justified with respect to s. 9 of the Charter either.

If, based on the reasons given above, s. 542(2) is simply declared to be of no force or effect pursuant to s. 52(1) of the Constitution Act, 1982, it will mean that as of the date this judgment is released, judges will be compelled to release into the community all insanity acquittees, including those who may well be a danger to the public. Because of the serious consequences of finding s. 542(2) to be of no force and effect, there will be a period of temporary validity which will extend for a period of six months.

Disposition

For the reasons given above, the appropriate disposition in the circumstances of this case is a judicial stay of proceedings. Accordingly, I would allow the appeal and enter a stay of proceedings.

Appeal allowed; stay of proceedings entered.

Regina v. LePage

ONTARIO COURT OF APPEAL   OCTOBER 3, 1997

BACKGROUND

In 1977, LePage was charged with possession of a weapon for a purpose dangerous to the public peace. At trial, he was found not guilty by reason of insanity. He was detained in a psychiatric facility until 1992, when he was charged with uttering threats against individuals in the psychiatric facility; he was then placed in the local jail. LePage pleaded guilty to the charges. After his conviction, but prior to sentencing, he sought a declaration that sections 672.47 and 672.54 of the Criminal Code were invalid under the Charter and were of no force and effect. The trial judge ruled that section 672.54 of the Code infringed the accused's equality rights under section 15 of the Charter and that it could not be saved by the application of section 1 of the Charter. He struck down section 672.54 but suspended the implementation of this ruling for six months. The Crown appealed to the Ontario Court of Appeal.

MAIN ISSUE

Does section 672.54 of the Criminal Code, which articulates the criteria that govern the post-verdict disposition of those accused persons found NCRMD, infringe section 15(1) of the Charter and, if so, can it be saved by the application of section 1 of the Charter?

JUDGMENTS

The *majority* judgment was delivered by Justice Doherty (with whom Justice Charron agreed). The *concurring* judgment of Justice Goudge has been omitted.

DOHERTY, J.: —

II

7   This is an appeal by the Crown. The Crown and supporting intervenors submit that s. 672.54 does not limit the equality rights in s. 15(1) of the Charter. Alternatively, they submit that if those rights are limited, the limitation is justified under s. 1 of the Charter. Only s. 15 of the Charter is in play on this appeal. Section 15(1) provides:

> 15(1) Every individual is equal before and under the law and has the right to the equal protection and equal benefit of the law without discrimination and, in particular, without discrimination based on race, national or ethnic origin, colour, religion, sex, age or mental or physical disability.

8   Section 672.54 applies to both persons found NCR and persons found unfit to stand trial

on account of mental disorder. This appeal is concerned only with those found NCR and not with those found unfit to stand trial.

III

13 The appropriate response to those who engage in criminal activity, while incapable because of mental disorder of conforming to the criminal law, has always posed a conundrum for the criminal law. Any criminal law response must recognize the absence of criminal culpability, but at the same time offer adequate protection for the community from those who engage in criminal activity while mentally incapable of conforming to the criminal law. The present Criminal Code attempts to meet those two goals by providing for a verdict of not criminally responsible on account of mental disorder (NCR), followed by a post-verdict inquiry into the risk posed by the person found NCR culminating in a disposition intended to reflect the risk, if any, posed by that person.

14 In declaring Parliament's response unconstitutional, Howden J. found that the post-verdict provisions of Part XX.1 proceeded from a presumption of dangerousness applicable to all persons found NCR. That presumption, he held, was a reflection of the historic stereotyping which equated mental disorder with dangerousness. According to Howden J., this stereotypical notion that those suffering from a mental disorder are dangerous "has become ingrained in the criminal law as a general perception" (p. 75).

15 I part company with Howden J. on this fundamental point. I find no presumption of dangerousness in Part XX.1 of the Criminal Code. The only presumption I find in the legislation is that everyone found NCR must undergo a further proceeding to assess the risk, if any, which they pose to the community. I do not regard this assumption as a manifestation of the negative stereotyping from which the mentally disabled have no doubt suffered and continue to suffer in our society. In my view, the post-verdict assessment of risk is not only fully justified by the NCR finding, but is demanded if the criminal law is to maintain the confidence of

the community and to protect society from those who commit criminal acts while insane.

IV

16 In determining whether s. 672.54 limits Mr. Lepage's equality rights, I will address three components of the Criminal Code scheme governing those found NCR:

- the trial stage terminating in the verdict of NCR;
- the requirement of a post-verdict disposition hearing;
- the criteria governing the post-verdict disposition.

The Trial Stage

17 An accused charged with a criminal offence may plead guilty or not guilty. If the accused pleads not guilty, he or she may defend the charge by claiming the exemption from criminal liability created by s. 16 of the Criminal Code.

20 It is important when considering the ultimate question of the constitutionality of s. 672.54, to bear in mind exactly what an NCR finding entails. The present language of s. 16 makes it clear that it creates an exemption from criminal culpability. A person who meets the s. 16 criteria is exempted from the normal operation of the criminal law because of an inability to conform to that law. As a consequence of that exemption, an accused must be removed from the normal criminal law process. That accused can neither be convicted nor acquitted. Section 672.34 describes the nature of an NCR verdict:

> 672.34 Where the jury, or the judge or provincial court judge where there is no jury, finds that an accused committed the act or made the omission that formed the basis of the offence charged, but was at the time suffering from mental disorder so as to be exempt from criminal responsibility by virtue of subsection 16(1), *the*

jury or the judge shall render a verdict that the accused committed the act or made the omission but is not criminally responsible on account of mental disorder. [Emphasis added.]

21 Sections 672.35, 672.36, and 672.37 elaborate on the consequences of a finding of NCR. These sections reinforce the conclusion that a verdict of NCR is neither the equivalent of a conviction, nor of an acquittal. The verdict shares some of the characteristics of an acquittal (e.g., see s. 672.35(a)), and in some ways is more akin to a conviction (e.g., s. 672.35(b)(c)).

22 Under the present legislation, it is a misnomer to refer to persons found NCR as "NCR acquittees." It is also potentially misleading. An acquittal implies that the accused was appropriately judged under the criminal law standard and that the Crown failed to prove the requisite elements of the offence. An NCR verdict denies the very application of that standard to the accused because of the accused's inability to conform to that standard due to a mental disorder, and recognizes that the standard cannot, as a matter of fundamental justice, be applied to the accused.

23 Similarly, comparisons between persons found NCR and convicted persons are unhelpful. Convicted persons are held accountable as persons who are properly held to the criminal law standard. The sentence imposed must reflect that accountability. Those found NCR are not responsible for their acts and cannot be held accountable. I find it illogical to recognize the constitutional need to exempt persons found NCR from the imposition of criminal responsibility, while at the same time looking for some symmetry between the treatment of the exempt and those found properly culpable in the eyes of the criminal law.

24 The scope of the s. 16 exemption is also significant to the assessment of the constitutionality of s. 672.54. Not everyone who suffers from a mental disability will be exempt from criminal liability under s. 16. To qualify for the exemption, the accused must meet specific criteria.

♦ The accused must have suffered from a mental disorder at the time of the commission of the alleged offence.

♦ The mental disorder must have rendered the accused incapable, when the act was committed, of either appreciating the nature and quality of the act or of knowing that it was wrong.

26 In my view, the vast majority of disorders which qualify as a disease of the mind will carry with them some risk of recurrence. The exclusion of transitory conditions brought on by external causes from the ambit of the phrase "disease of the mind" fortifies that conclusion: *R. v. Rabey* (1977), 37 C.C.C.(2d) 461, 79 D.L.R. (3d) 414 (Ont. C.A.), affirmed (1980), 54 C.C.C. (2d) 1, 114 D.L.R. (3d) 193 (S.C.C.). The risk of recurrence which informs the definition of the term "disease of the mind," and hence the scope of the s. 16 exemption, becomes important when one addresses the constitutionality of the requirement that all persons found NCR must face a further inquiry before their ultimate fate can be determined.

27 Not only does the s. 16 exemption apply only to those who suffer from a disease of the mind, but it reaches only those who, because of that disease, are *incapable* of appreciating the nature and quality of their act or are *incapable* of knowing that the act was wrong. An impairment, even a substantial one, of these cognitive or normative functions will not suffice. Nor does the mere failure to engage in the cognitive functions or comprehend the wrongness of one's conduct on a particular occasion give rise to the s. 16 exemption. Outright incapacity on account of mental disorder must exist.

30 Clearly, the NCR verdict draws a distinction between accused who are found NCR and all other accused. It is equally clear that the distinction flows in part from a finding that the accused suffered from a mental disorder. A mental disorder is a mental disability, one of the enumerated grounds in s. 15(1) of the Charter: *R. v. Swain* (1991), 63 C.C.C. (3d) 481 (S.C.C.) at p. 521. It has, however, been authoritatively held that the NCR verdict is not *per se* discriminatory within the meaning of s. 15(1): *R. v. Swain, supra*, at pp. 520–24; see also *Winko v. British Columbia (Forensic Psychiatric Institute)* (1996), 112 C.C.C. (3d) 31 (B.C.C.A) at 58–59, leave to appeal to S.C.C. granted May 8, 1997, [114 C.C.C. (3d) vi]. Given that the NCR verdict is premised on a finding that an accused must be exempted from criminal liability on account of mental disorder, it is hardly surprising that the criminal law requires a different verdict for those exempted from liability than for those who are not exempted. Indeed, the failure to provide for a verdict which distinguished between the exempt and non-exempt would give rise to substantial equality concerns. Neither Mr. LePage nor the intervenors who support him contend that the NCR verdict is discriminatory.

The Requirement of a Post-Verdict Disposition Hearing

31 A person found NCR is not finished with the criminal justice system. He remains an accused (s. 672.1). A disposition hearing must be held either before the trial judge or the Review Board (s. 672.45, s. 672.47). The Review Board consists of at least one legally trained person, one psychiatrist, and one other person (s. 672.38 to s. 672.41). Generally speaking, Part XX.1 directs that the trial judge make a disposition where feasible, and where the trial judge cannot do so, the Review Board is directed to make a disposition as soon as practicable. This post-verdict inquiry is an exercise of the preventative component of the criminal law.

34 After a finding of NCR, a trial judge can do three things. She may direct an assessment of the mental condition of the accused; she may proceed with a disposition hearing either with or without an assessment order; and she may decline to make a disposition order. The trial judge may decline to make a disposition order even where she has ordered an assessment and embarked on a disposition hearing.

35 If the trial judge follows the first option, the accused will be assessed by the person or service named in the assessment order (s. 672.13). Subject to the exception set out in s. 672.16(3), there is a presumption against custody where an assessment order is made. The accused can be held in custody for the purpose of the assessment only if one of the conditions found in s. 672.16(1) is met. While an assessment order is in effect, neither a bail nor a detention order can be made (s. 672.17). Nor, as Howden J. suggested (at p. 77), is an assessment order automatic. The trial judge must be satisfied that there are reasonable grounds to believe that a report is necessary to determine the appropriate disposition (s. 672.11(d)).

36 The provisions relating to assessment orders belie the contention that the NCR verdict creates a presumption of dangerousness. Any assessment order must be justified under the statutory criteria and, unless one of the statutory conditions is met or s. 672.16(3) applies, the accused cannot be placed in custody for the purpose of that assessment. These provisions recognize the potential need for a mental assessment of a person found NCR so that a proper disposition order can be made, but they leave the question of any limit on the accused's liberty during the assessment process to a case-by-case determination based on articulated statutory grounds.

37 The trial judge must conduct a disposition hearing if the prosecution or the accused so request, and she may do so on her own motion (s. 672.45(1)). The trial judge must also proceed to make a disposition order if satisfied that she "can readily do so" and that the disposition should be made "without delay" (s. 672.45(2)). The Criminal Code makes no specific provision for the release or detention of the accused pending the disposition order by the trial judge. In my view, however, in the absence of any provision to the contrary and given the clear language of s. 672.46 (see below), the outstanding bail or release order made prior to the verdict will control until the trial judge makes a disposition, unless an assessment order has been made or either party shows cause why the outstanding order should be varied. As in the case of accused who are subject to an assessment order, there is no presumption that an accused is danger-ous or should be confined pending the outcome of his disposition hearing. Any restraint on the liberty of the accused pending the disposition order will depend on the application of the generally applica-ble bail provisions to the specific facts of the case.

38 If a trial judge concludes that she is unable to make a disposition order, then the Review Board must conduct a disposition hearing and make an order "as soon as practicable" and, in any event, within 45 days, unless the court extends that period to 90 days (s. 672.47(1)(2)).

41 There is no "immediate detention" if the trial judge declines to make a disposition order. Section 672.46(1) provides to the contrary and directs that any pretrial order for the release or detention of the accused remains in effect pending the disposition hearing before the Review Board.

42 Section 672.46(2) provides for a variation by a judge of the pre-existing release or detention order upon "cause being shown." Either party may apply for a variation. The Review Board has no power to alter the status of an accused prior to dis-position.

43 Where the initial disposition order is made by the Review Board and not the trial judge, the accused's status pending that disposition will be controlled by the generally applicable bail provi-sions. Any restriction of the accused's liberty must be justified under those provisions. The accused will have had a full opportunity to challenge any proposed restraint on his liberty at the initial bail hearing and at any subsequent application by the Crown to vary the accused's bail. If the accused is not content with the bail or detention order in effect at the time of the NCR verdict, the accused may move to vary that order between verdict and disposition.

44 On my review of the relevant provisions of Part XX.1, I find no "presumption" of dangerous-ness or detention flowing from the NCR verdict. To the contrary, any presumption favours the *status quo* pending disposition. Any restraint of the accused's liberty must be justified under specific statutory provisions relating to bail or assessment orders and will be imposed only after an inquiry into the specific circumstances of the case and the accused.

45 In rejecting the position that the require-ment of a post-verdict disposition hearing carries with it a presumption of dangerousness or a pre-sumption in favour of detention, I do not suggest that Part XX.1 does not create a distinction between those found NCR and all other accused. Clearly, it does. Only those found NCR are subject to the further inquiry mandated by Part XX.1. Pending the disposition, those found NCR are potentially subject to further restraints on their lib-erty and a compulsory mental assessment. These are significant distinctions between NCR accused and all other accused and are based in part on the finding that NCR accused have suffered from a mental disorder.

46 There can be no doubt but that Part XX.1 distinguishes between some accused and other accused on the basis of mental disability. The ques-tion remains whether these distinctions are dis-criminatory within the meaning of s. 15(1) of the Charter. That question must be answered having regard to the scheme as established under the applicable legislation. For the reasons set out above, I do not regard that scheme as creating any pre-sumption of dangerousness or any presumption in favour of detention pending disposition. The scheme requires a post-verdict assessment of risk. It is properly characterized as a "risk assessment scheme" and not a "detention review system."

51 The question then becomes: Does the requirement that all persons found NCR undergo a risk assessment, upon which their ultimate disposi-tion will be based, reflect stereotypical assumptions about the mentally disabled, or does it reflect an individualized assessment based on the merits of each case?

52 An NCR verdict tells us two things:

- the accused has been proven beyond a reason-able doubt to have committed a criminal act;
- the accused has been proven on the balance of probabilities to have suffered from a mental dis-

order which rendered him incapable of conforming to the dictates of the criminal law at the time when he committed the criminal act.

53 Both of these facts are established by admissible evidence after a trial where the full rigour of the procedural due process requirements of the criminal law is engaged. Both findings are grounded in the specifics of an individual case and are the antithesis of assumptions which reflect generalized conclusions based on the placement of an individual within a certain group or classification.

54 In my opinion, it is axiomatic that a person who committed a criminal act when he was unable, on account of mental disorder, to conform to the dictates of the criminal law posed a danger to the community when he committed the act. That danger existed not just because the person committed the criminal act. It is the commission of the act coupled with the incapacity to comply with the criminal law because of a mental disorder that created the danger. The danger to the community existed, in my view, even where the particular criminal act was not serious or did not pose an immediate danger to the community.

55 The NCR verdict does not compel any conclusion with respect to the accused's mental state or dangerousness at the time of the verdict. The trial inquiry looks backward to the time when the criminal act was committed by the accused. Some persons found NCR pose dangers of varying degrees to the community at the time of the NCR verdict. Others pose no danger when found NCR: *R. v. Swain*, *supra*, at pp. 537–38. However, the fact that the particular mental disability constituted a mental disorder, and hence a disease of the mind, does provide cause for concern about the continued existence of that condition or its recurrence. Those concerns further fuel the need for some inquiry into the condition of the NCR accused at the time of the verdict.

56 How is the criminal law to distinguish between those NCR accused who continue to pose a danger to the community and are properly the subject of further restraint, and those who pose no

such risk at the time of the verdict? I can think of no way except by means of a post-verdict inquiry into the risk, if any, posed by each and every person found NCR. The need for that inquiry proceeds not from any assumption that persons suffering from mental disorder are dangerous, but from the findings made at the accused's trial and the uncertainty as to his condition at the time of the verdict. A risk assessment designed to determine the danger, if any, posed by an NCR accused is the only rational response available if the criminal law is to both protect the community from those NCR accused who remain dangerous and prevent unwarranted restrictions on the liberty of those found NCR.

57 In my opinion, it is only by means of an individualized inquiry into the risk posed by each NCR accused that dispositions based on stereotypical assumptions can be avoided. Part XX.1 requires that each NCR accused be treated as an individual and that an inquiry be made into each NCR accused's "merits and capacities" insofar as they are relevant to an assessment of the risk the NCR accused poses to the community at the time of the verdict.

58 The risk assessment scheme contemplated by Part XX.1 recognizes that proven past dangerousness, combined with present uncertainty as to the mental condition of an accused, warrants an inquiry to determine what risk, if any, the NCR accused poses to the community. At the same time, Part XX.1 demands that any restraint on the accused's liberty pending that assessment be justified under statutory criteria which require an individualized assessment of the accused and the circumstances of the offence. None of these criteria make any assumption about the dangerousness of an NCR accused at the time of the verdict. Part XX.1 also demands that the eventual disposition be the product of an inquiry which looks at the circumstances of each case and each accused individually. In doing so, it avoids the shortcomings of the previous system, which was found unconstitutional in *Swain*, *supra*. In short, the inquiry requirement in Part XX.1 "treats individuals as individuals."

The Criteria Governing the Post-Verdict Disposition

59 A disposition may be made by the trial judge or the Review Board. In every case, save where the trial judge orders an absolute discharge, the Review Board must hold an inquiry and make a disposition within 90 days of the verdict (s. 672.47). Prior to the Review Board's order, the accused will be subject to a bail or detention order, an assessment order, or a disposition order made by the trial judge.

60 The constitution of the Board provides both legal and psychiatric expertise. Its members are familiar with the available facilities, the information needed to make an appropriate disposition, and the issues which must be addressed in arriving at a disposition. Howden J.'s finding that the scheme is unconstitutional and the submissions of counsel relate exclusively to the criteria governing the making of the disposition order. Those criteria are found in s. 672.54 and apply to disposition orders made by the trial judge or the Review Board.

61 Section 672.54 contemplates three possible dispositions:

- an absolute discharge (s. 672.54(a));
- a discharge subject to conditions (s. 672.54(b));
- detention in a hospital with or without conditions (s. 672.54(c)).

62 In deciding which disposition to impose, the court or Review Board must take into consideration:

- the need to protect the public from dangerous persons;
- the mental condition of the accused;
- the reintegration of the accused into society;
- the other needs of the accused.

63 The section requires a two-step inquiry. First, the court or Review Board must decide whether "in the opinion of the court or the Review Board, the accused is not a significant threat to the safety of the public." If the court or Review Board forms that opinion, it must discharge the accused absolutely. An accused who is absolutely discharged is no longer subject to any of the provisions of Part XX.1. If the court or Review Board does not form the opinion that the accused is not a significant threat to the safety of the public, it must proceed to the second stage of the inquiry. At that stage, it may impose either a conditional discharge or order the accused detained in a hospital. In choosing between these two alternatives, the court or Review Board must make the disposition which is "least onerous and least restrictive to the accused." Consequently, an order detaining an accused in a hospital can only be made where the court or Review Board is satisfied, having regard to the considerations enumerated in s. 672.54, that detention in a hospital is the least onerous and least restrictive disposition available: *Pinet v. Ontario* (1995), 100 C.C.C. (3d) 343 (C.A.).

64 The provisions permitting the imposition of conditions upon discharge (s. 672.54(b)) and the imposition of conditions as part of a hospital detention order (s. 672.54(c)) allow the court or Review Board to impose an almost infinite variety of orders tailored to the circumstances of each case. A conditional discharge may provide for release subject only to the requirement that the accused attend before the Board for further review at some later point. A conditional discharge may also provide for the release of an accused into the community on a variety of conditions which impose significant limits on the accused's freedom. In Ontario, an order detaining an accused in a hospital will require him to remain in one of 10 psychiatric units. Those units have a variety of facilities and three different security levels (maximum, medium, and low). The order requiring detention in a hospital may also include conditions which permit escorted or unescorted trips into the community for specific purposes and at specific times.

66 The disposition scheme established by Part XX.1 takes cognizance of the risk to the community, associated with the premature absolute release of those who will pose a danger to the community, by establishing a threshold requirement for an absolute release. That threshold requires the court or Board to be of the opinion that the accused is not a significant threat to the safety of the public. At the same time, the scheme recognizes the harm done to accused who are unnecessarily detained in a psychiatric facility. The scheme limits detention to situations where it is the "least onerous and restrictive" position available. Finally, the scheme permits the court or Review Board to tailor orders to the specific needs of each case and to make those orders sufficiently flexible to respond quickly where circumstances warrant a variation of the disposition.

69 The mental condition of the accused is but one of four factors to be considered by the court or Board in determining whether it is of the opinion that the accused is not a significant threat to the safety of the public and should, therefore, be discharged absolutely. The significance of the accused's mental condition to that determination will depend on many variables, including the nature of the mental disorder, if any, from which the accused suffers at the time of the inquiry, the available treatment, the accused's understanding of his mental condition, and the accused's willingness to conform to any proposed course of treatment. Some accused who suffer from a mental disorder will receive an absolute discharge. Most will not receive an absolute discharge. The point is, however, that the decision is not premised on the existence of a mental disability, but on an opinion formed after a consideration of the accused's mental state, the need to protect the public from dangerous persons, the need to reintegrate the accused into society, and the other needs of the accused.

70 A denial of an absolute discharge based solely on the finding that the accused suffers from a mental disorder would be discriminatory. It would also be in direct contravention of s. 672.54. That section makes risk to the public the factor which

distinguishes between those who receive an absolute discharge and those who do not. Unless the court or Review Board is of the opinion that the risk does not reach the level of posing a significant threat to the safety of the public, an NCR accused cannot be discharged absolutely regardless of his mental condition. The distinction drawn in s. 672.54 between those who are to be absolutely discharged and those who are not is based on the assessment of risk to the public occasioned by an absolute discharge and not by the existence of any mental disability. Mental disability is one of the factors to be considered in assessing the risk posed by the NCR accused. The distinction required under s. 672.54(a) is the result of an individualized assessment of risk. A distinction based on the risk posed by the NCR accused does not attract s. 15(1) scrutiny. That distinction is not based on any of the grounds enumerated in s. 15(1) or on any analogous ground: *Winko v. B.C. (Forensic Psychiatric Institute), supra,* at pp. 58–60.

V

78 I find no limitation on the NCR accused's equality rights arising out of the verdict itself, the requirement of a post-verdict risk assessment, or the criteria employed in determining the appropriate post-verdict disposition. Nor do I find such limitation when the three facets of the scheme are considered as a whole.

VI

81 I would allow the appeal, set aside the order of Howden J., and dismiss both the application for declaratory relief and the application for discharge upon the return of the writ of *habeas corpus.*

Appeal allowed.

Jacquard v. The Queen

SUPREME COURT OF CANADA   FEBRUARY 20, 1997

BACKGROUND

Jacquard was convicted at his trial of the offences of first degree murder and attempted murder. His appeal against his convictions to the Nova Scotia Court of Appeal was dismissed. He subsequently appealed to the Supreme Court of Canada against the judgment of the Court of Appeal.

MAIN ISSUES

(1) To what extent may mental disorder, falling short of establishing a defence of NCRMD under section 16 of the Code, negative the intent to kill or the elements of planning and deliberation that the Crown must prove in cases involving a charge of first degree murder? (2) What instructions should the trial judge be giving the jury in such cases?

JUDGMENTS

The *majority* judgment was delivered by Chief Justice Lamer (with whom Justices La Forest, L'Heureux-Dubé, and Gonthier agreed). The *dissenting* judgments of Justice Cory and Justice Sopinka (with whom Justice Major agreed) have been omitted.

LAMER C.J.C.: —

I. Factual and Procedural Background

3 December 17, 1992, was a fateful day for at least three people in Yarmouth, Nova Scotia. Alexander "Sandy" Hurlburt and his spouse, Barbara Wilkinson, went out for a special dinner in celebration of Ms. Wilkinson's 27th birthday. When they returned home, the appellant, Clayton Jacquard, Mr. Hurlburt's stepson from a previous relationship, was there to greet them. This came as no surprise because, although he did not live with them, Mr. Jacquard had spent the previous day and night at the couple's home, sleeping on the living room sofa during the course of the night.

4 Soon after Ms. Wilkinson retired to her bedroom, the night turned tragic. When she went to bed, she left her husband and the appellant playing cards and watching television in the living room. The next thing Ms. Wilkinson recalled was sitting up in bed screaming, having been shot, and seeing the appellant standing at the bedroom door with a gun pointing at her. After Ms. Wilkinson instinctively raised her hand to protect herself from further gunshot, the appellant fired once more and then left the room. Ms. Wilkinson then crawled from her bedroom to the living room where she was able to phone her mother and sister and then await the arrival of the police.

5   When the police arrived they found Ms. Wilkinson lying in the living room with serious shotgun wounds. She would survive, although she sustained permanent disability to her leg, hip, hand, and collarbone. By contrast, the police found Mr. Hurlburt dead in a pool of blood in the front hall with fatal shotgun wounds to his back and chest.

6   The appellant was charged with first degree murder and attempted murder contrary to ss. 235(1) and 239 of the Criminal Code, R.S.C. 1985, c. C-46.

7   At trial, the appellant filed an admission pursuant to s. 655 of the Criminal Code in which he indicated that he had fired the two gun shots that caused Mr. Hurlburt to die. He pleaded not guilty to the charges, however, on the grounds that: (1) under s. 16 of the Criminal Code he was not criminally responsible for his act because, at the time of the shooting, he was suffering from a mental disorder that rendered him incapable of appreciating the nature or quality of the act or knowing that it was wrong; and (2) he lacked the requisite intent to kill Mr. Hurlburt. Among other things, the appellant adduced the evidence of two psychiatrists who testified that, at the relevant time, the appellant suffered from Post Traumatic Stress Disorder, as a result of which he neither understood the nature or quality of his acts nor was capable of forming the intent to carry them out.

8   At the conclusion of the parties' respective cases, the trial judge gave his directions to the jury. In the course of his lengthy 62-page, 3-hour charge, the trial judge spent nearly 15 pages of text reviewing the evidence of the appellant's mental disorder as it related to the first prong of his "not criminally responsible" s. 16 defence. When subsequently discussing the issues of "planning and deliberation" (as required to substantiate a first degree murder conviction under s. 231(2) of the Criminal Code), the trial judge chose not to repeat himself. He said:

In considering whether the murder was planned and deliberate, you should consider all the evid . . . all the circumstances and all the evidence.

On the subject of both the ingredient of intention and whether or not Mr. Jacquard was or was not criminally responsible by reason of a mental disorder, I have reviewed the evidence at great length. I can see no reason to repeat what I already said to you.

There were no objections to the jury instructions at that time.

9   The jury convicted the appellant of both offences and he was sentenced to life imprisonment with no chance of parole for 25 years.

11   On April 11, 1995, the appellant filed a notice of application for leave to appeal to this Court. On October 12, 1995, leave to appeal was granted affirming the need to canvass the following issue raised by the appellant:

1. Did the Nova Scotia Court of Appeal err in holding that the Trial Judge had adequately instructed the jury on the essential elements of the various issues and related material evidence to those issues and in particular on the issue of planning and deliberation?

For the reasons outlined below, I am of the opinion that we should dismiss the appeal.

III. Analysis

A. The Mental Disorder Evidence

(1) THE NEED TO RESTATE THE EVIDENCE IN RELATION TO EACH ISSUE

13   It has been suggested that the trial judge should have restated the evidence of the appellant's mental disorder in its entirety and expressly told the jury how it should reconsider that evidence in relation to the other live legal issues on appeal, particularly the Crown's burden of proving that the appellant planned and deliberated over Sandy Hurlburt's murder. I am reluctant,

however, to conclude that a 62-page, 3-hour jury charge would have been improved had it been any longer. I cannot emphasize enough that the role of a trial judge in charging the jury is to decant and simplify.

14 Courts have recognized that there is no need to state evidence twice where once will do. In many cases, a trial judge need only review relevant evidence once and has no duty to review the evidence in a case in relation to every essential issue. As long as an appellate court, when looking at the trial judge's charge to the jury as a whole, concludes that the jury was left with a sufficient understanding of the facts as they relate to the relevant issues, the charge is proper.

15 In this case, the trial judge thoroughly canvassed the evidence of the appellant's mental disorder when he discussed the s. 16 defence. Later, when addressing the "planned and deliberate" issue, he decided not to repeat what he had already gone to great lengths to discuss. He said:

> In considering whether the murder was planned and deliberate, you should consider all the evid ... all the circumstances and all the evidence.
>
> On the subject of both the ingredient of intention and whether or not Mr. Jacquard was or was not criminally responsible by reason of a mental disorder, I have reviewed the evidence at great length. I can see no reason to repeat what I already said to you.

16 In my opinion, the trial judge was entitled not to restate this evidence of the appellant's mental disorder each time he addressed an issue in respect of which that evidence was relevant. By directing the jury to reconsider all of the circumstances and evidence, he fulfilled his obligation to relate the essential evidence of the appellant's mental disorder as it related to the "planned and deliberate" issue. Indeed, I resist the conclusion that restating the evidence would have improved the charge. In many cases restating the evidence only confounds the issues, making the charge less perfect and not more so.

(2) THE NEED TO REFER TO THE EVIDENCE AT THE APPROPRIATE TIME

17 Although not emphasized in his factum, the appellant's first argument at the oral hearing was that the trial judge failed to adequately convey to the jury that evidence of the appellant's mental disorder was relevant to determining whether the appellant intended to cause the death of Mr. Hurlburt.

18 It is true that the trial judge introduced the subject of intention in a general way. He said:

> In the end you will have to consider all the surrounding circumstances including what Mr. Jacquard, the accused, said and did, in order to decide whether the Crown has proven that Clayton Jacquard did, in fact, mean to cause the death of Mr. Hurlburt.

However, on at least two occasions later in his charge, the trial judge was clear and unequivocal in his instructions. First, when discussing intention and the included offence of manslaughter, he stated:

> Where Mr. Jacquard shot and killed Mr. Hurlburt, which is an unlawful act, but you are not satisfied beyond a reasonable doubt he had the specific intent to commit murder, then you will find the accused not guilty of murder but guilty of manslaughter. I also tell you that after considering whether Mr. Jacquard was not criminally responsible because of a mental disorder, as I asked you to determine first in your deliberations, if you are not satisfied on a balance of probabilities that Mr. Jacquard suffered from a mental disorder to the extent necessary for the special verdict of not criminally responsible on account of a mental disorder, I direct you to still consider the evidence of mental disorder along with the other evidence in determining whether or not Mr. Jacquard had the specific intent to commit the offence of murder. I direct your attention to consider all the evidence including the evidence of Doctor Rosenberg, Doctor Bradford and Doctor Akhtar.

Second, he later summarized in the context of attempted murder:

> I direct your attention to consider all the evidence, including the evidence of the three psychiatrists, particularly where they differed in their opinions, as to whether Mr. Jacquard, at the time of the offence, had the specific intent to commit murder or attempted murder.

20 Even if I were to conclude that the jury might initially have been left with the impression that the mental disorder evidence was not relevant to the topic of intention, the trial judge's subsequent comments resolved any alleged uncertainty. You must look at a jury charge in its entirety. The trial judge made it absolutely clear to the jury, prior to its deliberations, that intention could be negatived by the evidence of the accused's mental disorder. I thus fail to see how he was guilty of misdirection. Although this aspect of the charge may not have been perfect, it was certainly proper and fair.

(3) THE NEED TO PROPERLY CHARGE THE JURY ON HOW THE MENTAL DISORDER EVIDENCE APPLIED TO THE REMAINING LEGAL ISSUES

21 The appellant submits that, even if the jury understood that the evidence *was* relevant to each issue, it did not understand *how* it applied. In other words, the jury was not properly instructed on the legal issues themselves.

22 The appellant argues that the jury did not properly understand that, even if it fell short of establishing a s. 16 defence, or even if it failed to negate proof of intention, evidence of the appellant's mental disorder may still raise a reasonable doubt as to whether or not the accused had the capacity to plan and deliberate and did in fact plan and deliberate. It is alleged that the jury did not understand the meaning of "planned and deliberate" and did not recognize that it is a separate issue with a distinct burden of proof on the Crown. It is also alleged that the trial judge did not adequately

convey to the jury that a mental disorder could conceivably negative the elements of planning and deliberation without negativing proof that an accused intended to kill.

23 I am not persuaded by these arguments either. The trial judge made it clear that the Crown had the burden to prove planning and deliberation beyond a reasonable doubt, and that this was a different burden from that imposed on the accused under the s. 16 defence. At the outset of his charge, the trial judge discussed in considerable detail the burden of proof, reminding the jury that "[f]rom start to finish the burden is upon the Crown to prove beyond a reasonable doubt the guilt of the accused on these charges." After reading s. 16 to the jury he said:

> This means that you must presume Mr. Jacquard was not so mentally disordered as to be exempt from criminal responsibility at the time of the offence unless the contrary is proven. Since Mr. Jacquard is alleging that he was mentally disordered at the time of the offence, he has the burden or responsibility of proving the mental disorder defence. He must prove mental disorder on a balance of probabilities.
>
> There is a lesser standard of proof than proof . . . than beyond a reasonable doubt which I explained to you earlier. If you are satisfied that it is more likely than not that Mr. Jacquard was mentally disordered to the extent of being incapable of appreciating the nature and quality of his act [*sic*] or of knowing that they were wrong at the time of the offence, you must return a verdict of not criminally responsible on account of a mental disorder.

24 I agree with Chipman J.A. that "the jury could not possibly have been confused with respect to the burden of proof being on the Crown beyond a reasonable doubt with respect to all of the elements of first degree murder. The trial judge told the jury so in no uncertain terms" (p. 362).

25 There is also ample reason to conclude that the jurors fully understood that, even if they concluded that the appellant did not adequately establish a defence under s. 16, the other defences were still very much open to consider. At the conclusion of his s. 16 instructions, the trial judge warned the jury:

> If you find Mr. Jacquard did not suffer from a mental disorder that rendered him incapable of appreciating the nature and quality of his act [*sic*] or of knowing that they were wrong, I direct that you must then proceed to determine the remaining issues in count number one.

The trial judge then discussed the elements of count number one and later outlined what was incumbent upon the Crown to prove:

> I tell you as a matter of law, the Crown will not have discharged that burden of proof unless you are satisfied beyond a reasonable doubt that the only reasonable inference to be drawn from the proven facts (1) is that the accused intended to kill Sandy Hurlburt or to cause him bodily harm that he knew was likely to cause his death and was reckless whether death ensued or not; (2) that the murder of Sandy Hurlburt was planned and deliberate; and (3) the intention of the accused was to kill Barbara Marie Wilkinson.

27 It is true that some factor, such as a mental disorder, that is insufficient to negative the charge that the accused *intended* to kill, may nevertheless be sufficient to negative the elements of *planning and deliberation*. This is because one can intend to kill and yet be impulsive rather than considered in doing so. It requires less mental capacity simply to intend than it does to plan and deliberate.

31 There is no question that the trial judge treated the issue of planning and deliberation separately from all others and alerted the jury that the evidence of the appellant's mental disorder was relevant to its determination. Moreover, he indicated to the jury that neither "planning" nor "deliberation" is equivalent to "intentional." He told the jury that "a person can mean or intend to kill someone without having planned to kill the person." The effect of instructing the jury that the appellant could intend to do something without planning and deliberating is to make the jury understand that the appellant's mental disorder could conceivably have undermined his capacity to plan and deliberate without undermining his capacity to intend.

41 Applying a functional approach to the jury instructions in the greater context of the appellant's trial, I find that there is ample reason to conclude that the jury was properly instructed. The jury was fully apprised of the meaning, scope, and effect of the "planned and deliberate" requirement, and understood its responsibility to consider the evidence of the appellant's mental state in determining whether he had the capacity to "plan and deliberate" and whether he in fact did so.

Appeal dismissed.

Defences to a Criminal Charge: Part I
Mistake of Fact, Intoxication, Necessity, and Duress

INTRODUCTION

The six cases in this chapter provide examples of four important defences to a criminal charge: mistake of fact, intoxication, necessity, and duress.

The *Park* case (1995) represents a striking example of how the courts apply the defence of mistake of fact. The case involved a charge of sexual assault and a defence based on an allegedly mistaken belief of consent. The decision ultimately turned on the question of whether the trial judge should have left the defence of mistake of fact to the jury or, more specifically, whether the accused had established sufficient evidence to "give an air of reality" to the defence. This evidential burden applies to almost all of the defences available to an accused person within the framework of Canadian criminal law; therefore, the Supreme Court of Canada's analysis in the *Park* case is of relevance to all of the defences covered in Chapters 8 and 9. It should be noted, however, that, with the enactment of section 273.2 of the Criminal Code in 1992, the defendant's ability to raise the defence of honestly mistaken consent in relation to sexual assault charges has been significantly circumscribed by the imposition of a duty to "take all reasonable steps to ascertain that the complainant was consenting."

Daviault (1994) and *Robinson* (1996) are cases in which the accused raised the defence of intoxication. *Daviault* is an important and controversial decision of the Supreme Court of Canada. In this case, the Court held that, for the purposes of the defence of intoxication, the distinction between

crimes of specific and general (or basic) intent should be maintained. However, the Court ruled that while intoxication will normally not constitute a valid defence to a charge of a general intent offence (such as sexual assault), it will do so when the intoxication is so extreme that it produces a mental state akin to automatism or mental disorder (under section 16 of the Code). Subsequently, Parliament enacted section 33.1 of the Criminal Code, which effectively overturns the *Daviault* decision in any case where the accused is charged with an offence involving an assault or an interference (or threatened interference) with "the bodily integrity of another person." Whether section 33.1 is invalid under the Charter is a question that remains to be answered by the appellate courts.

In the *Robinson* case, the Supreme Court of Canada examined the application of the so-called "*Beard* rules" to charges involving crimes of specific intent (in this particular case, charges of second degree murder). The Supreme Court held that the ultimate issue in such a case is whether the accused actually formed the specific intent required (not whether he or she had the capacity to do so), and the Court indicated how a trial judge should instruct a jury to apply the *Beard* rules.

The *Perka* case (1984) concerns the defence of necessity. In *Perka*, the Supreme Court of Canada provided an extensive analysis of the basic elements and rationale of the defence. In particular, the Court emphasized that necessity should be viewed as an "excuse" rather than a "justification," and that the excuse should be based on the "normative involuntariness" of an action that is dictated by the necessity of circumstances rather than by the free will of the accused.

The final two cases, *Hibbert* (1995) and *Langlois* (1993), raise significant issues concerning the defence of duress. In *Hibbert*, the Supreme Court of Canada held that the underlying rationale of the defence of duress is exactly the same as that for the defence of necessity: namely, "normative involun-

tariness." The Court also made the important ruling that an *objective* test should be applied when determining whether the accused had a "safe avenue of escape" from the situation in which he or she was under the threat of death or bodily harm. In *Langlois*, the Québec Court of Appeal took the audacious step of declaring the statutory defence of duress, as defined in section 17 of the Code, to be invalid under the Charter.

Regina v. Park

SUPREME COURT OF CANADA   JUNE 22, 1995

BACKGROUND

Park was charged with sexual assault. At his trial, he advanced the defence that he had honestly, albeit mistakenly, believed that the complainant had consented to the sexual activity in question. The trial judge refused to put this defence to the jury and Park was convicted. Park appealed to the Alberta Court of Appeal, which overturned the conviction and ordered a new trial. The Crown subsequently appealed to the Supreme Court of Canada against the judgment of the Court of Appeal.

MAIN ISSUE

Was the trial judge acting in error when he refused to place the defence of honest, but mistaken, belief of consent before the members of the jury?

JUDGMENTS

Justice L'Heureux-Dubé delivered the *majority* judgment (with which Chief Justice Lamer and Justices La Forest, Gonthier, Cory, and McLachlin agreed, except in relation to the Mistake of Fact and Consent portion of the judgment).* Justice

Sopinka and Justice Iacobucci (with whom Justices Cory and Major agreed) delivered *concurring* judgments, which have been omitted.

....

1   LAMER C.J.C.: — I have read the reasons for judgment written by my colleague Justice L'Heureux-Dubé and, for the reasons given by her, I agree that the Crown's appeal should be allowed and the conviction restored. I would like, however, to express one reservation.

2   My reservation concerns the "mistake of fact and consent" section of the analysis by L'Heureux-Dubé J., which deals with the interaction of consent and mistake of fact in a sexual assault situation. I prefer to make no comment on this subject since it is not necessary to deal with these matters in deciding this appeal. As this court did not have the benefit of any argument on the aspects discussed by my colleague in this section, I would prefer to reserve these matters for another time.

3   L'HEUREUX-DUBÉ J.: — The respondent was charged with sexual assault as a result of events that took place at the complainant's home early in the morning of November 25, 1991. At trial, his

---

* The Chief Justice and the four other Justices made no comment on this section of Justice L'Heureux-Dubé's judgment because it was not necessary to decide the relevant issues in the appeal.

Adapted from *R. v. Park* (1995), 99 C.C.C. (3d), pp. 6–30. Copyright © by *Canada Law Book*. Reprinted with permission.

....

defence was that the complainant consented to the sexual activities engaged in or that, in the alternative, he held an honest but mistaken belief that she consented to those activities. The trial judge concluded that the facts of the case did not lend the mistaken belief defence any "air of reality," and therefore declined to put it to the jury. The respondent was convicted. On appeal, his conviction was overturned and a new trial ordered. The Crown appeals to this Court as of right on the question of both the nature and the proper application of the "air of reality" test to the mistake of fact defence in the context of a sexual assault.

II. Facts and Judgments

5   In early November 1991, the complainant and the respondent met in a parking lot when the respondent helped her remove her car from an icy spot. He asked for her phone number. She agreed. Approximately one week later, on November 12, they went out on a date and subsequently returned to her place. He says that they became quite intimate, removed substantially all of their clothing, fondled one another's private parts, talked of sex and birth control, and that she masturbated him to ejaculation. She maintains that they only kissed, talked of birth control, and talked about the fact that, as a born-again Christian, she did not believe in premarital sex. Nothing else happened and he left at around 9:45 P.M.

6   Thirteen days later, on November 25, the respondent, having driven all night from Winnipeg, called the complainant up at six in the morning from his cellular phone and asked if he could stop by. Although she had just gotten up for work, she assented since she thought he needed to talk. He arrived ten minutes later, having stopped to buy a condom at a nearby store. She greeted him at the door with a kiss on the cheek, clad only in her bathrobe. He entered and beckoned her to the couch and tried to kiss her. At this point, their stories diverge considerably.

7   According to her, she pulled away and, seeing the condom in his hand, asked if that was "why

[he] came over here." Distraught, she went to her room to take her sleeping two-year-old child off her bed and took her to another room to change the child's diapers. The respondent followed her. After she had finished, he beckoned the complainant into the bedroom. She followed, thinking that he wanted to "crash," since he had driven all night before arriving at her door. She began to look in her closet for clothes to wear to work when she turned around and saw that the respondent had taken his shirt off. She claims that he drew her to him and kissed her and then pushed her onto the bed. She resisted actively, both verbally and physically, but he was stronger. She described in considerable detail the assault. Feeling his weight atop her, she had a flashback to a previous traumatic experience and went into "shock." The next thing she remembered, he was pulling his penis out of her and ejaculating on her stomach. She fled to the bathroom, needing to vomit. He dressed and kissed her goodbye on the cheek as he left. The complainant did not go to work that day, but instead went directly to see her counsellor, who testified to the fact of her emotionally agitated state on that particular day.

8   By contrast, the respondent claims that they sat on her couch and kissed, and that he then asked to use the washroom. The complainant then took her sleeping child back to the child's bedroom, and the two of them entered the complainant's bedroom where they lay on the bed and began to kiss. She actively participated in the sexual activity. Her only resistance was that, when he pulled out the condom, she said "no, not yet." He therefore put the condom aside on the pillow. In his words, things then began to get "hot" and he prematurely ejaculated on her stomach. No intercourse took place. They talked for a short period of time. She got up and went to the bathroom. He dressed, kissed her goodbye and left.

9   At trial, the respondent asserted that the complainant consented to the sexual activity or, in the alternative, that he had an honest but mistaken belief that she was consenting. Both the complainant and the respondent testified. A report from the medical examination of the complainant

was admitted into evidence in an agreed-upon statement of facts. That report indicated no physical injury, but noted the presence of redness on the inner labia which could be consistent with either consensual or non-consensual intercourse. The trial judge refused to put the mistaken belief defence to the jury, finding there to be no air of reality to the defence, and concluding that the issue was simply one of "consent or no consent." Because of his ruling on the mistaken belief defence, he also instructed the jury to disregard all evidence of any sexual activity between the complainant and the respondent prior to the alleged incident, since it was not relevant to any other issue in the trial. The respondent was convicted.

10 McClung J.A., for the majority of the Alberta Court of Appeal, held the trial judge's failure to put the mistaken belief defence to the jury to be in error. He enumerated certain independent facts that, in his view, lent an air of reality to the defence of honest but mistaken belief in consent: the complainant's telephone overture to the respondent, the discussions of her use of birth control, and the fact that she met him with a kiss at 6:10 A.M. on November 25 wearing only her bathrobe. He also held the trial judge's instruction that the jury disregard the prior sexual activity to be in error, since it was relevant to the question of mistaken belief.

III. Analysis

11 The common law has long recognized that a trial judge need not put to the jury defences for which there is no real factual basis or evidentiary foundation. Courts must filter out irrelevant or specious defences, since their primary effect would not be to advance the quest for truth in the trial, but rather to confuse finders of fact and divert their attention from factual determinations that are pertinent to the issue of innocence or guilt. Since this court's judgment in *Pappajohn v. The Queen* (1980), 52 C.C.C. (2d) 481, 111 D.L.R. (3d) 1, [1980] 2 S.C.R. 120, the requirement that such a foundation exist for a defence before it is put to the jury has generally come to be known as the "air of reality" test.

12 In *R. v. Osolin* (1993), 86 C.C.C. (3d) 481, 109 D.L.R. (4th) 478, [1993] 4 S.C.R. 595, Cory J. noted that this test applies uniformly to all defences, and that its application to the defence of mistaken belief in consent was only a subset of this broad principle.

A. The Nature and Purpose of the "Air of Reality" Threshold

13 In *Pappajohn, supra*, at p. 509, McIntyre J. explained the air of reality test in the following manner:

> Before any obligation arises to put defences, there must be in the evidence some basis upon which the defence can rest and it is only where such an evidentiary basis is present that a trial judge must put a defence.

In *R. v. Bulmer* (1987), 33 C.C.C. (3d) 385 at p. 391, 39 D.L.R. (4th) 641, [1987] 1 S.C.R. 782, he further elaborated upon this standard:

> There will not be an air of reality about a mere statement that "I thought she was consenting" not supported to some degree by other evidence or circumstances arising in the case. If that mere assertion were sufficient to require a trial judge to put the "mistake of fact" defence, it would be a simple matter in any rape case to make such an assertion and, regardless of all other circumstances, require the defence to be put. It must be remembered that at this stage of the proceedings the trial judge is not in any way concerned with the question of guilt or innocence. *He is not concerned with the weight of evidence or with the credibility of evidence.* The question he must answer is this. In all the circumstances of the case, is there any reality in the defence? To answer this question, he must consider all the evidence, all the circumstances.

(Emphasis added.) The requirement that the trial judge not enter into assessments of credibility or weighing of evidence is an important factor in the application of this test. The test is the means by which a judge demarcates the limits of the jury's fact-finding responsibilities. A jury must not be invited to speculate on issues that are not realistically before it (*Osolin, supra,* at p. 531, *per* Cory J.):

> The term "air of reality" simply means that the trial judge must determine if the evidence put forward is such that, if believed, a reasonable jury properly charged could have acquitted. If the evidence meets that test, then the defence must be put to the jury. *This is no more than an example of the basic division of tasks between judge and jury.*

(Emphasis added.)

B. Application of the "Air of Reality" Threshold

1. ASSERTION OF AN HONEST BELIEF IN CONSENT

14 Some have interpreted this court's past jurisprudence as suggesting that an accused must actually allege a "belief" in consent, as opposed to asserting the presence of consent itself, in order for there to be a basis for the honest but mistaken belief defence. Both parties to the present appeal, in fact, devote significant argument to the question of whether the accused actually asserted such a belief or whether his failure to assert it precludes him from claiming that defence. Frankly, they are chasing a red herring.

15 The defence of mistake of fact was described in *Pappajohn, supra,* at p. 494, by Dickson J. (dissenting in the result):

> Mistake is a defence . . . where it prevents an accused from having the *mens rea* which the law requires for the very crime with which he is charged. Mistake of fact is more accurately seen as a negation of guilty intention than as the affirmation of a positive defence. *It avails an accused who acts innocently, pursuant to a flawed perception of the facts, and nonetheless commits the* actus reus *of the offence.* Mistake is a defence, though, in the sense that it is raised as an issue by an accused.

The Crown is rarely possessed of knowledge of the subjective factors which may have caused an accused to entertain a belief in a fallacious set of facts.

(Emphasis added.)

16 In the context of sexual assault, proof of the *actus reus* includes proof of the fact that the complainant was not, in fact, consenting. By the very nature of sexual assault, however, the issue of actual consent is almost always materially in dispute. For the accused to assert a belief which he acknowledges to be *mistaken* (i.e., a *mis*perception), he would essentially have to assert a belief that implicitly concedes the *actus reus* of the offence — i.e., the non-consent. It is inappropriate to suggest that an accused should have to assist the Crown in proving the *actus reus* of the offence, by admitting that "perhaps he was mistaken about her consent," in order to rely on the mistaken belief defence. Given that consent is, itself, a mental state experienced only by the complainant, an accused's assertion that the complainant consented must mean that he in fact *believed* she was consenting. The distinction between asserting a *belief* in consent and asserting consent, itself, is therefore both artificial and potentially misleading. Assault differs importantly from most other Code offences in its interaction with the mistake of fact defence. Under most other offences, mistake of fact will primarily arise in contexts in which the *actus reus* of the offence is beyond dispute. Assaults raise a unique problem in that the mental state of another person (i.e., consent or lack thereof) is an essential element that is relevant to both the *actus reus* <u>and</u> the *mens rea* of the offence — an element which almost invariably *is* materially in dispute.

17 Where the accused asserts that the complainant actually consented, then it is artificial to inquire further into whether he also expressed a belief that she was consenting. The absence or presence of an actual statement indicating a belief in consent is of no consequence in all but the most unusual of cases. Presuming that the accused is *de facto* asserting such a belief, the more fundamental question is whether that belief is an *honest* belief, capable of supporting the defence of honest but mistaken belief in consent.

2. THE "CORROBORATION" REQUIREMENT

18 Independent corroboration implies objectivity and reliability. Where there is "independent" evidence, particularly real evidence, corroborating an accused's testimony with respect to a particular defence, then a court can generally conclude that, as a matter of law, there is an "air of reality" to that defence. As a purely practical matter, courts have a more difficult time in deciding what to do in circumstances where there is an absence of "independent" corroborative evidence. Sexual assault, by virtue of the fact that it is often not witnessed by anyone other than the complainant and the accused, and by virtue of the fact that it does not require proof of visible physical injury to the complainant, raises special problems in this respect.

20 Essentially, for there to be an "air of reality" to the defence of honest but mistaken belief in consent, the totality of the evidence for the accused must be reasonably and realistically capable of supporting that defence. Although there is not, strictly speaking, a requirement that the evidence be corroborated, that evidence must amount to something more than a bare assertion. There must be some support for it in the circumstances. The search for support in the whole body of evidence or circumstances can complement any insufficiency in legal terms of the accused's testimony. The presence of "independent" evidence supporting the accused's testimony will only have the effect of improving the chances of the defence. The judge's role is limited to ascertaining whether the accused has discharged the evidentiary burden imposed by s. 265(4) of the Code.

21 As a corollary, in the absence of some other evidence supporting such a defence, it is difficult to imagine situations in which there will be sufficient evidence to put the defence of mistaken belief to the jury where an accused does not testify. Finally, for practical and policy reasons, which shall be discussed below, courts must be wary of being too ready to put the mistaken belief defence to the jury. We must recall that it is the rare exception rather than the general rule that a sexual assault will have been committed by accident.

3. DIAMETRICALLY OPPOSED STORIES

22 It is true that in cases where the defence of honest but mistaken belief is not put to the jury, there is often a considerable divergence between the evidence of the accused and that of the complainant. The significance of diametrically opposing stories is often misunderstood in two respects, however.

23 First, it is important to recall that the two individuals' stories are only relevant to guilt or innocence of sexual assault insofar as they relate in some way to the circumstances affecting the parties *at the time of the alleged assault*. Beyond evidence such as the location and time of the alleged assault and the conduct of the two parties at that time, this includes relevant and admissible background facts which explain how the accused could have honestly interpreted the complainant's conduct at the time of the alleged assault to mean that she was consenting.

24 An honest belief that the complainant *would* consent is not a defence to sexual assault where the accused is aware of, or wilfully blind or reckless as to, lack of consent at the time of the sexual activity. Only where an accused entertains an honest belief that the complainant actually *does* consent does this mistake render the sexual assault non-culpable. Absent some realistic showing of how earlier events could have influenced the accused's honest perceptions of the complainant's behaviour at the time of the actual assault, such evidence will not be capable of supporting, by itself, the defence of honest but mistaken belief in consent.

25 Secondly, the fact that stories are diametrically opposed, as well as the degree to which they are opposed, is but one factor in the air of reality determination. We must bear in mind that neither the version of the facts given by the complainant nor that given by the accused is necessarily a full and complete account of what actually took place and, as such, a jury may decide not to believe certain parts of each person's testimony. Thus, the question is whether, in the absence of other evidence lending an air of reality to the defence of honest mistake, a reasonable jury could cobble together some of the complainant's evidence and some of the accused's evidence to produce a sufficient basis for such a defence. Would the acceptance of one version necessarily involve the rejection of the other? Put another way, is it realistically possible for a properly instructed jury, acting judiciously, to splice some of each person's evidence with respect to the encounter, and settle upon a reasonably coherent set of facts, supported by the evidence, that is capable of sustaining the defence of mistaken belief in consent? If the stories cannot realistically be spliced in such a manner, then the issue really is purely one of credibility — of consent or no consent — and the defence of mistaken belief in consent should not be put to the jury.

26 To summarize, when the complainant and the accused give similar versions of the facts, and the only material contradiction is in their interpretation of what happened, then the defence of honest but mistaken belief in consent should generally be put to the jury, except in cases where the accused's conduct demonstrates recklessness or wilful blindness to the absence of consent. On the other hand, courts have generally refused to put the defence of honest but mistaken belief in consent to the jury when the accused clearly bases his defence on voluntary consent, and he also testifies that the complainant was an active, eager, or willing partner, whereas the complainant testifies that she vigorously resisted. In such cases, the question is generally simply one of credibility, of consent or no consent.

C. Absence of an Air of Reality

27 It is apparent from the problems that judges, practitioners, and academics have all encountered in finding a satisfactory means by which to apply the "air of reality" test that it is, indeed, a somewhat elusive standard to put into practice. There is more than one way, though, to approach every problem. Although it may be difficult to put into positive terms that which is necessary to satisfy the "air of reality" test, framing the test negatively can be a more fruitful endeavour. In other words, though it may be difficult to define in precise terms and as a matter of law the constituent components of "air of reality," it can be a simpler task to delimit with some degree of certainty when an "air of reality" is *absent*.

30 Building upon this approach, it is possible to say that there is no air of reality to a particular defence, and therefore no need to put it to the jury, under the following circumstances:

(1) the totality of the evidence for the accused is incapable of amounting to the defence being sought; or

(2) the totality of the evidence for the accused is clearly, logically inconsistent with the totality of evidence that is not materially in dispute.

It goes without saying, of course, that these standards should be viewed realistically, and not evaluated according to purely speculative or hypothetical extremes. We must recall that a defence should not be put to the jury unless a reasonable jury, properly instructed and acting judiciously, could acquit on that basis.

D. Mistake of Fact and Consent

38 This court recently concluded that a finding of lack of consent does not, as a matter of law, require some minimal word or gesture of objection: *R. v. M. (M.L.)* (1994), 89 C.C.C. (3d) 96*n*, [1994] 2 S.C.R. 3*n*, 30 C.R. (4th) 153. Passivity is, in essence, capable of communicating lack of consent. Although it is not strictly necessary to address this issue in order to resolve the present appeal, it seems to me that many of the difficulties relating to both the nature and the application of the "air of reality" test to honest belief defences may flow from

the manner in which the common law approaches the *mens rea* of the offence of sexual assault. Briefly put, the current common law approach to consent may perpetuate social stereotypes that have historically victimized women and undermined their equal right to bodily integrity and human dignity.

39 The *actus reus* of sexual assault requires that the Crown demonstrate a touching of a sexual nature, combined with a lack of actual consent to that touching. The *mens rea* for sexual assault is established by showing that the accused intended to touch the complainant in a manner that is sexual, and knew of, or was reckless or wilfully blind to, the fact that the complainant was not consenting to that touching. Our law typically takes this to mean that the accused must be shown to be aware of, or reckless or wilfully blind to, the fact that non-consent was communicated. I shall elaborate immediately below on why, in my view, we must accept that the *mens rea* for sexual assault is also established by showing that the accused was aware of, or reckless or wilfully blind to, the fact that consent was not communicated. In other words, the *mens rea* of sexual assault is not only satisfied when it is shown that the accused knew that the complainant was essentially saying "no," but is also satisfied when it is shown that the accused knew that the complainant was essentially not saying "yes."

40 Few would dispute that there is a clear communication gap between how most women *experience* consent, and how many men *perceive* consent. Some of this gap is attributable to genuine, often gender-based, miscommunication between the parties. Another portion of this gap, however, can be attributed to the myths and stereotypes that many men hold about consent. As Robin D. Wiener has observed in "Shifting the Communication Burden: A Meaningful Consent Standard in Rape" (1983), 6 Harv. Women's L.J. 143 at p. 147:

> Because both men and women are socialized to accept coercive sexuality as the norm in sexual behavior, men often see extreme forms of this aggressive behavior as seduction, rather than rape.

A great many incidents women consider rape are, in effect, considered "normal" by both male perpetrators and the male-dominated legal system.

The current approach to consent may perpetuate this unfortunate phenomenon.

42 In my view, the primary concern animating and underlying the present offence of sexual assault is the belief that women have an inherent right to exercise full control over their own bodies, and to engage only in sexual activity that they wish to engage in. If this is the case, then our approach to consent must evolve accordingly, for it may be out of phase with that conceptualization of the law.

43 Consideration of *communication* of consent has always implicitly informed our approach to how knowledge of absence of consent relates to the *mens rea* of the offence of sexual assault. In fact, since consent is, itself, a private mental state, we go about inferring it in much the same way as we would infer *mens rea*. Namely, we look to verbal and non-verbal cues and then draw inferences about a particular mental state by evaluating the individual's behaviour in light of the totality of the circumstances. A finder of fact employs these techniques to determine whether a complainant has, in fact, not consented to a sexual touching. Insofar as the *actus reus* of the offence of sexual assault is concerned, the inquiry stops there. The *mens rea* of sexual assault, however, requires proof of the accused's awareness of, or recklessness or wilful blindness to, this absence of consent. The inquiry into absence of consent for the purposes of establishing the *mens rea* of the offence must therefore go one step further, and delve into the *accused's perception* of the absence of consent. Since mistake of fact goes to the *mens rea* of the offence, an honest mistake of fact by the accused in this respect may therefore indicate that he possessed a non-culpable state of mind.

44 As I mentioned earlier, however, circumstances are not relevant to the defence of honest but mistaken belief where they are only capable of supporting a belief on the part of the accused that the complainant *would* consent, rather than being capa-

ble of supporting his belief that she does, in fact, consent. An accused cannot say that he believed the complainant to be consenting without pointing out the basis for that belief. As a practical matter, therefore, the principal considerations that are relevant to this defence are (1) the complainant's actual communicative behaviour, and (2) the totality of the admissible and relevant evidence explaining how the accused *perceived* that behaviour to communicate consent. Everything else is ancillary.

45 Non-consensual sexual touching is criminal unless, at the least, the accused honestly believes that consent has been communicated with respect to that touching. Thus, as a practical matter, the *mens rea* of the offence does not relate so much to the complainant's frame of mind as it does to the complainant's communication of that frame of mind and to the accused's *perception of that communication*. Furthermore, although consent may exist in the mind of the woman without being communicated in any form, it cannot be accepted by a reasonable finder of fact as having been *honestly perceived* by the accused without first identifying the behaviour that led the accused ostensibly to hold this perception. If the accused is unable to point to evidence tending to show that the complainant's consent was communicated, then he risks a jury concluding that he was aware of, or reckless or wilfully blind to, the complainant's absence of consent.

46 Under such an analytic approach, although the communication gap between the sexes may still avail confusion and miscommunication, the consequences will accrue more equally to both. Women, as a practical matter, still run the risk of being sexually assaulted unless they communicate non-consent in a manner that is sufficiently clear for others to understand. Men, by contrast, must assume the responsibility for that part of the communication gap that is driven by androcentric myths and stereotypes, rather than by genuine misunderstanding due to gender-based miscommunication.

47 The assumption that if a woman is not consenting then she will say so is only helpful if we further assume that men *perceive* non-consent in

the same way that women *communicate* it. The elusive and multifacetted character of sex-speak, however, demonstrates this latter assumption to be patently incorrect (Weiner [*sic*], *supra*, at pp. 148–9):

> A woman may believe she has communicated her unwillingness to have sex — and other women would agree, thus making it a "reasonable" female expression. Her male partner might still believe she is willing — and other men would agree with his interpretation, thus making it a "reasonable" male interpretation. The woman, who believes that she *has* conveyed her lack of consent, may interpret the man's persistence as an indication that he does not care if she objects and plans to have sex despite her lack of consent. She may then feel frightened by the man's persistence, and may submit against her will.

(Emphasis in original.) Acknowledging the reality of this communication gap between reasonable women and reasonable men requires us to discard the assumption that voluntariness — defined only in terms of force, fear, or fraud — is a fair proxy for consent in the absence of communicated non-consent. It is not. As long as the effect of our approach to the *mens rea* of sexual assault reinforces the view that sexual activity is consensual in the absence of communicated non-consent, the damaging communication gap between the sexes, and the terrible costs that flow from it, will continue unacknowledged and will be perpetuated rather than narrowed. In order to give full and meaningful effect to women's right to control their own bodies, we must recognize that awareness of, or recklessness or wilful blindness to, an absence of communicated consent is sufficient to found the *mens rea* of the offence of sexual assault.

48 In my view, finders of fact will benefit from focusing their attentions on communication, and honest perception of that communication, when determining whether the *mens rea* of the offence has been made out. Such an approach will enable them to separate more effectively the wheat from the chaff — the myth and the stereotype from the reality — in determining whether the accused was aware of the complainant's absence of consent, or whether he could have entertained an honest but mistaken belief as to her consent. It will help them to identify, and filter out, stereotypical beliefs on the part of the accused that lead him to override non-consent, or that lead him to be reckless towards whether a woman is consenting or not. I believe that it may therefore lead to fairer, more accurate factual determinations. I believe that it will also take women's and men's distinct realities more equitably into account.

49   There is nothing preventing the common law governing consent from evolving to reflect contemporary social mores and realities. In fact, common law approaches to consent have always been strongly informed by public policy considerations.

51   The majority of this court recently concluded in *Dagenais v. Canadian Broadcasting Corp.* (1994), 94 C.C.C. (3d) 289, 120 D.L.R. (4th) 12, [1994] 3 S.C.R. 835, that the common law must develop in a way that is consistent with Charter values. It follows that the common law governing the *mens rea* of sexual assault must be approached having regard to, *inter alia*, s. 15 of the Charter. As was the case in *R. v. Lavallee* (1990), 55 C.C.C. (3d) 97, [1990] 1 S.C.R. 852, 76 C.R. (3d) 329, this court must strive to ensure that criminal law is responsive to women's realities, rather than a vehicle for the perpetuation of historic repression and disadvantage. A doctor who operates in the absence of the patient's informed and communicated consent risks being charged with assault. Awareness of, or recklessness or wilful blindness to, the absence of that communication is culpable in such situations. I see no reason why an accused charged with sexual assault should not be held to an identical standard.

IV. Application to the Facts

52   In the present appeal, there was no air of reality to the accused's defence of mistaken belief in consent. The factors listed by McClung J.A. as lending an air of reality to that defence — the com-

plainant's telephone overture to the respondent, the discussions of her use of birth control, the sexual activity engaged in thirteen days earlier, and the fact that she met him with a kiss at 6:10 A.M. on November 25 wearing only her bathrobe — are all only capable, if anything, of supporting a belief on the part of the respondent that the complainant *would* consent, not a belief that she did *in fact* consent. None of these factors address or relate in any realistic way to the events that actually took place at the time of the alleged sexual assault. They are therefore incapable of supporting a defence of honest but mistaken belief in consent.

53   What *is* relevant to a possible defence of honest but mistaken belief is the account of the events that took place in the bedroom, as well as any additional information explaining why the respondent might have honestly interpreted those events at that time to be consistent with consent. In certain cases, evidence of prior sexual activity between the two parties may be relevant in this respect. In the present case, however, the dissimilarities between the alleged assault and the acts that took place in the encounter thirteen days earlier can only lead one to conclude that evidence of that encounter was neither relevant to, nor capable of supporting, an honest belief on the part of the accused that the complainant was consenting at the time of the assault.

54   In the present case, moreover, the respondent's evidence is very sketchy as to the events that took place in the bedroom. He asserts that the complainant was a willing participant, that she only resisted with respect to the timing of the use of the condom, and that "as things were going on, it was getting hot," leading him to ejaculate on her stomach. He asserts that intercourse never even took place. The complainant, on the other hand, claims to have vigorously resisted him, both verbally, by saying repeatedly "No, Darryl" and "I don't want this," and physically. His strength and considerably greater weight, however, were too much for her and caused her then to go into a state of shock, during which he penetrated her.

55   There is nothing in the totality of this evidence, coming from either the respondent or the

complainant, to lend any air of reality to the possibility that the respondent may have held a mistaken belief as to her consent. Nor, for that matter, would it have been possible for a reasonable jury to splice together some of her evidence and some of his with respect to the encounter, and to settle upon a reasonably coherent set of facts that could support the defence of mistaken belief in consent. A reasonable jury, properly instructed and acting judiciously, could not come to a conclusion both that the complainant did not consent to the sexual activity and that the respondent could have had a mistaken belief about her non-consent. For all of these reasons, the trial judge was correct in refusing to put the defence of mistake of fact to the jury.

56   As such, I would allow the Crown's appeal and restore the conviction.

Appeal allowed; conviction restored.

....

Daviault v. The Queen

SUPREME COURT OF CANADA   SEPTEMBER 30, 1994

BACKGROUND

Daviault was acquitted at his trial on a charge of sexual assault. The Crown's appeal to the Québec Court of Appeal was allowed and a conviction was substituted. However, Daviault subsequently appealed to the Supreme Court of Canada against the judgment of the Court of Appeal.*

MAIN ISSUE

Does the Charter require that a defendant should be granted a valid defence to a charge of an offence of *general* intent if, at the time of the alleged offence, he or she was in an extreme state of self-induced intoxication that was akin to automatism or mental disorder?

JUDGMENTS

Justice Cory delivered the *majority* judgment (with which Chief Justice Lamer and Justices La Forest, L'Heureux-Dubé, McLachlin, and Iacobucci agreed). A *dissenting* judgment was delivered by Justice Sopinka (with whom Justices Gonthier and Major agreed).

SOPINKA J. (dissenting): —

Facts
....

The facts which give rise to this appeal are not in dispute. The complainant is a 65-year-old woman who is partially paralyzed and thus confined to a wheelchair. She knew the appellant through his wife, who was the complainant's dressmaker and ran errands for her. The complainant testified that at approximately 6:00 P.M. on May 30, 1989, at her request, the appellant arrived at her home carrying a 40-ounce bottle of brandy. The complainant drank part of a glass of brandy and then fell asleep in her wheelchair. When she awoke during the night to go to the bathroom, the appellant appeared, grabbed her chair, wheeled her into the bedroom, threw her on the bed and sexually assaulted her. The appellant left the apartment at about 4:00 A.M. The complainant subsequently discovered that the bottle of brandy was empty. The trial judge found as a fact that the appellant had drunk the rest of the bottle between 6:00 P.M. and 3:00 A.M.

The appellant was a chronic alcoholic. He testified that he had spent the day at a bar where he had

---

* Note that, subsequent to this decision, Parliament enacted section 33.1 of the Criminal Code, which came into effect in 1996.

....

Adapted from *R. v. Daviault* (1994), 93 C.C.C. (3d), pp. 26–27, 30, 46–70. Copyright © 1994 by *Canada Law Book*. Reprinted with permission.

consumed seven or eight bottles of beer. He recalled having a glass of brandy upon his arrival at the complainant's residence but had no recollection of what occurred between then and when he awoke nude in the complainant's bed. He denied sexually assaulting her.

The defence called a pharmacologist, Louis Léonard, to testify as an expert witness. Mr. Léonard testified that the appellant's alcoholic history made him less susceptible to the effects of alcohol. He hypothesized that, if the appellant had consumed seven or eight beers during the day and then 35 ounces of brandy on the evening in question, his blood-alcohol content would have been between 400 and 600 milligrams per 100 millilitres of blood. That blood-alcohol ratio would cause death or a coma in an ordinary person. Mr. Léonard testified that an individual with this level of alcohol in his blood might suffer an episode of "l'amnésie-automatisme," also known as a "blackout." In such a state the individual loses contact with reality, and the brain is temporarily dissociated from normal functioning. The individual has no awareness of his actions when he is in such a state and will likely have no memory of them the next day.

Mr. Léonard further testified that it is difficult to distinguish between a person in a blackout and someone who is simply acting under the influence of alcohol. He stated that if a person acting under the influence of alcohol behaves in a manner which requires higher cognitive functions or reflection, it is unlikely that the person is in a blackout. On the other hand, if the person departs from his normal behaviour to act in a gratuitous or violent manner, it is more likely that he is in a blackout.

The appellant was charged with one count of sexual assault. The trial judge found as a fact that the appellant had committed the offence as described by the complainant. However, he acquitted the appellant because he had a reasonable doubt about whether the appellant, by virtue of his extreme intoxication, had possessed the minimal intent necessary to commit the offence of sexual assault. The Québec Court of Appeal overturned this ruling. The appellant now appeals to this court as of right, pursuant to s. 691(2)(a) of the Criminal Code, R.S.C. 1985, c. C-46.

Analysis

Sexual assault is a crime of general intent. In *Leary v. The Queen* (1977), 33 C.C.C. (2d) 473, 74 D.L.R. (3d) 103, [1978] 1 S.C.R. 29 (S.C.C.), a majority of this court held that drunkenness is not a defence to a crime of general intent. I agree with the Court of Appeal's decision that the trial judge was bound by the decision in *Leary*. Furthermore, I reject the appellant's submission that *Leary* ought to be overruled.

The final alternative to the *Leary* rule is to create a new defence of automatism caused by voluntary intoxication which would have to be proved by the defence on the balance of probabilities. I do not favour this course of action. Permitting an accused to raise such a defence would ignore the fact that those who commit criminal offences after voluntarily becoming intoxicated are not blameless. In my view, such individuals possess a culpable state of mind which deserves to be considered a form of *mens rea*. It is not inconsistent with the principles of fundamental justice to punish such individuals for the crimes which they commit.

Conclusion

For all of these reasons, in my opinion the best course is for the court to reaffirm the traditional rule that voluntary intoxication does not constitute a defence to an offence of general intent, subject to the comments I have made with respect to improvements in the definition and application of the distinction between offences of specific and general intent. If a different approach is considered desirable because the *Leary* approach does not comport with social policy, Parliament is free to intervene. It has been suggested that Parliament should create a new offence of dangerous intoxication. Such legislation could be coupled with amendments to the Criminal Code to extend the defence of drunkenness to some or all offences to which it does not apply. Such changes, however, are for Parliament and not for this Court to make.

CORY J.: —

Issue

Can a state of drunkenness which is so extreme that an accused is in a condition that closely resembles automatism or a disease of the mind, as defined in s. 16 of the Criminal Code, R.S.C. 1985, c. C-46, constitute a basis for defending a crime which requires not a specific but only a general intent? That is the troubling question that is raised on this appeal.

The facts of this case and the judgments below are set out in the reasons of Justice Sopinka. Although I agree with my colleague on a number of issues, I cannot agree with his conclusion that it is consistent with the principles of fundamental justice and the presumption of innocence for the courts to eliminate the mental element in crimes of general intent. Nor do I agree that self-induced intoxication is a sufficiently blameworthy state of mind to justify culpability, and to substitute it for the mental element that is an essential requirement of those crimes. In my opinion, the principles embodied in our Canadian Charter of Rights and Freedoms, and more specifically in ss. 7 and 11(d), mandate a limited exception to, or some flexibility in, the application of the *Leary* rule. This would permit evidence of extreme intoxication akin to automatism or insanity to be considered in determining whether the accused possessed the minimal mental element required for crimes of general intent.

Analysis

The Physical and Mental Aspects of Criminal Acts

For my purposes, it is sufficient to say that for a great many years it has been understood that, unless the legislator provides otherwise, a crime must consist of the following elements. First, a physical element which consists of committing a prohibited act, creating a prohibited state of affairs, or omitting to do that which is required by the law. Secondly, the conduct in question must be willed; this is usually referred to as voluntariness. Some writers classify this element as part of the *actus reus*, others prefer to associate it with *mens rea*; however, all seem to agree that it is required. If persons other than lawyers were asked what constituted willed or voluntary conduct, they would respond that such an act or conduct must involve a mental element. It is the mental element, that is, the act of will, which makes the act or conduct willed or voluntary. In *R. v. Théroux* (1993), 79 C.C.C. (3d) 449 at p. 458, 100 D.L.R. (4th) 624 at p. 634, [1993] 2 S.C.R. 5 (S.C.C.), McLachlin J. had this to say concerning the *actus reus*:

> The term *mens rea*, properly understood, does not encompass all of the mental elements of crime. The *actus reus* has its own mental element; the act must be the voluntary act of the accused for the *actus reus* to exist. *Mens rea*, on the other hand, refers to the guilty mind, the wrongful intention, of the accused. Its function in criminal law is to prevent the conviction of the morally innocent — those who do not understand or intend the consequences of their acts. Typically, *mens rea* is concerned with the consequences of the prohibited *actus reus*.

The definition of *actus reus* is thus established. Yet I should add that, as will be seen later, the mental aspect involved in willed or voluntary conduct may overlap to some extent in both the concept of *mens rea* and *actus reus*. Finally, then there must be a contemporaneous mental element comprising an intention to carry out the prohibited physical act or omission to act; that is to say, a particular state of mind such as the intent to cause, or some foresight of, the results of the act or the state of affairs.

With this concept of a crime established, it soon came to be accepted that in certain situations a person who committed a prohibited physical act still could not be found guilty. A number of examples come to mind. For instance, if a person in a state of automatism as a result of a blow on the head committed a prohibited act that he was not consciously aware of committing, he could not be found guilty since the mental element involved in committing a willed voluntary act and the mental element of intending to commit the act were absent. Thus, neither the requisite *actus reus* or *mens rea* for the offence was present. The result would be the same in the case of a person who had an unexpected reaction to medication which rendered him totally unaware of his actions.

A review of the history of the defence of intoxication shows that, originally, intoxication was never a defence to any crime. However, with the evolution of criminal law, this rule came to be progressively relaxed, and the defence of intoxication was admitted for crimes of specific intent. Although one of the justifications for this was the courts' preoccupation with the harshness of criminal liability and criminal sanctions, clearly this development was also influenced by the development of the requirements for mental elements in crimes. The defence of intoxication was based on the recognition and the belief that alcohol affected mental processes and the formulation of intention. In my view, the need for this historical expansion is justified and emphasized by the increased concern for the protection of fundamental rights enshrined in the Charter.

It can thus be seen that with the development of principles recognizing constituent elements of crimes, particularly the need for a mental element, there came the realization that persons who lack the requisite mental element for a crime should not be found guilty of committing that crime. For centuries it has been recognized that both the physical and the mental elements are an integral part of a criminal act. It has long been a fundamental concept of our criminal law.

This appeal is concerned with situations of intoxication that are so extreme that they are akin to automatism. Such a state would render an accused incapable of either performing a willed act or of forming the minimal intent required for a general intent offence. I will approach the issue primarily on the basis that the extreme intoxication renders an accused incapable of forming the requisite minimum intent.

Categorization of Crimes as Requiring Either a Specific Intent or a General Intent

The distinction between crimes of specific and general intent has been acknowledged and approved by this court on numerous occasions. The categorization of crimes as being either specific or general intent offences, and the consequences that flow from that categorization, are now well established in this court. However, as he observes, we are not dealing here with ordinary cases of intoxication but with the limited situation of very extreme intoxication and the need, under the Charter, to create an exception in situation where intoxication is such that the mental element is negated. Sopinka J. sees no need for such an exception. This is where I must disagree with my colleague.

Drunkenness as a Factor in the Consideration of Criminal Liability

This issue has been the subject of many judicial decisions in commonwealth countries. It is useful here to contrast the two opposite positions which have emerged in the absence of Charter considerations. The first position is illustrated by the decision of this court in *Leary, supra*, and also corresponds to the English position. The second position is that which prevails in Australia and New Zealand. It is best illustrated by *R. v. O'Connor* (1980), 4 A. Crim R. 348.

LEARY V. THE QUEEN

Leary was charged with rape. In the course of his instructions, the trial judge advised the jury that "drunkenness is no defence to a charge of this sort." This position was taken on the grounds that rape was a crime of general intent and that in such a crime, the mental element could not be negated by drunkenness. The majority in this court confirmed that rape was, indeed, a crime of general intent and that the *mens rea* could not be affected by drunkenness.

The supporters of the *Leary* decision are of the view that self-induced intoxication should not be used as a means of avoiding criminal liability for offences requiring only a general intent. They contend that society simply cannot afford to take a different position since intoxication would always be the basis for a defence despite the fact that the accused had consumed alcohol with the knowledge of its possible aggravating effects. Supporters of the *Leary* decision argue that to permit such a defence would "open the floodgates" for the presentation of frivolous and unmeritorious defences.

Those who oppose the decision contend that it punishes an accused for being drunk by illogically imputing to him liability for a crime committed when he was drunk. Further, it is said that the effect of that decision is to deny an accused person the ability to negate his very awareness of committing the prohibited physical acts. That is to say, the accused might, as a result of his drinking, be in a state similar to automatism and, thus, completely unaware of his actions, yet he would be unable to put this forward as a factor for the jury to consider because his condition arose from his drinking. In such cases, the accused's intention to drink is substituted for the intention to commit the prohibited act. This result is said to be fundamentally unfair. Further, it is argued that the floodgates argument should not have been accepted because juries would not acquit unless there was clear evidence that the drunkenness was of such a severity that they had a reasonable doubt as to whether the accused was even aware that he had committed the prohibited act.

THE *O'CONNOR* CASE — A POSITION TAKEN CONTRARY TO *LEARY*

O'Connor, supra, (1980), 54 A.L.J.R. 349, is a decision of the High Court of Australia. There, the majority concluded that for all offences requiring proof of a mental element, evidence of intoxica-tion, whether self-induced or not, was relevant and admissible in determining whether the requisite mental element was present. The majority went on to observe that evidence of intoxication which merely tends to establish loss of inhibition or weakening of the capacity for self-control would not provide a basis for denying that the mental element of an offence was present. However, where there was evidence that the accused was unconscious or that his mind was a blank through drunkenness at the time of the offence, this should be left to the jury in resolving the question as to whether there had been a voluntary act on the part of the accused.

Earlier, the Court of Appeal of New Zealand, in *R. v. Kamipeli,* [1975] 2 N.Z.L.R. 610, came to a similar conclusion. Thus, the courts of Australia and New Zealand have come to a conclusion that is diametrically opposed to that reached in *Director of Public Prosecutions v. Majewski,* [1977] A.C. 433, and *Leary.*

Passage of the Charter and Subsequent Cases of This Court

The passage of the Charter makes it necessary to consider whether the decision in *Leary* contravenes ss. 7 or 11(d) of the Charter.

There have been some statements by this court which indicate that one aspect of the decision in *Leary* does infringe these provisions of the Charter. The first occurred in *R. v. Bernard* (1988), 45 C.C.C. (3d) 1, [1988] 2 S.C.R. 833, 67 C.R. (3d) 113 (S.C.C.). Bernard was charged with sexual assault causing bodily harm. He was tried by judge and jury and found guilty. Bernard admitted forcing the complainant to have sexual intercourse with him but stated that his drunkenness caused him to attack her. The issue was whether self-induced intoxication should be considered by the jury along with all the other relevant evidence in determining whether the prosecution had proved beyond a reasonable doubt the *mens rea* required by the offence. Bernard's appeal was dismissed by a majority of the court. They all agreed that, as the defence of intoxication had not been made out on the evidence,

s. 613(1)(b)(iii) (now s. 686(1)(b)(iii) of the Criminal Code) could be applied.

Wilson J. (L'Heureux-Dubé J. concurring) advocated a modification of the rule set out in *Leary*. Her reasoning proceeds in this way. Sexual assault causing bodily harm is an offence of general intent which requires only a minimal intent to apply force. Ordinarily the Crown can establish the requisite mental state by means of the inferences to be drawn from the actions of the accused. Wilson J. found that the *Leary* rule was perfectly consistent with an onus resting upon the Crown to prove the minimal intent which should accompany the doing of the prohibited act in general intent offences, but she would have applied it in a more flexible form. In her view, evidence of intoxication could properly go before a jury in general intent offences if it demonstrated such extreme intoxication that there was an absence of awareness which was akin to a state of insanity or automatism. Only in such cases would she find that the evidence was capable of raising a reasonable doubt as to the existence of the minimal intent required for a general intent offence.

She also noted that she had some real concerns about the validity of the use of self-induced intoxication as a substituted form of *mens rea* under the Charter. More specifically, she thought it would be unlikely that proof of the substituted element would lead inexorably to a conclusion that the minimum intent existed at the time of the commission of the criminal act.

The same position was put forward by Wilson J., again concurred in by L'Heureux-Dubé J., in *R. v. Penno* (1990), 59 C.C.C. (3d) 344, [1990] 2 S.C.R. 865, 80 C.R. (3d) 97 (S.C.C.). In my view, this position has much to commend it and should be adopted.

The Alternative Options

What options are available with regard to the admissibility and significance of evidence of drunkenness as it may pertain to the mental element in general intent offences? One choice would be to continue to apply the *Leary* rule. Yet, as I will attempt to demonstrate in the next section, the rule violates the Charter and cannot be justified. Thus, this choice is unacceptable.

Another route would be to follow the *O'Connor* decision. Evidence relating to drunkenness would then go to the jury along with all other relevant evidence in determining whether the mental element requirement had been met. It is this path that is enthusiastically recommended by the majority of writers in the field. Yet it cannot be followed. It is now well established by this court that there are two categories of offences: those requiring a specific intent and others which call for nothing more than a general intent. To follow *O'Connor* would mean that all evidence of intoxication of any degree would always go to the jury in general intent offences. This, in my view, is unnecessary. Further, in *Bernard, supra*, the majority of this court rejected this approach.

A third alternative, which I find compelling, is that proposed by Wilson J. in *Bernard*.

How the *Leary* Rule Violates ss. 7 and 11(d) of the Charter

What then is the rule of law established by the decision in *Leary*? The conclusion of the majority in that case establishes that, even in a situation where the level of intoxication reached by the accused is sufficient to raise a reasonable doubt as to his capacity to form the minimal mental element required for the general intent offence for which he is being tried, he still cannot be acquitted. In such a situation, self-induced intoxication is substituted for the mental element of the crime. The result of the decision in *Leary*, applied to this case, is that the intentional act of the accused to voluntarily become intoxicated is substituted for the intention to commit the sexual assault or for the recklessness of the accused with regard to the assault. This is a true substitution of *mens rea*. First, it would be rare that the events transpiring from the consumption of alcohol through to the commission of the crime could be seen as one continuous series of events or as a single transaction. Secondly, the requisite mental element, or *mens rea*, cannot necessarily be inferred from the physical act, or *actus reus*, when the very voluntariness or consciousness of that act may be put in question by the extreme intoxication of the accused.

It has not been established that there is such a connection between the consumption of alcohol and the crime of assault that it can be said that drinking leads inevitably to the assault. Experience may suggest that alcohol makes it easier for violence to occur by diminishing the sense of what is acceptable behaviour. However, studies indicate that it is not in itself a cause of violence. For example, in the [Saskatchewan Alcohol and Drug Abuse Commission] Research Report of 1989, the following appears at p. 8:

> While it is widely recognized that alcohol and drug abuse are associated with criminality, neither the extent of this association nor its nature has been clearly identified.

> . . . But more research is required in order to establish with confidence the nature or extent to which such offences are drug related. However, research conducted elsewhere would suggest that, at most, 10% of violent offences in Saskatchewan are drug related.

Alcohol abuse, although it frequently accompanies violent behaviour, is not, in and of itself, a cause of violence.

Alcohol abuse can best be viewed as a "facilitator" of violence. That is to say that in our culture, alcohol abuse makes it easier for violence to occur, either by blurring the boundaries between what is and what is not acceptable behaviour, or by removing conscious recognition of rules governing acceptable behaviour altogether.

In addition, in some instances alcohol or drug abuse may serve as a conscious accompanier of violent behaviour in that some offenders use alcohol or drug abuse to excuse a violent act (e.g., some instances of wife battering).

There is no simple causal relationship between alcohol or drug abuse and violent behaviour (Brain, 1986). Patterns of violent behaviour are shaped by a host of physiological, psychological, situational and socio-cultural factors. Among the various socio-cultural factors which shape patterns of substance abuse and violence, especially important are gender, age, socio-economic status and ethnicity (Coid, 1986).

In my view, the strict application of the *Leary* rule offends both ss. 7 and 11(d) of the Charter for a number of reasons. The mental aspect of an offence, or *mens rea*, has long been recognized as an integral part of crime. The concept is fundamental to our criminal law. That element may be minimal in general intent offences; nonetheless, it exists. In this case, the requisite mental element is simply an intention to commit the sexual assault or recklessness as to whether the actions will constitute an assault. The necessary mental element can ordinarily be inferred from the proof that the assault was committed by the accused. However, the substituted *mens rea* of an intention to become drunk cannot establish the *mens rea* to commit the assault.

The consumption of alcohol simply cannot lead inexorably to the conclusion that the accused possessed the requisite mental element to commit a sexual assault, or any other crime. Rather, the substituted *mens rea* rule has the effect of eliminating the minimal mental element required for sexual assault. Furthermore, *mens rea* for a crime is so well-recognized that to eliminate that mental element, an integral part of the crime, would be to deprive an accused of fundamental justice: see *R. v. Vaillancourt* (1987), 39 C.C.C. (3d) 118, 47 D.L.R. (4th) 399, [1987] 2 S.C.R. 636 (S.C.C.).

In that same case it was found that s. 11(d) would be infringed in those situations where an accused could be convicted despite the existence of reasonable doubt pertaining to one of the essential elements of the offence: see *Vaillancourt, supra*, at pp. 134–5 C.C.C., pp. 415–6 D.L.R. That would be the result if the *Leary* rule was to be strictly applied. For example, an accused in an extreme state of intoxication akin to automatism or mental illness would have to be found guilty although there was reasonable doubt as to the voluntary nature of the act committed by the accused. This would clearly infringe both ss. 7 and 11(d) of the Charter. In my view, the mental element of voluntariness is a fundamental aspect of the crime which cannot be taken away by a judicially developed policy. It simply cannot be automatically inferred that there would be an objective foresight that the consequences of voluntary intoxication would lead to the commission of the offence. It follows that it cannot be said that a reasonable person, let alone an accused who might be a young person inexperienced with alcohol, would expect that such intoxication would lead to either a state akin to automatism or to the commission of a sexual assault. Nor is it likely that someone can really intend to get so intoxicated that they would reach a state of insanity or automatism.

It was argued by the respondent that the "blameworthy" nature of voluntary intoxication is such that it should be determined that there can be no violation of the Charter if the *Leary* approach is adopted. I cannot accept that contention. Voluntary intoxication is not yet a crime. Further, it is difficult to conclude that such behaviour should always constitute a fault to which criminal sanctions should apply. However, assuming that voluntary intoxication is reprehensible, it does not follow that its consequences in any given situation are either voluntary or predictable. Studies demonstrate that the consumption of alcohol is not the cause of the crime. A person intending to drink cannot be said to be intending to commit a sexual assault.

In summary, I am of the view that to deny that even a very minimal mental element is required for sexual assault offends the Charter in a manner that is so drastic and so contrary to the principles of fundamental justice that it cannot be justified under s. 1 of the Charter. The experience of other jurisdictions which have completely abandoned the *Leary* rule, coupled with the fact that, under the proposed approach, the defence would be available only in the rarest of cases, demonstrate that there is no urgent policy or pressing objective which needs to be addressed. Studies on the relationship between intoxication and crime do not establish any rational link. Finally, as the *Leary* rule applies to all crimes of general intent, it cannot be said to be well tailored to address a particular objective and it would not meet either the proportionality or the minimum impairment requirements.

What then should be the fate of the *Leary* rule?

Justifications for the Adoption of the Flexible Approach Suggested by Wilson J.

As I have said, the position adopted by Wilson J. in *Bernard* has much to commend it and should be adopted.

Far more writers have supported the approach adopted in *O'Connor*. In my view, the most vehement and cogent criticism of both *Majewski* and *Leary* is that they substitute proof of drunkenness for proof of the requisite mental element. The authors deplore the division of crimes into those requiring a specific intent and those which mandate no more than a general intent. They are also critical of the resulting presumption of recklessness, and of the loss of a requirement of a true *mens rea* for the offence. They would prefer an approach that would permit evidence of drunkenness to go to the jury together with all the other relevant evidence in determining whether the requisite *mens rea* had been established.

I find further support for adopting the approach suggested by Wilson J. in studies pertaining to the effect of the *O'Connor* and *Kamipeli* decisions which have been undertaken in Australia and New Zealand: reference to these studies can be found in the English Law Commission's "Intoxication and Criminal Liability," Consultation Paper No. 127 at pp. 60–3 (1993). One of these studies was conducted in New South Wales, by means of a survey of approximately 510 trials. The author, Judge George Smith, concluded, at p. 277, that:

> Those figures disclose that a "defence" of intoxication which could not have been relied upon pre-*O'Connor* was raised in eleven cases or 2.16 per cent of the total. Acquittals followed in three cases or 0.59 per cent of the total, but only in one case or 0.2 per cent of the total could it be said with any certainty that the issue of intoxication was the factor which brought about the acquittal.

> ....

> Certainly my inquiries would indicate that the decision in *O'Connor's* case, far from opening any floodgates, has at most permitted an occasional drip to escape from the tap.

That study clearly indicates that the *O'Connor* decision has not had an effect of any significance on trials or on the number of acquittals arising from evidence of severe intoxication.

Given the minimal nature of the mental element required for crimes of general intent, even those who are significantly drunk will usually be able to form the requisite *mens rea* and will be found to have acted voluntarily. In reality it is only those who can demonstrate that they were in such an extreme degree of intoxication that they were in a state akin to automatism or insanity that might expect to raise a reasonable doubt as to their ability to form the minimal mental element required for a general intent offence. Neither an insane person nor one in a state of automatism is capable of forming the minimum intent required for a general intent offence. Similarly, as the words themselves imply, "drunkenness akin to insanity or automatism" describes a person so severely intoxicated that he is incapable of forming even the minimal intent required of a general intent offence. The phrase refers to a person so drunk that he is an automaton. As such, he may be capable of voluntary acts such as moving his arms and legs but is quite incapable

of forming the most basic or simple intent required to perform the act prohibited by a general intent offence.

It is obvious that it will only be on rare occasions that evidence of such an extreme state of intoxication can be advanced and perhaps only on still rarer occasions is it likely to be successful. Nonetheless, the adoption of this alternative would avoid infringement of the Charter.

I would add that it is always open to Parliament to fashion a remedy which would make it a crime to commit a prohibited act while drunk.

The appellant in this case is an elderly alcoholic. It is difficult if not impossible to present him in a sympathetic light. Yet any rule on intoxication must apply to all accused, including the young and inexperienced drinker. The strict rule in *Leary* is not a minor or technical infringement but a substantial breach of the Charter eliminating the mental elements of crimes of general intent in situations where the accused is in an extreme state of intoxication. I would think that this judge-made rule should be applied flexibly, as suggested by Wilson J., so as to comply with the Charter. Such an approach would mean that except in those rare situations where the degree of intoxication is so severe it is akin to automatism, that drunkenness will not be a defence to crimes of general intent.

It should not be forgotten that if the flexible "Wilson" approach is taken, the defence will only be put forward in those rare circumstances of extreme intoxication. Since that state must be shown to be akin to automatism or insanity, I would suggest that the accused should be called upon to establish it on the balance of probabilities. Drunkenness of the extreme degree required in order for it to become relevant will only occur on rare occasions. It is only the accused who can give evidence as to the amount of alcohol consumed and its effect upon him. Expert evidence would be required to confirm that the accused was probably in a state akin to automatism or insanity as a result of his drinking.

Extreme intoxication akin to automatism or insanity should, like insanity, be established by the accused on a balance of probabilities.

....

Thus, it is appropriate to place an evidentiary and legal burden on the accused to establish, on a balance of probabilities, that he was in a state of extreme intoxication that was akin to automatism or insanity at the time he committed the offence.

RESULT IF THE MENTAL ELEMENT RELATES SOLELY TO THE *ACTUS REUS* WHICH REQUIRES THAT THE PROHIBITED ACT BE PERFORMED VOLUNTARILY

Should it be thought that the mental element involved relates to the *actus reus* rather than the *mens rea*, then the result must be the same. The *actus reus* requires that the prohibited criminal act be performed voluntarily as a willed act. A person in a state of automatism cannot perform a voluntary willed act since the automatism has deprived the person of the ability to carry out such an act. It follows that someone must also be deprived of that ability. Thus, a fundamental aspect of the *actus reus* of the criminal act is absent. It would equally infringe s. 7 of the Charter if an accused who was not acting voluntarily could be convicted of a criminal offence. Here again the voluntary act of becoming intoxicated cannot be substituted for the voluntary action involved in sexual assault. To do so would violate the principle set out in *Vaillancourt, supra*. Once again, to convict in the fact of such a fundamental denial of natural justice could not be justified under s. 1 of the Charter.

Summary of Proposed Remedy

In my view, the Charter could be complied with, in crimes requiring only a general intent, if the accused were permitted to establish that, at the time of the offence, he was in a state of extreme intoxication akin to automatism or insanity. Just as in a situation where it is sought to establish a state of insanity, the accused must bear the burden of establishing, on the balance of probabilities, that he was in that extreme state of intoxication. This will undoubtedly require the testimony of an expert. Obviously, it will be a rare situation where an accused is able to establish such an extreme degree of intoxication. Yet, permitting such a procedure would mean that a defence would remain open that, due to the extreme degree of intoxication, the minimal mental element required by a general intent offence had not been established. To permit this rare and limited defence in general intent offences is required so that the common law principles of intoxication can comply with the Charter.

Disposition

In the result, I would allow the appeal, set aside the order of the Court of Appeal and direct a new trial.

Appeal allowed; new trial ordered.

Regina v. Robinson

SUPREME COURT OF CANADA   MARCH 21, 1996

BACKGROUND

Robinson was convicted of second degree murder by a jury at his trial. The B.C. Court of Appeal subsequently allowed Robinson's appeal against his conviction. However, the Crown appealed to the Supreme Court of Canada against the judgment of the Court of Appeal.

MAIN ISSUES

(1) Did the trial judge err in law when he directed the members of the jury in relation to the defence of intoxication? (2) Do the so-called *Beard* rules, as interpreted by the Supreme Court of Canada in the *MacAskill* case (1931),* infringe sections 7 and 11(d) of the Charter; and, if so, are they salvaged by the application of section 1 of the Charter? (3) If the *Beard* rules, as interpreted in *MacAskill*, are invalid, what new rule should replace them; and, in particular, how should judges instruct juries in cases which raise the defence of intoxication?

JUDGMENTS

The *majority* judgment was delivered by Chief Justice Laskin (with whom Justices La Forest, Sopinka, Gonthier, Cory, McLachlin, Iacobucci, and Major agreed). The *dissenting* judgment of Justice L'Heureux-Dubé has been omitted.

LAMER C.J.C.: —

I. Introduction

1   In March of 1920, Britain's House of Lords handed down judgment in the now famous *Beard* case (*Director of Public Prosecutions v. Beard*, [1920] A.C. 479 [1920] All E.R. 21, 14 Cr. App. R. 159). The issue before the court concerned the manner in which a jury should be instructed on the relationship between intoxication and intent. Lord Birkenhead, in speaking for the court, formulated rules that evidence of intoxication is to be considered by a jury only in those cases where its effect was to render the accused incapable of forming the requisite intent. In *MacAskill v. The King* (1931), 55 C.C.C. 81, [1931] 3 D.L.R. 166, *sub nom. McAskill v. The King*, [1931] S.C.R. 330, the *Beard* rules were incorporated into our law and they have been, for the most part, applied by this court ever since.

2   I am of the view that the time has finally come for this court to review the adequacy of

---

* [1931] S.C.R. 330.

MacAskill in light of earlier opinions expressed by Laskin and Dickson C.JJ., the Canadian Charter of Rights and Freedoms, and other relevant developments in this area in our provincial appellate courts and other common law countries.

II. Summary of the Facts

3 Clark Hall was found stabbed to death, seated in a chair in his own apartment, on January 22, 1991. He was 52 years old. The autopsy revealed that he had suffered at least 12 blunt trauma wounds to the head, which together would result in unconsciousness, but not death. Death was caused by three stab wounds to the upper part of the stomach, any one of which would have been fatal. The deceased had a blood alcohol level of 293 milligrams of alcohol per 100 millilitres of blood. The police found an empty litre-bottle of red wine in his apartment.

4 According to the respondent's statement to the police, he stabbed the deceased in self-defence. The deceased apparently said something to the respondent who then struck the deceased on the head with a rock from his pocket. The respondent then went to the kitchen, returned with a bread knife and was standing with the knife in his right hand. The respondent remembered stabbing the deceased two times and pushing him back into his chair.

6 In final submissions to the jury, defence counsel submitted that the most important issue in the case was how the jury was going to deal with the defence of intoxication. Crown counsel conceded that the respondent was under some degree of influence of intoxication. In his charge to the jury, the trial judge told them that intoxication in this case was "significant" and there was evidence that the respondent "consumed a considerable amount of alcohol before the alleged killing of Mr. Clark Hall."

7 The respondent was convicted of second degree murder by a jury. He appealed his conviction to the British Columbia Court of Appeal primarily on the basis that the trial judge had

misdirected the jury on the manner in which they could use the evidence of intoxication as it related to the requisite intent for murder. The British Columbia Court of Appeal allowed the appeal and the Crown appealed that decision to this court.

IV. Analysis

(i) The *Beard* Rules: Capacity Is the Only Relevant Inquiry

9 Arthur Beard was convicted of murder and sentenced to death in the rape and killing of a 13-year-old girl. Beard's position at trial was that he was only guilty of manslaughter as his self-induced intoxication rendered him incapable of knowing that what he was doing was likely to inflict serious injury. The case eventually found its way to Britain's House of Lords on a point of law described by Lord Birkenhead at p. 493 as one of "undoubted importance in the administration of the criminal law" — the manner in which juries should be instructed concerning evidence of intoxication.

10 It is important to recall that until the early 19th century, the law of England was such that drunkenness was never a mitigating factor in assessing liability. This rigid rule was slowly relaxed over the next century in cases involving serious offences such as murder to reflect the harshness of the sentence which often included the death penalty.

11 In delivering his speech in *Beard, supra*, at pp. 501–502, Lord Birkenhead reviewed the developments over the last century and formulated the following famous rules of intoxication which he believed properly reflected the current state of the English law:

> . . . That evidence of drunkenness which renders the accused *incapable of forming the specific intent* essential to constitute the crime should be taken into consideration with the other facts proved in order to determine whether or not he had this intent.
>
> . . . That evidence of drunkenness falling short of a proved incapacity in the accused *to form the*

intent necessary to constitute the crime, and merely establishing that his mind was affected by drink so that he more readily gave way to some violent passion, does not rebut the presumption that a man intends the natural consequences of his acts.

(Emphasis added.) Under these rules, intoxication is not a relevant factor for triers of fact to consider except in those cases where the alcohol or drugs has removed the accused's capacity to form the requisite intent.

(ii) The Incorporation of *Beard* into Our Common Law: *MacAskill* and Its Progeny

12 Some 11 years after the decision in *Beard*, this court was given an opportunity to consider the manner in which juries should be instructed on the circumstances under which intoxication could reduce a charge of murder to manslaughter in *MacAskill, supra*. MacAskill had been convicted of murder and sentenced to death. In ruling on the propriety of the trial judge's charge to the jury, this court held, at p. 82 C.C.C., p.168 D.L.R., that the *Beard* "propositions embody the rules governing us on this appeal." Duff J. (as he then was) stated at p. 84 C.C.C., p 169 D.L.R.:

> The right direction . . . is that evidence of drunkenness rendering the accused incapable of the state of mind defined by that subsection [s. 259(b)] may be taken into account with the other facts of the case for the purpose of determining whether or not, in fact, the accused had the intent necessary to bring the case within that subsection; but that the existence of drunkenness not involving such incapacity is not a defence.

13 The only modification to the *Beard* rules came in *Malanik v. The Queen* (1952), 103 C.C.C. 1 at pp. 4–5, [1952] 2 S.C.R. 335, 14 C.R. 367, where this court held that the word "proved" should be removed from its rules. In other words, intoxication should be treated like any other

defence where there is simply an evidentiary burden on the accused to adduce some evidence capable of raising a reasonable doubt.

14 In *Bradley v. The Queen* (1956), 116 C.C.C. 341, 6 D.L.R. (2d) 385, [1956] S.C.R. 723, the following observation concerning the presumption that a person intends the natural consequences of his or her acts contained in the *Beard* rules was made (at p. 368 C.C.C., p. 410 D.L.R.):

> . . . it may be said that, when dealing generally with the presumption that a man is presumed to intend the natural consequences of his act, certain statements of the charge could be objectionable . . .

However, the court did not find it necessary to make a modification to this aspect of the *Beard* rules in that case. Therefore, I wish to take the opportunity in this case to hold that the presumption of intent, to which *Beard* refers, should only be interpreted and referred to as a common sense and logical inference that the jury can but is not compelled to make.

15 Since *MacAskill*, the *Beard* rules and "capacity" language have been approved of and relied on in many decisions of this court.

(iii) Should *MacAskill* Be Overruled?

16 The important issue raised by this appeal is whether the Court should now overrule the *Beard* rules of intoxication incorporated in *MacAskill* and its progeny. It is clear that this court may overrule its own decisions. However, as Dickson J. (as he then was) remarked in *Bernard*, at p. 14, "[t]here must be compelling circumstances to justify departure from a prior decision."

(a) THE OPINIONS OF FORMER CHIEF JUSTICES LASKIN AND DICKSON

19 In the early 1970s, Laskin J., as he then was, writing in dissent along with Hall and Spence JJ. in *Perrault v. The Queen*, [1970] 5 C.C.C. 217 at p. 225, 12 D.L.R. (3d) 480 at pp. 488–9, [1971] S.C.R. 196, was the first to recognize that the real question was one of intent in fact, and that even where the evidence of intoxication did not rise to the level of incapacity, it could still be relevant to intent in fact and therefore should not be rejected.

21 Similar views began to be expressed by Dickson J. in the late 1970s. In *Mulligan v. The Queen* (1976), 28 C.C.C. (2d) 266, 66 D.L.R. (3d) 627, [1977] 1 S.C.R. 612, Dickson J., alone in dissent, argued that the critical inquiry, notwithstanding the issue of capacity, is whether the accused had the requisite intent in fact, and therefore that all relevant evidence bearing on that issue, including evidence of intoxication, should be considered by the triers of fact.

23 In 1988, similar views were again expressed by now Dickson C.J.C., again in dissent, in *Bernard*, reasons in which I concurred:

> In principle, therefore, intoxication is relevant to the mental element in crime, and should be considered, together with all other evidence, in determining whether the Crown has proved the requisite mental state beyond a reasonable doubt.

24 By the 1980s, it was thus clear to some members of this court that the validity of *Beard* and *MacAskill* was now prone to a challenge.

26 Finally, this court's decision in *R. v. Cooper* (1993), 78 C.C.C. (3d) 289, [1993] 1 S.C.R. 146, 18 C.R. (4th) 1, confirmed that the issue of the validity of *Beard* and *MacAskill* was still an open one that would need to be soon addressed by this court.

(b) DEVELOPMENTS IN OUR PROVINCIAL APPELLATE COURTS

27 In deciding that the time has come to overrule *MacAskill*, I am cognizant of the fact that the *Beard* rules are no longer followed by any provincial appellate court in this country that has considered the issue. In place of the *Beard* rules, two different approaches have developed over the years.

28 The Ontario Court of Appeal was the first provincial appellate court to develop an alternative

approach. In *R. v. Dees* (1978), 40 C.C.C. (2d) 58, Arnup J.A., for the Court of Appeal, dissatisfied with the *Beard* rules, stated at p. 66:

> The ultimate question must always be: did the accused have the requisite intent? Of course, if he lacked the capacity to form that intent, then he did not have the intent, but the converse proposition does not follow, i.e., it does not follow that just because he had the capacity, he also had the specific intent.

29 The Ontario approach culminated in Martin J.A.'s decision in *R. v. MacKinlay*, (1986), 28 C.C.C. (3d) 306, 53 C.R. (3d) 105, 15 O.A.C. 241 (C.A.). Under *MacKinlay*, a jury is to be instructed as follows (at pp. 321–2):

> Where intoxication is in issue, I think it would be helpful for the trial judge to draw the jury's attention to the common knowledge of the effects of the consumption of alcohol. He should first instruct the jury that intoxication causing a person to cast off restraint and act in a manner in which he would not have acted if sober affords no excuse for the commission of a crime while in that state if he had the intent required to constitute the crime. He should then instruct the jury that where a specific intent is necessary to constitute the crime, the crime is not committed if the accused lacked the specific intent essential to constitute the crime. In considering whether the Crown has proved beyond a reasonable doubt that the accused had the specific intent required to constitute the crime charged, they should take into account the accused's consumption of alcohol or drugs along with the other facts which throw light on the accused's intent. It would, as a general rule, be desirable for the judge to refer to the evidence as to the consumption of alcohol or drugs and to the other facts which throw light on the accused's intention. If the accused by reason of intoxication was incapable of forming the required intent, then obviously he could not have it. If the jury entertain a reasonable doubt whether the accused by reason

of intoxication had the capacity to form the necessary intent, then the necessary intent has not been
proved. If they are satisfied beyond a reasonable
doubt that the accused had the capacity to form
the necessary intent, *they must then go on to consider whether, taking into account the consumption
of liquor and the other facts, the prosecution has satisfied them beyond a reasonable doubt that the accused
in fact had the required intent.*

(Underlining added; italics in original.)

30   The *MacKinlay* charge has been approved
of in Saskatchewan, Manitoba, Newfoundland,
and Nova Scotia.

31   The *MacKinlay* charge received an endorse-
ment by this court in *Cooper, supra*. In that case,
the trial judge charged the jury in accordance with
the spirit of *MacKinlay* and this court noted at p.
302 that, in the context of the case, the "respondent had the benefit of a charge that was the most
favourable to his position."

32   In *R. v. Korzepa* (1991), 64 C.C.C. (3d)
489, 13 W.C.B. (2d) 204, the British Columbia
Court of Appeal rejected *MacKinlay* as unfaithful to
Beard and other cases in this court. However, some
two years later in *R. v. Canute* (1993), 80 C.C.C.
(3d) 403, 20 C.R. (4th) 312, 43 W.A.C. 277, that
court, faced with a constitutional challenge directed
at *Beard* and *MacAskill*, agreed that the *Beard* rules
were unconstitutional because they created a form of
constructive liability that violated ss. 7 and 11(d) of
the Charter and did not constitute a reasonable limit
under s. 1. In deciding on the appropriate charge
that should replace *Beard*, the court in that case went
further than *MacKinlay* and recommended that all
references to capacity be removed. The *Canute*
approach was approved of by the Québec Court of
Appeal in *R. v. Cormier* (1993), 86 C.C.C. (3d) 163,
[1993] R.J.Q. 2723, 59 Q.A.C. 1.

(c) DEVELOPMENTS IN ENGLAND, NEW ZEALAND, AND AUSTRALIA

35   In most common law countries, *Beard*'s
"capacity" language has fallen out of favour.

Instead, intoxication is simply a factor jurors can
consider in assessing whether the prosecution has
proved beyond a reasonable doubt that the accused
had the required intent.

(d) ACADEMIC COMMENTARY

39   Most of the academic commentary in Canada
also favours abandoning the *Beard* rules.

(e) THE CHARTER

40   It is my opinion that the *Beard* rules incorporated in *MacAskill* are inconsistent with our Charter.

41   The *Beard* rules put an accused in jeopardy
of being convicted despite the fact that a reasonable
doubt could exist in the minds of the jurors on the
issue of actual intent. Under these rules, if the jury
is satisfied that the accused's voluntary intoxication
did not render the accused incapable of forming
the intent, then they would be compelled to convict despite the fact that the evidence of intoxication raised a reasonable doubt as to whether the
accused possessed the requisite intent. *MacAskill*
precludes the jury from acting on that reasonable
doubt, and therefore the *Beard* rules violate ss. 7
and 11(d).

42   Having reached the conclusion that the
Beard rules are a restriction on an accused's legal
rights, we must next assess whether the restriction
constitutes a reasonable limit under s. 1 of the
Charter. Since we are dealing with a judge-made
rule rather than with a legislative enactment, I am
of the view that a strict application of the *Oakes* test
(*R. v. Oakes* (1986), 24 C.C.C. (3d) 321, 26
D.L.R. (4th) 200, [1986] 1 S.C.R. 103, and in particular of the proportionality prong of that test, is
appropriate.

43   There is no question that the protection of
the public from intoxicated offenders is of sufficient importance to warrant overriding a constitutionally protected right or freedom. I am also of the
view that there is a rational connection between the
"capacity" restriction of the defence contained in
the impugned common law rule and its objective.

44 However, in my opinion, the restriction fails the proportionality prong because it does not impair an accused's ss. 7 and 11(d) rights as little as is reasonably possible. In the case at bar, there is more than minimal impairment of ss. 7 and 11(d) because the *Beard* rules lead to the result that *all* accused persons who had the capacity to form the requisite intent will be unable to rely on their state of intoxication despite the fact that that state might create a reasonable doubt in the minds of the triers of fact as to whether the accused actually intended to kill or cause bodily harm with subjective foresight of death. The objective of protecting society can be met by ensuring that only those who have the necessary blameworthy intent be imprisoned rather than through the creation of a rule which threatens to cast the criminal net too far. It is also important to point out in this context that society is also protected because the defence is one of mitigation rather than of exculpation. In other words, even if the defence is successful, the accused will nonetheless be convicted of manslaughter which carries a maximum sentence of life imprisonment.

45 I therefore conclude that the common law rule which limits the defence of intoxication to the capacity of an accused to form the specific intent is contrary to ss. 7 and 11(d) of the Charter and not a reasonable limit under s. 1.

46 Consequently, I am of the view, particularly giving due consideration to ss. 7 and 11(d) of the Charter, that there are, to quote Dickson C.J.C., "compelling circumstances to justify" overruling this court's decision in *MacAskill* concerning the relationship between intoxication and intent.

(iv) What New Rule Should Replace *MacAskill*?

47 Having reached the conclusion that the *Beard* rules are constitutionally infirm and that therefore *MacAskill* should now be overruled, we need to determine what new common law rule should be put in its place. It is our duty as judges to ensure that the common law develops in a manner consistent with the supreme law of our country.

48 How then should juries be instructed on the use they can make of evidence of intoxication? I am of the view that before a trial judge is required by law to charge the jury on intoxication, he or she must be satisfied that the effect of the intoxication was such that its effect *might* have impaired the accused's foresight of consequences sufficiently to raise a reasonable doubt. Once a judge is satisfied that this threshold is met, he or she must then make it clear to the jury that the issue before them is whether the Crown has satisfied them beyond a reasonable doubt that the accused had the requisite intent. In the case of murder, the issue is whether the accused intended to kill or cause bodily harm with the foresight that the likely consequence was death.

49 Therefore, a *Canute*-type charge is a useful model for trial judges to follow as it omits any reference to "capacity" or "capability" and focuses the jury on the question of "intent in fact." In most murder cases, the focus for the trier of fact will be on the foreseeability prong of s. 229(a)(ii) of the Criminal Code, R.S.C. 1985, c. C-46, that is, on determining whether the accused foresaw that his or her actions were likely to cause the death of the victim. For example, consider the case where an accused and another individual engage in a fight outside a bar. During the fight, the accused pins the other individual to the ground and delivers a kick to the head, which kills that person. In that type of a case, the jury will likely struggle, assuming they reject any self-defence or provocation claim, with the question of whether that accused foresaw that his or her actions would likely cause the death of the other individual. At this level of inquiry, the need for the jury to consider issues of capacity will rarely arise since a level of impairment falling short of incapacity will often be sufficient to raise a reasonable doubt on the question of foreseeability.

51 Those who would favour a two-stage charge even in these types of cases argue that such a charge is necessary in order to put in context for the jury the evidence of experts who often testify in "capacity" terms. While it is true that experts will testify in terms of the effect of alcohol or other intoxicants on capacity if so questioned, this need not always be the case. We could simply have experts only testify about such things as the effects of alcohol on the functioning of the brain. Experts could also testify by way of a hypothetical and be asked whether in their opinion, taking into consideration all of the relevant facts, the hypothetical person would have foreseen that his or her actions would likely cause death.

52 I should not want to be taken as suggesting that reference to "capacity" as part of a two-step procedure will never be appropriate in a charge to the jury. Indeed, in cases where the only question is whether the accused intended to kill the victim (s. 229(a)(i) of the Code), while the accused is entitled to rely on any evidence of intoxication to argue that he or she lacked the requisite intent and is entitled to receive such an instruction from the trial judge (assuming of course that there is an "air of reality" to the defence), it is my opinion that intoxication short of incapacity will in most cases rarely raise a reasonable doubt in the minds of jurors. For example, in a case where an accused points a shotgun within a few inches of someone's head and pulls the trigger, it is difficult to conceive of a successful intoxication defence unless the jury is satisfied that the accused was so drunk that he or she was not capable of forming an intent to kill. It is in these types of cases where it may be appropriate for trial judges to use a two-step, *MacKinlay*-type charge. In addition, I suspect that most accused will want the trial judge to refer to capacity since his or her defence will likely be one of incapacity.

53 Furthermore, there may well be some other cases where a two-step charge will be helpful to the jury, for example, where there has been expert evidence concerning issues of capacity, where the evidence reveals that the accused consumed a considerable amount of alcohol, or where the accused specifically requests a "capacity" charge as part of his or her defence. If a two-step charge is used and the charge is later challenged on appeal, the role of an appellate court will be to review the charge and determine whether there is a reasonable possibility that the jury may have been misled into believing that a determination of capacity was the *only* relevant inquiry.

54 It may be of some assistance to summarize my conclusions in the following manner:

1. A *MacAskill* charge which only refers to capacity is constitutionally infirm and constitutes reversible error.

2. A *Canute*-type charge which only asks the jury to consider whether the evidence of intoxication, along with all of the other evidence in the case, impacted on whether the accused possessed the requisite specific intent is to be preferred for the reasons set out at paras. 49 to 51.

3. In certain cases, in light of the particular facts of the case and/or in light of the expert evidence called, it may be appropriate to charge *both* with regard to the capacity to form the requisite intent *and* with regard to the need to determine in *all* the circumstances whether the requisite intent was in fact formed by the accused. In these circumstances, a jury might be instructed that their overall duty is to determine whether or not the accused possessed the requisite intent for the crime. If on the basis of the expert evidence the jury is left with a reasonable doubt as to whether, as a result of the consumption of alcohol, the accused had the capacity to form the requisite intent, then that ends the inquiry and the accused must be acquitted of the offence, and consideration must then be given to any included lesser offences. However, if the jury is not left in a reasonable doubt as a result of the expert evidence as to the capacity to form the intent, then of course they *must* consider and take into account all the surrounding circumstances and the evidence pertaining to those circumstances in determining whether or not the accused possessed the requisite intent for the offence.

V. Application of the Analysis to This Case

(a) The Charge on Intoxication

55   I am of the view that the trial judge's charge to the jury in this case incorrectly instructed them on the relationship between intoxication and intent in fact. The trial judge began his charge as follows:

> You must first consider whether the mind of the accused was so affected by his consumption of alcohol that he did not have the *ability to form* the specific intent to cause death or bodily harm that he knew was likely to cause death and was reckless.

(Emphasis added.)

56   At no time did the trial judge further instruct them that, even if they were satisfied that the appellant had the ability to form the intent, they were then to consider whether he *in fact* had the intent in light of the evidence of drunkenness.

60   I am thus satisfied that there is a reasonable possibility that the trial judge's charge to the jury on the defence of intoxication, when read as a whole, may have misled the jury into believing that a verdict of manslaughter could only have been arrived at if they had a reasonable doubt about whether the respondent had the capacity to form the requisite intent as a result of his drinking.

(b) The Charge on the "Common Sense Inference"

61   The trial judge charged the jury on the common sense inference as follows:

> In the course of my remarks I said that you might rely on the presumption that sometimes that people have been known to mean the natural and probable consequences of their acts. That is a presumption that need not be followed. It is a permissive one only. It is maybe some help, but the real question is one of subjective foresee-

ability on the part of Mr. Robinson that he would cause bodily harm that he knows was likely to cause death, and is reckless whether death ensues or not or that he meant to cause death. That's the key issue. It is intent here and if you have reasonable doubt in that, I have told you about the lesser included offence of manslaughter. . .

62   While the trial judge incorrectly used the term "presumption" in discussing the common sense inference that a sane and sober person intends the natural consequences of his or her actions, I think he made it sufficiently clear to the jury that they were not obligated to follow it. Moreover, when the trial judge first introduced the common sense inference, he did not use the word "presumption." Consequently, when this error is read in the context of the charge as a whole, I agree with the appellant that we should find no reversible error on this issue.

63   The respondent's principal argument on this point was that the trial judge failed to discuss the evidence of intoxication when he referred to the common sense inference.

65   The respondent correctly argues, in my view, that where there is some evidence of intoxication, a trial judge must link his or her instructions on intoxication with the instructions on the common sense inference so that the jury is specifically instructed that evidence of intoxication can rebut the inference. In both the model charges set out in *MacKinlay* and *Canute*, this approach is taken. This instruction is critical since in most cases jurors are likely to rely on the inference to find intent. Moreover, if no instruction is given, then a confused jury may see a conflict between the inference and the defence and resolve that conflict in favour of their own evaluation of common sense: see *Korzepa*, at p. 505. Therefore, an instruction which does not link the common sense inference with the evidence of intoxication constitutes reversible error. In this case, the trial judge's failure to make this linkage constitutes reversible error.

VI. Disposition

70 In my opinion, the appeal should be dismissed. I am not satisfied that at the end of the day, the jury would have adequately understood the issues concerning intoxication and intent or the law and evidence relating to those issues: see *Cooper, supra,* at pp. 300–301.

71 The appellant Crown has urged us to apply the curative proviso contained in s. 686(1)(b)(iii) of the Code to cure any errors made in the trial judge's charge to the jury. However, I am of the view that in a case such as this, s. 686(1)(b)(iii) should not be applied since the accused was denied a defence he was entitled to in law. I reach this conclusion as a matter of fairness and logic. In this case, there existed an "air of reality" for the intoxication defence, which meant that there was some evidence upon which a properly instructed jury could reasonably have reached a verdict of manslaughter. The respondent was precluded by the trial judge's instructions from having a jury of his peers assess whether, as a result of his intoxication, he did not have the specific intent to kill the deceased. It is not the role of this court to reweigh the evidence and consider issues of credibility, in this type of a case, in order to determine whether a reasonable jury properly instructed would have reached the same verdict as rendered by the jury.

Appeal dismissed.

CASE

35

....

Perka et al. v. The Queen

SUPREME COURT OF CANADA   OCTOBER 11, 1984

BACKGROUND

The accused, who relied on the defence of necessity, were acquitted at their trial on charges of
importing and possession of narcotics for the purpose of trafficking. The B.C. Court of Appeal
allowed the Crown's appeal, set aside the acquittal,
and ordered a new trial. The accused subsequently
appealed to the Supreme Court of Canada against
the judgment of the Court of Appeal.

MAIN ISSUES

(1) What are the nature and limits of the defence of
necessity? (2) What is the legal rationale underlying
the defence of necessity? (3) Should the accused
lose the benefit of the defence of necessity if they
were willingly involved in a joint criminal enterprise? (4) Did the trial judge instruct the jury correctly in relation to the question of whether the
accused had any reasonable, legal alternative to the
course of action that they took?

JUDGMENT

The judgment of the *majority* of the Supreme
Court of Canada was delivered by Justice Dickson
(with whom Justices Ritchie, Chouinard, and
Lamer agreed). The judgments of Justices Ritchie
and Wilson have been omitted.

....

DICKSON J.: — In this case we consider (i) a recurring legal problem, the "necessity" defence;
(ii) what is commonly known as the "botanical" or
"*cannabis* species" defence.

I. Facts

The appellants are drug smugglers. At trial, they
led evidence that in early 1979 three of the appellants were employed, with 16 crew members, to
deliver, by ship (the "Samarkanda") a load of
cannabis (marijuana) worth $6 000 000 or
$7 000 000 from a point in international waters off
the coast of Columbia, South America, to a drop-
point in international waters 200 miles off the
coast of Alaska. The ship left Tumaco, Columbia,
empty, with a port-clearance document stating the
destination to be Juneau, Alaska. For three weeks
the ship remained in international waters off the
coast of Columbia. While there, a DC-6 aircraft
made four trips, dropping into the water shrimp-
nets with a total of 634 bales of *cannabis*, which
were retrieved by the ship's long-boats.

A "communications" package was also dropped
from a light aircraft, giving instructions for a rendezvous with another vessel, the "Julia B," which
was to pick up the cargo of *cannabis* from the
"Samarkanda" in international waters off the coast
of Alaska. *En route*, according to the defence evi-

dence, the vessel began to encounter a series of problems; engine breakdowns, overheating generators, and malfunctioning navigation devices, aggravated by deteriorating weather. In the meantime, the fourth appellant, Nelson, part-owner of the illicit cargo, and three other persons left Seattle in a small boat, the "Whitecap," intending to rendezvous with the "Samarkanda" at the drop-point in Alaska. The problems of the "Samarkanda" intensified as fuel was consumed. The vessel became lighter, the intakes in the hull for sea-water, used as a coolant, lost suction and took in air instead, causing the generators to overheat. At this point the vessel was 180 miles from the Canadian coastline. The weather worsened. There were eight-to-ten-foot swells and a rising wind. It was finally decided for the safety of ship and crew to seek refuge on the Canadian shoreline for the purpose of making temporary repairs. The "Whitecap" found a sheltered cove on the west coast of Vancouver Island, "No Name Bay." The "Samarkanda" followed the "Whitecap" into the bay but later grounded amidships on a rock because the depth sounder was not working. The tide ran out. The vessel listed severely to starboard, to the extent that the captain, fearing the vessel was going to capsize, ordered the men to off-load the cargo. This is a brief summary of the defence evidence.

Early on the morning of May 22, 1979, police officers entered No Name Bay in a marked police boat with siren sounding. The "Samarkanda" and the "Whitecap" were arrested, as were all the appellants except Perka and Nelson, the same morning. The vessels and 33.49 tons of *cannabis* marijuana were seized by the police officers.

Charged with importing *cannabis* into Canada and with possession for the purpose of trafficking, the appellants claimed they did not plan to import into Canada or to leave their cargo of *cannabis* in Canada. They had planned to make repairs and leave. Expert witnesses on marine matters called by the defence testified that the decision to come ashore was, in the opinion of one witness, expedient and prudent, and in the opinion of another, essential. At trial, counsel for

the Crown alleged that the evidence of the ship's distress was a recent fabrication. Crown counsel relied on the circumstances under which the appellants were arrested to belie the "necessity" defence; when the police arrived on the scene most of the marijuana was already onshore, along with plastic ground sheets, battery-operated lights, liquor, food, clothing, camp stoves, and sleeping-bags. Nevertheless, the jury believed the appellants and acquitted them.

The acquittal was reversed on appeal. After the close of the case for the accused at trial, the Crown had applied to call rebuttal evidence with respect to the condition of the vessel. The trial judge refused the Crown's application. He held that the defence evidence relating to the happenings on the engine-room should not have caught the prosecution by surprise, and, in the circumstances, the conditions for calling rebuttal evidence had not been met. At trial the defence also relied upon a "botanical defence," arguing that the Crown had failed to prove that the ship's cargo was *"cannabis sativa* L," as provided for in the schedule to the Narcotic Control Act, R.S.C. 1970, c. N-1. Thus the appellants had committed no offence. The trial judge withdrew the botanical defence from the jury. On appeal by the Crown, the Court of Appeal, in allowing the appeal, held that the trial judge had erred in refusing to grant leave to the Crown to call rebuttal evidence and, on the cross-appeal, held that the judge was correct in withdrawing the botanical defence from the jury.

The appellants have now appealed to this Court. In addition to claiming that the Court of Appeal erred in reversing the trial judge on the rebuttal issue, the appellants contend that the Court of Appeal applied the wrong standard in ordering a new trial. The appellants also contend that the botanical defence should have been left with the jury. The Crown, of course, takes the opposite position on each of these questions and has raised one of its own: whether the trial judge erred in charging the jury with respect to the necessity defence.

II. The Necessity Defence

(a) History and Background

From earliest times it has been maintained that in some situations the force of circumstances makes it unrealistic and unjust to attach criminal liability to actions which, on their face, violate the law. Aristotle, *Ethics* (Book III, 1110 a), discusses the jettisoning of cargo from a ship in distress and remarks that "any sensible man does so" to secure the safety of himself and his crew.

In those jurisdictions in which such a general principle has been recognized or codified, it is most often referred to by the term "necessity." Classic and harrowing instances which have been cited to illustrate the arguments both for and against the principle include the mother who steals food for her starving child, the shipwrecked mariners who resort to cannibalism (*R. v. Dudley and Stephens* (1884), 14 Q.B.D. 273), or throw passengers overboard to lighten a sinking lifeboat (*United States v. Holmes* (1842), 26 Fed. Cas. 360), and the more mundane case of the motorist who exceeds the speed-limit taking an injured person to the hospital.

In the United States, a general defence of necessity has been recognized in the statutory law of a number of states and has found its way into the Model Penal Code of the American Law Institute.

In England, opinion as to the existence of a general defence of necessity has varied. While Glanville Williams (6 C.L.P. 216 (1953)) has been able to assert "with some assurance" that the defence of necessity is recognized by English law, the authors of Smith & Hogan, *Criminal Law*, 4th ed. (1978), at pp. 193–4, state that: "The better view appears to be that a general defence of necessity is not recognized by the English courts at the present time."

In Canada, the existence and the extent of a general defence of necessity was discussed by this Court in *Morgentaler v. The Queen* (1975), 20 C.C.C. (2d) 449, 53 D.L.R. (3d) 161, [1976] 1 S.C.R. 616. As to whether or not the defence exists at all, I had occasion to say, at p. 497 C.C.C., p. 209 D.L.R., p. 678 S.C.R.:

On the authorities it is manifestly difficult to be categorical and state that there is a law of necessity, paramount over other laws, relieving obedience from the letter of the law. If it does exist, it can go no further than to justify non-compliance in urgent situations of clear and imminent peril when compliance with the law is demonstrably impossible.

Subsequent to *Morgentaler*, the courts appear to have assumed that a defence of necessity does exist in Canada. On the later trial of Dr. Morgentaler, the defence of necessity was again raised on a charge of procuring a miscarriage. Some admissible evidence was made in support of the plea and the case went to the jury, which rendered a verdict of not guilty. An appeal by the Crown from the acquittal failed: *R. v. Morgentaler* (1976), 27 C.C.C. (2d) 81, 64 D.L.R. (3d) 718, 33 C.R.N.S. 244; leave to appeal to this Court was refused [1976] 1 S.C.R. x.

In the present appeal, the Crown does not challenge the appellants' claim that necessity is a common law defence preserved by Criminal Code, s. 7(3). Rather, the Crown claims the trial judge erred in (1) instructing the jury on the defence in light of the facts, and (2) imposing the burden of disproof of the defence upon the Crown, rather than imposing the burden of proof on the appellants.

(b) The Conceptual Foundation of the Defence

Criminal theory recognizes a distinction between "justifications" and "excuses." A "justification" challenges the wrongfulness of an action which technically constitutes a crime. The police officer who shoots the hostage-taker, the innocent object of an assault who uses force to defend himself against his assailant, the good Samaritan who commandeers a car and breaks the speed laws to rush an accident victim to the hospital: these are all actors whose actions we consider *rightful*, not wrongful. For such actions, people are often praised, as motivated by some great or noble object. The concept of punishment often seems incompatible with the social approval bestowed on the doer.

In contrast, an "excuse" concedes the wrongfulness of the action but asserts that the circumstances under which it was done are such that it ought not to be attributed to the actor. The perpetrator who is incapable, owing to a disease of the mind, of appreciating the nature and consequences of his acts, the person who labours under a mistake of fact, the drunkard, the sleepwalker: these are all actors of whose "criminal" actions we disapprove intensely, but whom, in appropriate circumstances, our law will not punish.

Packer, *The Limits of the Criminal Sanction* (1968), expresses the distinction thus at p. 113:

> . . . conduct that we choose not to treat as criminal is "justifiable" if our reason for treating it as non-criminal is predominantly that it is conduct that we applaud, or at least do not actively seek to discourage: conduct is "excusable" if we deplore it but for some extrinsic reason conclude that it is not politic to punish it.

It is still my opinion that, "[n]o system of positive law can recognize any principle which would entitle a person to violate the law because on his view the law conflicted with some higher social value." The Criminal Code has specified a number of identifiable situations in which an actor is justified in committing what would otherwise be a criminal offence. To go beyond that and hold that ostensibly illegal acts can be validated on the basis of their expediency would import an undue subjectivity into the criminal law. It would invite the courts to second-guess the Legislature and to assess the relative merits of social policies underlying criminal prohibitions. Neither is a role which fits well with the judicial function. Such a doctrine could well become the last resort of scoundrels and, in the words of Edmund Davies L.J. in *Southwark London Borough Council v. Williams et al.*, [1971] Ch. 734 [at p. 746], it could "very easily become simply a mask for anarchy."

Conceptualized as an "excuse," however, the residual defence of necessity is, in my view, much less open to criticism. It rests on a realistic assessment of human weakness, recognizing that a liberal and humane criminal law cannot hold people to the strict obedience of laws in emergency situations where normal human instincts, whether of self-preservation or of altruism, overwhelmingly impel disobedience. The objectivity of the criminal law is preserved; such acts are still wrongful, but in the circumstances they are excusable. Praise is indeed not bestowed, but pardon is, when one does a wrongful act under pressure which, in the words of Aristotle in *The Nicomachean Ethics* (translator Rees, p. 49), "overstrains human nature and which no one could withstand."

George Fletcher, *Rethinking Criminal Law*, describes this view of necessity as "compulsion of circumstance," which description points to the conceptual link between necessity as an excuse and the familiar criminal law requirement that in order to engage criminal liability, the actions constituting the *actus reus* of an offence must be voluntary. Literally, this voluntariness requirement simply refers to the need that the prohibited physical acts must have been under the conscious control of the actor. Without such control, there is, for purposes of the criminal law, no act. The excuse of necessity does not go to voluntariness in this sense. The lost Alpinist who, on the point of freezing to death, breaks open an isolated mountain cabin is not literally behaving in an involuntary fashion. He has control over his actions to the extent of being physically capable of abstaining from the act. Realistically, however, his act is not a "voluntary" one. His "choice" to break the law is no true choice at all; it is remorselessly compelled by normal human instincts. This sort of involuntariness is often described as "moral or normative involuntariness." Its place in criminal theory is described by Fletcher at pp. 804–5 as follows:

> The notion of voluntariness adds a valuable dimension to the theory of excuses. That conduct is involuntary — even in the normative sense — explains why it cannot fairly be punished. Indeed, H.L.A. Hart builds his theory of excuses on the principle that the distribution of punishment

should be reserved for those who voluntarily break the law. Of the arguments he advances for this principle of justice, the most explicit is that it is preferable to live in a society where we have the maximum opportunity to choose whether we shall become the subject of criminal liability. In addition, Hart intimates that it is ideologically desirable for the government to treat its citizens as self-actuating, choosing agents. This principle of respect for individual autonomy is implicitly confirmed whenever those who lack an adequate choice are excused for their offences.

I agree with this formulation of the *rationale* for excuses in the criminal law. In my view, this *rationale* extends beyond specific codified excuses and embraces the residual excuse known as the defence of necessity. At the heart of this defence is the perceived injustice of punishing violations of the law in circumstances in which the person had no other viable or reasonable choice available; the act was wrong but it is excused because it was realistically unavoidable.

Punishment of such acts, as Fletcher notes at p. 813, can be seen as purposeless as well as unjust:

> . . . involuntary conduct cannot be deterred and therefore it is pointless and wasteful to punish involuntary actors. This theory. . . of pointless punishment, carries considerable weight in current Anglo-American legal thought.

Relating necessity to the principle that the law ought not to punish involuntary acts leads to a conceptualization of the defence that integrates it into the normal rules for criminal liability rather than constituting it as a *sui generis* exception and threatening to engulf large portions of the criminal law. Such a conceptualization accords with our traditional legal, moral, and philosophic views as to what sorts of acts and what sorts of actors ought to be punished. In this formulation it is a defence which I do not hesitate to acknowledge and would not hesitate to apply to relevant facts capable of satisfying its necessary prerequisites.

(c) Limitations on the Defence

If the defence of necessity is to form a valid and consistent part of our criminal law, it must, as has been universally recognized, be strictly controlled and scrupulously limited to situations that correspond to its underlying *rationale*. That *rationale*, as I have indicated, is the recognition that it is inappropriate to punish actions which are normatively "involuntary." The appropriate controls and limitations on the defence of necessity are, therefore, addressed to ensuring that the acts for which the benefit of the excuse of necessity is sought are truly "involuntary" in the requisite sense.

In *Morgentaler v. The Queen* (1975), 20 C.C.C. (2d) 449 at p. 497, 53 D.L.R. (3d) 161 at p. 209, [1976] 1 S.C.R. 616 at p. 678, I was of the view that any defence of necessity was restricted to instances of non-compliance "in urgent situations of clear and imminent peril when compliance with the law is demonstrably impossible." In my opinion, this restriction focuses directly on the "involuntariness" of the purportedly necessitous behaviour by providing a number of tests for determining whether the wrongful act was truly the only realistic reaction open to the actor, or whether he was in fact making what in fairness could be called a choice. If he was making a choice, then the wrongful act cannot have been involuntary in the relevant sense.

The requirement that the situation be urgent and the peril be imminent tests whether it was indeed unavoidable for the actor to act at all. At a minimum the situation must be so emergent and the peril must be so pressing that normal human instincts cry out for action and make a counsel of patience unreasonable.

The requirement that compliance with the law be "demonstrably impossible" takes this assessment one step further. Given that the accused had to act, could he nevertheless realistically have acted to avoid the peril or prevent the harm without breaking the law? *Was there a legal way out?* If there is a reasonable legal alternative to disobeying the law, then the decision to disobey becomes a voluntary one, impelled by some consideration beyond the dictates of "necessity" and human instincts.

The importance of this requirement that there be no reasonable legal alternatives cannot be over-stressed.

Even if the requirements for urgency and "no legal way out" are met, there is clearly a further consideration. There must be some way of assuring proportionality. No rational criminal justice system, no matter how humane or liberal, could excuse the infliction of a greater harm to allow the actor to avert a lesser evil. In such circumstances we expect the individual to bear the harm and refrain from acting illegally. If he cannot control himself, we will not excuse him.

I would therefore add to the preceding requirements a stipulation of proportionality expressible, as it was in *Mortgentaler*, by the proviso that the harm inflicted must be less than the harm sought to be avoided.

(d) Illegality or Contributory Fault

The Crown submits that there is an additional limitation on the availability of the defence of necessity. Citing *R. v. Salvador, Wannamaker, Campbell and Nunes* (1981), 59 C.C.C. (2d) 521, 21 C.R. (3d) 1, 45 N.S.R. (2d) 192 (N.S.S.C.A.D.), it argues that because the appellants were committing a crime when their necessitous circumstances arose, they should be denied the defence of necessity as a matter of law.

Were it indeed accurate that the fact of doing something illegal when the necessitous circumstances arise will deny one the benefit of the necessity defence, I would nevertheless doubt that this principle would be relevant to the present case. The accused here (as, incidentally, was also apparently the case in *Salvador*) were not doing anything illegal under Canadian law when the necessity arose. They were on the high seas. They were conspiring to import marijuana into the United States, not Canada. If such a limitation on the necessity defence were to be formulated, in my view, the accused should, at a minimum, be violating some law of the forum, not just the law of a foreign State.

In any event, I have considerable doubt as to the cogency of such a limitation. If the conduct in which an accused was engaging at the time the peril arose was illegal, then it should clearly be punished, but I fail to see the relevance of its illegal character to the question of whether the accused's subsequent conduct in dealing with this emergent peril ought to be excused on the basis of necessity. At most the illegality — or if one adopts Jones J.A.'s approach, the immorality — of the preceding conduct will colour the subsequent conduct in response to the emergency as also wrongful. But that wrongfulness is never in any doubt. Necessity goes to *excuse* conduct, not to *justify* it. Where it is found to apply, it carries with it no implicit vindication of the deed to which it attaches. That cannot be over-emphasized. Were the defence of necessity to succeed in the present case, it would not in any way amount to a vindication of importing controlled substances nor to a critique of the law prohibiting such importation. It would also have nothing to say against importing as compared to obeying the law. The question, as I have said, is never whether what the accused has done is wrongful. It is always and by definition wrongful. The question is whether what he has done is voluntary. Except in the limited sense I intend to discuss below, I do not see the relevance of the legality or even the morality of what the accused was doing at the time the emergency arose to this question of the voluntariness of the subsequent conduct.

In my view, the accused's fault in bringing about the situation later invoked to excuse his conduct *can* be relevant to the availability of the defence of necessity, but not in the sweeping way suggested by some of the commentators and in some of the statutory formulations. Insofar as the accused's "fault" reflects on the moral quality of the action taken to meet the emergency, it is irrelevant to the issue of the availability of the defence on the same basis as the illegality or immorality of the actions preceding the emergency are irrelevant. If this fault is capable of attracting criminal or civil liability in its own right, the culprit should be appropriately sanctioned. I see no basis, however, for "transferring" such liability to the actions taken in response to the emergency, especially where to do so would result in attaching criminal consequences on the basis of negligence to actions which would otherwise be excused.

In my view, the better approach to the relationship of fault to the availability of necessity as a defence is based once again on the question of whether the actions sought to be excused were truly "involuntary." If the necessitous situation was clearly foreseeable to a reasonable observer, if the actor contemplated or ought to have contemplated that his actions would likely give rise to an emergency requiring the breaking of the law, then I doubt whether what confronted the accused was in the relevant sense an emergency. His response was in that sense not "involuntary." "Contributory fault" of this nature, but only of this nature, is a relevant consideration to the availability of the defence.

If the accused's "fault" consists of actions whose clear consequences were in the situation that actually ensued, then he was not "really" confronted with an emergency which compelled him to commit the unlawful act he now seeks to have excused. In such situations the defence is unavailable. Mere negligence, however, or the simple fact that he was engaged in illegal or immoral conduct when the emergency arose will not disentitle an individual to rely on the defence of necessity.

(e) Onus of Proof

Although necessity is spoken of as a defence, in the sense that it is raised by the accused, the Crown always bears the burden of proving a voluntary act. The prosecution must prove every element of the crime charged. One such element is the voluntariness of the act. Normally, voluntariness can be presumed, but if the accused places before the court, through his own witnesses or through cross-examination of Crown witnesses, evidence sufficient to raise an issue that the situation created by external forces was so emergent that failure to act could endanger life or health, and, upon any reasonable view of the facts, compliance with the law was impossible, then the Crown must be prepared to meet that issue. There is no onus of proof on the accused.

(f) Preliminary Conclusions as to the Defence of Necessity

It is now possible to summarize a number of conclusions as to the defence of necessity in terms of its nature, basis, and limitations:

(1) the defence of necessity could be conceptualized as either a justification or an excuse;

(2) it should be recognized in Canada as an excuse, operating by virtue of s. 7(3) of the Criminal Code;

(3) necessity as an excuse implies no vindication of the deeds of the actor;

(4) the criterion is the moral involuntariness of the wrongful action;

(5) this involuntariness is measured on the basis of society's expectation of appropriate and normal resistance to pressure;

(6) negligence or involvement in criminal or immoral activity does not disentitle the actor to the excuse of necessity;

(7) actions or circumstances which indicate that the wrongful deed was not truly involuntary do disentitle;

(8) the existence of a reasonable legal alternative similarly disentitles; to be involuntary the act must be inevitable, unavoidable, and afford no reasonable opportunity for an alternative course of action that does not involve a breach of the law;

(9) the defence only applies in circumstances of imminent risk where the action was taken to avoid a direct and immediate peril;

(10) where the accused places before the court sufficient evidence to raise the issue, the onus is on the Crown to meet it beyond a reasonable doubt.

(g) The Judge's Charge

The trial judge concluded that there was before him an adequate body of evidence to raise the issue of necessity and proceeded to direct the jury with respect to the defence. As I have earlier indicated, the Crown disputes whether the defence was open to the accused in the circumstances of the case and submits further that if it was in fact available, the trial judge erred in his direction.

In my view, the trial judge was correct in concluding that on the evidence before him he should instruct the jury with regard to necessity. There was evidence before him from which a jury might conclude that the accused's actions in coming ashore with their cargo of *cannabis* were aimed at self-preservation in response to an overwhelming emergency. I have already indicated that in my view they were not engaged in conduct that was illegal under Canadian criminal law at the time the emergency arose, and that even if they were, the fact alone would not disentitle them to raise the defence. The question then becomes whether the trial judge erred in charging the jury in the terms that he did.

The summary of conclusions with regard to necessity in the foregoing section indicates that for the defence to succeed, an accused's actions must be, in the relevant sense, an "involuntary" response to an imminent and overwhelming peril. The defence cannot succeed if the response was disproportional to the peril or if it was not "involuntary" in the sense that the emergency was not "real" or not imminent or that there was a reasonable alternative response that was not illegal.

In the course of his charge on the issue of necessity, the trial judge instructed the jury, using the specific words that appear in *Morgentaler v. The Queen* (1975), 20 C.C.C. (2d) 449, 53 D.L.R. (3d) 161, [1976] 1 S.C.R. 616, to the effect that they must find facts which amount to "an urgent situation of clear and imminent peril when compliance with the law is demonstrably impossible" in order for the appellants' non-compliance with the law against importation and possession of *cannabis* to be excused. That is the correct test. It is, with respect, however, my view that in explaining the meaning and application of this test, the trial judge fell into error.

The trial judge was obliged, in my opinion, to direct the jury's attention to a number of issues pertinent to the test for necessity. Was the emergency a real one? Did it constitute an immediate threat of the harm purportedly feared? Was the response proportionate? In comparing this response to the danger that motivated it, was the danger one that society would reasonably expect the average person to withstand? Was there any reasonable legal alternative to the illegal response open to the accused? Although the trial judge did not explicitly pose each and every one of these questions, in my view his charge was adequate to bring the consideration underlying them to the jury's attention on every issue except the last one, the question of a reasonable alternative.

In his charge, the trial judge did not advert to this requirement. He did tell the jury that they must find facts capable of showing that "compliance with the law was demonstrably impossible . . ." but on his recharge he put before the jury a significantly different test. The test, he said, is:

> . . . can you find facts from this evidence, and that means all the evidence, of course, that the situation of the Samarkanda at sea was so appallingly dire and dangerous to life that a reasonable doubt arises as to whether or not their decision was justified?

And again, at the conclusion of the recharge:

> There is no need for the evidence to show you that a certainty of death would result unless the action complained of by the Crown was taken. It doesn't go so far as that. You have to look at it as reasonable people and decide, on any reasonable view of the matter, would these people have been justified in doing what they did? That is all that necessity means.

Both of these passages imply that the crucial consideration was whether the accused acted reasonably in coming into shore with their load of *cannabis* rather than facing death at sea. That is not sufficient as a test. Even if it does deal with the reality of the peril, its imminence and the proportionality of putting into shore, it does not deal at all with the question of whether there existed any other reasonable responses to the peril that were not illegal. Indeed, aside from the initial repetition of the *Morgentaler* formula, the trial judge did not advert to this consideration at all, nor did he direct the jury's attention to the relevance of evidence indicating the possibility of such alternative courses of action. In these respects I believe he erred in law. He did not properly put the question of a "legal way out" before the jury.

In my view, this was a serious error and omission going to the heart of the defence of necessity. The error justifies a new trial.

III. The Botanical Defence

The Narcotic Control Act, s. 2, defines "*cannabis* (marijuana)" as "*Cannabis sativa* L." At trial, the

appellants presented expert testimony to the effect that there are three species of *cannabis* — *cannabis sativa* L., *cannabis indica* Lam., and *cannabis ruderalis* Jan. The Crown countered with expert testimony that there is only one species of *cannabis* — the prohibited *cannabis sativa* L.

The trial judge was correct in withdrawing the appellants' botanical defence from the jury.

V. Conclusion

On the basis of all the above, it is my conclusion that the Court of Appeal was correct in the result in ordering a new trial and was correct in sustaining the trial judge's decision to withhold the botanical defence from the jury.

I would dismiss the appeals.

Hibbert v. The Queen

SUPREME COURT OF CANADA   JULY 20, 1995

BACKGROUND

At his trial, Hibbert, who relied on the defence of duress, was acquitted of attempted murder but convicted of the included offence of aggravated assault. Hibbert's appeal to the Ontario Court of Appeal was dismissed. He subsequently appealed to the Supreme Court of Canada against the judgment of the Court of Appeal.

MAIN ISSUES

(1) What is the legal *rationale* underlying the defence of duress? (2) Does duress operate as a defence because it may negative *mens rea*? (3) Should an *objective* standard be applied when considering whether an accused person who claims the benefit of the common law defence of duress had a "safe avenue of escape"?

JUDGMENT

The judgment of the Supreme Court of Canada was delivered by Chief Justice Lamer. (The other members of the Court were Justices La Forest, L'Heureux-Dubé, Sopinka, Gonthier, Cory, McLachlin, Iacobucci, and Major.)

LAMER C.J.C.: —

I. Factual Background

2   On November 25, 1991, shortly before 1:00 A.M., Fitzroy Cohen was shot four times with a semi-automatic handgun as he stood in the lobby of the apartment building he lived in. The shots were fired by Mark Bailey, an acquaintance of Cohen whom Cohen knew by his street names, "Quasi" or "Dogheart." At the time of the shooting, Bailey was accompanied by the appellant, Lawrence Hibbert, who was a close friend of Cohen. Cohen had descended from his apartment to the lobby at the appellant's request, unaware that Bailey was waiting below with gun in hand.

3   Cohen survived the shooting. At the appellant's trial, Cohen testified that for some time, prior to the shooting, he had been aware that Bailey was seeking a confrontation with him. Bailey, Cohen believed, was seeking revenge for an incident that had taken place the previous year, in which Bailey had been robbed by a rival drug dealer named Andrew Reid while Cohen and several others stood by, watching and laughing. Cohen testified that he had been told that Bailey had subsequently

attacked one of the men involved in the robbery on a busy street, firing several shots at him (but missing). He also knew that Andrew Reid had been murdered. Cohen said that he had told the appellant, whom he described as his "best friend," about the robbery of Bailey.

4 The appellant, who testified at trial, stated that at the time of the shooting he owed Bailey $100 as payment for drugs he had purchased from him some months earlier. He testified that he had been attempting to avoid Bailey, but that on the evening of November 24, 1991, he had accidentally run into him in the lobby of an apartment building in Etobicoke where he had gone to visit friends. Bailey had approached the appellant and indicated that he was armed with a handgun. The appellant testified that Bailey ordered him to take him to Cohen's apartment. When he refused, the appellant stated, Bailey had led him to the basement and punched him in the face several times. The appellant testified that he feared for his life, and that he believed that Bailey would shoot him if he continued to refuse to assist him. He stated that it was this fear that led him to agree to lead Bailey to Cohen's apartment.

5 Bailey and the appellant went out to Bailey's car, where Bailey's girlfriend and another young woman were waiting. The appellant got into the back seat, while Bailey drove. At trial, one of the young women recalled that the appellant had made a remark to the effect that "this might be the last time I'm going to see you."

6 Bailey dropped the two women off at their apartment, and told the appellant to get into the front seat. The appellant testified that they stopped at a telephone booth, and that Bailey ordered him to call Cohen and ask him to meet him downstairs in 20 minutes. The appellant did so, telling Cohen that he "had something for him." According to the appellant, Bailey stood by the phone booth during his conversation with Cohen and could hear what the appellant said to Cohen. Cohen and his girlfriend, Beverley St. Hillaire, confirmed that they had received a telephone call from the appellant, essentially as the appellant described. They testified

that the appellant had sounded "normal," but that he had been more abrupt than he usually was.

7 Bailey and Hibbert arrived at Cohen's apartment building approximately half an hour after making the phone call. The appellant testified that Bailey drew his gun and pointed it at him as they got out of the car. They went to the front door of the building where, following Bailey's orders, the appellant called Cohen's apartment on the building intercom, while Bailey kept his gun trained on him. The appellant's testimony, which was confirmed by Cohen, was that ordinarily when visiting Cohen he would not use the building's front door, but would instead enter the building through a side door that could be opened from the outside using a technique Cohen had taught him. Cohen also confirmed the appellant's testimony that he had asked Cohen to "come down" to the lobby, but that he had not asked Cohen to "buzz him in" (i.e., press a button on the intercom that would unlock the building's outer door). The appellant testified that he had hoped that Cohen would not unlock the building's front door, so that when he came downstairs he would see Bailey through the locked glass outer door and have a chance to retreat to safety. However, Cohen buzzed the outer door open without being asked to do so, and Bailey and the appellant went into the lobby.

8 According to the testimony of both Cohen and Hibbert, Cohen took the stairs from his second-floor apartment to the lobby. When he emerged into the lobby, he was met by Bailey, who grabbed him and pointed the gun at his chest, saying "You're dead now, pussy." Bailey led Cohen into the ground floor hallway, where (according to both Cohen and the appellant's testimony) he turned to Hibbert and told him to "stay some place where I [can] see you." After a brief exchange of words with Cohen, Bailey pushed Cohen away and fired four shots at him, striking him in the groin, legs, and buttocks. Saying "Come, Pigeon" (the appellant's nickname), Bailey and the appellant left the building by the side door. Cohen testified that during the incident the appellant said nothing and made no effort to intervene. He described the

appellant as "all sweating," and said that the appellant was unable to look at him. The appellant,
however, testified that he had repeatedly pleaded
with Bailey, "Quasi, don't kill him."

9 The appellant testified that from the
moment he first encountered Bailey that evening,
he had believed Bailey would shoot him if he
refused to co-operate, and stated that he had been
"terrified" throughout his time in Bailey's company.
Under cross-examination, he declared that he
believed that he had had no opportunity to run
away or warn Cohen without being shot.

10 After leaving the building, Bailey drove the
appellant back to Etobicoke. The appellant testified
that Bailey threatened to kill him if he went to the
police. The next morning, he turned himself in to
the police. Bailey, however, was never apprehended.

11 The appellant was charged with attempted
murder. On March 19, 1992, following a trial by
jury in the Ontario Court of Justice (General Division) presided over by Webber J., he was acquitted
of this charge, but was convicted of the included
offence of aggravated assault and sentenced to four
years' imprisonment. On July 15, 1993, his appeal
of his conviction to the Court of Appeal for
Ontario was dismissed, although the court allowed
his appeal from sentence, reducing his sentence
from four years to time served (some 15 months).

IV. Grounds for Appeal

16 Lawrence Hibbert appeals his conviction to
this court on the grounds that the trial judge's
charge to the jury on the issue of duress contained
several errors. First, he argues, the trial judge erred
by instructing the jury that the defence of duress
operated by "negativing common intention." The
appellant objects further to the trial judge's statement that the defence of duress was unavailable to
an accused who failed to avail himself or herself of a
"safe avenue of escape." As an alternative to the latter argument, the appellant submits that even if the
"safe avenue of escape" rule exists, the trial judge
erred by not advising the jury that the existence or
non-existence of such an avenue was to be deter-

mined by reference to the appellant's subjective
belief.

V. Analysis

B. The Relationship between *Mens Rea* and the Defence of Duress

(1) THE COMMON LAW DEFENCE OF DURESS IN
CANADA

18 The defence of "duress *per minas*" ("duress by
threat") has a long history at common law. In spite
of the defence's antiquity, however, many important aspects of its nature and its details have
remained unresolved, or have been shrouded with
uncertainty.

19 In Canada, a defence of duress was
included in the first Criminal Code enacted in
1892 (S.C. 1892, c. 29). For many years, it seems
to have been generally assumed (although never
conclusively established) that the existence of a
codified version of the defence of duress left no
room for further development of the common law
defence in Canada. In *R. v. Paquette* (1976), 30
C.C.C. (2d) 417, 70 D.L.R. (3d) 129, [1977] 2
S.C.R. 189, however, this court determined that
s. 17 of the Code does not constitute an exhaustive
codification of the law of duress. Rather, the court
held, s. 17 applies only to persons who commit
offences as *principals*. Accordingly, it remains open
to persons who are liable as *parties* to offences to
invoke the common law defence of duress, which
remains in existence by virtue of s. 8(3) of the Code
(which preserves those common law defences not
expressly altered or eliminated by Parliament). The
common law rules governing situations of duress
thus remain an important aspect of Canadian criminal law.

20 The holding in *Paquette* that the common
law defence of duress is available to persons liable as
parties is clear and unambiguous, and has stood as
the law in Canada for almost 20 years. The case has
a second aspect, however, that is less firmly established, having given rise to differing interpretations, and having been the subject of considerable

debate in the legal community. The controversy stems from certain comments made by Martland J. on the issue of the relationship between duress and the *mens rea* for party liability under s. 21(2) of the Code.

21 As noted above, the main holding of the court was that s. 17 applied only to principals and not to parties, from which it followed that Paquette could rely on the common law defence of duress, to which the restrictions set out in s. 17 did not apply. Martland J. went on, however, to make an observation regarding duress and the mental element of party liability under s. 21(2) of the Code, stating (at p. 423):

> A person whose actions have been dictated by fear of death or of grievous bodily injury cannot be said to have formed a *genuine* common intention to carry out an unlawful purpose with the person who has threatened him with those consequences if he fails to co-operate.

(Emphasis added.) Thus, Martland J. evidently did not intend to suggest that duress provides a defence at common law *only* when the accused's culpable mental state can be said to have been "negated." Instead, he appears to have been holding out an alternative route by which a person charged as a party under s. 21(2) could escape criminal liability, distinct from the "defence of duress" *per se* — that is, a "defence" founded not on concepts of excuse or justification, but based instead on the absence of an essential element of the offence.

22 Seen in this way, *Paquette* stands for the proposition that duress can provide a "defence" in either of two distinct ways — as an excuse, or by "negating" *mens rea*. In the present case, the appellant argues that this is a correct view of the law, and submits that the trial judge erred by not placing both alternatives before the jury. What falls to be considered, therefore, is the validity of the proposition that the *mens rea* for party liability under the Criminal Code can be "negated" by threats of death or bodily harm. That is, the court is called upon to reconsider whether the second aspect of our judg-

ment in *Paquette* reflects a correct understanding of the law of duress in Canada.

(2) DURESS AND *MENS REA*

23 That threats of death or serious bodily harm can have an effect on a person's state of mind is indisputable. However, it is also readily apparent that a person who carries out the *actus reus* of a criminal offence in response to such threats will not necessarily lack the *mens rea* for that offence. Whether he or she does or not will depend both on what the mental element of the offence in question happens to be and on the facts of the particular case. As a practical matter, though, situations where duress will operate to "negate" *mens rea* will be exceptional, for the simple reason that the types of mental states that are capable of being "negated" by duress are not often found in the definitions of criminal offences.

24 In general, a person who performs an action in response to a threat will *know* what he or she is doing, and will be aware of the probable consequences of his or her actions. Whether or not he or she *desires* the occurrence of these consequences will depend on the particular circumstances. For example, a person who is forced at gunpoint to drive a group of armed ruffians to a bank will usually know that the likely result of his or her actions will be that an attempt will be made to rob the bank, but he or she may not desire this result — indeed, he or she may strongly wish that the robbers' plans are ultimately foiled, if this could occur without risk to his or her own safety. In contrast, a person who is told that his or her child is being held hostage at another location and will be killed unless the robbery is successful will almost certainly have an active subjective desire that the robbery succeed. While the existence of threats clearly has a bearing on the *motive* underlying each actor's respective decision to assist in the robbery, only the first actor can be said not to *desire* that the robbery take place, and neither actor can be said not to have knowledge of the consequences of their actions. To determine whether *mens rea* is "negated" in a particular case, therefore, the first question that must be asked is whether the mental element of the offence in question is defined in such a way that either an actor's motives or his or her immediate desires have any direct relevance.

25 As Dickson J. (as he then was) observed in *Lewis v. The Queen* (1979), 47 C.C.C. (2d) 24 at p. 33, 98 D.L.R. (3d) 111, [1979] 2 S.C.R. 821, "[t]he mental element of a crime ordinarily involves no reference to motive." Instead, he noted, "[i]n most criminal trials, the mental element, the *mens rea* with which the court is concerned, relates to 'intent.'" Intention, however, is distinct from desire or subjective wish. Parliament is, of course, entitled to define the mental element of criminal offences in whatever manner it sees fit (subject, of course, to the requirements of s. 7 of the Canadian Charter of Rights and Freedoms). Thus, Parliament could choose to make it an element of a given offence that the perpetrator have some particular *desire* at the time of the commission of the *actus reus*, or even make it a precondition for liability that an actor have a particular *motive* for performing a prohibited act.

(3) THE *MENS REA* REQUIREMENTS FOR PARTY LIABILITY UNDER SECTION 21

(a) SECTION 21(1)(b)

26 As noted earlier, s. 21(1)(b) imposes criminal liability as a party on anyone who "does or omits to do anything for the purpose of aiding any person to commit" an offence. Although a person who is a party to an offence is guilty of committing *that* offence, rather than a separate crime (as is the case for accessories after the fact), s. 21(1)(b) contains its own *mens rea* requirement, distinct from that applicable to the principal who actually commits the underlying offence. As the subsection states, party liability as an "aider" requires acts or omissions "for the purpose" of aiding the commission of the offence.

27 It is impossible to ascribe a single fixed meaning to the term "purpose." In ordinary usage, the word is employed in two distinct senses. One

can speak of an actor doing something "on purpose" (as opposed to by accident), thereby equating purpose with "immediate intention." The term is also used, however, to indicate the ultimate ends an actor seeks to achieve, which imports the idea of "desire" into the definition. This dual sense is apparent in the word's dictionary definition. For instance, the Oxford English Dictionary (2nd ed. 1989) defines "purpose" alternatively as "[t]hat which one sets before oneself as a thing to be done or attained; the object which one has in view" and as "[t]he action or fact of intending or meaning to do something; intention, resolution, determination." The first of these definitions reflects the notion of one's "purpose" as relating to one's ultimate object or desire, while the latter conveys the notion of "purpose" as being synonymous with "intention."

31 When Parliament drafts a statute in language that, on its face, supports more than one meaning, it is appropriate for a court to consider which of the alternative interpretations that are available best accords with Parliament's intention. As I will explain, I am of the view that in the context of s. 21(1)(b) of the Code, the second of the two meanings of "purpose" discussed above — that is, the interpretation that equates "purpose" with "intention" — best reflects the legislative intent underlying the subsection. In contrast, adopting the first interpretation of "purpose" (the "purpose" equals "desire" interpretation) to describe the *mens rea* for aiding in s. 21(1)(b) would, in my view, create a number of theoretical and practical difficulties that Parliament is unlikely to have envisioned or intended.

32 The problems associated with the "purpose equals desire" interpretation are several. First, incorporating the accused's feelings about the desirability of the commission of an offence by the principal into the definition of the *mens rea* for "aiding" can result in distinctions being made which appear arbitrary and unreasonable in light of the policy underlying s. 21(1)(b). As Professor Colvin notes in *Principles of Criminal Law*, 2nd ed. (Scarborough, Ont: Thomson Professional Publishing

Canada, 1991), under the "purpose equals desire" interpretation, a person would not be guilty of aiding in the commission of an offence if he or she were "genuinely opposed or indifferent to it" (p. 123). The reason for the aider's indifference or opposition would be immaterial. The perverse consequences that flow from this are clearly illustrated by the following hypothetical situation described by Mewett and Manning:

> If a man is approached by a friend who tells him that he is going to rob a bank and would like to use his car as the getaway vehicle for which he will pay him $100, when that person is . . . charged under s. 21 for doing something for the purpose of aiding his friend to commit the offence, can he say "My purpose was not to aid the robbery but to make $100"? His argument would be that while he knew that he was helping the robbery, his desire was to obtain $100 and he did not care one way or the other whether the robbery was successful or not.

(*Criminal Law*, 2nd ed. (Toronto: Butterworths, 1985), at p. 112.) I agree with the authors' conclusion that "[t]hat would seem an absurd result" (p. 112). As I noted in *R. v. McIntosh* (1995), 95 C.C.C. (3d) 481 at p. 495, [1995] 1 S.C.R. 686, 36 C.R. (4th) 171, "[a]bsurdity is a factor to consider in the interpretation of ambiguous statutory provisions." In my view, the absurdity that would flow from the equation of "purpose" with "desire" cannot legitimately be ascribed to Parliamentary intention. This serves to cast considerable doubt on the correctness of this interpretation of the word "purpose" in this context, especially when one recalls that there exists an alternative interpretation of the word that can just as accurately be said to reflect its "plain meaning," under which this absurdity would be avoided.

38 Finally, I am satisfied that the interpretation of the *mens rea* for liability under s. 21(1)(b) that I am proposing will not result in unjust convictions in cases involving coercion by threats of death or bodily harm, since in these cases the common law defence of duress will remain available to the accused. As I will explain shortly, this defence, properly understood, provides an excuse to persons who assist in the commission of offences as a result of threats of serious violence. On the other hand, interpreting "purpose" as equivalent to "desire" in s. 21(1)(b) would result in the introduction of unnecessary complication into the law. Under such an interpretation, juries in duress cases would have to be provided with extremely complex instructions that would, in the end, have very little, if any, impact on the final determination of guilt or innocence.

39 For these reasons, I conclude that the expression "for the purpose of aiding" in s. 21(1)(b), properly understood, does not require that the accused actively view the commission of the offence he or she is aiding as desirable in and of itself. As a result, the *mens rea* for aiding under s. 21(1)(b) is not susceptible of being "negated" by duress. The trial judge's charge to the jury in the present case was thus incorrect in two respects. First, the reference to the relevant mental state in the present case as being a "common intention to carry out an unlawful purpose" was erroneous since, unlike *Paquette*, what was at issue in the present case was s. 21(1)(b), as opposed to s. 21(2). Second, in light of the mental element for commission of an offence under s. 21(1)(b), the suggestion that duress might "negate" the accused's *mens rea* was also incorrect.

(b) SECTION 21(2) AND THE DECISION IN *PAQUETTE*

40 The preceding discussion suffices to resolve the question of the relation between duress and *mens rea* that directly arises in the present case. As I indicated earlier, however, I believe that in the interests of avoiding undue confusion in the law that applies to duress cases, I should proceed further and look expressly at the question of whether the interpretation of s. 21(2)'s mental element that was adopted by the Court in *Paquette, supra*, remains correct in light of the interpretation of s. 21(1)(b) I am now adopting.

41 As was the case with the term "purpose" in s. 21(1)(b), the phrase "intention in common" is capable of being understood in more than one sense. One possible interpretation is that "intention in common" means no more than that the two persons must have in mind the same unlawful purpose. Alternatively, however, it might be argued that the requirement of "commonality" requires that the two persons' intentions match in greater detail — in particular, that their motives or subjective views as to the desirability of the commission of the "unlawful purpose" match up. If this latter interpretation were adopted, it could be argued that although persons who assist others to commit criminal acts as a result of threats made by the others would "intend" to provide such assistance, their intention would not be "in common" with the intentions of the threatener, due to the different motives and, possibly, views as to the immediate desirability of the criminal activity at issue. In contrast, under the former interpretation, a person would fall within the ambit of s. 21(2) if they intended to assist in the commission of the same offence envisioned by the principal, regardless of the fact that their intention might be due solely to the principal's threats. Of course, it would be open to such a person to avoid criminal liability through the common law defence of duress.

42 I have come to the conclusion that, in the context of s. 21(2), the first interpretation discussed above is more consistent both with Parliament's intention and with the interpretation of s. 21(1)(b) I have adopted in these reasons. Many of the factors I considered earlier in the course of determining the meaning to be ascribed to the term "purpose" in s. 21(1)(b) apply with similar force to the problem of interpreting s. 21(2). Parliament's purpose in enacting s. 21(2) is clear. Parliament has chosen to impose liability on persons who engage in criminal conduct with others for additional criminal acts that could be foreseen as likely to be committed in furtherance of the underlying offence (within the limits imposed by the Charter: see *R. v. Logan*, (1990), 58 C.C.C. (3d) 391, 73 D.L.R. (4th) 40, [1990] 2 S.C.R. 731). Interpreting the expression "intention in common" as connoting a mutuality of motives and desires

between the party and the principal would restrict the scope of this section in a manner that is difficult to justify on the basis of Parliamentary intention. As was the case with the interpretation of "purpose" in s. 21(1)(b), adopting this interpretation of "intention in common" would remove all manner of persons from the scope of s. 21(2) in addition to those whose intention is the product of threats of death or serious bodily harm since, once again, the *reason* for the divergence in motive and desire would be immaterial to the question of whether the party's and principal's "intentions" matched to a sufficient degree. This result, I believe, can no more be ascribed to Parliament's intention than could the similar result that would flow from equating "purpose" with "desire" in s. 21(1)(b), which I discussed earlier. In my opinion, a much more plausible interpretation of Parliament's purpose is that the "commonality" qualification on the subsection's mental element is simply meant to ensure that accused persons are not convicted of crimes committed in furtherance of offences to which *they* are not party to.

43 Furthermore, as was the case with s. 21(1)(b), the interpretation of s. 21(2)'s *mens rea* requirement that was adopted by the court in *Paquette* is not essential as a means of ensuring the avoidance of unjust convictions in duress cases, since here, as in cases involving s. 21(1)(b), accused persons who act under duress have recourse to the protection from criminal liability provided by the common law defence of duress.

44 For these reasons, I am of the view that the comments of Martland J. in *Paquette, supra*, on the relation between duress and *mens rea* in the context of s. 21(2) can no longer be considered the law in Canada.

(4) CONCLUSIONS ON DURESS AND *MENS REA*

45 The conclusions that can be extracted from the discussion in the previous sections may be summarized as follows:

1. The fact that a person who commits a criminal act does so as a result of threats of death or bod-

ily harm can in some instances be relevant to the question of whether he or she possessed the *mens rea* necessary to commit an offence. Whether or not this is so will depend, among other things, on the structure of the particular offence in question — that is, on whether or not the mental state specified by Parliament in its definition of the offence is such that the presence of coercion can, as a matter of logic, have a bearing on the existence of *mens rea*. If the offence is one where the presence of duress is of potential relevance to the existence of *mens rea*, the accused is entitled to point to the presence of threats when arguing that the Crown has not proven beyond a reasonable doubt that he or she possessed the mental state required for liability.

2. A person who commits a criminal act under threats of death or bodily harm may also be able to invoke an excuse-based defence (either the statutory defence set out in s. 17 or the common law defence of duress, depending on whether the accused is charged as a principal or as a party). This is so regardless of whether or not the offence at issue is one where the presence of coercion also has a bearing on the existence of *mens rea*.

3. The mental states specified in ss. 21(1)(b) and 21(2) of the Criminal Code are not susceptible to being "negated" by duress. Consequently, it is not open to persons charged under these sections to argue that because their acts were coerced by threats, they lacked the requisite *mens rea*. Such persons may, however, seek to have their conduct *excused* through the operation of the common law defence of duress.

C. The "Safe Avenue of Escape" Requirement in the Common Law of Duress

46 The second and third issues raised by the appellant have to do with the so-called "safe avenue of escape" rule. The court must decide whether such a rule in fact exists, and, if it does, whether the availability of a "safe avenue" is to be determined on an objective or subjective basis.

(1) THE RELATION BETWEEN DURESS AND OTHER EXCUSES

47 As I have explained, the common law defence of duress, properly understood, is not based on the idea that coercion negates *mens rea*. Rather, it is one of a number of defences that operate by justifying or excusing what would otherwise be criminal conduct.

50 The defences of self-defence, necessity, and duress all arise under circumstances where a person is subjected to an external danger, and commits an act that would otherwise be criminal as a way of avoiding the harm the danger presents. In the case of self-defence and duress, it is the intentional threats of another person that are the source of the danger, while in the case of necessity, the danger is due to other causes, such as forces of nature, human conduct other than intentional threats of bodily harm, etc. In cases of self-defence, the victim of the otherwise criminal act at issue is himself or herself the *originator* of the threat that causes the actor to commit what would otherwise be an assault or culpable homicide (bearing in mind, of course, that the victim's threats may themselves have been provoked by the conduct of the accused). In this sense, he or she is the author of his or her own deserts, a factor which arguably warrants special consideration in the law. In cases of duress and necessity, however, the victims of the otherwise criminal act (to the extent that a victim can be identified) are *third parties*, who are not themselves responsible for the threats or circumstances of necessity that motivated the accused's actions. For this reason, analogies between the defence of necessity and duress would appear to be the most clearly supportable, and thus the most likely to be instructive.

51 In Canada, of course, a distinction between the two defences exists as a result of the fact that the defence of duress has been partially codified (in relation to principals) by s. 17, while necessity remains a purely common law defence: *Perka v. The Queen* (1984), 14 C.C.C. (3d) 385, 13 D.L.R. (4th) 1, [1984] 2 S.C.R. 232. In the present case, however, we are concerned only with those cases of duress falling outside the ambit of s. 17, where the common law remains applicable — that is, cases of party liability (*Paquette, supra*). In my view, the clear similarities between the factual circumstances in which the common law defence of duress and the common law defence of necessity arise, imply that comparisons between the two remain highly relevant, notwithstanding the existence of a partially codified version of the defence of duress applicable in other situations. It would, I believe, be highly anomalous if the common law defence of duress were to be understood as based on substantially different juridical principles from the common law defence of necessity.

52   In *Perka, supra*, the status of the defence of necessity in the common law of Canada was firmly established.

53   Dickson J. approved of this theoretical foundation for excuses, stating (at p. 250):

> I agree with this formulation of the rationale for excuses in the criminal law. In my view, this *rationale* extends beyond specific codified excuses and embraces the residual excuse known as the defence of necessity. At the heart of this defence is the perceived injustice of punishing violations of the law in circumstances in which the person had no other viable or reasonable choice available; the act was wrong but it is excused because it was realistically unavoidable.

Dickson J. proceeded to establish several preconditions that must be satisfied before the defence of necessity could be invoked. He was of the view that there were three primary requirements: first, that there be an "urgent situation of clear and imminent peril"; second, that "compliance with the law [be] demonstrably impossible"; and third, that there be proportionality between the danger facing the accused and the harm caused by his or her unlawful acts.

54   As I noted earlier, the common law defences of necessity and duress apply to essentially similar factual situations. Indeed, to repeat Lord Simon of

Glaisdale's observation in *Director of Public Prosecutions for Northern Ireland v. Lynch*, [1975] A.C. 653, "[d]uress is . . . merely a particular application of the doctrine of 'necessity.'" In my view, the similarities between the two defences are so great that consistency and logic require that they be understood as based on the same juristic principles. Indeed, to do otherwise would be to promote incoherence and anomaly in the criminal law. In the case of necessity, the court has already considered the various alternative theoretical positions available (in *Perka, supra*), and has expounded a conceptualization of the defence of necessity as an excuse, based on the idea of normative involuntariness. In my opinion, the need for consistency and coherence in the law dictates that the common law defence of duress also be based on this juridical foundation. If the defence is viewed in this light, the answers to the questions posed in the present appeal can be seen to follow readily from the reasons of Dickson J. in *Perka*.

(a) THE SAFE AVENUE OF ESCAPE REQUIREMENT

55   The so-called "safe avenue of escape" requirement in the law of duress is, in my view, simply a specific example of a more general requirement, analogous to that in the defence of necessity identified by Dickson J. — the requirement that compliance with the law be "demonstrably impossible." As Dickson J. explained, this requirement can be derived directly from the underlying concept of normative involuntariness upon which the defence of necessity is based. As I am of the view that the defence of duress must be seen as being based upon this same theoretical foundation, it follows that the defence of duress includes a similar requirement — namely, a requirement that it can only be invoked if, to adopt Dickson J.'s phrase, there is "no legal way out" of the situation of duress the accused faces. The rule that the defence of duress is unavailable if a "safe avenue of escape" was open to the accused is simply a specific instance of this general requirement — if the accused could have escaped without undue danger, the decision to commit an offence

becomes, as Dickson J. observed in the context of necessity, "a voluntary one, impelled by some consideration beyond the dictates of necessity and human instincts."

(b) IS THE EXISTENCE OF A SAFE AVENUE OF ESCAPE TO BE DETERMINED SUBJECTIVELY OR OBJECTIVELY?

56 The remaining question on this appeal raises a potentially more difficult issue, namely, the question of whether the existence of a "safe avenue of escape" is to be determined objectively or on the basis of the accused's own subjective knowledge and awareness at the time. How this question is answered depends, in my view, on how one conceives of the notion of "normative involuntariness" upon which the defence of duress is based. That is, is an action "normatively involuntary" when the actor *believes* that he has no real choice, or is this the case only when there is *in fact* no reasonable alternative course of action available?

57 As Dickson J.'s reasons in *Perka* suggest, a degree of objectivity is inherent to excuses that are based on the notion of normative involuntariness, to the extent that this concept turns on the objective availability, or lack of availability, of true choice. Indeed, Dickson J. clearly indicates that the operative standard for the defence of necessity is to be an objective one, based on whether "there is a *reasonable* legal alternative to disobeying the law."

59 This court has previously indicated that when assessing the reasonableness of an accused's conduct for the purposes of determining whether he or she should be excused from criminal responsibility, it is appropriate to employ an objective standard that takes into account the particular circumstances of the accused, including his or her ability to perceive the existence of alternative courses of action. For instance, in *R. v. Lavallee* (1990), 55 C.C.C. (3d) 97, [1990] 1 S.C.R. 852, 76 C.R. (3d) 329, a self-defence case, Wilson J., writing for a majority of the court, declared (at p. 125):

I think the question the jury must ask itself [in a case of self-defence] is whether, given the history, circumstances and perceptions of the appellant, her belief that she could not preserve herself from being killed by [her "common-law" spouse] that night except by killing him first was reasonable.

Similarly, in *R. v. Pétel* (1994), 87 C.C.C. (3d) 97 at p. 103, [1994] 1 S.C.R. 3, 26 C.R. (4th) 145, I stated that in assessing self-defence "the jury must seek to determine how the accused perceived the relevant facts and whether that perception was reasonable."

60 The defences of self-defence, duress, and necessity are essentially similar, so much so that consistency demands that each defence's "reasonableness" requirement be assessed on the same basis. Accordingly, I am of the view that while the question of whether a "safe avenue of escape" was open to an accused who pleads duress should be assessed on an objective basis, the appropriate objective standard to be employed is one that takes into account the particular circumstances and human frailties of the accused.

(2) CONCLUSIONS ON DURESS AND "SAFE AVENUE OF ESCAPE" REQUIREMENT

62 My conclusions on the second and third issues raised by the appellant can thus be summarized as follows. An accused person cannot rely on the common law defence of duress if he or she had an opportunity to safely extricate himself or herself from the situation of duress. The rationale for this rule is simply that in such circumstances the condition of "normative involuntariness" that provides the theoretical basis for both the defences of duress and necessity is absent — if the accused had the chance to take action that would have allowed him or her to avoid committing an offence, it cannot be said that he or she had no real choice when deciding whether or not to break the law. Furthermore, I believe that the internal logic of the excuse-based defence, which has theoretical underpinnings directly analogous to those that support the defence of necessity (as set out in *Perka, supra*), suggests that the question of whether or not a safe avenue of escape existed is to be determined according to an objective standard. When considering the perceptions of a "reasonable person," however, the personal circumstances of the accused are relevant and important, and should be taken into account.

D. Assessing the Charge to the Jury

64 In the present case, Webber J. was confronted with the difficult and unenviable task of charging the jury on a very complex area of the common law. With the greatest of respect, I am of the view that his charge to the jury contained several instructions that, when read with reference to the law as set out in this court's current decision, now can be identified as incorrect. In his charge, the trial judge told the jurors that "if Hibbert joined in the common plot to shoot Cohen, under threats of death or grievous bodily harm, that would negative his having a common intention with Quasi to shoot Cohen, and [*sic*] you must find Hibbert not guilty." In my respectful view, these instructions contained several errors. First, the reference to "common intention" — an expression descriptive of the mental element in s. 21(2) — was misplaced, in light of the trial judge's earlier instruction that s. 21(1)(b) was "the portion of s. 21 that applies to this particular case." Second, as I have explained, it was incorrect to instruct the jury that the *mens rea* for party liability under s. 21(1)(b) could be "negated" by duress. Thirdly, and most importantly, the jury was not told that even if the appellant possessed the requisite *mens rea*, his conduct could be *excused* by

operation of the common law defence of duress if the jurors were of the view that the necessary conditions for this defence's application were present.

67 Although the errors identified above are in themselves sufficient, in my opinion, to entitle the appellant to a new trial, I will briefly address the other points raised by the appellant. As I have explained, I am of the view that the trial judge did not err in instructing the jury that the appellant could not rely on the defence of duress if the Crown established that he had failed to avail himself of a safe avenue of escape. Furthermore, while I believe the trial judge should have instructed the jury that the existence of such an avenue was to be determined objectively, taking into account the personal circumstances of the appellant, on the particular facts of this case, I am not persuaded that his failure to do so affected the jury's decision, since there was no indication, on the facts, that any of the appellant's personal attributes or frailties rendered him unable to identify any safe avenues of escape that would have been apparent to a reasonable person of ordinary capacities and abilities.

VI. Conclusion

68 With respect, I am of the view that the trial judge erred in his instructions to the jury on the law of duress. Since I do not believe that it can be said that this error necessarily had no impact on the jury's verdict, I believe that there should be a new trial. Accordingly, the appeal is allowed, the appellant's conviction is set aside, and a new trial is ordered.

Appeal allowed; new trial ordered.

Regina v. Langlois

QUÉBEC COURT OF APPEAL   FEBRUARY 12, 1993

BACKGROUND

Langlois was acquitted by the trial judge of charges of conspiracy, trafficking, and possession of narcotics for the purpose of trafficking and illegally selling drugs contrary to the Food and Drugs Act. The Crown subsequently appealed against the acquittal to the Québec Court of Appeal.

MAIN ISSUES

(1) Is section 17 of the Criminal Code, which defines the statutory defence of duress, invalid under the Charter? (2) What are the basic elements of the common law defence of duress?

JUDGMENT

The judgment of the Québec Court of Appeal was delivered by Justice Fish. (The other members of the Court were Justices Tyndale and Mailhot.)

....

FISH J.A.: — This case concerns the current state of the defence of duress, or compulsion by threats, in Canada.

Respondent was caught smuggling drugs into the penitentiary where he worked. He successfully invoked the common law defence of duress at his trial. We are asked on this appeal to set aside respondent's acquittal on the ground that the trial judge misapplied the law of duress. For the reasons that follow, I would decline to intervene.

I

The common law defence of duress has been denied in Canada, since 1967, to every one who "actually commits" any offence, however compelling the threats, however minor the crime: *R. v. Carker*, [1967] 2 C.C.C. 190, [1967] S.C.R. 114, 2 C.R.N.S. 16 (S.C.C.).

Yet the defence has remained available for virtually all offences (other than murder, attempted murder, and some forms of treason) to aiders and abettors, and to those charged in virtue of s. 21(2) of the Criminal Code (for forming an intention in common with another person to carry out an unlawful purpose), unless the accused was in fact a "co-perpetrator": *R. v. Robins* (1982), 66 C.C.C. (2d) 550 (Que. C.A.), discussed below.

Section 17 of the Criminal Code, on the other hand, sets out a defence of compulsion by threats that applies to "principals," or those who "actually commit the offence," but not to aiders or abetttors: *R. v. Paquette* (1976), 30 C.C.C. (2d) 417 at p. 421, 70 D.L.R. (3d) 129, [1977] 2 S.C.R. 189 (S.C.C.).

This statutory defence is more liberal in some respects than the common law defence of duress, but it is more limited in others. Two restrictive conditions are of particular concern here. The first is that s. 17, by its express terms, can only be invoked by an accused who acted "under compulsion by threats of *immediate* death or bodily harm." Secondly, the defence only avails where the threats are "from a person who is *present when the offence is committed.*"

In the present case, it is conceded that the accused personally delivered and transported drugs. He thus "actually committed" the offences with which he was charged.

It is undecided whether s. 17 is restricted to threats of harm to the accused alone. Even if it extends to threats of death or injury to third persons, such as members of the accused's family, respondent Langlois cannot invoke s. 17, since he did not act under threats of *immediate* death or injury from a person who was *present when the offences were committed.*

If s. 17 is unconstitutional, however, the common law defence of duress becomes available to respondent in virtue of s. 8(3) of the Code.

The principal remaining issues would then be whether the trial judge, bearing in mind respondent's evidential burden, properly left the defence of duress to the jury and, assuming this to be so, whether the judge's charge adequately laid out its constituent elements.

My conclusion, for the moment put briefly, is that s. 17 of the Criminal Code violates the principle of fundamental justice that a person should not be found guilty of a crime if he or she is morally blameless.

In my view, a person is morally blameless if he or she commits a wrongful act that is "normatively involuntary" within the meaning of *R. v. Perka* (1984), 14 C.C.C. (3d) 385, 13 D.L.R. (4th) 1, [1984] 2 S.C.R. 232 (S.C.C.). An accused whose offence is normatively involuntary cannot, in a criminal law context, be said to be personally at fault and, as the Supreme Court of Canada has recently again recognized, it "is axiomatic that in

criminal law there should be no responsibility without personal fault": *per* Sopinka J., speaking for the court in *R. v. DeSousa* (1992), 76 C.C.C. (3d) 124 at p. 134, 95 D.L.R. (4th) 595, [1992] 2 S.C.R. 944 (S.C.C.).

Yet s. 17 denies the defence of compulsion to persons who commit any of the excluded offences as a result of credible threats of immediate death made by a person present when the offence is committed. It therefore requires the conviction of persons who commit those offences in a morally blameless and normatively involuntary manner.

However forceful and paralyzing the threat, however fleeting and reparable the wrong, s. 17 would thus remain inaccessible to any person who is compelled to perform a prohibited act by threats of grave injury to a member of his or her family from a person who, though absent when the crime is committed, remains none the less positioned to actualize the threats soon if not immediately.

These limits imposed by s. 17 on an accused's right not to be punished for morally blameless behaviour are, in my opinion, not "demonstrably justified in a free and democratic society," within the meaning of s. 1 of the Canadian Charter of Rights and Freedoms.

In the result, I believe the common law defence of duress was in principle open to respondent. I believe as well that the trial judge properly explained the essential elements of that defence to the jury. In this matter, the defence of duress was accepted and respondent was acquitted.

The verdict of a properly instructed jury is, in my view, no less reliable when the jury acquits than when the jury convicts.

II

Respondent Serge Langlois, then a recreation officer at Archambault Penitentiary, was searched upon his arrival for work on March 24, 1984.

The authorities found in his boots 282.6 grams of hashish and 1547 tablets of diazepam (valium). A search of his briefcase and of his parked pickup truck resulted in the discovery and seizure of letters addressed to imprisoned members of the Hell's Angels motorcycle gang, $1000 in cash, Hell's Angels clothing and stationery, video and audio cassettes intended for inmates of the penitentiary, and an additional 2076 valium pills.

Langlois admitted in a written statement that he had also smuggled four or five pieces of hashish into the penitentiary some 10 days earlier.

Respondent, who testified at trial, called evidence of good character and made a defence of compulsion by threats, or duress.

He claimed to have received several anonymous telephone calls in which the caller asked him if his wife and children were well. A further caller told him that if he were ordered to do something, he had best not complain to the police if he did not wish to jeopardize the safety of his wife and children.

One day, an inmate by the name of Fernandez gave him a book of matches, told him to go to the address written inside and to bring what he received there into the penitentiary.

Langlois went to the address, a nude dancing club, received the drugs mentioned earlier and returned to his home for the night. The next day, he brought the contraband with him to work.

The same procedure was followed a second time, leading to his search and arrest.

Langlois testified that he did not report these incidents to the police because he feared for his family and did not believe that the police could give them timely and adequate protection. He did not believe that he had a sufficient delay to flee with his family and to hide them.

In respect of the first episode, Langlois was charged with conspiracy with Raymond Fernandez to traffic in hashish, trafficking in the hashish, and possession for the purposes of trafficking.

With respect to the hashish found in his possession at the time of his arrest, Langlois was charged with conspiracy, trafficking, and possession for the purposes of trafficking. He was charged in a seventh count with illegally selling 3623 diazepam pills, thereby committing an indictable offence under s. 26(b) of the Food and Drugs Act, R.S.C. 1970, c. F-27.

Langlois was acquitted in 1987 by a jury at St-Jérôme on all seven counts of the indictment.

III

Essentially, as I mentioned at the outset, this appeal turns on the constitutionality of s. 17 of the Criminal Code and on the availability to respondent of the common law defence of duress.

A quarter century ago, in *Carker, supra*, the Supreme Court of Canada held unanimously that:

> . . . the common law rules and principles respecting "duress" as an excuse or defence have been codified and exhaustively defined in s. 17 [of the Criminal Code] . . .

Seven years later, in *Paquette, supra*, the Supreme Court, again unanimous, rejected a Crown submission that (at p. 420) ". . . the principles of law applicable to the excuse or defence of duress or compulsion are exhaustively codified in s. 17 . . . of the Criminal Code . . ." and explained that ". . . the application of s. 17 is limited to cases in which the person seeking to rely upon it has himself committed an offence."

In the present matter, the trial judge considered the distinction between *Carker* and *Paquette* (A.F., p. 6) [translation]: ". . . totally illogical and artificial and fundamentally unreasonable in the light of the Canadian Charter of Rights which states clearly that there is no discrimination between people."

After referring to respondent's right under s. 15 of the Charter to "equal protection and equal benefit of the law without discrimination," the judge decided that respondent was not precluded by s. 17 of the Code from invoking the wider common law defence of duress.

Before this court, respondent relies on s. 17 rather than s. 15 of the Charter.

Next, appellant urges us to overrule or "set aside" the judgment of the Supreme Court of Canada in *Paquette*.

The appellant asks us to find that *Paquette* has produced [translation] "an obvious illogicality," has had [translation] "an inequitable result," has lost its raison d'être, was based on English authority since rejected by the House of Lords, and should therefore now itself be overruled.

Despite his full and able argument, counsel for appellant has failed to persuade me that the outcome of this appeal can be made to depend on *Paquette*, or that we would be entitled in this case to interpret the law in a manner that contradicts a previous decision of the Supreme Court of Canada.

That court, however, has not since the advent of the Charter determined the constitutionality of s. 17 of the Criminal Code. We are therefore entitled, indeed bound, to face that issue here, and I turn to it now.

IV

No one charged in Canada with the commission as actual perpetrator (or, in view of *Robins*, as "co-perpetrator") of *any offence* may ever invoke the common law defence of duress or otherwise be excused on the ground of compulsion by threats unless:

(1) the threats were of *immediate* death of bodily harm, and
(2) the author of the threats was *present when the offence was committed.*

Moreover, no one prosecuted as perpetrator or co-perpetrator, *even if he or she satisfied these two conditions* and *believes that the threats will be carried out*, may *under any circumstances* invoke the common law defence of duress *or the defence of compulsion under s. 17* on a charge of robbery, sexual assault, unlawfully causing bodily harm, assault causing bodily harm, aggravated assault, or arson, let alone murder, treason, piracy, or aggravated sexual assault.

Turning to other offences excluded by s. 17, it is important to recall that "bodily harm" in this context means "any hurt or injury to the complainant that interferes with the health or comfort of the complainant and that is more than merely transient or trifling in nature": see s. 267(2) of the Criminal Code. Thus, the offence of unlawfully causing bodily harm is complete upon proof that the accused, *intentionally or not*, caused such harm while committing *any objectively dangerous act*, prohibited by *federal or provincial law*: see the recent and unanimous judgment of the Supreme Court of Canada in *DeSousa, supra*, especially at pp. 133 and 142.

Sopinka J., speaking for the court in *DeSousa*, confirmed that (at p. 140) "both assault and assault causing bodily harm have identical *mens rea* requirements and the element of causing bodily harm is merely used to classify the offence," and further, that (at p. 141) "the mental element of an offence attaches only to the underlying offence and not to the aggravating circumstances."

Because of s. 17 of the Criminal Code, no one in Canada may therefore be excused for yielding to the gravest of threats, if that person, in order to avoid actualization of those threats, is driven to commit any objectively dangerous federal or provincial offence that causes another person discomfort, albeit minor, though neither "transient" nor "trifling."

The restrictive and anomalous character of the law of duress or compulsion in Canada has been the subject of extensive academic comment. Don Stuart has observed, comparing s. 17 to corresponding rules in other jurisdictions, that it excepts an unusually large number of offences (*Canadian Criminal Law: A Treatise,* 2nd ed., p. 395 (1987)).

Because of its narrow compass, s. 17 has the potential, in my view, of mandating a conviction despite the normatively involuntary character of the accused's *actus reus*. It has replaced the common law defence of duress by a statutory substitute that has proved, in cases such as *Carker, supra*, to be virtually inaccessible.

And, in this light, I again find that s. 17, on any reading of its provisions, constricts unacceptably the right of an accused not to be punished for performing a prohibited act "in emergency situations where normal human instincts, whether of self-preservation or of altruism, overwhelmingly compel disobedience": *Perka, supra*.

V

Delivering the judgment of the Supreme Court of Canada in *DeSousa, supra,* Sopinka J. stated (at p. 134):

> It is axiomatic that in criminal law there should be no responsibility without personal fault. A fault requirement was asserted to be a fundamental aspect of our common law by this court in *R. v. Sault Ste. Marie (City)* (1978), 40 C.C.C. (2d) 353 . . . and as a matter of constitutional law under s. 7 of the Charter in *Reference re: s. 94(2) of Motor Vehicle Act* (1985), 23 C.C.C. (3d) 289 . . .

Sopinka J. reiterated that:

> The criminal law is based on proof of personal fault and this concept is jealously guarded when a court is asked to interpret criminal provisions, especially those with potentially serious penal consequences.

Again (at p. 140):

> The requirement of fault in regard to a meaningful aspect of the *actus reus* is necessary to prevent punishing the mentally, *and morally,* innocent and is in keeping with a long line of cases of this court . . .

(My emphasis.) And finally, after referring to (at p. 141) "the constitutional aversion to punishing the morally innocent" (at p. 142): "In punishing for unforeseen consequences, the law is not punishing the morally innocent but those who cause injury through *avoidable* unlawful action" (my emphasis).

Conviction for a criminal offence requires, as a principle of fundamental justice, an element of moral blameworthiness. The Supreme Court has not yet had occasion to deal with this requirement in the context of compulsion by threats. It did, however, canvass the issue in *Perka, supra,* at p. 403, where the court considered the "largely analogous" defence of necessity.

In my view, s. 17 of the Criminal Code, to the extent that it does not satisfy the standard of moral blameworthiness adopted by the Supreme Court in *Perka,* violates the principles of fundamental justice enshrined in s. 7 of the Canadian Charter of Rights and Freedoms.

VI

The defence of compulsion by threats, or duress, is founded on the same underlying considerations as the defence of compulsion by circumstances, or necessity.

Lord Simon of Glaisdale, in *Director of Public Prosecutions for Northern Ireland v. Lynch,* [1975] A.C. 653 at p. 692 (H.L.), explained the close connection between the two defences as follows:

> The only difference is that in duress the force constraining the choice is a human threat, whereas in "necessity" it can be any circumstance constituting a threat to life (or, perhaps, limb). Duress is, thus considered, merely a particular application of the doctrine of "necessity."

Since the defence of duress or compulsion, which concerns us in this case, is so closely related, legally and philosophically, to the defence of necessity considered in *Perka, supra,* I believe the outcome of the present matter is in large measure dictated by the principles of law laid down in *Perka.*

Whether a prohibited act results from compulsion by circumstances or compulsion by threats, does not seem to me to materially alter "the perceived injustice of punishing violations of the law in circumstances in which the person had no other viable or reasonable choice available": *per* Dickson J., in *Perka, supra,* at pp. 398–9.

Section 17 of the Criminal Code permits this perceived injustice to become an inescapable reality in two main ways: first, where the threats made, though not of *immediate* death or injury, or not from a person who is present when the prohibited act is done, would have caused any reasonable person to behave exactly as did the accused; secondly, where the accused was truly compelled, within the meaning of *Perka*, to commit one of the excluded offences.

In the present case, respondent seeks to invoke the common law defence of duress in virtue of s. 8(3) of the Criminal Code. He may avail himself of that defence only if s. 17 of the Code is shown to be unconstitutional and inoperative.

Respondent claims that he acted under threats of injury to members of his family. The threats were not made by a person present when the crime was committed. Nor were they threats of immediate death or injury. Respondent's defence therefore cannot comply with the mandatory conditions of s. 17. In effect, he is deprived by the narrow compass of that provision from invoking any defence of compulsion by threats.

As I stated earlier, the requirements of s. 17 that respondent is unable to satisfy create a real risk of criminal conviction for normatively involuntary acts. They expose to penal consequences behaviour that may well be morally blameless. Section 17 therefore violates principles of fundamental justice venerated equally by ancient and contemporary philosophers. These principles were recently reaffirmed, in relation to the defence of necessity, by the Supreme Court of Canada in *Perka, supra*. In my view, they apply equally to compulsion by threats or duress.

In my respectful view, s. 17 does not pass constitutional muster. It should therefore be declared inoperative, leaving open to all parties — those who commit the offence and those who aid in its commission — the common law defence of duress.

VII

In *R. v. Mena* (1987), 34 C.C.C. (3d) 304 at p. 319, 57 C.R. (3d) 172, 2 W.C.B. (2d) 58 (Ont. C.A.), writing for the court, Martin J.A. noted that: "The common law, with respect to the defence of duress, is in a somewhat unsatisfactory state."

Notably, at common law, there is no requirement that the threats be made by a person who is present at the scene of the crime. It has been said that the threat must be "immediate" or "imminent" and that persons threatened must resort to the protection of the law if they can do so: Smith and Hogan, *Criminal Law*, 6th ed., p. 235 (1988). While the defence is not available to those who have "an obvious safe avenue of escape" (*Mena*, at p. 322), I agree with Martin J.A. that the operative test is "whether the accused failed to avail himself or herself of some opportunity to escape or to render the threat ineffective" (at p. 323).

VIII

The trial judge, in opening the common law defence in this case, directed the jury that duress involved three essential requirements (A.F., p. 79).

First, there had to be either explicit or implicit threats of death or serious injury.

Secondly, the threats had to be "immediate": respondent had no right to yield to threats if he had an obvious safe avenue of escape. He had a duty to try, by all possible means, to avoid committing the crime, to escape (p. 80).

The judge reviewed the evidence on this issue in a fair and careful way (pp. 80–3), and again directed the jury, as to this second element of duress, to ask itself whether the accused could validly claim that he had no safe avenue of escape.

Essentially, the trial judge appears to have invited the jury to apply an objective standard in determining whether the respondent had an obvious and safe way of escape. This seems to be in accord with the authorities: see *Mena, supra*, at p. 322. However, the issue is not free from controversy.

In any event, as I mentioned earlier, the trial judge directed the jury to apply an essentially objective standard as to the availability of an avenue of escape, and in this regard I see no room for complaint by the Crown.

As to the third element, the judge directed the jury that a person subjected to threats was expected to show reasonable courage (A.F., p. 83) [translation]:

. . . the law does not protect a person who commits criminal offences due to threats if that person does not show normal and reasonable courage in the particular circumstances of his situation.

The jury was then told that society expects a higher standard or additional degree of courage from someone who has chosen a calling that normally requires courage, such as a police officer. Penitentiary employees were also expected to show "the kind of courage one does not demand of an accountant or schoolteacher" (p. 84).

The jury was thus to ask itself whether Langlois [translation]:

. . . had shown the resolution, the determination and the self-control that an officer in a penitentiary should normally possess. If he did not possess those qualities, did he have the duty to resign and find another position in a less demanding field instead of keeping his position?

Lack of courage is not a legitimate excuse for committing a crime . . .

Finally, I agree with Martin J.A., who concluded in *Mena, supra,* that, at least in principle (at p. 323), "whether the accused had failed to avail himself of an opportunity to escape, which was reasonably open to him, is a question for the jury."

In this case, the trial judge gave careful consideration to the Crown's submission concerning respondent's evidential burden on the defence of duress. He concluded that there was an air of reality to the defence and that it should therefore go to the jury.

Another judge might perhaps have taken a less indulgent view, but in the absence of any material misdirection as to the elements required to found a defence of duress, I would not interfere.

Taken as a whole, I think it can fairly be said that the judge's charge to the jury subjected respon-

dent's defence to the tests laid down, for necessity, in *Perka, supra,* [at p. 407]:

Was the emergency a real one? Did it constitute an immediate threat of the harm purportedly feared? Was the response proportionate? In comparing this response to the danger that motivated it, was the danger one that society would reasonably expect the average person to withstand? Was there any reasonable legal alternative to the illegal response open to the accused?

And as I said near the outset, the verdict of a properly directed jury is no less reliable in the case of an acquittal than in the event of conviction.

IX

There have been calls in England, as we have seen, for a fresh parliamentary look at the common law defence of duress. Similar views have been expressed in Canada with respect both to the common law and to the statutory defence under s. 17 of the Criminal Code.

Paquette, supra, may well have introduced unforeseen anomalies into the law. That case can be seen, however, as a judicial initiative constrained by the law as it then stood.

Under the Charter, different considerations obtain. Courts are now mandated to determine whether impugned statutory provisions satisfy Canadian constitutional requirements, including adherence to the principles of fundamental justice.

For the reasons given, I believe s. 17 of the Criminal Code fails that test and should therefore be declared inoperative.

I have also concluded that appellant has established no reversible error in the judge's charge to the jury in this case.

Accordingly, I would dismiss the appeal.

Appeal dismissed.

Defences to a Criminal Charge: Part II
Provocation, Self-Defence, and Consent

INTRODUCTION

In this chapter, there are five cases that illustrate the application of the following significant defences to a criminal charge: provocation, self-defence, and consent.

The *Thibert* case (1996) constitutes an important statement by the Supreme Court of Canada concerning the precise nature and extent of the defence of provocation. In particular, the case provides guidance for the interpretation of the Criminal Code requirement [section 232(2)] that the provocation must be "sufficient to deprive an *ordinary person* of the power of self-control" (emphasis added), in order for it to qualify as a valid defence.

Lavallee (1990) and *Pétel* (1994) both raise fundamental questions about the nature of the defence of self-defence in Canada. In particular, these cases involve self-defence under the terms of section 34(2) of the Code, which applies when the accused has caused the death of another person during an act of alleged self-defence. In the famous case of *Lavallee*, the Supreme Court of Canada attempted to ensure that the judicial interpretation of section 34(2) takes into account the realities facing those women who are threatened by abusive partners. More specifically, the Supreme Court held that, in

order to assist trial courts in making the determination as to whether the accused acted *reasonably* when she killed her abuser, trial courts may admit expert testimony concerning the so-called "battered-wife syndrome." Furthermore, the Court ruled in *Lavallee* that an abused woman whose life has been threatened does not have to wait until the attack actually commences before she is permitted to take forceful action in her self-defence. In *Pétel*, in circumstances somewhat different to those that existed in the *Lavallee* case, the Supreme Court of Canada once again articulated the view that section 34(2) did not impose a requirement that the assailant's attack be "imminent" before the right to act in self-defence comes into play.

The final two cases concern the circumstances in which a defendant may raise the consent of his or her alleged victim as a defence to a charge of assault. In the *Jobidon* case (1991), the Supreme Court of Canada ruled that, in general, consent is not a defence to a charge of assault when anything more than trivial bodily harm is intended by the accused. On the other hand, in the *Leclerc* case, the Ontario Court of Appeal explored the parameters of one of the exceptions to the general rule expounded in *Jobidon*: the defence of implied consent in the context of contact sports, such as hockey.

Thibert v. The Queen

SUPREME COURT OF CANADA   JANUARY 25, 1996

BACKGROUND

Thibert was convicted at his trial of second degree murder. His appeal to the Alberta Court of Appeal was dismissed. However, Thibert's subsequent appeal to the Supreme Court of Canada was allowed and a new trial ordered.

MAIN ISSUES

(1) What factors should be considered by the jury when applying the "ordinary-person" test contained in section 232(2) of the Criminal Code? (2) Did the victim have a "legal right" to do what he did within the meaning of section 232(3)?

JUDGMENTS

The *majority* judgment was delivered by Justice Cory (with whom Justices Sopinka and McLachlin agreed). Justice Major's *dissenting* judgment (with which Justice Iacobucci agreed) has been omitted.

1 CORY J.: — The sole question to be considered on this appeal is whether the trial judge was correct in leaving the defence of provocation with the jury. Put another way, the issue is whether there was any evidence upon which a reasonable jury acting judi-

cially and properly instructed could find that there had been provocation.

2 If the trial judge was correct in leaving provocation with the jury, then it is conceded that there must be a new trial. This is the result of the failure to instruct the jury that there was no onus resting upon the appellant to establish the defence, but rather that it rested upon the Crown to establish beyond a reasonable doubt that there had not been provocation. If, on the other hand, it was inappropriate for the trial judge to leave the defence of provocation to the jury, then the fact that he erred in the instructions pertaining to provocation was immaterial and it would be appropriate to find that no substantial wrong or miscarriage had been occasioned by the error.

The Defence of Provocation

3 The Criminal Code has always provided a defence of provocation which may reduce the crime of murder to manslaughter. It is found at present in s. 232 of the Criminal Code.

4 The section specifies that there is both an objective and a subjective element to the defence. Both must be satisfied if the defence is to be invoked. First, there must be a wrongful act or insult of such a nature that it is sufficient to deprive an ordinary person of the power of self-control as the objective element. Second, the subjective element requires that the accused act upon that insult on the sudden and before there was time for his passion to cool. The objective aspect would at first reading appear to be contradictory for, as legal writers have noted, the "ordinary" person does not kill. Yet, I think the objective element should be taken as an attempt to weigh in the balance those very human frailties which sometimes lead people to act irrationally and impulsively against the need to protect society by discouraging acts of homicidal violence.

When Should the Defence of Provocation Be Left to the Jury?

6   Before the defence of provocation is left to the jury, the trial judge must be satisfied (a) that there is *some* evidence to suggest that the particular wrongful act or insult alleged by the accused would have caused an ordinary person to be deprived of self-control and (b) that there is some evidence showing that the accused was actually deprived of his or her self-control by that act or insult. This threshold test can be readily met, so long as there is some evidence that the objective and subjective elements may be satisfied. If there is, the defence must then be left with the jury.

7   It is true that the objective and subjective requirements mandated by section 232 are clearly questions of fact which the jury must decide. Nonetheless, the trial judge must still determine if there is *any* evidence upon which a reasonable jury properly instructed and acting judicially could find that there had been provocation. If the trial judge is satisfied that there is such evidence, then the defence must be put to the jury to determine what weight, if any, should be attached to that evidence. Obviously, the trial judge should not weigh the sufficiency of the evidence. This is the function reserved for the jury. A trial judge considering whether the evidence has met the threshold test must also take into account the nature of the wrongful act or insult and how that act or insult should be viewed in the context of the case.

THE WRONGFUL ACT OR INSULT

8   *Taylor v. The King* (1947), 89 C.C.C. 209 at p. 223, [1948] 1 D.L.R. 545 at p. 557, [1947] S.C.R. 462, adopted *The Oxford English Dictionary* definition of "insult" and found it to mean:

> ". . . an act, or the action, of attacking or assailing; an open and sudden attack or assault without formal preparations; injuriously contemptuous speech or behaviour; scornful utterance or action intended to wound self-respect; an affront; indignity."

THE OBJECTIVE ELEMENT OF THE TEST: HOW ORDINARY IS THE "ORDINARY PERSON" AND WOULD THAT PERSON HAVE BEEN PROVOKED BY THE WRONGFUL ACT OR INSULT?

9   In earlier cases, both in England and in Canada, the concept of the ordinary person was very narrowly defined. This narrow approach required a court to completely ignore all the particular features of the accused whether mental or physical, even for the purpose of assessing the gravity of the insult.

11   The courts in England and Canada have changed their position. They now permit the inclusion of many of the characteristics of the accused in the "ordinary person" standard which must be met in the objective test. It was recognized that if the objective test was to be usefully applied, the jury or fact finder must take into consideration features such as the age, sex, and racial origin of the accused. Obviously, the effect of calling a black person a "two-bit nigger punk," as in *Olbey v. The Queen* (1979), 50 C.C.C. (2d) 257, 105 D.L.R. (3d) 385, [1980] 1 S.C.R. 1008, would be far greater than if the same demeaning epithet was applied to a white man.

12   *Director of Public Prosecutions v. Camplin,* [1978] A.C. 705 (H.L.), was the turning point in England. In that case a 15-year-old male was raped and then mocked. The accused picked up a frying pan and struck and fatally injured his assailant.

Section 3 of the Homicide Act, 1957 (U.K.), 5 & 6 Eliz. 2, c. 11, provided that "the jury shall take into account everything both done and said according to the effect which, in their opinion, it would have on a reasonable man." Lord Diplock, at p. 718, interpreted the section in this way:

> . . . the reasonable man referred to . . . is a person having the power of self-control to be expected of an ordinary person of the sex and age of the accused, but in other respects sharing such of the accused's characteristics as they think would affect the gravity of the provocation to him . . .

14   In Canada, the courts have also sought to attain a proper balance in the interpretation of the provocation section. It has been properly recognized that the objective element of the test exists to ensure that the criminal law encourages reasonable and responsible behaviour. A consideration of the defence of provocation must always bear this principle in mind. On the other hand, if the test is to be applied sensibly and with sensitivity, then the ordinary person must be taken to be of the same age, and sex, and must share with the accused such other factors as would give the act or insult in question a special significance. In other words, all the relevant background circumstances should be considered. In the context of other cases, it may properly be found that other factors should be considered. It is how such an "ordinary" person with those characteristics would react to the situation which confronted the accused that should be used as the basis for considering the objective element.

15   The problem was considered by this court in *R. v. Hill* (1996), 25 C.C.C. (3d) 322, 27 D.L.R. (4th) 187, [1986] 1 S.C.R. 313. There, a 16-year-old male fought off the homosexual advances of an older man who was his "Big Brother." The narrow "ordinary person" test was rejected and a more contextual one adopted. Dickson C.J.C., writing for the majority of the court, held that the age and sex of the accused are important considerations in the objective branch of the test. At p. 335 C.C.C., p. 201 D.L.R., he noted that "particular characteristics that are not peculiar or idiosyncratic can be ascribed to an ordinary person without subverting the logic of the objective test of provocation." Although it was not necessary in the circumstances of that case to go beyond a consideration of the age and sex of the accused, Dickson C.J.C. did state that the jury should "assess what an ordinary person would have done if subjected to the same circumstances as the accused" (p. 336 C.C.C., p. 201 D.L.R.). Thus, although characteristics such as a propensity to drunken rages or short-tempered violence cannot be taken into account, other characteristics may properly be considered without in any way demeaning or subverting the aim of the objective test to encourage responsible behaviour. So, too, it is proper for the jury to consider the background of the relationship between the deceased and the accused, including earlier insults which culminated in the final provocative actions or words. For a jury to take this into account would not adversely affect the objective aspect of the test.

16   The provincial courts of appeal have widened, I believe correctly, the approach to the objective element in order to consider the background relationship between the deceased and the accused.

18   In my view, so long as the provocation section remains in the Criminal Code in its present form, certain characteristics will have to be assigned to the "ordinary person" in assessing the objective element. The "ordinary person" must be of the same age, and sex, and share with the accused such other factors as would give the act or insult in question a special significance and have experienced the same series of acts or insults as those experienced by the accused.

19   In summary then, the wrongful act or insult must be one which could, in light of the past history of the relationship between the accused and the deceased, deprive an ordinary person, of the same age and sex, and sharing with the accused such other factors as would give the act or insult in question a special significance, of the power of self-control.

THE SUBJECTIVE ELEMENT

20   In *R. v. Tripodi* (1955), 112 C.C.C. 66, [1955] 4 D.L.R. 445, [1955] S.C.R. 438, Rand J. interpreted "sudden provocation" to mean that "the wrongful act or insult must strike upon a mind unprepared for it, that it must make an unexpected impact that takes the understanding by surprise and sets the passions aflame" (p. 68 C.C.C., p. 447 D.L.R). To this definition, I would add that the background and history of the relationship between the accused and the deceased should be taken into consideration. This is particularly appropriate if it reveals a long history of insults, levelled at the accused by the deceased. This is so even if the insults might induce a desire for revenge so long as immediately before the last insult, the accused did not intend to kill.

Bearing in Mind the Principles Pertaining to Provocation, Was There Any Evidence Adduced in This Case Which Required the Trial Judge to Leave That Defence with the Jury?

22   In this case, there is no doubt that the relationship of the wife of the accused with the deceased was the dominating factor in the tragic killing. Obviously, events leading to the breakup of the marriage can never warrant taking the life of another. Affairs cannot justify murder. Yet the provocation defence section has always been and is presently a part of the Criminal Code. Any recognition of human frailties must take into account that these very situations may lead to insults that could give rise to provocation. Some European penal codes recognize "crimes of passion" as falling within a special category. Indeed many of the Canadian cases which have considered the applicability of the defence arise from such situations. See, for example, the cases of *R. v. Daniels* (1983), 7 C.C.C. (3d) 542, [1983] N.W.T.R. 193, 47 A.R. 149 (N.W.T. C.A.), and *R. v. Conway* (1985), 17 C.C.C. (3d) 481, 14 W.C.B. 7 (Ont. C.A.). The defence of provocation does no more than recognize human frailties. Reality and the past experience of the ages recognize that this sort of situation

may lead to acts of provocation. Each case must be considered in the context of its particular facts to determine if the evidence meets the requisite threshold test necessary to establish provocation.

THE OBJECTIVE ELEMENT OF THE TEST

23   In this case, it is appropriate to take into account the history of the relationship between the accused and the deceased. The accused's wife had, on a prior occasion, planned to leave him for the deceased but he had managed to convince her to return to him. He hoped to accomplish the same result when his wife left him for the deceased on this second occasion. At the time of the shooting he was distraught and had been without sleep for some 34 hours. When he turned into the parking lot of his wife's employer, he still wished to talk to her in private. Later, when the deceased held his wife by her shoulders in a proprietary and possessive manner and moved her back and forth in front of him while he taunted the accused to shoot him, a situation was created in which the accused could have believed that the deceased was mocking him and preventing him from his having the private conversation with his wife which was so vitally important to him.

24   Taking into account the past history between the deceased and the accused, a jury could find the actions of the deceased to be taunting and insulting. It might be found that, under the same circumstances, an ordinary person who was a married man, faced with the breakup of his marriage, would have been provoked by the actions of the deceased so as to cause him to lose his power of self-control. There was some evidence, therefore, that would satisfy the objective element of the test. Next it remains to be seen whether there was evidence that could fulfil the subjective element of the test.

THE SUBJECTIVE ELEMENT OF THE TEST

25   It must be determined whether there was evidence that the appellant was actually provoked. Once again it is necessary to take into account the past history involving the accused, the deceased, and his wife. Further, it cannot be forgotten that the accused hadn't slept for some 34 hours and that he described himself as being devastated, stressed out, and suicidal. He emphasized how important it was to him to talk to his wife in private, away from the deceased. It was in this manner that he successfully persuaded his wife to stay with him on the earlier occasion. When his wife returned to her employer's parking lot and the deceased came out of the building, he testified that his thoughts were "here is the man that won't give me a half hour alone with my wife after 21 years and he has had her for 24 hours the night before."

26 It was when the deceased put his arm around his wife's waist and started leading her back towards the building that the appellant removed the rifle from the car. He testified that he did so as a bluff. He hoped it would make them take him more seriously and succeed in convincing his wife to accompany him so that they could talk privately. From this point, the deceased's actions could be construed as a conscious attempt to test the appellant's limits. When he saw that the appellant had a gun, he advanced towards him. The appellant's wife was in front of the deceased and the deceased had his hands on her shoulders. The appellant recalled that the deceased was swinging Mrs. Thibert from side to side like a moving target. While doing this, the deceased was laughing and grinning at the appellant. He also dared the appellant to fire and taunted him by saying: "Come on big fellow, shoot me. You want to shoot me? Go ahead and shoot me." The deceased continued to approach the appellant, proceeding as fast as he could. In turn, the appellant kept backing up and told the deceased to "stay back," but the deceased continued to approach him. The appellant testified that he remembered wanting to scream because the deceased would not stop coming towards him. The appellant's eyes were tightly closed when he fired the gun. The time the appellant held the gun until he fired was not long. The events unfolded very quickly, in a matter of moments, seconds, not minutes.

27 The respondent submitted that "[r]ejection in the context of a romantic relationship will not constitute a basis for the provocation defence." This is correct. If the appellant had simply brooded over the unhappy situation, put a rifle in his car and gone looking for the deceased, then the history of the deceased's relationship with the wife of the accused could not be used as a basis for a defence of provocation because the necessary final act of provocation was missing. However, in this case, rejection is not the most significant or overriding factor. The appellant sought to avoid the deceased in order to talk privately with his wife. The evidence indicates that the confrontation with the deceased in the parking lot was unexpected. The appellant had gone to some lengths to avoid meeting the deceased.

28 In my view, there was evidence upon which a reasonable jury acting judicially and properly instructed could have concluded that the defence of provocation was applicable. Next it must be considered whether the acts of the deceased were those which he had a legal right to do and thus within the exemption described in s. 232(3).

Were the Acts of the Deceased Ones Which He Had a Legal Right to Do But Which Were Nevertheless Insulting?

29 It will be remembered that s. 232(3) provides that "no one shall be deemed to have given provocation to another by doing anything that he had a legal right to do." In the context of the provocation defence, the phrase "legal right" has been defined as meaning a right which is sanctioned by law as distinct from something which a person may do without incurring legal liability. Thus, the defence of provocation is open to someone who is "insulted." The words or act put forward as provocation need not be words or act which are specifically prohibited by the law.

30 Thus, while the actions of the deceased in the parking lot were clearly not prohibited by law, they could nonetheless be found by a jury to constitute insulting behaviour. In light of the past history, possessive or affectionate behaviour by the deceased towards the appellant's wife coupled with his taunting remarks could be considered to be insulting. A jury

could infer that it was the taunting of the appellant by the deceased, who was preventing him from talking privately with his wife, which was the last straw that led him to fire the rifle suddenly before his passion had cooled. While the deceased's conduct might not have been specifically prohibited nor susceptible to a remedy, it was not sanctioned by any legal right.

31 In summary, there was some evidence upon which a reasonable jury acting judicially and properly instructed could find that the defence of provocation was applicable. It was appropriate for the trial judge to leave his defence with the jury. Once it was determined the defence should be left, then the trial judge was required to correctly relate the principles of reasonable doubt as they applied to that defence.

Some General Comments

THE EFFECT OF LEAVING THE DEFENCE OF PROVOCATION WITH THE JURY

32 It must be remembered that to find that there was evidence which justified leaving the defence to the jury is far from concluding that the jury should or would act upon that evidence. The defence is simply something that the jury will have to assess. The great good sense of jurors will undoubtedly lead them to consider all the facts, including the presence of the loaded gun in the car. Further, it must be remembered that the defence of provocation goes no farther than to reduce the conviction for murder to one of manslaughter. This is hardly an insignificant crime when it is remembered that life imprisonment can be imposed as punishment.

Disposition

35 In the result, I would allow the appeal, set aside the decision of the Court of Appeal and direct a new trial on the charge of second degree murder.

Appeal allowed; new trial ordered.

Lavallee v. The Queen

SUPREME COURT OF CANADA   MAY 3, 1990

BACKGROUND

At her trial in the Manitoba Court of Queen's Bench, Lavallee was acquitted by a jury of a charge of murder. The Crown appealed the accused's acquittal to the Manitoba Court of Appeal, which overturned the jury's verdict and ordered a new trial. Lavallee appealed against the Court of Appeal's judgment to the Supreme Court of Canada.

MAIN ISSUES

(1) Was the trial judge correct when he permitted the introduction of expert evidence concerning the so-called "battered-wife syndrome" in order to assist the jury in their task of determining whether the accused acted in self-defence, under the provisions of section 34(2) of the Criminal Code? (2) Did the trial judge provide the jury with adequate instructions concerning the extent to which they should rely on such expert testimony?

JUDGMENTS

The *majority* judgment was delivered by Justice Wilson (with whom Chief Justice Dickson and Justices Lamer, L'Heureux-Dubé, Gonthier, and McLachlin agreed). Justice Sopinka delivered a *concurring* judgment, which has been omitted.

WILSON J.: —

1. The Facts

The appellant, who was 22 years old at the time, had been living with Kevin Rust for some three to four years. Their residence was the scene of a boisterous party on August 30, 1986. In the early hours of August 31st after most of the guests had departed, the appellant and Rust had an argument in the upstairs bedroom, which was used by the appellant. Rust was killed by a single shot in the back of the head from a .303 calibre rifle fired by the appellant as he was leaving the room.

The appellant did not testify, but her statement made to police on the night of the shooting was put in evidence. Portions of it read as follows:

> I went upstairs and hid in my closet from Kevin. I was so scared . . . My window was open and I could hear Kevin asking questions about what I was doing and what I was saying. Next thing I know, he was coming up the stairs for me. He came into my bedroom and said, "Wench, where are you?" And he turned on my light and he said, "Your purse is on the floor" and he kicked it. OK, then he turned and he saw me in the closet. He wanted me to come out but I didn't want to come

out because I was scared. He grabbed me by the arm right there. There's a bruise on my face also where he slapped me. He didn't slap me right then; first he yelled at me, then he pushed me and I pushed him back and he hit me twice on the right-hand side of my head. I was scared. All I thought about was all the other times he used to beat me. I was scared. I was shaking as usual. The rest is a blank. All I remember is he gave me the gun and a shot was fired through my screen. This is all so fast. And then the guns were in another room and he loaded it the second shot and gave it to me. And I was going to shoot myself. I pointed it to myself, I was so upset. OK and then he went and I was sitting on the bed and he started going like this with his finger [the appellant made a shaking motion with an index finger] and said something like "You're my old lady and you do as you're told" or something like that. He said, "Wait till everybody leaves, you'll get it then," and he said something to the effect of "Either you kill me or I'll get you" — that was what it was. He kind of smiled and then he turned around. I shot him but I aimed out. I thought I aimed above him and a piece of his head went that way.

The relationship between the appellant and Rust was volatile and punctuated by frequent arguments and violence. They would apparently fight for two or three days at a time or several times a week. Considerable evidence was led at trial indicating that the appellant was frequently a victim of physical abuse at the hands of Rust. Between 1983 and 1986, the appellant made several trips to hospital for injuries including severe bruises, a fractured nose, multiple contusions, and a black eye.

At one point on the night of his death, Rust chased the appellant outside the house, and a mutual friend, Norman Kolish, testified that the appellant pleaded with Rust to "leave me alone" and sought Kolish's protection by trying to hide behind him. A neighbour overheard Rust and the appellant arguing and described the tone of the former as "argumentative" and the latter as "scared."

Later, between the first and second gunshot, he testified that he could hear that "somebody was beating up somebody" and the screams were female. Another neighbour testified to hearing noises like gunshots and then a woman's voice sounding upset saying, "Fuck. He punched me in the face. He punched me in the face." He looked out the window and saw a woman matching the description of the appellant.

Three witnesses who attended the party testified to hearing sounds of yelling, pushing, shoving, and thumping coming from upstairs prior to the gunshots. It is not disputed that two shots were fired by the appellant. The first one went through a window screen. It is not clear where Rust was at the time. The appellant in her statement says that he was upstairs, while another witness places him in the basement. The second shot was the fatal one. The arresting officer testified that en route to the police station the appellant made various comments in the police car, including "He said if I didn't kill him first, he would kill me. I hope he lives. I really love him," and "He told me he was gonna kill me when everyone left."

The expert evidence which forms the subject matter of the appeal came from Dr. Fred Shane, a psychiatrist with extensive professional experience in the treatment of battered wives. At the request of defence counsel, Dr. Shane prepared a psychiatric assessment of the appellant. The substance of Dr. Shane's opinion was that the appellant had been terrorized by Rust to the point of feeling trapped, vulnerable, worthless, and unable to escape the relationship despite the violence. At the same time, the continuing pattern of abuse put her life in danger. In Dr. Shane's opinion, the appellant's shooting of the deceased was a final desperate act by a woman who sincerely believed that she would be killed that night.

Dr. Shane stated that his opinion was based on four hours of formal interviews with the appellant, a police report of the incident (including the appellant's statement), hospital reports documenting eight of her visits to emergency departments between 1983 and 1985, and an interview with the appellant's mother. In the course of his testimony, Dr. Shane related many things told to him by the appellant, for which there was no admissible evidence. They were not in the appellant's statement to the police and she did not testify at trial.

4. Issues on Appeal

The issues before this court are as follows:

1. Did the majority of the Manitoba Court of Appeal err in concluding that the jury should have considered the plea of self-defence absent the expert evidence of Dr. Shane?
2. Did the majority of the Manitoba Court of Appeal err in holding that the trial judge's charge to the jury with respect to Dr. Shane's expert evidence did not meet the requirements set out by this court in *Abbey*, thus warranting a new trial?

5. Analysis

(i) Admissibility of Expert Evidence

This court addressed the admissibility of expert psychiatric evidence in criminal cases in *R. v. Abbey, supra*, (1982), 68 C.C.C. (2d) 394 (S.C.C.). At p. 409 of the unanimous judgment, Dickson J. (as he then was) stated the rule as follows:

> With respect to matters calling for special knowledge, an expert in the field may draw inferences and state his opinion. An expert's function is precisely this: to provide the judge and jury with a ready-made inference which the judge and jury, due to the technical nature of the facts, are unable to formulate. "An expert's opinion is admissible to furnish the Court with scientific information which is likely to be outside the experience and knowledge of a judge or jury. If on the proven facts a judge or jury can form their own conclusions without help, then the opinion of the expert is unnecessary."

Where expert evidence is tendered in such fields as engineering or pathology, the paucity of the lay person's knowledge is uncontentious. The long-standing recognition that psychiatric or psychological testimony also falls within the realm of expert evidence is predicated on the realization that in some circumstances the average person may not have sufficient knowledge of or experience with human behaviour to draw an appropriate inference from the facts before him or her.

The need for expert evidence in these areas can, however, be obfuscated by the belief that judges and juries are thoroughly knowledgeable about "human nature" and that no more is needed. They are, so to speak, their own experts on human behaviour. This, in effect, was the primary submission of the Crown to this court.

The bare facts of this case, which I think are amply supported by the evidence, are that the appellant was repeatedly abused by the deceased but did not leave him (although she twice pointed a gun at him), and ultimately shot him in the back of the head as he was leaving her room. The Crown submits that these facts disclose all the information a jury needs in order to decide whether or not the appellant acted in self-defence. I have no hesitation in rejecting the Crown's submission.

Expert evidence on the psychological effect of battering on wives and common law partners must, it seems to me, be both relevant and necessary in the context of the present case. How can the mental state of the appellant be appreciated without it? The average member of the public (or of the jury) can be forgiven for asking: Why would a woman put up with this kind of treatment? Why should she continue to live with such a man? How could she love a partner who beat her to the point of requiring hospitalization? We would expect the woman to pack her bags and go. Where is her self-respect? Why does she not cut loose and make a new life for herself? Such is the reaction of the average person confronted with the so-called "battered wife syndrome." We need help to understand it and help is available from trained professionals.

Expert testimony on the psychological effects of battering have been admitted in American courts in recent years. In *State v. Kelly*, 478 A.2d 364, at p. 378 (1984), the New Jersey Supreme Court commended the value of expert testimony in these terms:

> It is aimed at an area where the purported common knowledge of the jury may be very much mistaken, an area where jurors' logic, drawn from their own experience, may lead to a wholly incorrect conclusion, an area where expert knowledge would enable the jurors to disregard their prior conclusions as being common myths rather than common knowledge.

The court concludes at p. 379 that the battering relationship is "subject to a large group of myths and stereotypes." As such, it is "beyond the ken of the average juror and thus is suitable for explanation through expert testimony." I share that view.

(ii) The Relevance of Expert Testimony to the Elements of Self-Defence

In my view, there are two elements of the defence under s. 34(2) of the Code which merit scrutiny for present purposes. The first is the temporal connection in s. 34(2)(a) between the apprehension of death or grievous bodily harm and the act allegedly taken in self-defence. Was the appellant "under reasonable apprehension of death or grievous bodily harm" from Rust as he was walking out of the room? The second is the assessment in s. 34(2)(b) of the magnitude of the force used by the accused. Was the accused's belief that she could not "otherwise preserve herself from death or grievous bodily harm" except by shooting the deceased based "on reasonable grounds"?

The feature common to both para. (a) and para. (b) is the imposition of an objective standard of reasonableness on the apprehension of death and the need to repel the assault with deadly force. If it strains credulity to imagine what the "ordinary man" would do in the position of a battered spouse, it is probably because men do not typically find themselves in that situation. Some women do, however. The definition of what is reasonable must be adapted to circumstances which are, by and large, foreign to the world inhabited by the hypothetical "reasonable man."

A. REASONABLE APPREHENSION OF DEATH

Section 34(2)(a) requires that an accused who intentionally causes death or grievous bodily harm in repelling an assault is justified if he or she does so "under reasonable apprehension of death or grievous bodily harm." In the present case, the assault precipitating the appellant's alleged defensive act was Rust's threat to kill her when everyone else had gone.

It will be observed that s. 34(2)(a) does not actually stipulate that the accused apprehend *imminent* danger when he or she acts. Case law has, however, read that requirement into the defence. The sense in which "imminent" is used conjures up the image of "an uplifted knife" or a pointed gun. The rationale for the imminence rule seems obvious. The law of self-defence is designed to ensure that the use of defensive force is really necessary. It justifies the act because the defender reasonably believed that he or she had no alternative but to take the attacker's life. If there is a significant time interval between the original unlawful assault and the accused's response, one tends to suspect that the accused was motivated by revenge rather than self-defence. In the paradigmatic case of a one-time bar-room brawl between two men of equal size and strength, this inference makes sense. How can one feel endangered to the point of firing a gun at an unarmed man who utters a death threat, then turns his back and walks out of the room? One cannot be certain of the gravity of the threat or his capacity to carry it out. Besides, one can always take the opportunity to flee or to call the police. If he comes back and raises his fist, one can respond in kind if need be. These are the tacit assumptions that underlie the imminence rule.

In my view, expert testimony can cast doubt on these assumptions as they are applied in the context of a battered wife's efforts to repel an assault.

The appellant was routinely beaten over the course of her relationship with the man she ultimately killed. According to the testimony of Dr. Shane, these assaults were not entirely random in their occurrence. The following exchange during direct examination elicited a discernible pattern to the abuse:

Q. How did they react during the tension that preceded the beatings? How would her. . .

A. Well, typically before a beating there's usually some verbal interchange and there are threats and typically she would feel, you know, very threatened by him and for various reasons.

He didn't like the way she dressed or if she — didn't like the way she handled money or she wasn't paying him enough attention or she was looking at other men, all sorts of reasons, and she would be defending herself, trying to placate him, which was typical, saying, you know, trying to calm him down, trying to soothe him, you know, so nothing violent would happen and sometimes it would work. You know, as people's experiences indicated or as people who write about this process, if you will, have indicated.

But often, as reflected by what she has told me, and the information I have from other people, such as her mother, often it would fail and she would end up being beaten and assaulted.

Q. And that would be followed by this forgiveness state?

A. It typically would be followed by, you know, this make-up period.

Earlier in his testimony Dr. Shane explained how this "make-up" period would be characterized by contrite and affectionate behaviour by Rust:

In this particular case, she documented many times, after he would beat her, he would send her flowers and he would beg her for forgiveness and he would love her and then the relationship would come back to a sense of equilibrium, if you will. . .But then, because of the nature of the personalities, it would occur again.

The cycle described by Dr. Shane conforms to the Walker Cycle Theory of Violence named for clinical psychologist Dr. Lenore Walker, the pioneer researcher in the field of the battered wife syndrome. At pp. 95–6 of Walker's *The Battered Woman Syndrome* (1984), she summarizes the Cycle Theory as follows:

A second major theory that was tested in this project is the Walker Cycle Theory of Violence (Walker, 1979). This tension reduction theory states that there are three distinct phases associated in a recurring battering cycle: (1) tension building, (2) the acute battering incident, and (3) loving contrition.

Dr. Walker defines a battered woman as a woman who has gone through the battering cycle at least twice.

Given the relational context in which the violence occurs, the mental state of an accused at the critical moment she pulls the trigger cannot be understood except in terms of the cumulative effect of months or years of brutality.

Another aspect of the cyclical nature of the abuse is that it begets a degree of predictability to the violence that is absent in an isolated violent encounter between two strangers. This also means that it may in fact be possible for a battered spouse to accurately predict the onset of violence before the first blow is struck, even if an outsider to the relationship cannot. Indeed, it has been suggested that a battered woman's knowledge of her partner's violence is so heightened that she is able to anticipate the nature and extent (though not the onset) of the violence by his conduct beforehand.

According to the appellant's statement to police, Rust actually handed her a shotgun and warned her that if she did not kill him, he would kill her. I note, in passing, a remarkable observation made by Dr. Walker in her 1984 study, *The Battered Woman Syndrome*. Writing about the fifty battered women she interviewed who had killed their partners, she comments at p. 40:

> Most of the time the women killed the men with a gun; usually one of several that belonged to him. *Many of the men actually dared or demanded the woman use the gun on him first, or else he said he'd kill her with it.*

(Emphasis added.)

Where evidence exists that an accused is in a battering relationship, expert testimony can assist the jury in determining whether the accused had a "reasonable" apprehension of death when she acted by explaining the heightened sensitivity of a battered woman to her partner's acts. Without such testimony I am skeptical that the average fact-finder would be capable of appreciating why her subjective fear may have been reasonable in the context of the relationship. After all, the hypothetical "reasonable man" observing only the final incident may have been unlikely to recognize the batterer's threat as potentially lethal.

The issue is not, however, what an outsider would have reasonably perceived but what the accused reasonably perceived, given her situation and her experience.

Even accepting that a battered woman may be uniquely sensitized to danger from her batterer, it may yet be contended that the law ought to require her to wait until the knife is uplifted, the gun pointed, or the fist clenched before her apprehension is deemed reasonable. This would allegedly reduce the risk that the woman is mistaken in her fear, although the law does not require her fear to be correct, only reasonable. In response to this contention, I need only point to the observation made by Huband J.A. that the evidence showed that when the appellant and Rust physically fought, the appellant "invariably got the worst of it." I do not think it is an unwarranted generalization to say that due to their size, strength, socialization, and lack of training, women are typically no match for men in hand-to-hand combat. The requirement imposed in *R. v. Whynot* (1983), 9 C.C.C. 449, 37 C.R.

(3d) 198, 61 N.S.R. (2d) 33 (C.A.), that a battered woman wait until the physical assault is "underway" before her apprehensions can be validated in law would, in the words of an American court, be tantamount to sentencing her to "murder by installment": *State v. Gallegos*, 719 P.2d 1268 at p. 1271 (1986) (N.M.).

B. LACK OF ALTERNATIVES TO SELF-HELP

Section 34(2) requires an accused who pleads self-defence to believe "on reasonable grounds" that it is not possible to otherwise preserve him or herself from death or grievous bodily harm. The obvious question is, if the violence was so intolerable, why did the appellant not leave her abuser long ago? This question does not really go to whether she had an alternative to killing the deceased at the critical moment. Rather, it plays on the popular myth already referred to that a woman who says she was battered yet stayed with her batterer was either not as badly beaten as she claimed or else she liked it. Nevertheless, to the extent that her failure to leave the abusive relationship earlier may be used in support of the proposition that she was free to leave at the final moment, expert testimony can provide useful insights. Dr. Shane attempted to explain in his testimony how and why, in the case at bar, the appellant remained with Rust:

> She had stayed in this relationship, I think, because of the strange, almost unbelievable, but yet it happens, relationship that sometimes develops between people who develop this very disturbed, I think, very disturbed quality of a relationship.
>
> The spouse who becomes battered, if you will, stays in the relationship probably because of a number of reasons.
>
> One is that the spouse gets beaten so badly — so badly — that he or she loses the motivation to react and becomes helpless and becomes powerless.
>
> It's almost like a concentration camp, if you will. You get paralyzed with fear.

The other thing that happens often in these types of relationships with human beings is that the person who beats or assaults, who batters, often tries — he makes up and begs for forgiveness. And this individual, who basically has a very disturbed or damaged self-esteem, all of a sudden feels that he or she — we'll use women in this case because it's so much more common — the spouse feels that she again can do the spouse a favour and it can make her feel needed and boost her self-esteem for a while and make her feel worthwhile and the spouse says he'll forgive her and whatnot.

Apparently, another manifestation of this victimization is a reluctance to disclose to others the fact or extent of the beatings. For example, the hospital records indicate that on each occasion the appellant attended the emergency department to be treated for various injuries, she explained the cause of those injuries as accidental. In his testimony Dr. Shane testified that the apellant admitted to him that she lied to hospital staff and others about the cause of her injuries. In Dr. Shane's opinion this was consistant with her over-all feeling of being trapped and helpless.

The account given by Dr. Shane comports with that documented in the literature. Reference is often made to it as a condition of "learned helplessness," a phrase coined by Dr. Charles Seligman, the psychologist who first developed the theory by experimenting on animals in the manner described by Dr. Shane in his testimony. A related theory used to explain the failure of women to leave battering relationships is described by psychologist and lawyer Charles Patrick Ewing in his book *Battered Women Who Kill* (1987). Ewing describes a phenomenon labelled "traumatic bonding" that has been observed between hostages and captors, battered children and their parents, concentration camp prisoners and guards, and batterers and their spouses. At pp. 19–20, he states:

> Given the clear power differential between battered women and their batterers and the intermittent nature of physical and psychological

abuse common to battering relationships, it seems fair to conclude. . . that many battered women are psychologically unable to leave their batterers because they have developed a traumatic bond with them.

This strong "affective bond" may be helpful in explaining not only why some battered women remain with their abusers but why they even profess to love them. Of course, as Dr. Ewing adds, environmental factors may also impair the woman's ability to leave — lack of job skills, the presence of children to care for, fear of retaliation by the man, etc., may each have a role to play in some cases.

I emphasize at this juncture that it is not for the jury to pass judgment on the fact that an accused battered woman stayed in the relationship. Still less is it entitled to conclude that she forfeited her right to self-defence for having done so. I would also point out that traditional self-defence doctrine does not require a person to retreat from her home instead of defending herself. A man's home may be his castle but it is also the woman's home even if it seems to her more like a prison in the circumstances.

The situation of the battered woman as described by Dr. Shane strikes me as somewhat analogous to that of a hostage. If the captor tells her that he will kill her in three days' time, is it potentially reasonable for her to seize an opportunity presented on the first day to kill the captor, or must she wait until he makes the attempt on the third day? I think the question the jury must ask itself is whether, given the history, circumstances, and perceptions of the appellant, her belief that she could not preserve herself from being killed by Rust that night except by killing him first was reasonable. To the extent that expert evidence can assist the jury in making that determination, I would find such testimony to be both relevant and necessary.

In light of the foregoing discussion, I would summarize as follows the principles upon which expert testimony is properly admitted in cases such as this:

1. Expert testimony is admissible to assist the fact-finder in drawing inferences in areas where the expert has relevant knowledge or experience beyond that of the lay person.
2. It is difficult for the lay person to comprehend the battered wife syndrome. It is commonly thought that battered women are not really beaten as badly as they claim, otherwise they would have left the relationship. Alternatively, some believe that women enjoy being beaten, that they have a masochist strain in them. Each of these stereotypes may adversely affect consideration of a battered woman's claim to have acted in self-defence in killing her mate.
3. Expert evidence can assist the jury in dispelling these myths.
4. Expert testimony relating to the ability of an accused to perceive danger from her mate may go to the issue of whether she "reasonably apprehended" death or grievous bodily harm on a particular occasion.
5. Expert testimony pertaining to why an accused remained in the battering relationship may be relevant in assessing the nature and extent of the alleged abuse.
6. By providing an explanation as to why an accused did not flee when she perceived her life to be in danger, expert testimony may also assist the jury in assessing the reasonableness of her belief that killing her batterer was the only way to save her own life.

Quite apart from Dr. Shane's testimony, there was ample evidence on which the trial judge could conclude that the appellant was battered repeatedly and brutally by Kevin Rust over the course of their relationship. The fact that she may have exhibited aggressive behaviour on occasion or tried (unsuccessfully) to leave does not detract from a finding of systematic and relentless abuse. In my view, the trial judge did not err in admitting Dr. Shane's expert testimony in order to assist the jury in determining whether the appellant had a reasonable apprehension of death or grievous bodily harm and believed on reasonable grounds that she had no alternative but to shoot Kevin Rust on the night in question.

Obviously the fact that the appellant was a battered woman does not entitle her to an acquittal. Battered women may well kill their partners other than in self-defence. The focus is not on who the woman is, but on what she did.

Ultimately, it is up to the jury to decide whether, *in fact*, the accused's perceptions and actions were reasonable. Expert evidence does not and cannot usurp that function of the jury. The jury is not compelled to accept the opinions proffered by the expert about the effects of battering on the mental state of victims generally or on the mental state of the accused in particular. But fairness and the integrity of the trial process demand that the jury have the opportunity to hear them.

(iii) Adequacy of Trial Judge's Charge to the Jury

The second issue raised in this case is the adequacy of the trial judge's charge to the jury with respect to the expert evidence furnished by Dr. Shane. It appears that Dr. Shane relied on various sources in formulating his opinion — his series of interviews with the appellant, an interview with her mother, a police report of the incident (including information regarding her statement to the police), and hospital records documenting eight of her visits to emergency departments between 1983 and 1986. Neither the appellant nor her mother testified at trial. The contents of their statements to Dr. Shane were hearsay.

In the case at bar the trial judge was clearly of the view that Dr. Shane's evidence was relevant. He would not have admitted it otherwise. As I stated above, in light of the evidence of the battering relationship which subsisted between the appellant and the deceased, the trial judge was correct in so doing.

With respect to the second point, the trial judge warned the jury generally that they could not "decide the case on the basis of things the witnesses did not see or hear," which would seem to include those matters which Dr. Shane neither saw nor heard.

The trial judge's instructions regarding the weight attributable to Dr. Shane's opinion also emphasize his distinction between admissible evidence and hearsay:

> *If the premises upon which the information is substantially based has not been proven in evidence, it is up to you to conclude that it is not safe to attach a great deal of weight to the opinion. An opinion of an expert depends, to a large extent, on the validity of the facts assumed by the evidence of the expert.*
>
> If there are some errors and the factual assumptions aren't too important to the eventual opinion, that's one thing. *If there are errors or matters not in evidence and those matters are substantial, in your view, in terms of the impact on the expert's opinion, then you will want to look at the value and weight of that expert's opinion very carefully.* It depends on how important you think the matters were that Dr. Shane relied on that are not in evidence.

(Emphasis added.)

Given that Dr. Shane relied extensively on his interview with the appellant, the trial judge drew particular attention to the additional element of credibility that could affect the quality of Dr. Shane's opinion: "It is the position of the Crown that Dr. Shane's opinion stands or falls on the veracity of Lyn Lavallee because he relied so heavily and extensively on what she told him and the evidence contained in the statement, Exhibit 16. That's for you to decide."

In my view, as long as there is some admissible evidence to establish the foundation for the expert's opinion, the trial judge cannot subsequently instruct the jury to completely ignore the testimony. The judge must, of course, warn the jury that the more the expert relies on facts not proved in evidence the less weight the jury may attribute to the opinion.

On my reading of the record, Dr. Shane had before him admissible evidence about the nature of the relationship between the appellant and Rust in the form of the appellant's statement to the police and the hospital records. In addition, there was substantial corroborative evidence provided at trial by Ezako, the emergency room doctor who testified to doubting the appellant's explanation of her injuries. There was also the evidence of the witnesses on the night of the shooting who testified to the appellant's frightened appearance, tone of voice, and conduct in dealing with Rust. The evidence pointed to the image of a woman who was brutally abused, who lied about the cause of her injuries, and who was incapable of leaving her abuser.

Where the factual basis of an expert's opinion is a mélange of admissible and inadmissible evidence, the duty of the trial judge is to caution the jury that the weight attributable to the expert testimony is directly related to the amount and quality of admissible evidence on which it relies. The trial judge openly acknowledged to counsel the inherent difficulty in discharging such a duty in the case at bar. In my view, the trial judge performed his task adequately in this regard. A new trial is not warranted on the basis of the trial judge's charge to the jury.

I would accordingly allow the appeal, set aside the order of the Court of Appeal, and restore the acquittal.

Appeal allowed; acquittal restored.

Regina v. Pétel

SUPREME COURT OF CANADA   JANUARY 20, 1994

BACKGROUND

Following the shooting death of an associate of her daughter's boyfriend, Pétel was charged with second degree murder. At her trial, Pétel was convicted of murder by a jury. She appealed against her conviction to the Québec Court of Appeal, which allowed her appeal and ordered a new trial. The Crown subsequently appealed to the Supreme Court of Canada against the judgment of the Court of Appeal.

MAIN ISSUE

Did the trial judge err when, in the context of Pétel's assertion that she acted in self-defence under section 34(2) of the Criminal Code, he responded to a question from the members of the jury as to whether they should differentiate between threats made to Pétel over a period of several months before the date of the fatal shooting and threats made on the actual evening of its occurrence?

JUDGMENTS

The *majority* judgment was delivered by Chief Justice Lamer (with whom Justices Sopinka, Cory, McLachlin, and Iacobucci agreed). The *dissenting*

judgment of Justice Gonthier (with whom Justices La Forest, L'Heureux-Dubé, and Major agreed) has been omitted.

....

LAMER C.J.C.: —

I. Facts

The respondent Colette Pétel is charged with the second degree murder of Alain Raymond. She is the mother of Josée Desjardins, who, at the time of the alleged offence, was Serge Edsell's girlfriend. Edsell and Raymond were jointly involved in drug trafficking.

Josée Desjardins and Serge Edsell met and began living together in March, 1989. In early May, after being evicted from the apartment where they were living, they moved in temporarily with the respondent. In her testimony the respondent described the terrible existence caused by Edsell's presence in her house, the fact that he was engaged in drug trafficking there and the comings and goings of his customers in the house. She said that Edsell was always angry, that he threatened her frequently, and that he beat his girlfriend, Josée Desjardins. The respondent even tried to commit suicide. However, this version of the facts was contradicted by the testimony of Josée Desjardins at the preliminary inquiry. (Desjardins was killed before the trial and so could not testify at it.) She denied that she had ever been beaten by Edsell.

In early July, the respondent moved in order to put an end to Edsell's presence in her house. This was unsuccessful, as Edsell continued to go to the respondent's home to conduct his drug trafficking operations.

On July 21, Edsell went to the respondent's home with a revolver, cocaine, and scales. He asked her to hide the weapon. He forced her to weigh some cocaine and then suggested he would kill her, together with her daughter and granddaughter. Shortly afterwards, Josée Desjardins arrived accompanied by Alain Raymond. At this point the respondent consumed a small amount of drugs and then went to get the weapon she had hidden in the bathroom. She fired at Edsell, who fell at once. Seeing that Raymond was lunging at her, she also fired at him. Edsell survived but Raymond died of his injuries. Josée Desjardins' version of the facts was slightly different. She said that the respondent fired on Edsell and then aimed at her own daughter. Raymond then tried to escape and that is when the respondent also shot him.

In her statements to the police immediately after these events, the respondent admitted firing at Edsell and Raymond and said she wished both of them dead.

V. Analysis

A. Elements of Self-Defence

The law on self-defence has often been criticized for its complexity and lack of coherence. When the courts interpret the provisions of the Criminal Code, they should therefore try to confine themselves to general principles and not unnecessarily create complex rules and subtle distinctions.

It can be seen from the wording of s. 34(2) of the Code that there are three constituent elements of self-defence, when as here the victim has died: (1) the existence of an unlawful assault; (2) a reasonable apprehension of a risk of death or grievous

bodily harm; and (3) a reasonable belief that it is not possible to preserve oneself from harm except by killing the adversary.

In all three cases the jury must seek to determine how the accused perceived the relevant facts and whether that perception was reasonable. Accordingly, this is an objective determination. With respect to the last two elements, this approach results from the language used in the Code and was confirmed by this court in *R. v. Reilly* (1984), 15 C.C.C. (3d) 1 at pp. 7–8, 13 D.L.R. (4th) 161, [1984] 2 S.C.R. 396:

> The subsection can only afford protection to the accused if he apprehended death or grievous bodily harm from the assault he was repelling and if he believed he could not preserve himself from death or grievous bodily harm otherwise than by the force he used. Nonetheless, his apprehension must be a *reasonable* one and his belief must *be based upon reasonable and probable grounds*. The subsection requires that the jury consider, and be guided by, what they decide, on the evidence, was the accused's appreciation of the situation and his belief as to the reaction it required, so long as there exists an objectively verifiable basis for his perception.

(Emphasis in original.)

Some doubt may still exist as to whether this passage from *Reilly* also applies to the existence of an assault. For my part, I think that the word "situation" refers to the three elements of s. 34(2). An honest but reasonable mistake as to the existence of an assault is therefore permitted. The existence of an assault must not be made a kind of prerequisite for the exercise of self-defence to be assessed without regard to the perception of the accused. This would amount in a sense to trying the victim before the accused. In a case involving self-defence, it is the accused's state of mind that must be examined, and it is the accused (and not the victim) who must be given the benefit of a reasonable doubt. The question that the jury must ask itself is therefore not "was the accused unlawfully assaulted?";

but rather "did the accused reasonably believe, in the circumstances, that she was being unlawfully assaulted?"

Moreover, *R. v. Lavallee* (1990), 55 C.C.C. (3d) 97, [1990] 1 S.C.R. 852, 76 C.R. (3d) 329, rejected the rule requiring that the apprehended danger be imminent. This alleged rule, which does not appear anywhere in the text of the Criminal Code, is in fact only a mere assumption based on common sense. As Wilson J. noted in *Lavallee*, this assumption undoubtedly derives from the paradigmatic case of self-defence, which is an altercation between two persons of equal strength. However, evidence may be presented (in particular, expert evidence) to rebut this presumption of fact. There is thus no formal requirement that the danger be imminent. Imminence is only one of the factors which the jury should weigh in determining whether the accused had a reasonable apprehension of danger and a reasonable belief that she could not extricate herself otherwise than by killing the attacker.

B. Charge to the Jury

In his charge the trial judge reiterated the three elements indicated by the wording of s. 34(2) of the Criminal Code, namely the existence of an assault, the apprehension of a danger of death or grievous bodily harm, and the impossibility of otherwise extricating oneself. He added that the accused must have intended to cause her attacker's death. Although it is not strictly speaking an element of self-defence, this fourth criterion was justified in the circumstances since this was a murder charge. In any event, the respondent does not deny that she intended to cause the death of Edsell and Raymond.

The judge also said that the jury should try to determine how the accused assessed the situation and compare that assessment with what a reasonable person placed in the same circumstances would have thought. To explain this, the judge repeated almost word for word two paragraphs from *Reilly*.

The judge then went on to summarize the main points in the evidence which could support the respondent's defence. He did not limit the relevance of a particular piece of evidence to its effect on only one of the elements of self-defence. Accordingly, one may conclude that the jury must have understood that they were to look at the evidence as a whole in considering each element of self-defence. This is exactly what s. 34(2) of the Criminal Code requires. Thus no fault may be found in the main charge given by the trial judge, a judge of great experience; on the contrary, it could serve as a model.

The same is not true, however, of the answer given by the judge to the question put to him by the jury regarding the relevance of the threats immediately preceding the incident of July 21st and the threats prior to that date.

The question asked by the jury was specific, as the jury had identified its concern: the threats made by the victim in the months preceding the incident and those made on the day itself and, it can be assumed, the distinction that should be made between the two types of threat or act. The question was general, however, in the sense that the jury did not indicate whether its concern related only to one element of self-defence. The question concerned the "definition of self-defence," without more detail. The judge nonetheless limited his answer to only one of the elements, the existence of an assault and the assailant's ability to carry it out. This led him to make two errors.

First, the judge's answer suggested that the only relevance of the threats prior to July 21st was in enabling the jury to determine whether there had actually been an assault on the evening of July 21st, that is, in the present case, death threats, and whether the assailant was in a position to carry out those threats. In a way, the judge treated the earlier threats like similar fact evidence of the present threats. Their only use would then be to make it more plausible that Edsell also made threats in the minutes preceding the shots fired by the accused. This, in my view, diverted the jury from the question it really should have been considering, namely the reasonable belief of the accused in the existence of an assault. Emphasizing the victims' acts rather than the accused's state of mind has the effect of depriving the latter of the benefit of any error, however reasonable. The jury's attention should not be diverted from its proper concern, the guilt of the accused, by an inquiry into the guilt of the victim.

Secondly, and this is the crucial point, the judge's answer might have led the jury to believe that the threats made before July 21st could serve no other purpose than to determine the existence of the assault and the assailant's ability, thus denying their relevance to reasonable apprehension of a danger of death or grievous bodily harm and to the belief that there was no solution but to kill the attacker. The judge said that the previous threats served to [translation] "assess the assault on the evening of July 21." He then explained what "assess the assault" meant (translation):

> . . . these previous acts or threats help you to determine whether Alain Raymond and Serge Edsell attempted or threatened . . . to apply force to Mrs. Pétel . . . *whether* the assailant had or caused . . . the alleged victim to believe on reasonable grounds that he had present ability to effect his purpose.

(Emphasis added.) The judge was in fact here repeating almost exactly the wording of s. 265(1)(b) of the Criminal Code. Although it is true that the previous threats can help the jury to decide *whether* threats were made immediately before the respondent shot Edsell and Raymond, they are also very relevant in determining what the respondent believed, not only concerning the existence of the threats, but also concerning her apprehension of the risk of death and her belief in the need to use deadly force. By failing to mention these two elements in his answer, the trial judge seriously limited the relevance of the earlier threats. In explaining how these threats could be used, he should actually have referred not only to s. 265(1)(b) but also, most importantly, to s. 34(2) of the Code.

The importance of failing to relate the earlier threats to the elements of self-defence cannot be underestimated. The threats made by Edsell throughout his cohabitation with the respondent are very relevant in determining whether the respondent had a reasonable apprehension of danger and a reasonable belief in the need to kill Edsell and Raymond. The threats prior to July 21st form an integral part of the circumstances on which the perception of the accused might have been based. The judge's answer to this question might thus have led the jury to disregard the entire atmosphere of terror which the respondent said pervaded her house. It is clear that the way in which a reasonable person would have acted cannot be assessed without taking into account these crucial circumstances. As Wilson J. noted in *Lavallee*, at p. 120: "The issue is not, however, what an outsider would have reasonably perceived but what the accused reasonably perceived, given her situation and her experience." By unduly limiting the relevance of the previous threats, the judge in a sense invited the jury to determine what an outsider would have done in the same situation as the respondent.

VI. Conclusion

The undisputed evidence that Edsell, her alleged attacker, handed over his weapon and asked his future victim to hide it, conduct that is odd, to say the least, for someone intending to kill, must have had a clear effect on the jury, indeed on any jury composed of reasonable individuals. In the Court of Appeal and in this court, however, counsel for the Crown did not argue that, given the evidence in this case, no substantial wrong or miscarriage of justice occurred, and that s. 686(1)(b)(iii) of the Criminal Code should thus be applied. The Crown has the burden of showing that this provision is applicable: *Colpitts v. The Queen*, [1966] 1 C.C.C. 146, 52 D.L.R. (2d) 416, [1965] S.C.R. 739. This court cannot apply it *proprio motu*. Having found an error of law in the judge's answer to the question by the jury, I must accordingly dismiss the appeal and affirm the order for a new trial.

Appeal dismissed.

Jobidon v. The Queen

SUPREME COURT OF CANADA   SEPTEMBER 26, 1991

BACKGROUND

At his trial, Jobidon was acquitted on a charge of manslaughter. The Crown appealed against the acquittal to the Ontario Court of Appeal which allowed the appeal, set aside the acquittal, and substituted a verdict of guilty on the manslaughter charge. Jobidon subsequently appealed to the Supreme Court of Canada against the judgment of the Court of Appeal.

MAIN ISSUE

Could the accused claim that the consent of the victim to engage in a fist fight constitutes a valid defence to a charge of assault or a charge of (unlawful act) manslaughter?

JUDGMENTS

The *majority* judgment was delivered by Justice Gonthier (with whom Justices La Forest, L'Heureux-Dubé, Cory, and Iacobucci agreed). The judgment of Justice Sopinka (with whom Justice Stevenson agreed) has been omitted.

GONTHIER J.: —

I. Statement of Facts

The appellant, Jules Jobidon, was charged with manslaughter for the unlawful act of killing Rodney Haggart — through the offence of assault (alternatively, through an act of criminal negligence). The incident leading to the charge was a fist fight between the two men, in a parking lot outside a hotel near Sudbury, Ontario, on September 19, 1986. At the date of the killing, Rodney Haggart was 25 years old.

The two men initiated their aggression in the bar of the hotel. With his brother and a few friends, Haggart was celebrating his impending marriage. He approached Jobidon, who was also in the hotel with friends, and started a fight with him. Haggart was larger than the appellant, and had previous training as a boxer. In this first encounter, Haggart was prevailing when the owner of the hotel separated the combatants and told Jobidon and his brother to leave the hotel. Jobidon and Haggart exchanged angry words in the lobby, and the trial

Adapted from *R. v. Jobidon* (1991), 66 C.C.C. (3d), pp. 462–497. Copyright © 1991 by *Canada Law Book*. Reprinted with permission.

judge found that the two men agreed the fight was not over.

Jobidon and his brother waited outside in the parking lot. When the Haggart party exited the hotel, their respective older brothers began fighting at the far end of the lot. Jobidon and Haggart argued. A crowd of people, many of whom had come outside to see the fight, gathered around them.

While Haggart and Jobidon stood facing each other, Jobidon struck Haggart with his fist, hitting him with great force on the head and face. Haggart was knocked backward onto the hood of a car. The trial judge determined that Haggart was rendered unconscious by this initial punch and that he appeared to be "out cold." He was not moving and offered no resistance to the appellant.

Immediately after throwing that first punch, Jobidon continued forward. In a brief flurry lasting no more than a few seconds, he struck the unconscious victim a further four to six times on the head. The trial judge found that there was no interval between Haggart's fall and the continued punching. The punches were part of "one single continuing transaction . . . one fluid event, punctuated by specific blows." The judge noted that the most reliable witness testified that it all happened so quickly he thought Haggart would bounce off the hood and resume the fight.

Instead, Haggart rolled off the hood and lay limp. He was taken to the hospital in a coma, where he died of severe contusions to the head. Medical evidence showed that he had sustained extensive bruising and abrasions to the head and neck. It was determined that the cause of death was one or more of the punches he had received at the hand of the appellant in the parking lot.

The trial judge found that Jobidon did not intend to kill Haggart, nor did he intend to cause the deceased serious bodily harm. However, the possibility of injury more serious than a bruise or bloody nose, such as a broken nose, was contemplated. Jobidon intentionally hit Haggart as hard as he could, but believed he was fighting fair. He did not depart intentionally from the kind of fight that Haggart had consented to. Jobidon believed that Haggart had consented to a fair fight, the object of which was to hit the other man as hard as physically possible until that person gave up or retreated. The trial judge also found that, although mistaken, and not supported by objective facts, Jobidon honestly believed that after Haggart had been struck onto the hood of the car, he was merely stunned, but still capable of fighting back, and still trying to fight.

Jobidon was tried before a judge of the Supreme Court of Ontario, and was found not guilty of manslaughter. The judge held that Haggart's consent negated assault, and held further that Jobidon had not been criminally negligent. The respondent appealed the judge's holding of assault to the Ontario Court of Appeal, which allowed the appeal, set aside the acquittal, and substituted a guilty verdict on the charge of manslaughter.

Issues on Appeal

The principal issue is whether absence of consent is a material element which must be proved by the Crown in all cases of assault or whether there are common law limitations which restrict or negate the legal effectiveness of consent in certain types of cases.

II. Analysis

1. The Evolution of the Offence of Assault in Canadian Criminal Law

The basic offence of assault originally came to post-Confederation Canada as a crime of common law. The Law Reform Commission of Canada described the relationship this way:

> Our law. . . derives from earlier English law. That law in turn was built on two foundation stones — the common law crimes of assault and battery. In consequence our present law is likewise built on these foundations, although both crimes are lumped together under the same name, "assault."

(Working Paper 38: Assault (1984), at p. 1.)

As a constituent element of numerous crimes, a common assault was any act in which one person intentionally caused another to apprehend immediate and unlawful violence. The traditional common law definition always assumed that absence of consent was a required element of the offence. As a general rule, an essential feature of assault is that it takes place against the victim's will. Thus, in most circumstances, it provided a valid defence to an accused. This makes sense when one acknowledges that the genuine consent of a complainant has traditionally been a defence to almost all forms of criminal responsibility.

Canada did not adopt its first criminal code until 1893. So, the English law was the primary foundation of Canadian criminal law. As Canadian courts gradually added to the English jurisprudence, our criminal common law increasingly became a blend of English and Canadian authorities. For decades, though, the definition of assault in Canadian criminal law remained virtually identical to the English common law version. That essential identity was not disturbed when Canada proclaimed its Criminal Code on July 1, 1893, since Canada's codification was very moderate, merely "expressing the common law in neat statutory language to be interpreted by common law judges."

The number of the assault provision was changed to 265 in the revision of the Criminal Code in 1985, R.S.C. 1985, c. C-46. The section now reads:

> 265(1) A person commits an assault when
> (a) without the consent of another person, he applies force intentionally to that other person, directly or indirectly;
>
> ....
>
> (2) This section applies to all forms of assault, including sexual assault, sexual assault with a weapon, threats to a third party or causing bodily harm and aggravated sexual assault.
> (3) For the purposes of this section, no consent is obtained where the complainant submits or does not resist by reason of

> (a) the application of force to the complainant or to a person other than the complainant;
> (b) threats or fear of the application of force to the complainant or to a person other than the complainant;
> (c) fraud; or
> (d) the exercise of authority.

It can be seen from this brief overview that the absence of consent to intentionally applied force was a material component of the offence of assault throughout its existence in Canada. But it is also evident that consent would not be legally effective in all circumstances. For instance, it would be vitiated by fraud. Various limitations on the validity of consent have a long lineage in the history of the offence. To observe those limitations, one must advert to the common law. Yet before turning to that jurisprudence, it is important to note the link between the offence of assault and the offence of manslaughter, since Jobidon was convicted of the latter offence.

2. The Nexus between Assault and Manslaughter

The connection between the two offences of assault and manslaughter is found in s. 222 (formerly s. 205) of the Code. That section provides a definition of manslaughter which is contingent on an unlawful act causing death:

> 222(4) Culpable homicide is murder or manslaughter or infanticide.
> (5) A person commits culpable homicide when he causes the death of a human being,
> (a) by means of an unlawful act;

The offence of assault is a foundation offence upon which other offences against the person are constructed. Of course, assault is also unlawful. It therefore follows from s. 222 that when an assault is committed and causes the death of a person, the assailant is thereby criminally liable for manslaughter.

It also follows that if consent acts as a defence to assault, it will indirectly act as a defence to a charge of manslaughter based on assault.

3. The Role and Scope of Consent in Assault

The controversy in this appeal stems from the apparent contradiction between the holding of the Ontario Court of Appeal in the instant appeal and the wording of s. 265(1)(a). By that wording, once the trial judge found that the deceased had consented to a fight with Jobidon, it appears as if he could not have committed the unlawful act of assault since s. 265(2) states a general rule that s. 265 applies to all forms of assault, including assault causing bodily harm. Consequently, given the reference to absence of consent in s. 265(1), proof of consent to a fist fight in which force is intentionally applied and which results in bodily harm would seem to serve as a defence for Jobidon. In that way, s. 265(1) and (2) also appear to support the appellant's position that absence of consent is a requirement to be proved by the Crown beyond a reasonable doubt, in each and every *instance* of assault. Given the *prima facie* appearance of support for the appellant's position, one might question how the Ontario Court of Appeal could hold that the deceased's consent to a fair fight did not preclude commission of the offence of assault.

That question would be well aimed. Provincial courts of appeal have grappled with the issue on numerous occasions in recent years, sometimes arriving at divergent conclusions. In 1984, the Law Reform Commission of Canada phrased the problem in more detailed terms (Working Paper 38 Assault, *op. cit.*, at p. 24):

> As regards the present law, it is clear that sometimes, as in the case of mere touching, consent is a defence, and that in general, where the contact is intended to cause death or serious harm, consent is no defence. It is also clear that even in circumstances going beyond mere touching (for example, in surgical operations

and in lawful sports) consent can prevent the force from being unlawful. *What is unclear is the extent to which the same rule applies or does not apply in Canada outside the operating theatre and the sports arena, for example, in sado-masochistic circumstances.*

(Emphasis added.) It is the purpose of the remaining analysis to clarify the role of consent in relation to a fist fight or brawl.

(a) THE GENERAL INFLUENCE OF THE COMMON LAW ON THE CODE'S DEFINITION OF ASSAULT

Although containing myriad provisions of a relatively detailed nature, the Criminal Code has been inspired by general principles of criminal responsibility. Section 265 is no exception. It speaks in a universal tone and sets out a general rule that one cannot commit assault if the other person agrees to the application of force.

However, while it is true that the general rule says all forms of assault are covered by the various clauses of s. 265, it does not attempt to define the *situations* or *forms of conduct* or *eventual consequences* which the law will recognize as being valid objects of consent for the purpose of the offence. It does not attempt to define the situations in which consent will or will not be legally effective. The present Code is silent in this regard.

Just as the common law has built up a rich jurisprudence around the concepts of agreement in contract law, and *volenti non fit injuria* in the law of negligence, it has also generated a body of law to illuminate the meaning of consent and to place certain limitations on its legal effectiveness in the criminal law. It has done this in respect of assault. In the same way that the common law established principles of public policy negating the legal effectiveness of certain types of contracts — contracts in restraint of trade, for example — it has also set limits on the types of harmful actions to which one can validly consent, and shelter an assailant from the sanctions of our criminal law.

There is no indication in s. 265 that the jurisprudence of the criminal common law was to be undermined by its enactment. There was no hint that traditional policy limits on consent, described below in greater detail, were to be ousted by s. 258 of the first Criminal Code of 1892, nor by enactment of its successor provision in s. 244 (now s. 265). This should not be surprising. As the foregoing sketch of the history of the offence demonstrates, far from intending to curtail the authority of that law, the Code was a partial expression of it.

All criminal offences in Canada are now defined in the Code (s. 9). But that does not mean the common law no longer illuminates these definitions nor gives content to the various principles of criminal responsibility those definitions draw from. As the Law Reform Commission of Canada has noted in its 31st report on recodification, the basic premises of our criminal law — the necessary conditions for criminal liability — are at present left to the common law. The Code itself, in s. 8, explicitly acknowledges the ongoing common law influence.

Section 8 expressly indicates that the common law rules and principles continue to apply, but only to the extent that they are not inconsistent with the Code or other Act of Parliament and have not been altered by them.

If s. 8(3) and its interaction with the common law can be used to develop entirely new defences not inconsistent with the Code, it surely authorizes the courts to look to pre-existing common law rules and principles to give meaning to, and explain the outlines and boundaries of, an existing defence or justification, indicating where they will not be recognized as legally effective — provided of course that there is no clear language in the Code which indicates that the Code has displaced the common law. That sort of language cannot be found in the Code. As such, the common law legitimately serves in this appeal as an archive in which one may locate situations or forms of conduct to which the law will not allow a person to consent.

(b) THE SPECIFIC RELATIONSHIP BETWEEN THE CODE AND THE COMMON LAW OF ASSAULT IN CASES OF FIST FIGHTS

(i) THE RELATIONSHIP BETWEEN CONSENT AND SECTION 265(3)

The appellant argued that the 1983 amendments to s. 265 reflected Parliament's intent to replace any common law doctrines that might have negated the legal effectiveness of consent to an act which would otherwise constitute assault. In particular, reference was made to s. 265(3), which sets out four factors that may vitiate consent: application of force, threats of force, fraud, or the exercise of authority. It was argued that because Parliament explicitly specified these factors, any others, even though they may have applied prior to 1983, could no longer be drawn from the common law. Since the trial judge found that Haggart had consented to the fight and did not hold that such consent was invalidated on any of the four grounds, it should be effective, and should serve as a defence to assault as the plain words of ss. 265(1) and 265(2) appear to require.

While at first glance the appellant's argument may seem cogent, it is ultimately unpersuasive. Parliament did not set foot into new territory when listing the four vitiating factors in s. 265(3). On the contrary, it will be seen that, for the most part, that list merely concretized, and made more explicit, basic limits on the legal effectiveness of consent which had for centuries formed part of the criminal law in England and in Canada. Their expression in the Code did not reflect an intent to remove the existing body of common law which already described those limitations and their respective scope. The Code just spelled them out more clearly, in a general form.

Since s. 8(3) of the Code expressly confirms the common law's continued authority and provides that exculpatory defences not expressly struck down by the Code continue to operate to exclude criminal liability, in this appeal, where the Code has not erased the common law limit in fist fights, it must continue to define the scope of legally effective consent.

Whether consent is formally categorized as part of the *actus reus* of the offence, or as a defence, its essential function remains unaltered — if consent is proved, or if absence of consent is not proved, an individual accused of assault will *generally* be able to rely on the consent of the complainant to bar a conviction. He will be able to lean on the consent as a defence to liability. This basic reality has been widely recognized. We have also observed, in the general interpretative section above, that the law confers on s. 8(3) an open and developmental view of the common law's role. Section 8(3) strongly suggests preservation of the common law approach to consent in assault.

Assault has been given a very encompassing definition in s. 265. It arises whenever a person intentionally applies force to a person "directly or indirectly," without the other's consent. The definition says nothing about the degree of harm which must be sustained. Nor does it refer to the motives for the touching. If taken at face value, this formulation would mean that the most trivial intended touching would constitute assault. As just one of many possible examples, a father would assault his daughter if he attempted to place a scarf around her neck to protect her from the cold but she did not consent to that touching, thinking the scarf ugly or undesirable. (Even an argument for implied consent would not seem to apply in a case like this.) That absurd consequence could not have been intended by Parliament. Rather, its intention must have been for the courts to explain the content of the offence, incrementally and over the course of time.

Furthermore, whereas the factors specified in s. 265(3) are readily identifiable, and are generally applicable to all sorts of situations, that is inherently not true of limitations based on policy considerations, which are fact-specific by nature. It would have been quite impractical, if not impossible, for Parliament to establish an adequate list of exceptions to apply to all situations, old and new. Policy-based limits are almost always the product of a balancing of individual autonomy (the freedom to choose to have force intentionally applied to oneself) and some larger societal interest. That balancing may be better performed in the light of actual situations, rather than in the abstract, as Parliament would be compelled to do.

With the offence of assault, that kind of balancing is a function the courts are well-suited to perform. They will continue to be faced with real situations in which complicated actions and motivations interact, as they have in the past. I do not accept the argument that by failing to enact a list of *objects* or *forms of conduct* to which one could not validly consent, Parliament intended to eliminate their role in the offence of assault and to rely only on the four factors specified in s. 265(3). Such a major departure from well-established policy calls for more than mere silence, particularly as such a list would have been unduly difficult and impractical to prescribe, and was unnecessary given their existing entrenchment in the common law. The common law is the register of the balancing function of the courts — a register Parliament has authorized the courts to administer in respect of policy-based limits on the role and scope of consent in s. 265 of the Code.

(ii) THE RELATIONSHIP BETWEEN CONSENT AND SECTION 265(2)

The appellant argues that the interpretation favouring limits on consent being advanced here would render s. 265(1)(a) ("without the consent of another") otiose and meaningless, insofar as s. 265(2) specifies that s. 265(1)(a) is to apply to all forms of assault, including assault causing bodily harm. However, this objection is not sustainable.

By specifying in s. 265(2) that s. 265 is to apply to all forms of assault, Parliament undoubtedly sought to ensure that the basic elements of the offence of assault in ss. 265(1)(a) to (c), the circumstances listed in s. 265(3) for vitiating consent due to a coerced or misinformed volition, and the required state of mind for raising a defence in s. 265(4), would be applied without exception, irrespective of the peculiar form of assault. That is plain. Yet it does not follow from that expression that Parliament intended to eliminate the common law prescription of objects or forms of conduct to which legally effective consent may not be given. Section 265 was deliberately left open in that regard, for the above reasons.

(c) COMMON LAW LIMITS IN FIST FIGHTS AND BRAWLS

Limits on consent to assault have long been recognized by English and Canadian courts. We have already seen the earliest antecedents of them in the English jurisprudence, in fist fights and otherwise; here we are concerned only with the former situation. In present times as well, the English courts have on the whole been very consistent when confronted by assaults arising from fist fights and brawls. Since the English cases have set the overall direction for the Canadian common law in the assault context, and apparently continues to do so, it is of particular relevance in the circumstances of this case. The Canadian authorities also favour limits on consent. However, in recent years there has evolved a mixed record across provincial courts of appeal. This appeal therefore presents a timely opportunity for clarification.

In 1980, the English Court of Appeal was asked to state the law in *Attorney-General's Reference* (No. 6 of 1980), [1981] 2 All E.R. 1057. It was a reference prompted by a street fight between two young men who, in a relatively calm fashion, had decided to settle differences between them by resorting to their fists. One suffered a bleeding nose and some bruises. The other was charged with assault, but acquitted. The question put to the appellate court was, at p. 1058: "'Where two persons fight (otherwise than in the courts of sport) in a public place, can it be a defence for one of those persons to a charge of assault arising out of the fight that the other consented to fight?'"

The court held that because it is not in the public interest that people should cause each other bodily harm for no good reason, consent is no answer to a charge of assault when "actual bodily harm is intended and/or caused" (p. 1059). This meant that most fights would be unlawful regardless of consent.

Only minor struggles, or rough but properly conducted sporting events — which may have some positive social value — were combative activities where consent would be an effective bar to a charge of assault. Of course, lawful chastisement and reasonable surgical interference were also activities in which the public interest does not require nullification of consent. In such cases the general rule applies: the Crown must prove absence of consent to get a conviction for assault. The English Court of Appeal added that the public nature of the forum in which the fight occurs is not determinative of the effectiveness of consent. Private fights deserved no more protection than public ones.

If determinative of this appeal, the English authorities would undoubtedly support the decision of the court below. Here, the assault occurred in circumstances which appear very nearly to have amounted to a disturbance of the peace. And there is no question that the punches thrown by Jobidon were intentional applications of force intended to cause the deceased bodily harm. Rodney Haggart's apparent consent would provide no defence to Jobidon in England.

(d) SUMMARY OF THE COMMON LAW

(i) THE ENGLISH POSITION

Attorney-General's Reference makes it clear that a conviction of assault will not be barred if "bodily harm is intended *and/or* caused." Since this test is framed in the alternative, consent could be nullified even in situations where the assailant did not intend to cause the injured person bodily harm but did so inadvertently. In Canada, however, this very broad formulation cannot strictly apply, since the definition of assault in s. 265 is explicitly restricted to *intentional* application of force. Any test in our law which incorporated the English perspective would of necessity have to confine itself to bodily harm intended *and* caused.

(ii) THE CANADIAN POSITION

The preceding analysis reveals division in the Canadian jurisprudence. Decisions by courts of appeal in Manitoba, Ontario, Nova Scotia, and (lately) Saskatchewan would nullify consent to intentionally inflicted bodily harm arising from a fist fight.

On the other side are decisions of appellate courts in New Brunswick, Québec, Saskatchewan, and Alberta.

Although there is certainly no crystal-clear position in the modern Canadian common law, still, when one takes into account the combined English and Canadian jurisprudence, when one keeps sight of the common law's centuries-old persistence to limit the legal effectiveness of consent to a fist fight, and when one understands that s. 265 has always incorporated that persistence, the scale tips rather heavily against the validity of a person's consent to the infliction of bodily injury in a fight.

The thrust of the English common law is particularly important in this regard because it has been consistent for many decades, indeed, centuries. It became an integral component of the Canadian common law and has remained so to this day.

(e) POLICY CONSIDERATIONS

Foremost among the policy considerations supporting the Crown is the social uselessness of fist fights. As the English Court of Appeal noted in the *Attorney-General's Reference*, it is not in the public interest that adults should willingly cause harm to one another without a good reason. There is precious little utility in fist fights or street brawls. These events are motivated by unchecked passion. They so often result in serious injury to the participants. Here, it resulted in a tragic death to a young man on his wedding day.

There was a time when pugilism was sheltered by the notion of "chivalry." Duelling was an activity not only condoned, but required by honour. Those days are fortunately long past. Our social norms no longer correlate strength of character with prowess at fisticuffs. Indeed, when we pride ourselves for making positive ethical and social strides, it tends to be on the basis of our developing reason. This is particularly true of the law, where reason is cast in a privileged light. Erasing long-standing limits on consent to assault would be a regressive step, one which would retard the advance of civilized norms of conduct.

Quite apart from the valueless nature of fist fights from the combatants' perspective, it should also be recognized that consensual fights may sometimes lead to larger brawls and to serious breaches of the public peace. In the instant case, this tendency was openly observable. At the prospect of a fight between Jobidon and the deceased, in a truly macabre fashion many patrons of the hotel deliberately moved to the parking lot to witness the gruesome event. That scene easily could have erupted in more widespread aggression between allies of the respective combatants. Indeed, it happened that the brothers of Jobidon and Haggart also took to each other with their fists.

Given the spontaneous, often drunken nature of many fist fights, I would not wish to push a deterrence rationale too far. Nonetheless, it seems reasonable to think that, in some cases, common law limitations on consent might serve some degree of deterrence to these sorts of activities.

Related to a deterrence rationale is the possibility that, by permitting a person to consent to force inflicted by the hand of another, in rare cases the latter may find he derives some form of pleasure from the activity, especially if he is doing so on a regular basis. It is perhaps not inconceivable that this kind of perversion could arise in a domestic or marital setting where one or more of the family members are of frail or unstable mental health.

Of course this appeal does not concern sadism or intentional killing. But it comes close to mutilation. In any event, the weight of the argument could hold true for fights. If aggressive individuals are legally permitted to get into consensual fist fights, and they take advantage of that licence from time to time, it may come to pass that they eventually lose all understanding that that activity is the subject of a powerful social taboo. They may too readily find their fists raised against a person whose consent they forgot to ascertain with full certitude. It is preferable that these sorts of omissions be strongly discouraged.

Wholly apart from deterrence, it is most unseemly from a moral point of view that the law would countenance, much less provide a back-handed sanction to, the sort of interaction displayed by the facts of this appeal. The sanctity of the human body should militate against the validity of consent to bodily harm inflicted in a fight.

The policy preference that people not be able to consent to intentionally inflicted harms is heard not only in the register of our common law. The Criminal Code also contains many examples of this propensity. As noted above, s. 14 of the Code vitiates the legal effectiveness of a person's consent to have death inflicted on him under any circumstances. The same policy appears to underlie ss. 150.1, 159, and 286 in respect of younger people, in the contexts of sexual offences, anal intercourse, and abduction, respectively. All this is to say that the notion of policy-based limits on the effectiveness of consent to some level of inflicted harms is not foreign. Parliament as well as the courts have been mindful of the need for such limits. Autonomy is not the only value which our law seeks to protect.

Some may see limiting the freedom of an adult to consent to applications of force in a fist fight as unduly paternalistic; a violation of individual self-rule. Yet while that view may commend itself to some, those persons cannot reasonably claim that the law does not know such limitations. All criminal law is "paternalistic" to some degree — top-down guidance is inherent in any prohibitive rule. That the common law has developed a strong resistance to recognizing the validity of consent to intentional applications of force in fist fights and brawls is merely one instance of the criminal law's concern that Canadian citizens treat each other humanely and with respect.

Finally, it must not be thought that by giving the green light to the common law, and a red light to consent to fights, this court is thereby negating the role of consent in all situations or activities in which people willingly expose themselves to intentionally applied force. No such sweeping conclusion is entailed. The determination being made is much narrower in scope.

(f) CONCLUSION

How, and to what extent is consent limited?

The law's willingness to vitiate consent on policy grounds is significantly limited. Common law cases restrict the extent to which consent may be nullified; as do the relevant policy considerations. The unique situation under examination in this case, a weaponless fist fight between two adults, provides another important boundary.

The limitation demanded by s. 265 as it applies to the circumstances of this appeal is one which *vitiates consent between adults intentionally to apply force causing serious hurt or non-trivial bodily harm to each other in the course of a fist fight or brawl.* (This test entails that a minor's apparent consent to an adult's intentional application of force in a fight would also be negated.) This is the extent of the limit which the common law requires in the factual circumstances of this appeal. It may be that further limitations will be found to apply in other circumstances. But such limits, if any, are better developed on a case-by-case basis, so that the unique features of the situation may exert a rational influence on the extent of the limit and on the justification for it.

Stated in this way, the policy of the common law will not affect the validity or effectiveness of freely given consent to participate in rough sporting activities, so long as the intentional applications of force to which one consents are within the customary norms and rules of the game. Unlike fist fights, sporting activities and games usually have a significant social value; they are worthwhile.

The court's majority determined that some forms of intentionally applied force will clearly fall within the scope of the rules of the game, and will therefore readily ground a finding of implied consent, to which effect should be given. On the other hand, very violent forms of force which clearly extend beyond the ordinary norms of conduct will not be recognized as legitimate conduct to which one can validly consent.

There is also nothing in the preceding formulation which would prevent a person from consenting to medical treatment or appropriate surgical interventions. Nor, for example, would it necessarily nullify consent between stuntmen who agree in advance to perform risky sparring or daredevil activities in the creation of a socially valuable cultural product. A charge of assault would be barred if the Crown failed to prove absence of consent in these situations, insofar as the activities have a positive social value and the intent of the actors is to produce a social benefit for the good of the people involved, and often for a wider group of people as well. This is a far cry from the situation presented in this appeal, where Jobidon's sole objective was to strike the deceased as hard as he physically could, until his opponent either gave up or retreated. Fist fights are worlds apart from these other forms of conduct.

Finally, the preceding formulation avoids nullification of consent to intentional applications of force which cause only minor hurt or trivial bodily harm. The bodily harm contemplated by the test is essentially equivalent to that contemplated by the definition found in s. 267(2) of the Code, dealing with the offence of assault causing bodily harm. The section defines bodily harm as "any hurt or injury to the complainant that interferes with the health or comfort of the complainant and that is more than merely transient or trifling in nature."

On this definition, combined with the fact that the test is restricted to cases involving adults, the phenomenon of the "ordinary" schoolyard scuffle, where boys or girls immaturely seek to resolve differences with their hands, will not come within the scope of the limitation. That has never been the policy of the law and I do not intend to disrupt the status quo. However, I would leave open the question as to whether boys or girls under the age of 18 who truly intend to harm one another, and ultimately cause more than trivial bodily harm, would be afforded the protection of a defence of consent. The appropriate result will undoubtedly depend on the peculiar circumstances of each case.

III. Disposition

I would uphold the decision of the Court of Appeal. The appeal is dismissed.

Appeal dismissed.

REGINA v. LECLERC

ONTARIO COURT OF APPEAL   SEPTEMBER 12, 1991

BACKGROUND

Leclerc was charged with aggravated assault follow-ing an industrial-league hockey game in which another player was paralyzed as a consequence of a severe spinal injury. At his trial, Leclerc was acquit-ted of the charge by a District Court Judge. The Crown subsequently appealed against the accused's acquittal to the Ontario Court of Appeal.

MAIN ISSUES

(1) Could the accused rely on the defence of implied consent and, if so, what is the scope of the implied consent? (2) Does the Crown have to prove that the accused deliberately intended to wound the injured player in order to gain a conviction?

JUDGMENT

The *judgment* of the Court was delivered by Justice Lacourcière (the other members of the Court were Justices Tarnopolsky and McKinlay).

....

LACOURCIÈRE J.A.: — This is an appeal by the Attorney-General of Ontario, pursuant to s. 676(1)(a) of the Criminal Code, against the acquit-tal of the respondent by a District Court judge on a charge of aggravated assault, alleged to have occurred during a hockey game. The question of law raised by the appellant is whether the learned trial judge erred in his interpretation of the *mens rea* requirement of the offence charged by placing an unduly onerous burden on the prosecution, which had the effect of requiring proof of a specific intent to cause serious injury, and whether this self-misdirection had the further effect of placing an incorrect and increased burden on the Crown as to the circumstances required to be proved in order to negative implied consent.

Overview of the Facts

The aggravated assault was alleged to have taken place in the course of a semifinal playoff hockey game in the Lanark Municipal Arena between con-tending teams in an industrial league, The Lanark Sportsmen's Recreational League. Under C.A.H.A. rules, no bodily contact is allowed. On March 3, 1989, a playoff game was held to determine the finalist team for the league championship. During the third period the respondent, who played in the forward position for the Calabogie team, pursued the complainant, James R. Conboy, a defenceman for Joe's Lake, the opposing team, who was attempting to retrieve the puck, which had been shot into his own end. There was a collision on the boards as the respondent hit the complainant in

....

the back with his hockey stick. The referee immediately blew his whistle and called a "match penalty" against the respondent for a deliberate attempt to injure. The game was halted. It was subsequently determined that the complainant had suffered a dislocation of a portion of the cervical spine: he was permanently paralyzed from the neck down.

The complainant and the Crown witnesses contended that the complainant was struck by the respondent with a cross-check to the back of his neck. The referee described the cross-check as "deliberate" and "vicious," with intent to injure. The respondent testified that he was skating fast after the puck and merely gave the complainant a push or a shove from behind to move him off the puck, which caused the latter to lose his balance and crash head first into the boards.

The learned trial judge reserved judgment after a four-day trial, ordered a transcript of the evidence, and later delivered carefully written reasons. I quote his summary of what he described as the undisputed facts:

> Shortly after the 14-minute mark of the third period, the Calabogie team dumped or snapped the puck into the Joe's Lake end. As the puck slid into the north west corner of the rink ultimately to a point very near the west end boards a few feet north of the Joe's Lake net, Jim Conboy, the Joe's Lake left defenceman, pivoted from a backward skating motion to skate in pursuit. He was skating in a westerly direction toward a point just north of his own net.
>
> At approximately the same time, Steven Leclerc had broken out of a pack of players outside the Joe's Lake blue line and skating at a high rate of speed was angling from the centre of the ice surface to the likely resting place of the puck just north of the Joe's Lake net. So fast was Leclerc moving that he gained some 20 to 25 feet in the approximately 75 feet he traversed as both players converged on the puck.
>
> As Conboy closed on the puck, Clifford, the goal tender, shouted, "Man On!" and Conboy

shifted to his right prior to his attempt to take possession and swing to his left behind the net. At that moment Leclerc's gloves and stick came in contact with Conboy's upper back, Conboy lost his balance and tumbled head first into the end boards, the top of his helmet violently contacting same a foot or two above the ice surface. His body recoiled from the boards in a twisted condition, semi-prone upon the ice. The violent contact with the end boards caused a fracture dislocation of Conboy's fourth and fifth cervical vertebrae provoking permanent paralysis.

> Immediately upon the contact between Leclerc and Conboy, the referee, Charles Harrison, blew his whistle and assessed Leclerc a five-minute match penalty for deliberate attempt to injure. Within moments he terminated the game to permit appropriate care to be given to the badly injured Conboy who remained conscious on the ice.

The learned trial judge described the disputed facts as relating to the manner, degree, and the location of the force applied by the respondent's glove and stick to the upper region of the complainant's back. He then meticulously analyzed the evidence of the referee, who characterized the cross-check as deliberate and vicious, and contrasted it to that of the linesman, whose evidence was that the cross-check was not vicious but had the effect of knocking the complainant off-balance, face first into the boards.

The learned trial judge clearly rejected the evidence of the referee. He did not accept the respondent's version entirely, but accepted the evidence of a witness whose opinion was that the respondent shoved the complainant in the back in order to push him off and avoid more violent contact in such close proximity to the end boards. He concluded that, even in the non-contact industrial league in which the respondent and the complainant played, "in practice all players expected and accepted the risks of contact inherent in the spirited play this level of hockey traditionally produced."

The Intent for Aggravated Assault

The appellant does not challenge the learned trial judge's comment to the effect that the prosecution was required to establish beyond a reasonable doubt that the application of force by the respondent was without the implied consent of the complainant, and that it was deliberate and intentional in law. However, the impugned self-instruction is as follows:

> The sole issue before this court is whether the conduct of the defendant, Leclerc, in the course of play in these circumstances constituted such a malicious, egregious, vicious breach of the accepted norm as to require the sanction of the criminal law. To paraphrase the judicial pronouncement in *Agar v. Canning*, hereinbefore alluded to — Did it exhibit or display a definite resolve to cause serious injury to another?
>
> Unless this court is convinced to a moral certainty on the evidence that the response to that question must be in the affirmative, the prosecution has not met the onus of proof. And to be so convinced, this court must find that that force be both of an egregious, vicious nature and be intentionally applied.

The case-law interpreting ss. 265 and 245.2 makes it clear that the essential intent required for an assault, as defined, remains the same for all forms of assault, including aggravated assault. Parliament intended that the severity of the punishment should increase to reflect the more serious consequences of the assault. It never intended that, on an indictment charging "aggravated assault," the prosecution would be required to prove that the accused intended to wound, maim, or disfigure the complainant or endanger his life.

To the extent, therefore, that the impugned wording of the self-direction quoted elevated the *mens rea* requirement to one of specific intent, it constituted an error in law. In order to determine whether the error of law influenced the findings of fact, it is necessary to examine the final conclusion of the learned trial judge:

> I hold that the push, shove or cross check was part of an instinctive reflex reaction executed by Leclerc while moving at a high rate of speed in a belated attempt to avoid more dreaded contact in such close proximity to the west end boards. It indeed violated the rules of the game but I find it lacked malicious design in that its object was not to inflict bodily harm but to minimize the prospect thereof. On all the testimony, I hold it constituted an ill-fated attempt by Leclerc to extricate himself from risk self-imposed by his intemperate zeal. It bore tragic consequences but these were neither contemplated or intended by him.

This passage suggests that the learned trial judge required the Crown to prove that the object of the respondent's push, shove, or cross-check was to inflict bodily harm on the complainant, and that the Crown had to prove that the tragic consequences thereof were either intended or contemplated. Later, in rejecting the prosecution's contention that the conduct of the accused met the standard required for a conviction on a charge of criminal assault in the course of a hockey game, the trial judge repeated what he regarded as an essential ingredient of the charge, namely "a definite resolve to cause serious injury." This is an error of law with respect to the required *mens rea* to support a charge of aggravated assault: this court will, in the dispositive part of the judgment, consider its effect on the verdict of acquittal.

The Implied Consent Issue

As previously mentioned, the learned trial judge found that the complainant, having agreed to compete in this particular hockey league, impliedly consented to those assaults which are inherent and reasonably incidental to the normal playing of the game at this level.

In *R. v. Cey* (1989), 48 C.C.C. (3d) 480, [1989] 5 W.W.R. 169, 75 Sask. R. 53, the Saskatchewan Court of Appeal was also considering a Crown appeal against the acquittal of the accused on a charge of assault causing bodily harm in the course of a hockey game. The sole issue before that court was whether the complainant, who had suffered serious injuries as a result of a body-check during the course of a hockey game, had or even could consent to the violence committed against him. The accused argued that the Crown had failed to negative consent as required by s. 244(1)(a) (now s. 265(1)(a)). He did not suggest, by way of defence, that he had an honest belief that the victim consented to the conduct that was the subject matter of the charge. Gerwing, J.A., writing for the majority, recognized that hockey players engage in and consent to various forms of conduct which, in circumstances other than a hockey arena, would amount to unlawful contact or a criminal offence. But she also said, at p. 488, that some sporting behaviour is so violent that it would be perverse to find that the participant had impliedly consented to subject himself or herself to it.

The problem that the courts face with respect to this issue is the scope of implied consent — that is, at what point does conduct in sporting activity fall outside the standards which players impliedly agree to as an acceptable part of the game? Gerwing, J.A., writing for the majority, stated at p. 490:

> Ordinarily consent, being a state of mind, is a wholly subjective matter to be determined accordingly, but when it comes to implied consent in the context of a team sport such as hockey, there cannot be as many different consents as there are players on the ice, and so the scope of the implied consent, having to be uniform, must be determined by reference to objective criteria.

The conclusion that the courts should endeavour to employ objective criteria in the analysis of whether a player could be said to have impliedly consented to the conduct which is the subject of the charge does not mean, however, that such criteria should be rigidly applied. Instead, regard must be had to the whole of the conditions under which the game is played. The criteria identified by the Saskatchewan Court of Appeal, which may be referred to so as to determine the scope of implied consent, include the setting of the game, the league, the age of the players, the conditions under which the game is played, the extent of the force employed, the degree of risk of injury and the probabilities of serious harm. That court went on to say at pp. 490–1:

> . . . in any given case, [in determining whether] the conduct complained of exceeds the scope of the prevailing implied consent, it is well to think in terms of (a) the nature of the act at issue and (b) the degree of force employed.
>
> It is well, too, to think in terms of what most deeply underlies the issue, namely, the risk of injury and the degrees thereof. Some forms of bodily contact carry with them such a high risk of injury and such a distinct probability of serious harm as to be beyond what, in fact, the players commonly consent to, or what, in law, they are capable of consenting to. Such are the violent acts referred to earlier.
>
> The conditions under which the game in question is played, the nature of the act which forms the subject matter of the charge, the extent of the force employed, the degree of risk of injury, and the probabilities of serious harm are, of course, all matters of fact to be determined with reference to the whole of the circumstances. In large part, they form the ingredients which ought to be looked to in determining whether in all of the circumstances the ambit of the consent at issue in any given case was exceeded.

To these criteria, which are not meant to be exhaustive, I would add whether the rules of the game contemplate contact or, as here, non-contact.

In the result, the majority concluded that some forms of contact in a sports match cannot be the subject of "true consent."

In her reasons, Gerwing, J.A. said, as well, at p. 493 that "the mere fact that a type of assault occurs with some frequency does not necessarily mean that it is not of such a severe nature that consent thereto is precluded."

I agree with the majority judgment in *R. v. Cey.* The weight of judicial authority appears to be that a player, by participating in a sport such as hockey, impliedly consents to some bodily contact necessarily incidental to the game, but not to overly violent attacks, all of which should be determined according to objective criteria. Conduct which evinces a deliberate purpose to inflict injury will generally be held to be outside of the immunity provided by the scope of implied consent in a sports arena. This is not to be taken to mean, as the trial judge apparently did in the case under appeal, that in order to negative implied consent, the prosecution has the burden of proving a deliberate purpose or resolve to inflict injury.

In the present case, the Crown argued forcibly that the scope of implied consent ought to be narrowed because the alleged assault occurred in the course of a recreational industrial game in which bodily contact was not permitted by the rules, and not in a professional contact league game. However, as found by the trial judge, the ideal of non-contact rules was frequently breached in a spirited game where bumps and other contacts resulted in many penalties. While the "no contact" rule is relevant in determining the scope of implied consent, it is not by itself determinative of the issue.

In the case under appeal, the ultimate question on the issue of implied consent, as in *R. v. Cey, supra,* is whether the cross-checking or push of the complainant across the neck in close proximity to the boards was so inherently dangerous as to be excluded from the implied consent. The question asked by the trial judge was whether the respondent's conduct exhibited or displayed a definite resolve to cause serious injury to another. In my opinion, the question of implied consent, which the Crown was required to negative, was not addressed properly in the court below. This error, together with the confusion in dealing with the *mens rea* requirement of aggravated assault, had the result of placing an inappropriate burden on the prosecution.

Disposition

The error in law does not automatically require the direction of a new trial. It becomes necessary to consider the effect of the self-misdirection in the light of the findings of fact which the learned trial judge made and which are supported by the evidence. Paraphrasing his view, the push, shove, or cross-check resulted directly from the respondent's loss of balance and was part of the respondent's "instinctive reflex reaction," which had the object of minimizing the risk of bodily harm created by his high speed in close proximity to the boards. He properly rejected the alternative Crown theory that the force of the blow to the neck of the victim was sufficient to establish criminal conduct.

Having regard to the clear findings of fact made by the trial judge as to the circumstances of that particular hockey game, the Crown has not satisfied me that the verdict of acquittal would not necessarily have been the same if there had been no self-misdirection in law.

I would accordingly dismiss the Attorney-General's appeal against the acquittal.

Appeal dismissed.

Ancio, [1984] 1 S.C.R. 225, 10 C.C.C. (3d) 385, 39 C.R. (3d) 1, 6 D.L.R. (4th) 577, 52 N.R. 161 (S.C.C.)

Butler, [1992] 1 S.C.R. 452, 70 C.C.C. (3d) 129, 11 C.R. (4th) 137 (S.C.C.)

Chaulk, [1990] 3 S.C.R. 1303, 62 C.C.C. (3d) 193, 2 C.R. (4th) 1, [1991] 2 W.W.R. 385, 119 N.R. 161 (S.C.C.)

Cooper, [1993] 1 S.C.R. 146, 78 C.C.C. (3d) 289, 18 C.R. (4th) 1, 146 N.R. 367 (S.C.C.)

Creighton, [1993] 3 S.C.R. 3, 83 C.C.C. (3d) 346, 23 C.R. (4th) 189, 105 D.L.R. (4th) 632, 157 N.R. 1 (S.C.C.)

Daviault, [1994] 3 S.C.R. 63, 93 C.C.C. (3d) 21, 33 C.R. (4th) 165 (S.C.C.)

DeSousa, [1992] 2 S.C.R. 944, 76 C.C.C. (3d) 124, 15 C.R. (4th) 66, 95 D.L.R. (4th) 595, 142 N.R. 1 (S.C.C.)

Gladstone (1996), 109 C.C.C. (3d) 193 (S.C.C.)

Greyeyes (1997), 116 C.C.C. (3d) 334, 148 D.L.R. (4th) 634 (S.C.C.)

Hatfield (1997), 115 C.C.C. (3d) 47 (Ont. C.A.)

Harbottle, [1993] 3 S.C.R. 306, 84 C.C.C. (3d) 1, 24 C.R. (4th) 137, 157 N.R. 349 (S.C.C.).

Hibbert, [1995] 2 S.C.R. 973, 99 C.C.C. (3d) 193, 40 C.R. (4th) 141 (S.C.C.)

Hundal, [1993] 1 S.C.R. 867, 79 C.C.C. (3d) 97, 19 C.R. (4th) 169, 149 N.R. 189, 43 M.V.R. (2d) 169 (S.C.C.)

Hydro-Québec (1997), 118 C.C.C. (3d) 97 (S.C.C.)

Jacquard (1997), 113 C.C.C. (3d) 1 (S.C.C.)

Jobidon, [1991] 2 S.C.R. 714, 66 C.C.C. (3d) 454, 7 C.R. (4th) 233, 128 N.R. 321 (S.C.C.)

Kitching and Adams (1976), 32 C.C.C. (2d) 159, [1976] 6 W.W.R. (Man. C.A.)

Langlois (1993), 80 C.C.C. (3d) 28, 19 C.R. (4th) 87, [1993] R.J.Q. 675 (Que. C.A.)

Lavallee, [1990] 1 S.C.R. 852, 55 C.C.C. (3d) 97, 76 C.R. (3d) 329, [1990] 4 W.W.R. 1, 108 N.R. 321 (S.C.C.)

Leclerc (1991), 67 C.C.C. (3d) 563, 7 C.R. (4th) 282, 4 O.R. (3d) 788 (Ont. C.A.)

LePage (1997), 119 C.C.C. (3d) 193, 152 D.L.R. (4th) 318 (Ont. C.A.)

Logan, [1990] 2 S.C.R. 731, 58 C.C.C. (3d) 391, 79 C.R. (3d) 169, 73 D.L.R. (4th) 40, 112 N.R. 144 (S.C.C.)

Martineau, [1990] 2 S.C.R. 633, 58 C.C.C. (3d) 353, 70 C.R. (3d) 129, [1990] 6 W.W.R. 97, 112 N.R. 83 (S.C.C.)

Morgentaler, Smolig and Scott, [1988] 1 S.C.R. 30, 37 C.C.C. (3d) 449, 62 C.R. (3d) 1

Oluwa (1996), 107 C.C.C. (3d) 236; (Supplementary Reasons) (1996), 110 C.C.C. (3d) 95 (B.C.C.A.)

Park, [1995] 2 S.C.R. 836, 99 C.C.C. (3d) 1, 39 C.R. (4th) 287 (S.C.C.)

Parks, [1992] 2 S.C.R. 871, 75 C.C.C. (3d) 287, 15 C.R. (4th) 289, 95 D.L.R. (4th) 27, 140 N.R. 161 (S.C.C.)

Perka, [1984] 2 S.C.R. 232, 14 C.C.C. (3d) 385, 42 C.R. (3d) 113, 13 D.L.R. (4th) 1, [1984] 6 W.W.R. 289 (S.C.C.)

Pétel, [1994] 1 S.C.R. 3, 87 C.C.C. (3d) 97, 26 C.R. (4th) 145, 162 N.R. 137 (S.C.C.)

Reference re: Section 94(2) of the Motor Vehicle Act, [1985] 2 S.C.R. 486, 23 C.C.C. (3d) 289, 48 C.R. (3d) 289, 24 D.L.R. (4th) 536, [1986] 1 W.W.R. 481, 69 B.C.L.R. 145, 36 M.V.R. 240 (S.C.C.)

Robinson, [1996] 1 S.C.R. 683, 105 C.C.C. (3d) 97, 46 C.R. (4th) 1 (S.C.C.)

Rodriguez v. British Columbia (Attorney-General), [1993] 3 S.C.R. 519, 85 C.C.C. (3d) 15, 24 C.R. (4th) 281, 107 D.L.R. (4th) 342, [1993] 7 W.W.R. 641, 82 B.C.L.R. (2d) 273 (S.C.C.)

Sansregret, [1985] 1 S.C.R. 570, 18 C.C.C. (3d) 223, 45 C.R. (3d) 193, 17 D.L.R. (4th) 577, [1985] 3 W.W.R. 701 (S.C.C.)

Sault Ste. Marie (City), [1978] 2 S.C.R. 1299, 40 C.C.C. (2d) 353, 3 C.R. (3d) 30, 21 N.R. 295 (S.C.C.)

Smithers, [1978] 1 S.C.R. 506, 34 C.C.C. (2d) 427, 75 D.L.R (3d) 321, 15 N.R. 287 (S.C.C.)

Swain, [1991] 1 S.C.R. 933, 63 C.C.C. (3d) 481, 5 C.R. (4th) 253, 125 N.R. 1 (S.C.C.)

Théroux, [1993] 2 S.C.R. 5, 79 C.C.C. (3d) 449, 19 C.R. (4th) 194, 100 D.L.R. (4th) 624 (S.C.C.)

Thibert, [1996] 1 S.C.R. 37, 104 C.C.C. (3d) 1, 45 C.R. (4th) 1 (S.C.C.)

Tutton and Tutton, [1989] 1 S.C.R. 1392, 48 C.C.C. (3d) 129, 69 C.R. (3d) 289, 98 N.R. 19, 13 M.V.R. (2d) 161 (S.C.C.)

United States of America v. Dynar, [1997] 2 S.C.R. 462, 115 C.C.C. (3d) 481, 8 C.R. (5th) 79 (S.C.C.)

Waite, [1989] 1 S.C.R. 1436, 48 C.C.C. (3d) 1, 69 C.R. (3d) 323, 98 N.R. 69, 13 M.V.R. (2d) 236 (S.C.C.).

Wholesale Travel Group Inc., [1991] 3 S.C.R. 154, 67 C.C.C. (3d) 193, 84 D.L.R. (4th) 161, 130 N.R. 1 (S.C.C.)